THE CUBAN REVOLUTION

THE CUBAN REVOLUTION

a critical perspective

by Sam Dolgoff

BLACK ROSE BOOKS   Montréal

BLACK ROSE BOOKS No. G34

Hardcover — ISBN: 0-919618-36-7
Paperback — ISBN: 0-919618-35-9

Canadian Cataloguing in Publication Data

Dolgoff, Sam, date
   The Cuban revolution

    ISBN 0-919618-35-9 pa.
    ISBN 0-919618-36-7 bd.

   1. Cuba — History — Rev., 1933.
   I. Title.

F1788.D.64   972.91'062   C77-000130-0.

Cover Design: Michael Carter

BLACK ROSE BOOKS LTD.
3934 rue St. Urbain
Montréal H2W 1V2, Québec

Printed and bound in Québec, Canada

CONTENTS

THE CUBAN REVOLUTION: AN ANARCHIST PERSPECTIVE

Between reactionary "pro-Batistianos" and "revolutionary Castro-ities," an adequate assessment of the Cuban Revolution must take into account another, largely ignored dimension, i.e., the history of Cuban anarchism and its influence on the development of the Cuban labor and socialist movements, the position of the Cuban anarchist movement with respect to the problems of the Cuban Revolution, and libertarian alternatives to Castroism.

Today's Cuban "socialism" differs from the humanistic and libertarian values of true socialism as does tyranny from freedom. There is not the remotest affinity between authoritarian socialism or its Castro variety and the libertarian traditions of the Cuban labor and socialist movements.

The character of the Latin American labor movement — like the Spanish revolutionary movement from which it derived its orientation — was originally shaped, not by Marxism, but by the principles of anarcho-syndicalism worked out by Bakunin and the libertarian wing of the International Workingmen's Association—the "First International"—founded in 1864.

The Latin American labor movement was, from its inception, greatly influenced by the ideology and revolutionary tactics of the Spanish anarcho-syndicalist movement. Even before 1870, there were organized anarchist and anarcho-syndicalist groups in Buenos Aires, Argentina; Mexico; Santiago, Chile; Montevideo, Uruguay; Rio de Janeiro and Sao Paulo, Brazil.

In 1891, a congress of trade unions in Buenos Aires organized the Federación Obrera Argentina which was in 1901 succeeded by the Federación Obrera Regional Argentina (FORA-Regional Labor Federation of Argentina) with 40,000 members, which in 1938 reached 300,000. The anarcho-sydicalist *La Protesta,* one of the best anarchist periodicals in the world, founded as a daily in 1897, often forced to publish clandestinely, is still being published as a monthly.

In Paraguay, anarcho-syndicalist groups formed in 1892, were in 1906 organized into the Federación Obrera Regional Paraguaya. The

1

anarcho-syndicalist unions of Chile in 1893 published the paper *El Oprimido* (The Oppressed). In the late 1920s the Chilean Administration of the IWW numbered 20,000 workers. Before then, many periodicals were published and the labor movement flourished. The journal *Alba*, organ of the Santiago Federation of Labor, was founded in 1905. The anarchist and anarcho-syndicalist groups and their publications were very popular with the workers in San Salvador, Guatemala, Nicaragua, and Costa Rica (where the anarchist paper *Renovación* first appeared in 1911).

To illustrate the scope of the anarcho-syndicalist movement in Latin America, attention is called to the organizations participating in the May 1929 Congress of all the Latin and South American anarcho-syndicalist groupings, convened by the FORA of Argentina in Buenos Aires. Besides the FORA, there were represented Paraguay, by the Centro Obrera Paraguaya; Bolivia, by the Federación Local de La Paz and the groups La Antorcha and Luz y Libertad; Mexico, by the Confederación General de Trabajadores; Guatemala, by the Comité Pro-Acción Sindical; Brazil, by the trade unions from seven constituent provinces; Costa Rica, by the organization, Hacia la Libertad; and the Chilean Administration of the IWW. These examples give only a sketchy idea of the extent of the movement. (sources: The Anarchist historian Max Nettlau's series of articles reprinted in *Reconstruir*, anarchist bi-monthly; Buenos Aires, 1972, #76, 77, 78, and Rudolf Rocker's *Anarcho-Syndicalism*, India edition, pgs. 183-184; no date)

Insofar as the history of anarcho-syndicalist movements in Argentina, Chile, Uruguay, Brazil and other Latin American lands are concerned, there is a voluminous literature in Spanish, and some, though by no means enough, works in English. Unfortunately there is scarcely anything, in any language, about the history of Cuban Anarcho-Syndicalism.

The anarcho-syndicalist origins of the Cuban labor movement and its influence is substantiated by the *Report on Cuba*, issued by the conservative International Bank for Reconstruction and Development:

> ...in the colonial days, labor leadership in Cuba came largely from anarcho-syndicalists of the Bakunin school. A strong thread of their ideology with its emphasis on 'direct action', its contempt for legality, its denial that there can be common interests for workers and employers, persists in the Cuban labor movement in modern times...it must be remembered that nearly all popular education of working people on how an economic system works and what might be done to improve it, came first from the anarcho-syndicalists...(quoted in *Background to Revolution: Development of Modern Cuba*; New York, 1966, p. 31, 32)

Even the communist historian Boris Nikirov concedes that

...the labor movement of Cuba has had a long tradition of radical orientation. Anarcho-Syndicalist influence was important from the late 1890s to the 1920s. (quoted ibid. p. 135) [Anarcho-syndicalist influence certainly spans a longer period.]

Even less is known about the anarcho-syndicalist roots of the Puerto Rican labor movement, which as in Cuba, traces back to the latter half of the 19th century. The editor of the excellent anthology of labor struggles and socialist ideology in Puerto Rico, A.G. Quintero Rivera asks:

...who even in Puerto Rico knows about readers in tobacco workrooms? [as in Cuba and Florida, workers paid readers to read works of social and general interest to them while they made cigars] Who knows that Puerto Rican study groups in the first decade of this century studied the works of the [anarchists] Bakunin, Kropotkin, Reclus and the history of the First International Workingmen's Association...that as early as 1890, Bakunin's *Federalism and Socialism* was published by anarchist groups in Puerto Rico and widely read by the workers?...

Quintero informs the reader that in 1897, the anarchist, Romero Rosa, a typographer, was one of the "principal founders of the first nationwide union in Puerto Rico—the Federación Regional Obrera." Together with Fernando Gómez Acosta, a carpenter, and José Ferrer y Ferrer, also a typographer, Romero Rosa founded the weekly *Ensayo Obrera* to spread anarcho-syndicalist ideas among the workers.

Louisa Capetillo, the Emma Goldman of Puerto Rico, whom Quintero calls a "legendary figure in the history of the Puerto Rican labor movement," was a gifted speaker and organizer who addressed countless meetings all over Puerto Rico in the late 1890s and early 1900s. She championed women's rights and preached free love (further defying convention by wearing pantaloons).

A prolific writer, Louisa Capetillo wrote—in Spanish—such libertarian essays as: *Humanity in the Future; My View of Freedom; Rights and Duties of Woman as Comrade, Mother and Free Human Being.* She also wrote and spoke extensively on art and the theater and carried on an extensive correspondence with foreign anarchists.

Between the years 1910 and 1920, anarchist and syndicalist periodicals were published in Puerto Rico and syndicalists carried on an intense agitation and militant action in labor struggles. (source: *Lucha Obrera en Puerto Rico;* 2nd edition, 1974, pgs. 1, 14, 34, 153, 156, 161.)

3

The example of Puerto Rico illustrates how little is known about the anarcho-syndicalist origins of the labor and socialist movements in the Caribbean area. This work tries to trace the remarkable influence of anarchism in the development of the Cuban revolutionary movement and to present the anarchist view of the Cuban Revolution.

CASTRO'S FRIENDLY CRITICS

From Waldo Frank to Rene Dumont

The repercussions of the Cuban Revolution are still being felt in Latin America and throughout the world. The character of the Revolution is being passionately debated. Many of Castro's original leftist and liberal supporters who have witnessed the gradual degeneration of the Revolution into a totalitarian dictatorship, have been forced, much against their inclinations, to accept this disappointing reality. In the process of accounting for the degeneration, these friendly critics clarify certain crucial facts about the Cuban Revolution which confirm the libertarian position, although most of them vehemently deny that this is indeed the case.

Still others, the more fanatical pro-Castroites, in trying to explain the dictatorial measures of the regime, fall into the most glaring contradictions—which serve only to emphasize the unpleasant facts they try to camouflage. A few typical examples are arranged chronologically to illustrate the progression of events.

Waldo Frank's *Cuba: A Prophetic Island* (New York, 1961) is particularly disappointing because he had always been a consistent anti-state communist, strongly influenced by libertarian ideas, which he amply demonstrated by his sympathetic attitude towards the CNT (anarcho-syndicalist union confederation of Spain). That Frank wth 40 years study of Spanish and Latin American history should have allowed his pro-Castro euphoria to becloud his judgment to the point where he could not recognize the obvious earmarks of a dictatorship in the making is unpardonable.

Although Frank was granted a two year subsidy by the Cuban government to write his book, he insists that his "only obligation was to seek the truth as I found it" (Preface). Nevertheless Frank's "unbiased" evaluation of Castro's personality and achievements rivals the tributes heaped upon Stalin by his sycophants. Thus:

> ...the Chevrolet rolled into the first streets of Matanzas...the crowd blocking Castro's way had, somehow, the shape of Castro...and what was the shape of Castro? Was it not Cuba itself? (p. 79) ...in his exquisite sensibilities...Castro is less the poet and the LOVER...to call Catro a dictator is dishonest semantics...(p. 141, Frank's emphasis)

In the very next paragraph Frank unwittingly marshalls crushing arguments against himself. Castro will not tolerate criticism:

> ...he likes to have intellectuals around him, not so much to discuss ideas as to fortify his actions and ideas...(p. 141) [In other words, Castro must, like Stalin, surround himself with fawning flatterers] Castro is not a dictator, [but]...there always comes a time, when leaders must dare, for the people's sake, to oppose the people...(p. 62) ...there are times of national fervor when an opposition press becomes a nuisance...[just because there are no elections in Cuba]...the opposition slanders Castro. [How dare they call him] "'totalitarian' 'communist'!?" (p. 16)
> ...[In spite of Frank's pro-Castro obsession, traces of anarcho-syndicalist influence come through]...the Cubans do not know that mere nationalization of their industries is no goal, that it may enthrone a bureaucracy even more rigid than capitalist possession. Nationalization is not necessarily true socialization, an end which demands [that there be workers in each industry to run these industries in coordination with the other sectors of the economy]. (p. 134)

Does Frank indict Castro for instituting nationalization? By no means! On the contrary, he considers that Castro's summary

> ...act of nationalization was an intelligent, courageous deed...to defend the Cuban Republic against those hostile forces that would destroy it...(p. 134) [Frank is even afraid] that...technicians from the Soviet Union will bring with them the communist ideology...equally alien, equally unwelcome...(p. 136) [But Frank hastens to dispel such fears]...the leaders are GOOD and what they are attempting to do is GOOD...they will tell you in plain words that they have not overthrown the overlordship of the United States in order to submit to a new master...the Soviet Union or anyone else...(p. 136) (Frank's emphasis)

6

Unfortunately, it turns out that the "good" men destined to save Cuba from totalitarian domination are themselves authoritarian communists: Armando Hart, Carlos Rafael Rodríguez, and irony of ironies! Castro himself, a few days after the American publication of Frank's book, confessed that "I am a Marxist-Leninist and will remain one until the last day of my life."

In spite of Castro's own statement that the so-called peasant cooperative farms (granjas del pueblo) are modeled after the Russian style "Kolkhozes," Frank still nurtures the forlorn hope that the:

> ...cooperative farms and industries of Cuba could well become the nuclei of a radical syndicalism, developed from the tradition of anarcho-syndicalism, which has long appealed to Spanish and Hispanic workers...far more than the crude kolkhoz within communism, libertarianism might flourish within a revived syndicalism...(p. 186)

In early 1963, members of the Cuban Libertarian Movement in Exile (CLME) addressed a letter to Pablo Casals, a co-sponsor of the Spanish Refugee Aid Committee, informing him that Waldo Frank, also a co-sponsor, had been commissioned by the Cuban Government to write a book in which he eulogized Castro. In its *Bulletin* for April 1963, the CLME published Casals's reply:

> ...like you, I too believe that all lovers of freedom...must condemn all dictatorship, "right," "left" or whatever the name...I feel strongly the anguish of the unfortunate people of Cuba, who, having suffered under the dictatorship of Batista, are now, anew, being subjected to the dictatorship of his successor, Fidel Castro...as to the attitude of Waldo Frank and his support of the Castro regime, I will immediately request the Spanish Refugee Aid Committee to order a thorough investigation of your charges, and if—as it seems—Waldo Frank violates the ideals of the organization, he be removed as member and co-sponsor ...With best wishes, Pablo Casals.

In 1964 *Monthly Review,* a Marxist-Leninist journal, published a special 96 page essay, *Inside the Cuban Revolution,* written by Adolfo Gilly, a fanatical "left wing" pro-Castro Argentine journalist who lived among the Cuban people for more than a year. Although Gilly acknowledges the deformation of the Cuban Revolution, he is "...still unconditionally on the side of the Revolution." (preface, p. vii) Gilly was nevertheless bitterly denounced by Castro. The following excerpts from his essay best illustrate the kind of muddled thinking which leads to the most glaring contradictions by "leftist" Castroite critics:

Statement: "the State defends the position...and concrete economic interests of the functionaries, the State itself, the Party and the union bureaucracy...the people have no direct power...the State creates and defends positions of privilege." (p. 42)
Contradiction: "The State is the workers' very own" (p. 46)

Statement: "Just as there has not appeared in the Cuban leadership any tendency that proposes self-management, neither has there appeared any which looks to the development of those bodies which in a socialist democracy express the will of the people; soviets, workers' councils, unions independent of the State, etc...." (p. 40-41)
Contradiction: "...in Cuba the masses feel that they have begun to govern their own lives..." (p. 78)

Statement: "When it comes to decisions of the government, it never allows dissent or criticism or proposals for change...nothing can be published without permission..." (p. 28)
Contradiction: "There is no country today where there is greater freedom and democracy than in Cuba." (ibid.)

Like Gilly, the editors of the *Monthly Review*, Leo Huberman and Paul Sweezy, also combine extravagant praise with what adds up to a devastating indictment of the Castro regime:

> ...the success achieved by the Cuban Revolution...the upsurge of mass living standard to create a quantity and quality of popular support for the Revolutionary Government...and its supreme leader Fidel Castro...has few, if any, parallels (*Socialism in Cuba*; N.Y., New York, 1970, p. 203, 204) ...there have been remarkable achievements in the economic field and there will be even more remarkable ones in the future...(p. 65)

Huberman and Sweezy then inadvertently deny their own statements:

> nearly everything is scarce in Cuba today (p. 129)...there is the continuing difficult economic situation. Daily life is hard, and after ten years many people are tired...tending to lose confidence in the leadership's ability to keep its optimistic promises...the ties that bind the masses to their paternalistic government are beginning to erode...(p. 217-218)

8

While the examples of the alleged economic "achievements" are indeed rare, the catastrophic collapse of the economy and the mass discontent for which the "Revolutionary Government" is directly responsible are overwhelmingly documented. (see pgs. 74, 81, 82, 86, 103, 107, 200, 205-207, 217-220)

> To create material incentives and reduce absenteeism the Revolutionary leadership, to its everlasting credit...has at no time committed the folly of restoring the capitalist wage system in which...whoever works harder gets more...Castro is quoted: "to offer a man more for doing his duty is to buy his conscience with money." (p. 145)

A few pages later, Huberman and Sweezy again refute themselves. The Revolution can be saved only if the capitalist wage system is restored. Now, the "...Revolution cannot afford to rely exclusively on political and moral incentives"; it will even have to resort to semi-militarization of work!" (p. 153)

The assertion that the "...Cuban Revolution has resorted to very little regimentation is refuted in the same paragraph:

> ...there are doubtless evidences of this in the large-scale mobilizations of voluntary labor...indeed, there are already signs of this regimentation in the growing role of the army in the economy bringing with it military concepts of organization and discipline...an example of this is the Che' Guevara Trail Blazers Brigade, organized along strictly military lines [which] has been clearing huge amounts of land...(p. 146) Cuba's system is clearly one of bureaucratic rule...[nor has the government worked out] an alternative...(p. 219-220)

For Huberman and Sweezy, the realization of socialism is, in effect, based upon the omnipotence of the State. The people are not the masters but the servants of the "revolutionary" leadership who graciously grant them the privilege of sharing "in the great decisions which shape their lives..." (p. 204)

To ignore the lessons of history and expect rulers to voluntarily surrender or even share power with their subjects is—to say the least—incredibly naive.

Herbert Matthews—foreign correspondent and later a senior editor of the *New York Times*, now retired—was granted his sensational interview with Fidel Castro in the Sierra Maestre on February 17, 1957. Matthews has since then been welcomed to Cuba and granted interviews with Castro and other leaders. His attitude towards the

Castro dictatorship resembles that of the doting parent who inflates the virtues of his offspring and invents excuses for the child's transgressions.

> ...Fidel's personality is overwhelming. He has done many things that enraged me. He has made colossal mistakes...but we must forgive him, he has to deal with difficult problems which no man could have tried to solve without making errors and causing harm to large sectors of Cuban society...(p. 4)

Not the least of the privileges accorded to despots is the right to make mistakes at the expense of ordinary mortals.

How Castro, who is "...a great orator...the greatest of his times," is "not able to express his emotions" (p. 44) is a peculiar failing that Matthews does not deem it necessary to explain.

Although his latest work (a big 486 page volume, *Revolution in Cuba;* New York, 1975) contains a great deal of valuable information about the situation in Cuba, it suffers from his clumsy efforts to reconcile his unabashed admiration for Castro with the brutal, bitter facts. Out of the chaotic mass of contradictions, absurdities and distortions, startling facts about the degeneration of the Cuban Revolution emerge. A few examples:

Castro is a dictator. His revolution is "autocratic," but it is still—strangely enough—"...a government by consensus, based upon popular support..." The support comes from the members of the Committees for the Defense of the Revolution (CDR) comprising "almost every able bodied adult in Cuba...everyone PARTICIPATES in the Cuban Revolution..." But this grass-roots consensus which is not "a democracy...has nothing to do with civil liberties..." (p. 15, Matthews' emphasis)

It should be obvious that a regime that has "nothing to do with civil rights" is by definition a dictatorship. It soon becomes apparent that this is indeed the case. Matthews notes that "...many Cubans are uneasy over the fact that the CDR [this model of participatory democracy]...is now completely under the control of the Communist Party of Cuba..." (p. 15, Matthews' emphasis)

> ...we Americans think of the Rights of Man in civic terms: equality before the law, non-discrimination, freedom of the press, sacredness of the home...In Cuba, as in Latin America, individual rights are cherished too (p. 7) But on page 129, Matthews reverses himself: "...I do not believe that the Cubans cared enough about civic freedoms to fight for them...the emphasis is not on civil liberties but on personal attributes: personal dignity, preservation of family life...

10

Matthews, however, tries to camouflage the fact that personal attributes cannot be exercised in Cuba because the State regiments the life of the individual from the cradle to the grave. He unintentionally documents this fact in his chapter on the Cultural Revolution.

On the flimsy and insulting pretext that the "...Cuban people do not have the Anglo-Saxon mania for privacy..." Matthews tries to minimize the fact that "Cuba is a goldfish bowl." (p. 15)

"Castro made the mistake at his Moncada trial in 1953 and in the Sierra Maestra in 1957, of promising to implement the liberal democratic consstitution of 1940." (p. 40) Castro did not make a mistake. He knew full well and later openly confessed (in his "I am a Marxist-Leninist" speech, Dec. 1, 1961) that Batista could be overthrown and his clique come to power, only on the basis of a democratic program acceptable to the anti-Castro bourgeoisie, The Church and other non-radical forces. "...in the circumstances [comments Matthews] to get them to accept a revolution was an...impossibility..." (p. 125) Castro is an astute politician. He did not make the mistake of antagonizing these elements by prematurely initiating expropriation of property and other radical measures. He waited until his regime was strong enough to neutralize, and if necessary, smother the opposition.

Matthews even tries to condone Castro's atrocities. For him the crimes committed by the Castro regime in the first ten years of the Revolution—1959-1970—"has only historic meaning today...they

were in Fidel's breathtaking word [?] an apprenticeship..." (p. 2) In short, the Dictator was learning his trade at the expense of his victims!

In connection with the restoration of the death penalty and the execution of prisoners without a fair trial, Matthews asserts that "...I was in Cuba twice while executions were going on and I did not then, nor ever, heard or read of an innocent man being condemned..." (p. 134) But Matthews himself unwittingly presents overwhelming evidence to the contrary:

> ...I felt critical over the summary nature of Cuban trials. Herman Marks, a native of Milwaukee, reportedly with a criminal record, was the executioner at the Cabañas fortress in Havana...he became a captain in Che' Guevara's column. He was used to avoid killing by Cubans. He was like a butcher killing cattle in an abattoir...(p. 135)...ordinary courts lost much of their authority. Lawyers who defended those accused of being counter-revolutionaries ran the danger of prosecution themselves...(p. 143). Habeas corpus was suspended in 1959. (p. 142)

...the evidence in the Matos case [see below] could not stand up in a Western court of law...but we must not blame the dictators...this was a Cuban court of law in the midst of a perilous revolution...the vilification of Castro in the Matos case is unjustified...(p. 142) The prisons were filled to overflowing. The interrogation rooms of G2, Castro's secret police, were scarcelessly less vile than the torture chambers of Batista's SIM... there were more prisoners now than Batista ever had...(Hugh Thomas quoted by Matthews, p. 142)

It is impossible to understand how Matthews, in view of his own evidence, could deny that such atrocities did take place and then reverse himself. His attitude is all the more incomprehensible, when in respect to the Matos case, he, at the request of Matos' family, tried to intercede with Castro on their behalf and his plea was ignored. (see p. 142)

Castro's refusal to honor "his repeated promises to hold elections for a multi-party democratic government" is justified on the pretext that this outrageous violation of elementary rights would crystallize a "strong congressional opposition to Castro's revolutionary policies at every step." But Castro is a better dictator than Franco was because "he never perpetrated the hypocrisy of a plebiscite as in Franco Spain..."! (p. 147)

After revealing that "Havana University was stripped of whatever autonomy remained to it in July 1960 and purged...and two thirds of the professors went into exile...", Matthews tries to condone these crimes because "...as with so much happening, unscrupulous means had to be used to achieve desirable ends..." As if means can ever be separated from ends! Matthews himself admits that the "University became an organ of the Marxist-Leninist government, but it also became a disciplined, serious, center of learning, which in the 1970s is undergoing an extraordinary rebirth..." (p. 183)

With respect to the criminal mismanagement of the economy and the proliferation of a new bureaucracy, Matthews gives examples:

...the Central Planning Board (Jucesplan) was created to control the economy as a whole but it did little of practical value...Fidel, Ché, and a few others had the real authority which they failed to coordinate or use systematically...There was a decline in the national income...too many cattle were slaughtered in 1961, bringing severe shortages from 1962 onwards...rationing of foodstuffs was instituted in the summer of 1961...something had gone seriously wrong with the economy. Even in World War II, there was no need for rationing...Ché Guevara, then Minister of Industry, reported many errors...much of what they were planning was impossible. Naturally a huge bureaucracy evolved... (pgs. 167-169)

Reasonable people, taking into account the accumulating mountain of evidence, naturally came to realize that the Cuban Revolution was over. Not Matthews. His faith remains undimmed: "...they were all so young! The group had any amount of faith...honesty and energy..." Matthews comes to the ridiculous conclusion that although the "economy was failing...the Revolution was succeeding..." The blundering despots who are largely responsible for the collapse of the Revolution "...put the Revolution on the rocky, unevenly advancing path it has followed since then..." (p. 167-169)

Reviewing all the vast literature about the Cuban Revolution is beyond the scope of this work. We center our discussion on René Dumont's analysis because it is by far, the most profound, and especially, because it is, in important areas, relevant to the position of the Cuban anarchists and anarcho-syndicalists—a position formulated long before Dumont's two books were published. (see his *Cuba: Socialism and Development*; New York 1970, and *Is Cuba Socialist?* New York 1974)

We will summarize Dumont's critique of Castro and his policies; the libertarian content of his constructive proposals; and how he departs from the libertarian implications of his work and contradicts himself.

Dumont's Critique

From the jacket blurb of *Is Cuba Socialist?* we gather that the significance of Dumont's book lies not so much:

> ...in his richly detailed...devasting portrait of economic disorder and militarization but [primarily because it] comes from a friend of the Revolution, who at earlier times praised Castro's efforts to create a socialist nation...Dumont, a distinguished agronomist, a veteran [pro-communist] activist, who in the 1960s paid [on Castro's invitation] several long visits as an expert adviser to, and sympathizer with, Castro's Cuba...

The book "created a sensation throughout Europe" because for Dumont to dispute the infallibility of Castro, or even dare deny the socialist nature of the Cuban Revolution, is, for the Castroites, a heresy comparable to a papal encyclical questioning the existence of God The phrasing of the chapter headings alone, constitutes a devastating indictment of the Castro regime:

STATIST: CENTRALIZATION: HERETICAL REVOLUTION
CENTRALIZED PLANNING WITH BUREAUCRACY: 1961-
1968

THE PARTY: DESIGNATED RATHER THAN ELECTED
THE STATE: SUBORDINATED TO THE PARTY?
COMMUNISM: A MILITARY SOCIETY OR PERSONAL
   POWER
AN AGRARIAN DRILL FIELD: THE GUEVARA BRIGADE
THE DEATH OF THE FARM
THE ARMY APPRAISES POETS
NEW MAN OR MODEL SOLDIER?
RE-STALINIZATION: PRIVILEGES AND THE NEW BU-
   REAUCRACY
PROTO-SOCIALISM WITH A NEW FACE
IS CUBA SOCIALIST?

That the answer is a resounding NO!, can be gathered from the text, which also explains why both Dumont and his books are banned in Cuba. What follows is a representative selection of Dumont's critical remarks. (Unless otherwise noted, all quotations are from *Is Cuba Socialist?)*

Workers and Unions

> ...note should be taken of the diminishing role of the unions which are due to disappear entirely since the state is—in principle—supposed to be the State of the workers...(p. 52) The government's decisions seem to be intended *FOR* the people, but it was not government *BY* the people...they used to have a capitalist boss, and now they have another boss...the State. (p. 22, Dumont's emphasis)

Dumont quotes Armando Hart, a member of the political bureau of the Popular People's (Communist) Party who speculated hopefully that it would be a good idea:

> ...if all the labor force were in encampments, like columns of soldiers...the development of the Cuban economy would be accelerated by the militarization of the labor force...it is toward this that we must work...(p. 94)
> In mid-1969,...the Minister of Labor warned that severe measures would be taken against...undisciplined work, absenteeism, and negligence...a month later, in September, the government promulgated a law under which each worker must have a dossier and work book in which will be noted the places in which he works, his comings and goings, etc. (p. 114)

14

The Boss

> ...the number one man in Cuba is Castro. Castro is Prime Minister of the Revolutionary Government, Commander In Chief of the Armed Forces, and First Secretary of the Cuban Communist Party...As an official, one's job depends upon Castro's confidence and on personal connections...leadership of the essential agencies is placed in the hands of men in whom the Boss [Castro] has confidence (p. 51)...Cuban society remains authoritarian and hierarchized; Fidel maneuvers it as he sees fit. The result is a militaristic society...(34)
> In public everybody is for Castro. In private his partisans are less numerous. Everybody goes to the demonstrations in the Plaza de la Revolucion. It is obligatory (p. 59)...Castro has confidence only in himself. He is no longer content with claims to military and political fame. He has to feel himself the leader in both scientific research and agricultural practice [about which he knows next to nothing] (p. 107) Nobody dares oppose him if he wants to hold his job. (p. 108)...when he throws his beret on the ground and flies into one of his rages, everybody quakes and fears reprisals... (p. 111)

Censorship and Spying

> There exists vigilance [spying] with the increasing control of neighborhoods by the Committees for the Defense of the Revolution [CDRs] standing in for and helping the police. Everybody belongs to the CDRs, unless he wants to miss out on many advantages...Capitalism robs the worker of his dignity...Police inquisition in the Cuban Revolution again denies it to the poorest worker...(p. 119) [In exposing press censorship, Dumont quotes Marx] "...the censored press CONSTANTLY lies." I challenge *Granma* to publish this [Marx's] sentence...[*Granma* is the official organ of the Communist Party of Cuba.]

Dumont cites the case of Heberto Padilla, the renowned Cuban poet and former editor of *Granma*. Padilla had been relieved of his editorial post because he commented favorably on the work of Guillermo Cabrera Infante, a prominent poet, who was at that time out of favor with the Party.

In 1968 Padilla was awarded the Casa de la Americas literary prize for his collection of critical poetry *Out of the Game* (two examples are reprinted below). The Writers Union published the book, including their disclaimer, charging that the poems were against the Revolution.

15

Padilla's verses were judged Counter-Revolutionary by *Granma* and the weekly newspaper of the Cuban Army, *Verde Olivo* (Olive Green--color of the uniform).

On March 27, 1971, Padilla was jailed for 37 days. He was also denied work for a year. His case aroused a world-wide storm of protest by prominent pro-Castro and other intellectuals and writers. Dumont in true Stalinist fashion confesses that he was guilty of adopting "counter-revolutionary" attitudes and in the words of Dumont "...providing information to CIA agents like myself and K.S. Karol (p. 120ff.; Karol is a friendly critic of Castro, was like Dumont invited to visit Cuba by Castro, and author of *Guerrillas in Power*).

Out of the Game

The Poet, get rid of him
He has nothing to do around here
He does not play the game
lacks enthusiasm
He does not make his message clear
    does not even notice the miracles.
He spends the whole day thinking
always finds something to object to
That fellow, get rid of him
Remove the party pooper
    the summer malcontent
    who wears dark glasses in the new dawn
    of time without history
He is even out of date
He likes only the old Louis Armstrong
Humming, at most, a song of Pete Seeger
He sings the 'Guantanamera' through clenched teeth
No one can make him talk
No one can make him smile
    each time the spectacle begins

Instructions for Admission into a New Society

In the first place: optimism.
Secondly: be correct, circumspect, submissive.
(Having undergone all the sports tests)
and to finish, march
as do all the other members:
one step forward,
two or three backwards:
but always applauding

Education

> ...the new man is a model soldier, ever obedient to his leaders...
> children are enrolled in organizations as soon as ten years old...
> young teachers are subjected to programs that smack of the
> convent and the barracks: 'WORK AND Shut Up!' 'The Leaders
> Are Always Right!' 'Fidel Doesn't Argue!' (p. 122) Technological
> training was under the control of the Vice-Minister of the Armed
> Forces. Military training was given at all levels. By the time they
> are eight, young people march in step...(p. 92)

Cuba: A Military Dictatorship

> ...In Cuba the military are taking over command of the
> economy...(p. 179)...it is becoming clearer and clearer that the
> army is transforming Cuban society. (p. 84) Militarization was
> urged not only to eliminate inefficiency and disorganization, but to
> cope with the passive resistance of a growing number of workers.
> (p. 100)
> ...it became increasingly difficult to distinguish between the
> Communist Party and the army, since they both wore uniforms
> and carried revolvers...This sort of Cuban communism is
> devilishly close to army life...This military society...follows a
> path leading away from participation of the people; it leads to a
> hierarchized society with an authoritarian leadership headed by
> Castro who decides all problems, political, conomic and
> technical...(p. 112-113)

Agriculture is Militarized

Under the heading Agrarian Reform Law and Cooperatives, Dumont
deplores that the

> ...estates confiscated in 1960 were cooperatives in name
> only...they were state farms...by August 1960, after my second
> visit, the cooperative formula was definitively set aside without
> those involved being advised or consulted (p. 22) [Dumont quotes
> law 43]: "the INRA [National Institute of Agrarian Reform] will
> APPOINT their administrators...and the workers will accept and
> respect [whatever commands the INRA] will dictate." (p. 47)
> [Dumont remarks that] "the workers have the mentality of paid
> employees...their boss is the state." (p. 22) [Dumont concludes
> that] "Cuban agriculture is certainly becoming more and more

17

militarized...all important jobs are entrusted to the army, headed by a Major, Captain or a First Lieutenant.''
(p. 96)

Dumont's Libertarian Socialistic Proposals

The typical attitude of the Marxist-Leninist left toward the Cuban Revolution was perhaps best summarized in one of its well known organs the *New Left Review* (issue #3, 1960) in the course of an ecstatic review of *Cuba: Anatomy of a Revolution* by Huberman and Sweezy, editors of the Marxist-Leninist *Monthly Review*:

> ...as a result of the final period of nationalization completed this past October, Cuba has become a sovereign socialist state...the first nation to have achieved socialism without benefit of Marxist-Leninist orientation...

Dumont rejects this brand of "socialism." He does not equate socialism with nationalization. Although a professed Marxist-Leninist, Dumont touches on anarchist themes insofar as he advocates a decentralist voluntaristic variety of socialism, not only because it is desirable, but also because it is eminently more practical than nationalization and other authoritarian alternatives. As an expert agronomist, Dumont concentrates on the problems of the agrarian revolution. But his general conclusions are applicable to the whole economic setup. He insists that "...socialism demands true popular participation at all levels of decision making..." (p. 140)

> ...an agrarian socialism does not require collectivization from above...I sought a solution that would tend to more decentralization, more responsibility at the base...self-management of basic units...(p. 97) [To stimulate the creativity of the individual and encourage him to take the initiative in the self-management of a cooperative society]...socialism must learn to be more respectful of his dignity and therefore of his autonomy. (*Cuba: Socialism and Development*, p. 161)
> ...the moral incentive would be respect for his individuality as a worker, the irreplaceable feeling on the part of the worker that he is PARTICIPATING in the management of the enterprise, that he PERSONALLY contributes to the decisions about the nature and quality of his work...more initiative, more autonomy, more responsibility...(*Is Cuba Socialist?* p. 137; emphasis Dumont's)

In Russia the anarchists bitterly criticized the Bolsheviks because they extirpated the grass-roots voluntary organizations and set up a state dictatorship. Dumont, too, does not think:

> ...it is a good idea to suppress pre-revolutionary cooperatives which are useful for the training of management personnel [and believes that] the cooperative formula...applies to handwork, distribution, small-scale industry, shops, services, etc. [where] the workers take better care of the material belonging to the group than that which belongs to the state...(*Cuba: Socialism and Development*, p. 163)

Under headings like "An Agrarian Socialism With Little Work Collectives;" "A Multiplicity of Socialist Patterns of Change" (*Cuba: Socialism and Development,* p. 160-170) Dumont's proposals read almost like excerpts from Kropotkin's anarchist classic, *Fields, Factories and Workshops:*

> ...in 1960 I suggested that the hypertrophied city of Havana be surrounded with a 'green belt' of market gardens and fruit farms as far as the adaptability of land and availability of water allowed. I urged a second concentric belt for the production of sweet potatoes, potatoes, plantains, etc. and that a dairy farm should be established. Other cities could have adopted the same plan...I even suggested a plan by which each major agricultural unit could suppply itself with a significant portion of its food supply. The prolongation and aggravation of scarcities only emphasized the value of this project which was never undertaken. (*Is Cuba Socialist?* p. 33)
> ...if every family that wanted to had been able to have a small garden plot, it could have raised a good portion of its own food... (p. 66.) The workers would organize their own work themselves. The farm groups would evolve not so much as giant cooperatives as TOWARD A FEDERATION OF SMALL COOPERATIVES. ...(*Socialism and Development, p. 160; emphasis Dumont's)*

Dumont: Spurious Libertarian

Unfortunately, Dumont's modifications negate his libertarianism and render his work useless to arrest the deformation of the Revolution and guide it in a libertarian direction. He makes this unmistakeably clear:

> ...Democratic Centralism which elsewhere has too often been the cover [read consequences] for totalitarianism, which would take

19

on a new meaning [back to Lenin the architect of "communist" tyranny]. Within this structure [cooperatives] the top echelon [i.e. the state] would be responsible for the economic plan...for the allotment of state funds [which gives the state life and death power over the cooperatives simply by granting or witholding funds]...the heads of cooperatives would be APPOINTED [until] such time as they were elected within a cooperative framework [until as in Russia the State "will wither away"?] (*Cuba: Socialism*... p. 160; our emphasis)

Wanted: A Libertarian Caudillo

Dumont unwittingly endorses de facto paternalism on the part of Castro. For example:

...if Castro could rid himself of his mystics and utopians and surround himself with real representatives of the people, he [Castro the savior] COULD LEAD the Cuban People to prosperity...(p. 122; our emphasis)...[Since Castro]...would not accept control from below because he enjoyed personal power too long to GIVE IT UP GRADUALLY...it is therefore up to the country's political leaders, especially Raúl Castro, Dórticos, Rafael Rodríguez, Armando Hart and Blas Roca, to advise Castro to do so IF THEY HAVE THE COURAGE AND IF THEY REALIZE THAT THE PRESENT PERSONAL DICTATOR-SHIP may lead to catastrophe...(p. 140-141, Dumont's emphasis)

Since they have neither "the will nor the courage" to take Dumont's advice, the situation is hopeless. Is it at all likely that these hardened, cynical politicians who make up the "innermost ruling group," would, no more than Castro himself, "accept control from below," since they too "enjoyed power too long to give it up gradually"? Is it at all likely that this "communist bourgeoisie...which clings to power by flattering Castro," whose very lives depend on Castro's good will, would summon up "the courage" to correct Castro? (p. 141)

That a realistic observer like Dumont could entertain the faintest hope that these puppets would willingly sacrifice themselves, is hard to understand. Especially, when Dumont himself cautions us "not to forget that despotism and its paternalistic variety has always been badly enlightened...and power corrupts...", and in the very next paragraph flatly contradicts himself by suggesting that the remedy for Castro's de facto "...absolute monarchy is a more modern version of what I will simplify in calling...LIMITED IF NOT CONSTI-TUTIONAL MONARCHY..." (p. 141, our emphasis)

20

Disregarding contrary evidence such as: the massacre of the Kronstadt sailors; the exile, persecution and murder of political prisoners by Lenin's secret police and other crimes for which Lenin is directly responsible; Dumont, nevertheless, asserts that the "...freedom of discussion and popular control advised [but never practised] by Lenin has been forgotten by the Castroites...Lenin's theory of democratic centralism has been interpreted to justify the unlimited dictatorship of personal power..." (p. 116)

Dumont, like the other Marxist-Leninists, whitewashes Lenin's crimes. He ignores the incontestable fact that it was Lenin himself who set the precedent followed on a wider scale by his successor Stalin. Dumont's remedy for the chronic afflictions of the Castro regime does not even begin to measure up to his excellent diagnosis.

Like his colleague K.S. Karol, Dumont assumes a similar self-contradictory attitude in respect to the Chinese Revolution, oscillating between extravagant praise and severe criticism:

> ...developing countries will most certainly find in China the basis for a new faith in Man and in his possibilities for progress. Socialist consciousness has attained a very high level...the people are almost exclusively concerned [not with personal affairs but] with the general interest...

Dumont then contradicts himself devastatingly exposing the true character of Mao's despotism:

> ...fundamental decisions, such as foreign policy and the economic plan are all made by the top hierarchy and a small minority of managers...without consultation or intervention of the famous 'popular' control called for [but never practiced] by Lenin...

Dumont then immediately proceeds to justify these outrageous violations of elementary rights by pointing to the "...hypocrisy of the false friends of democracy..." As if one evil automatically justifies another Dumont:

> ...salutes the devotion of the Chinese rulers to the welfare of the nation and the workers...if we prefer for OURSELVES more freedom of information and only formal democracy, IT IS SURELY NOT FOR US TO PRESCRIBE WHAT IS BEST FOR THE CHINESE...

(above quotes from *L'Utopie ou la Mort;* Paris, 1973, pgs. 156-158; Dumont's emphasis)

21

If Dumont were consistent, he would at least add that the totalitarian despots who rule China also have no right to "prescribe what is best for" THE CHINESE PEOPLE.

Like Dumont, the other loyal leftist critics of the Cuban Revolution do not realize that their own analysis leads inevitably to the conclusion that NO STATE CAN EVER PLAY A REVOLUTIONARY ROLE. It is their inability to grasp this fact. It is their orientation that enmeshes the Marxist-Leninists in a series of massive and insoluble contradictions. Their writings project a distorted, utterly false image of the Cuban Revolution; they are never a guide to meaningful alternatives.

THE CHARACTER OF THE CUBAN REVOLUTION

A Non-Social Revolution

The myth, induced by the revolutionary euphoria of the pro-Castro left, that a genuine social-revolution took place in Cuba, is based on a number of major fallacies. Among them is the idea that a social revolution can take place in a small semi-developed island, a country with a population of about eight million, totally dependent for the uninterrupted flow of vital supplies upon either of the great super-powers, Russia or the U.S. They assume falsely that these voracious powers will not take advantage of Cuba's situation to promote their own selfish interests. There can be no more convincing evidence of this tragic impossibility than Castro's sycophantic attitude toward his benefactor, the Soviet Union, going so far as to applaud Russia's invasion of Czechoslovakia in 1968, a crime certainly on a par with the military coup in Chile, which Castro rightfully condemned. To assume, furthermore, that the Cuban social revolution can be miraculously achieved without simultaneous uprisings in Latin America and elsewhere, is both naive and irresponsible.

Nationalization Versus Socialism

To equate nationalization of the economy and social services instituted from above by the decree of a "revolutionary government" or a *caudillo*, with true socialism is a dangerous illusion. Nationalization and similar measures, under the name of "welfare-ism," are common. They are widespread, and in many cases deep-going programs, instituted by democratic "welfare" states or "bene-volent" dictators as an *antidote* to revolution, and are by no means equivalent to socialism.

23

Russia and Cuba: Two Revolutions Compared

Another fallacy about the nature of the Cuban Revolution can perhaps be best illustrated by contrasting the early stages of the Russian Revolution of 1917 with the Cuban events. Analogies between the Russian and Cuban Revolutions—like analogies in general—fail to take into account certain important differences:

Czarism was OVERTHROWN by the spontaneous revolts of the peasant and proletarian masses only after a prolonged and bloody civil war.

In Cuba, the Batista regime COLLAPSED WITHOUT A STRUGGLE for lack of popular support. There were no peasant revolts. No general strikes. Theodor Draper (and many other observers) argues persuasively that since there were at least "500,000 agricultural workers in Cuba" there could not have been many peasants in a

> ...guerrilla force that never amounted to more than a thousand...there was nothing comparable in Cuba to the classic peasant revolution led by Zapata in Mexico in 1910...there was no national peasant uprising. Outside the immediate vicinity of the guerrilla forces, revolutionary activity, in the country as a whole, was largely a middle class phenomenon, with some working class support, but without working class organizations...(*Castroism: Theory and Practice*; New York, 1965, p. 74-75) [This takes on added significance when we consider that the unions comprised ONE MILLION out of a total population of about six million when the Revolution began, Jan. 1, 1959.]

In Russia, the masses made the social revolution BEFORE the establishment of the Bolshevik government. Lenin climbed to power by voicing the demands of, and legalizing the social revolutionary DEEDS of the workers and peasants: "All Power to the Soviets," "The Land to the Peasants," "The Factories to the Workers," etc. In Cuba, Castro, for fear of losing popular support, carefully avoided a social-revolutionary platform—assuming that he had one. Unlike Lenin, he came to power because he promised to put into effect the bourgeois-democratic program.

History is full of unexpected twists and turns. Ironically enough, these two *different* revolutions had similar results: Both Lenin and Castro betrayed their respective revolutions, instituted totalitarian regimes and ruled by decree from above.

The well-known anarcho-syndicalist writer and activist, Augustin Souchy, makes a cogent comparison between the Spanish Revolution (1936-1939) and the Cuban Revolution (both of which he personally witnessed):

...while in Spain, the confiscation of the land and the organization of the collectives was initiated and carried through by the peasants themselves; in Cuba, social-economic transformation was initiated, not by the people, but by Castro and his comrades-in-arms. It is this distinction that accounts for the different development of the two revolutions; Spain, mass revolution from the bottom up; Cuba, revolution from the top down by decree...(see *Cuba: An Eyewitness Report,* below)

Which brings to mind the celebrated phrase of the "Apostle" of Cuban independence, José Martí: *"To Change the Master Is Not To Be Free."*

Revolution the Latin American Way

The Cuban Revolution draws its specific character from a variety of sources. While not a Latin American "palace revolution" which produced no deep seated social changes, it nevertheless relates to the tradition of miltarism and bogus paternalism of Latin American "Caudillismo," the "Man on Horseback." "Caudillismo"—"right" or "left," "revolutionary" or "reactionary"—is a chronic affliction in Latin America since the wars for independence initiated by Simón Bolívar in 1810. The "revolutionary caudillo" Juan Perón of Argentina, catapulted to power by "leftist" army officers, was deposed by "rightist" military officers. Maurice Halperin calls attention to the "...expropriation of vast properties in Peru in 1968 and in Bolivia in 1969 by the very generals who had destroyed Cuban supported guerrilla uprisings in their respective countries..." (*The Rise and Fall of Fidel Castro;* University of California, 1972, p. 118)

The militarization of Cuban society by a revolutionary dictatorship headed by the "Caudillo" of the Cuban Revolution, Fidel Castro, follows, in general, the Latin American pattern. Like other revolutionary Latin American "Caudillos," Castro would come to power only on the basis of programs designed to win the indispensable support of the masses. Edwin Lieuwen marshalls impressive evidence:

> ...In Chile in 1924, Major Carlos Ibáñez established a military dictatorship [that] was notably successful in combining authoritarian rule with policies aimed at meeting popular demands for greater social justice. Successful but short lived revolutions took place during 1936 under the leadership of radical young officers inspired by ideas of social reform and authoritarian nationalism.. In Bolivia a clique of radical young officers came to power. Major David Toro and Colonel Germán Busch successfully headed regimes that had social revolution as their goals...they catered to

25

the downtrodden and pledged to build a new nation. Toro and Busch based their dictatorial regimes on attempts to win mass support...(*Arms and Politics in Latin America*; New York, 1961, pgs. 60, 62, 78, 79)

When in 1968, a "revolutionary" military Junta seized power in Peru, the new military government proclaimed the fundamental principle underlying all "radical" military regimes:

...the final aim of the State, being the welfare of the nation; and the armed forces being the instrument which the State uses to impose its policies, therefore,...in order to arrive at collective prosperity, the armed forces have the mission to watch over the social welfare, the final aim of the State... (quoted, *Modes of Political Change in Latin America,* ed. Paul Sigmund, New York, 1970, p. 201)

Dr. Carlos Delgado, Director of the Information Bureau of the Revolutionary Government of Peru, after stressing that the revolution was "...initiated from above" by decree, boasted that the dictatorship in "...the last four and a half years" accomplished more for the betterment of the people than in the "whole epoch of Republican rule." The revolution was hailed, boasted Delgado, even by the French Marxist thinker, Henri Lefebvre, as one of the most important historical events of the contemporary world..." (see *Reconstruir,* anarchist bi-monthly, Buenos Aires, Nov.-Dec. 1974)

There is an umbilical connection between militarism and the State, fully compatible with, and indispensable to, all varieties of State "socialism"—or more accurately State Capitalism. George Pendle (and other observers) with respect to Perón's social and welfare programs initiated to woo mass support concludes that:

...Perón's National Institute of Social Security...converted Argentina to one of the most advanced countries in South America...it was not surprising that the majority of workers preferred Peron to their traditional leaders...they felt that Perón accomplished more for them in a few years than the Socialist Party achieved in decades...(*Argentina;* Oxford University Press, London, 1965, pgs. 97, 99)
...In Havana Premier Fidel Castro proclaimed three days of mourning and Cuban officials termed Perón's death a blow to all Latin America...(*New York Times,* July 2, 1974) This cynical proclamation was not made solely for tactical reasons, but in recognition of the affinity between the Casro and Perón regimes. As early as 1961, there

26

were already informal contacts between Ché Guevara and Ángel Borlenghi "...a number two man in Perón's government and his Minister of the Interior for eight years...Ché told Borlenghi that there's no question about it that Peron was the most advanced embodiment of political and economic reform in Argentina...and under Ché's guidance a rapport was established between the Cuban Revolution and the Perónist movement...Ché had in his possession a letter from Perón expressing admiration for Castro and the Cuban Revolution and Ché had raised the question of inviting Perón to settle in Havana..." (quoted by Halperin, from Ricardo Rojo's work, *My Friend Ché*; ibid. p. 329-330)

> Herbert Matthews supplements Rojo's revelations:...the Argentine journalist Jorge Massetti who went into the Sierra Maestra in 1958, became friends with Guevara. He was trained for guerrilla warfare in the Sierra Maestra and in 1964 was killed in a guerrilla raid in Argentina...Massetti was credited with convincing Guevara that Perónism approximated his own ideas. Hilda Gadea—Guevara's first wife—wrote that for Ernesto Guevara, the fall of Perón Sept. 1955 was a heavy blow. Ché and Massetti blamed it,...'on North American Imperialists'...(ibid. p. 258)

[Carmelo Mesa-Lago notes the connection between State Socialism and militarism. Castro enthusiastically hailed] "...the Peruvian Social Revolution as a progressive military group playing a revolutionary role..." (*Cuba in the 1970s:* University of New Mexico Press, 1975, p. 111) In an interview, Castro emphatically maintained that social revolution is compatible with military dictatorship, not only in Peru, but also in Portugal and Panama.

> [When the military junta in Peru] took power...the first thing they did was to implement agrarian reform which was MUCH MORE RADICAL than the agrarian reform we initiated in Cuba. It put a much lower limit on the size of properties; organized cooperatives, agricultural communities;...they also pushed in other fields—in the field of education, social development, industrialization...We must also see the example of Portugal where the military played a decisive role in political change...and are on their way to finding solutions...we have Peru and Panama—where the military are acting as catalysts in favor of the revolution...(Castro quoted by Frank and Kirby Jones, *With Fidel*; New York, 1975, p. 195-196)

[The evidence sustains Donald Druze's conclusion that]...the programs of modern 'caudillos' embodies so many features of centralism and National Socialism, that it almost inevitably blends into communism...(*Latin America: An Interpretive History*; New York, 1972, p. 570)

Militarism flourishes in Cuba as in Latin America. Castro projected militarism to a degree unequalled by his predecessor, Batista: total domination of social, economic and political life. In the Spring of 1959, a few months after the Revolution of January 1st, Castro, who appointed himself the "Lider Maximo" ("Caudillo") of the Revolution and Commander-in-Chief of the Armed Forces, promised to cut the size of the army in half and ultimately to disband and replace it by civilian militias and police. "The last thing I am," said Castro, "is a military man...ours is a country without generals and colonels..."

Within a year after the disintegration of the Batista Army, Castro turned Cuba into a thoroughly militarized state, with the most formidable armed force of any in Latin America. For the first time in Cuban history, compulsory military service was instituted. Now, Cuba has adopted the traditional hierarchical ranking system of conventional armies. The Cuban army differs in no essential respect from the armies of both "capitalist" and "socialist" imperialist powers.

"Communism" a la Castro

Insofar as relations with the communists are concerned, Theodore Draper notes the striking resemblance between the policies of Batista and Castro:

> ...Batista paid off the communists for their support, by among other things, permitting them to set up an official trade union federation, the Confederación de Trabajadores de Cuba (CTC) with Lázaro Peña as its Secretary-General. In 1961, Castro paid off the communists for their support, by, among other things, permitting Lazaro Pena to come back officially as Secretary-General of the CTC...(ibid. p. 204)

If we accept at face value Castro's conversion to "communism," his "communism" embodies the Latin American version of Stalinism, absolute personal dictatorship. But "Caudillos" are not primarily ideologues. They are, above all, political adventurers. In their lust for power, they are not guided by ethical considerations, as they claim. In this respect, there is no essential difference between capitalist states and "revolutionary socialist states." All dictators conceal their true visage behind the facade of a political party, paying lip service to goals supposedly popular with the masses. Castro became a "communist" because he considered that his survival in power depended on cementing cordial relations with his saviors, the "socialist" countries (former enemies) and by extension with Batista's former allies, the domestic "communists." To promote his ends, Castro established relations with Franco Spain and the Vatican. Nor did he hesitate to side with the Arab oil magnates—lords over their impoverished subjects—in the mid-east disputes, or to endorse the Russian invasion of Czecho-Slovakia.

The Real Revolution Is Yet To Come

Albert Camus observed:

> ...the major event of the twentieth century has been the abandonment of the values of liberty on the part of the revolutionary movement, the weakening of Libertarian Socialism, vis-a-vis Caesarist and militaristic socialism. Since then, a great hope has disappeared from the world, to be replaced by a deep sense of emptiness in the hearts of all who yearn for freedom... *(Neither Victims Nor Executioners)*

Whether Castro is working out his own unique brand of "Cuban Socialism" is a relatively minor question. Even if Castro had no connection with the communist movement, his mania for personal power would lead inevitably to the establishment of an "independent" totalitarian regime. What is decisive is that the Cuban Revolution follows the pattern established in this century by the aborted Russian Revolution of 1917. This pattern is the counter-revolution of the State.

THE IDEOLOGY OF SPANISH ANARCHISM

To understand the character of Cuban anarchism it is first necessary to summarize the main principles of Spanish anarcho-syndicalism from which the Cuban revolutionary movement derives its orientation. These principles were formulated by Bakunin and the libertarian sections of the old "First" International Workingmen's Association (IWMA) founded in 1864. Francisco Tomas, one of the organizers of the Spanish Region of the IWMA, reported that "...relations with the Cuban sections were frequent after 1881..." (Max Nettlau: *Reconstruir,* Jan. 15, 1975)

The Declaration of Principles of the International Alliance of Socialist Democracy, drafted by Bakunin in 1868 could be called the "Magna Carta" of Spanish Anarchism. The most relevant paragraph reads:

> ...The Alliance seeks the complete and definitive abolition of classes and the political, economic, and social equality of both sexes. It wants the land and the instruments of labor like all other property [not personal belongings] to be converted into the collective property of the whole society for the utilization [not ownership] by workers: that is, by agricultural and industrial societies [unions] and federations. It affirms that existing political and authoritarian states, which are to be reduced to simple administrative functions dealing with public utilities, must eventually be replaced by a worldwide union of free associations, agricultural and industrial...

Bakunin stressed that the organization of the free society must be based on the "...various functions of daily life and of different kinds of labor...organized by professions and trades..." (Program of The International, 1871) He envisioned that the "free productive associations," which will include members of cooperatives, community

31

and neighborhood groups, cultural associations etc., will voluntarily organize "according to their needs and skills." They will eventually "...transcend all national boundaries and form an immense world-wide federation..." *(Revolutionary Catechism* 1866)

The Resolution of the Basel Congress of the IWMA (1869) after repeating that the wage system must be replaced by the "federation of free producers..." sketched out a form of organization, which, in the main, corresponded to the structure of the libertarian economy established in wide areas during the Spanish Revolution of 1936-1939:

> ...the structure of the new economy was simple: Each factory organized a new administration manned by its own technical and administrative workers. Factories in the same industry in each locality organized themselves into the local Federations of their particular industry. All the local Federations organized themselves into the Local Economic Council of the territorial community in which all the work places were represented [coordination, exchange, sanitation, culture, transportation, public utilities and the whole range of public services including distribution of commodities by consumer cooperatives and other associations.] Both the Local Federations of each industry and the Local Economic Councils were organized regionally and nationally into parallel National Federations of Industry and National Economic Federations... (Diego Abad de Santillan, anarchist writer, Minister of Economy of Catalonia during Spanish Revolution. *Por Que Perdimos la Guerra;* Buenos Aires, 1940, p. 82)

Adapting Bakuninist conceptions to Spanish conditions the Spanish anarcho-syndicalists between the founding Congress of the Federation of the Spanish Region of the IWMA (Barcelona, 1870) and the Madrid Congress of 1874, worked out the basic principles and organization of Spanish anarcho-syndicalism. (Rejecting the artificial national boundaries imposed by capitalism and the State to segregate and divide the workers into hostile camps, the IWMA designated its affiliated organizations of different countries as "Regional Federations of the IWMA") Briefly stated, the leading principles could be formulated in the following manner:

The working class must build a new world based on workers' self-management of the economy, collective ownership and administration of social wealth, full individual, sexual and cultural freedom based upon the principle of federalism. Federalism means coordination through free agreement, locally, regionally, nationally and internationally constituting a vast coordinated network of voluntary alliances embracing the totality of social life. Under federalism the associated groups and organizations reap the benefits of unity while still exercising autonomy within their own spheres. Through federation the people expand the range of their own freedoms. ﹀

This can be accomplished only by the Social Revolution which will forever do away with private property in the means of production and distribution; abolish the State and its satellite institutions, the armed forces, the church, the bureaucracy and all forms of domination and exploitation of man by man. "...on the ruins of capitalism, the State and the Church we will build an anarchist society; the free association of free workers' associations..."

Parliamentary action, collaboration with any form of the State is rejected:

> ...all governments are evil. To ask a worker what kind of government he prefers is to ask him what executioner he prefers... the great United States Republic is an example. There is no king nor emperor, but there are the giant trusts: the kings of Gold, of Steel, of Cotton...

While the means of production, (land, mines transportation, etc.) must become the property of the whole society, "...only the workers' collectives will have the use of these facilities..." In this respect differing from true communism where goods and services will be distributed according to NEED.

In such a society the authoritarian institutions which foster the "...spirit of nationalism and break the natural solidarity of mankind..." will disappear to be replaced by the world-wide commonwealth of labor. The free society will "...harmonize freedom with justice and achieve solidarity..." (quotes are from Anselmo Lorenzo's *El Proletariado Militante*, pgs. 80, 81, 178, 179, 192. Mexico City, Ediciones Vertice, no date)

The revolutionary "direct action" tendency in the Spanish labor movement has always rejected parliamentarianism and class collaboration with the employers and the State in favor of direct action on the economic front. The tactics of the general strike, partial strikes, passive "folded arms" strikes, the boycott, sabotage and insurrections were developed by the workers in the course of bitter class struggles long before the founding of the IWMA. The IWMA itself arose in response to the need for international solidarity in strikes.

Clara E. Lida and other historians trace the ideas and tactics of revolutionary syndicalism in Spain from the early 1800s to the revolution of 1854 and the great Catalonian general strike a year later, fifteen years before the organization of the IWMA in Spain. (*Anarquismo y Revolucion en Espana*, Madrid, 1972) The lessons learned in the course of bitter class struggles made the Spanish proletariat receptive to the ideas of Bakunin. They were inspired by the great watchword of the IWMA: "The emancipation of the working class is the task of the workers themselves."

Bakunin formulated a fundamental principle of anarcho-syndicalism: that in the process of struggling for better conditions within existing capitalist society and "studying economic science...the workers' organizations bear within themselves the living seeds of the new social order which is to replace the bourgeois world...they are creating not only the ideas, but also the facts of the future itself..." (quoted, Rudolf Rocker, *Anarcho-Syndicalism*, p. 88, India edition)

At the Basel Congress of the IWMA the Spanish delegates (and the other libertarian sections) also emphasized the twofold task of anarcho-syndicalism: the unions of the workers must not only carry on the daily struggle for their economic, social and cultural betterment within the existing exploitative system. They must prepare themselves to take over the self-management of social and economic life and become the living cells of the new, free society.

The structure of the Federation of the Spanish Region was designed to assure the greatest possible amount of freedom and autonomy commensurate with indispensable and effective coordination. To prevent the growth of bureaucracy there were no paid officials. All union affairs were conducted after working hours. When this was not possible, delegates were paid only for the time lost away from work. The power of the Federal Commission and the General Congresses were strictly limited only to carrying out the instructions of the membership, never to set policy. Decisions had to be ratified by the majority of the membership. The agenda for conferences, congresses of local, provincial and national assemblies were prepared and thoroughly discussed months in advance. In line with this tradition the CNT (National Confederation of Labor) with over a million members in 1936, had only one paid official — the General Secretary.

The Madrid Congress of the CNT (Dec. 1919) unanimously adopted an anarchist-communist Declaration of Principles stating that "...in accord with the essential postulates of the First International (IWMA) the aim of the CNT of Spain is the realization of Comunismo Libertario..." (José Peirats: *La CNT en la Revolucion Espanola*-Toulouse, 1951, p. 5) The Declaration of Principles of the IWMA reorganized by the anarcho-syndicalists in 1922 also proclaimed that "...its goal is the reorganization of social life on the basis of Free Communism..."

Strongly influenced by the ideas of Peter Kropotkin, who worked out the sociology of anarchism, the anarchist Isaac Puente (killed on the Saragossa front during the Spanish Civil War—1936-1939) envisaged the structure of an anarchist society on the basis of "From each according to his ability; to each according to his needs."

34

...Libertarian Communism is the organization of society without the state and without capitalism. To establish Libertarian Communism it will not be necessary to invent artificial social organizations. The new society will naturally emerge from "the shell of the old." The elements of the future society are already planted in the old existing order. They are the Union [in European usage, the Syndicate] and the Free Commune [sometimes called "free municipality"] which are old, deeply rooted, non-statist popular institutions, spontaneously organized, and embracing all towns and villages in urban and rural areas. Within the Free Commune, there is also room for cooperative associations of artisans, farmers and other groups or individuals who prefer to remain independent or form their own groupings to meet their own needs [providing, of course, that they do not exploit hired labor for wages]..."

"...the terms 'libertarian' and 'communism' denote the fusion of two inseparable concepts, the indispensable prerequisites for the free society: collectivism and individual freedom..." *(El Communismo Anarchico)*

Although the impact of Spanish anarchist ideas on Cuban labor was indeed great, it is not to be inferred that they were artificially grafted to the Cuban revolutionary movement. These ideas were adapted to Cuban conditions. Anarcho-syndicalist principles were accepted, not because they were imported from Spain (the masses did not know where these ideas came from) but because they corresponded to the aspirations and experiences of the Cuban workers on Cuban soil.

ANARCHISM IN CUBA: THE FORERUNNERS

Both anarchist ideas and the development of the Cuban labor movement trace back to the middle of the nineteenth century. Even today's Cuban communists recognize that:

> ...in spite of the efforts of Paul Lafargue (Marx's son-in-law, stationed in Spain) and other marxists, the proletariat of the peninsula (Spain and Portugal) were strongly influenced by anarchist and anarcho-syndicalist ideas. And these ideas carried over to Cuba in the last quarter of the 19th and first quarter of the 20th century, decisively influencing the Cuban labor movement which was invariable anarchist..." (Serge Aguirre; *Cuba Socialista*—a Castroite monthly—September, 1965.)
> ...During the whole epoch (from the 1890s until after the Russian Revolution) it was the anarcho-syndicalists who led the class struggles in Cuba, and the anarchist ideological influence that prevailed...)" (Julio de Riverend, *Cuba Socialista,* Feb. 1965)

Anarchism in the Colonial Period

In Cuba the anarchist movement did not, as in some countries, develop independently of the labor movement. They grew so closely together that it is impossible to trace the history of one without the other. The forerunners and organizers of the Cuban labor movement were the Spanish anarcho-syndicalist exiles who in the 1880s came to Cuba. It was they who gave the Cuban labor movement its distinct social revolutionary orientation, spreading the anarcho-syndicalist ideas of Bakunin and the Spanish internationalists—men like Enrique Messinier, Enrique Roig 'San Martín, and Enrique Cresci.

One of the early labor organizations was the Sociedades Económicos de Amigos del País (Economic Society of the Friends of the Country). We lack detailed information about the ideology of the Association of Tobacco Workers of Havana organized in 1866—but it was vaguely syndicalistic. The workers were passionately interested in self-education. The tobacco workers of Havana (like their countrymen in Florida) paid readers to read works of general interest to them while they worked. During the reader's rest period they avidly discussed what they had learned. An employer rash enough to interfere with these proceedings would be unceremoniously escorted from his premises.

In 1885, an informal federation of unions, Circular de Trabajadores de la Habana (workers' clubs) was organized. Two years later, it held a Congress in which two opposing groups, "reformists versus radicals" heatedly debated the future orientation of their organization.

The anarchist propaganda groups stressed the necessity for organization along anarcho-syndicalist lines, rejecting Marxian ideas on the necessity for parliamentary-political action by social-democratic political parties. In 1886, the Workers' Center was founded to spread the ideas of anarcho-syndicalism through its organ *El Productor,* (The Producer) founded and edited by the anarchist Enrique Roig San Martín.

In 1892, the first Workers' Congress celebrated the First of May by demonstrations for the independence of Cuba, which provoked the premature closing of the Congress by the Spanish authorities. The resolutions for the independence of Cuba were drafted by the anarchists Enrique Cresci, Enrique Suárez and Eduardo González. The Congress approved a resolution stating that "...the working class will not be emancipated until it embraces revolutionary socialism, which cannot be an obstacle for the triumph of the independence of our country..." (quoted by Maurice Halperin: *The Rise and Fall of Fidel Castro*, University of California 1972, p. 4)

Around 1874 the revered "apostle" of Cuban independence, José Martí, frequently referred to anarchist groups named for Fermín Salvochea, Bakunin and others. In his paper, *La Patria*, he printed articles by the anarchist Elisée Reclus and others. Martí wrote:

"...we live in a period of struggle between capitalists and workers...a militant alliance of workers will be a tremendous event. They are now creating it..." (quoted Halperin, ibid. p. 6-7)

The anarchist Carlos M. Balino, active among the tobacco workers of Florida, was an associate of Jose Martí. And the Enrique Roig Club included the anarchist and socialist supporters of Marti. We cite these facts to demonstrate the social-revolutionary character of the independence movement which was not merely nationalistic.

Enrique Messenier became the first president of the Liga General de Trabajadores, organized by the anarchists in the 1890s. This period also marked general strikes of longshoremen in Cardenas, Regla and Havana. The Liga conducted the first general strike for the eight hour day, which was brutally suppressed by the government.

A contemporary intimate account of the state of the Cuban anarchist movement during the crucial years preceding independence can be gleaned from the report of Pedro Esteve, a pioneer of the 20th century anarchist movement which flourished in the United States. *(A Los Anarquistas de Espana y Cuba;* Reported to the International Anarchist Congress, Chicago 1893; published by *El Despertar,* Paterson, New Jersey, 1900.) Esteve was in close touch with the Cuban anarchists in Cuba and with the Spanish anarchist exiles in Cuba. The following remarks were based upon a frustrated propaganda tour cut short by the police after a three month stay.

> The authorities tried to cripple, and if possible, extirpate our movement, not by outright violence—which would have aroused a storm of protest—but by a no less effective, persistent and devilishly clever campaign of petty harassments (landlords were pressured not to rent premises for our meetings.) While not resorting to open censorship, our weekly *La Alarma* was forced to suspend publication. It reappeared under the name *Archivo Social* and was again suppressed. Our Circulo de Trabajadores Workers' Center was closed down on false charges concocted by the "sanitation inspectors" etc., etc.)
>
> The attentats of Emil Henry and other anarchist terrorists which precipitated the brutal persecution of the anarchist movement in Europe, likewise became the pretext for the Cuban government's crackdown on our movement...

Esteve recounts the effects of racism on the healthy development of the Cuban labor and socialist movements, for, in spite of the abolition of slavery and proclamation of equal rights, rampant racial discrimination was still common.

> ...not even the exemplary conduct of the anarchists who unfailingly welcomed the negroes on equal terms at meetings, schools and all other functions on a person to person basis, sufficed for a long time to shake the belief that all whites were their natural enemies...Nevertheless we continued our agitation with dedication and attracted to our ranks genuine proletarian elements. We held meetings in various Havana neighborhoods and in other cities and villages. We were invited to explain our ideas in

39

non-academic popular schools, and in our Center, we gave popular courses in sociology and other subjects...we also initiated other projects of workers' education...at the invitation of workers in the La Rosa de Santiago cigar factory, I gave a well received talk on anarchism...these are only a few examples...little by little, anarchists who had been inactive for a long time returned, and new adherents came to us...our movement revived slowly, but on firmer foundations...

Struggle for Independence: 1868-1895

1868 marked the beginning of the ten-year guerrilla war for independence from Spanish colonial domination, "El Grito de Yara." On October 10, 1868, Carlos Manuel de Cespedes, a wealthy sugar plantation owner in Oriente province attacked the village of Yara with less than 40 men. The attack was repulsed and only 12 men survived. "El Grito de Yara," ("The Call To Rebellion") became the symbol and watchword of the struggle for independence. More than 200,000 militants were killed in the ten-year war, uncounted thousands were wounded. Total casualties could not be estimated. The most prominent military leaders of the independence movement were General Máximo Goméz and Antonio Maceo. In 1869 Cespedes was elected President of the Provisional Republic. This, and El Grito de Yara earned him the title "Father of Independence."

Spain sent General Valeriano Weyler, "The Butcher," to extirpate the independence movement. He locked hundreds of thousands of men women and children into concentration camps. In Havana alone, 52,000 people perished. In rebel areas, cattle and crops were destroyed to starve out the freedom fighters and their families. The peasants retaliated by burning down vast Spanish owned sugar plantations. Weyler was recalled to Spain in 1879.

After the abolition of slavery in 1880, the big landlords expected the Spanish government to compensate them for the losses entailed by the emancipation of the slaves. But the condition of the workers remained practically unchanged. The *Revista de Agricultura* wrote:

> ...A worker in a sugar mill camp awoke at 2 a.m., drank a glass of hot water for breakfast, worked till 11 a.m. After a two hour lunch break the worker went back and worked till 6 p.m., ate supper and then worked several hours more...(quoted in Castro organ *Cuba Socialista* clipping—no date)

Anarchists in the Struggle for Independence

The most militant elements in the insurrections of 1895 for the independence of Cuba were primarily the peasants (and to a relatively lesser extent the numerically inferior urban workers). From the beginning to the end of the war for independence the international anarchist movement supported the revolts, and many young anarchists came to Cuba to fight with the Cuban people. Many anarchists were in the forefront of these struggles, among them Rafael Garcia, Armando Andre (one of the commanders of the rebel army, later murdered by the Machado assassins) and Enrique Cresci.

Anarchist participation in the independence struggles was based upon the following considerations: For the exploited, oppressed masses, bourgeois independence was of secondary importance. For them, abolition of colonial despotism also signified the end of their age-long servitude, and with it, the inauguration of a new era of economic equality, social justice and personal freedom. The people's struggle for independence simultaneously took on a social-revolutionary character. Anarchist propaganda, and above all ACTION, encouraged the masses to turn the struggle for political independence into the struggle for the Social Revolution.

Cuban Independence: The Expansion of U.S. Imperialism

The U.S. imperialists feared the social-revolution of the Cuban people as much as their Spanish colonial and domestic exploiters. In this connection the views of two well qualified historians are well worth quoting:

> ...during the negotiations for the treaty of peace after the victory over Spain [in the Spanish-American War, 1898] Spain expressed fear that if left to itself the island...might be prey to frequent revolutions with the result that neither property nor personal rights would be protected. To save Cuba from the possible consequences of 'premature' independence, Spain wished to have the United States keep at least a degree of control sufficient to insure order...
> (Chester Lloyd Jones; quoted in *Background to Revolution*, New York, 1966, p. 63)

Professor Jones points out that the United States shared Spain's fear of Revolution in Cuba and agreed to "...discharge its obligations under international law..." (p. 64)

And Professor William Appleton Williams sums up the true motivations of U.S. imperialism in respect to Cuban independence:

> ...the United States sought the prompt and permanent pacification of the island...to insure military control...and

facilitate and safeguard United States economic predominance...
the United States thereby set itself in opposition to the Cuban
revolutionaries as well as the Spanish government...Cuba was to
be reconstructed along lines satisfactory to the United States, and
only finally handed over to the Cubans after such vital limits on
their freedom of action and development had been established to
insure indefinite American predominance...(quoted in anthology
Background to Revolution; pgs. 188-190)

Independence to the Outbreak of World War I: 1898-1914

With the defeat of Spain in the Spanish-American War, Cuba
became an independent republic. It was the revolutionary masses of
Cuba, the humble peasants and urban workers, who by their heroism
undermined Spanish rule and made possible the easy victory of the
United States.

Between 1898 and 1902, the American military occupied and
governed Cuba on the pretext that a transition period was necessary to
prepare Cuba for self-rule. The American troops left after the first
presidential election. But the Platt amendment of 1901 granted the U.S.
the right to intervene in Cuban affairs and permanently occupy the
Guantanámo Bay naval base. (The administration of the Isle of Pines
was revoked in 1925.)

Tomás Estrada Palma was elected President of the new republic in
1902. His fraudulent re-election in 1906 and the "liberal" coup which
deposed him created the pretext for the second intervention of U.S.
troops. The administration of Palma's successor José Miguel Gómez
(1909-1912) was incredibly corrupt. He boasted, "...in all my life, I
have been jovial in spirit, with a smile on my lips..." Hubert Herring
remarks: "...with a smile, Gómez emptied the treasury and allowed
his Cuban and American cronies to fatten on concessions..." (*History
of Latin America*; New York, 1955, p. 401) The new independent
republic turned out to be just, or almost as reactionary as the deposed
colonial despotism of Spain. Scarcely less bitter was the struggle
between the oppressed people of Cuba and the corrupt new State with
its bureaucracy and its military and police forces.

In the Spring of 1900, during the United States occupation, the group
publishing *El Mundo Ideal* (The Ideal Society), invited the well known
anarchist Errico Malatesta to tour Cuba and speak to the workers and
peasants. But the Government expelled him. Upon leaving Cuba,
Malatesta wrote a farewell letter to his Cuban comrades, from which
we excerpt the following passages:

"...Upon leaving this country for which I harbor a strong

affection permit me to salute the valiant Cuban workers, black and white, native and foreign, who extended me so cordial a welcome...

"...I have, for a very long time, admired the self-sacrifice and heroism with which you have fought for the freedom of your country. Now I have learned to appreciate your clear intelligence, your spirit of progress and your truly remarkable culture, so rare in people who have been so cruelly oppressed. And I leave with the conviction that you will soon take your place among the most advanced elements in all countries fighting for the real emancipation of humanity..."

"...I assume that the libertarians fighting against the existing government will not put another government in its place; but each one will understand that if in the war for independence this spirit of hostility to all governments incarnated in every libertarian, will now make it impossible to impose upon the Cuban people the same Spanish laws, which martyrs like Marti, Cresci, Maceo, and thousands of other Cubans died to abolish..." *(Solidaridad*

Gastronomica—Anarcho-Syndicalist food workers union organ, Aug. 15, 1955)

In 1902, Havana tobacco workers, organized by Gonzales Lozana and other anarchists, called a general strrike, the first under the Republic. This action, the famous "strike of the apprentices," sought to end the exploitation of apprentices, whose status had been, in effect, that of indentured servants bound to their employers for a given period. The tobacco workers were joined by the Havana port workers. The government tried to break the strike by force, provoking a violent battle in which twenty workers were killed. Using the threat of U.S. intervention, the government finally broke the strike.

The period between 1903 and 1914 was marked by many strikes in which the anarchist actively participated. Among the more important we list:

1903. During a major strike of sugar workers, the anarchists Casanas and Montero y Sarria were murdered by order of the then Governor of Las Villas Province, José Miguel Gómez, later President of Cuba. The long Moneda General Strike, led by the anarchists (Feb. 20th to July 15th) was called because the workers refused to accept payment in devalued Spanish pesetas. They demanded payment in American dollars worth more in purchasing power. Also in 1907, the anarchist weekly *Tierra!* was severely persecuted for inciting a railway strike for the eight hour day and other demands. The Tobacco workers again went on strike, this time for 145 days. They were joined by maritime, construction and other workers.

1910-1912. Anarcho-syndicalists played an important part in the strike of Havana and Cienfuegos sewer workers of June 1910. The bitter 1912 restaurant and cafe workers strike also involved anarchist militants. One of the most active strikers was Hilario Alonso. Other strikes of the period included the bricklayers strike for the eight hour day; the railway workers' strike; the violent Havana tunnel workers strike and the deportation of Spanish anarchists and syndicalists who were particularly militant.

During these years the anarchist movement flourished. The weekly *Tierra!* with its excellent articles from the pen of the most distinguished Cuban and Spanish writers; the libertarian journal, *El Ideal,* and the widespread circulation of works by Éliseé Reclus, Kropotkin and other anarchists in popular priced editions.

This period also marked the significant growth of the workers' cooperative movement in which the anarchists were very active. Payment of a moderate monthly fee gave workers the use of recreation and cultural facilities, medical services and other benefits. The movement reached a total of 200,000 members. In spite of the opposition of industrialists, the workers organized producers' and consumers' housing and other cooperatives.

The anarchists also spearheaded the organization of agrarian cooperatives, a movement which the Castro government crushed in favor of State farms. The libertarian movement of Cuba had always given top priority, not only to the organization of urban workers, but also to peasant struggles. They built up peasant organizations throughout Cuba—in San Cristobal, Las Placios, Pinar del Rio—wherever there was the slightest opportunity. In Realengo 18, Ventas de Casanova, Santa Lucia and El Vinculo anarchist militants like Marcelo Salinas, Modesto Barbieto, Alfredo Pérez and many others fought bravely. Our unforgettable comrades Sabino Pupo Millan and Niceto Peréz were militant peasant revolutionaries in the immense sugar plantations of Santa Lucia, and in Camaguey. During this period, and at least up to 1925, anarchists were the only militants influential among sugar workers. Millan was murdered October 20, 1945, by paid assassins of the Monati Sugar Company for stirring peasant resistance and organizing peasant cooperatives. Perez was also assassinated; the Peasant Federation of Cuba commemorated the date of his murder as "The Day of the Peasant: a day of struggle for the demands of the hungry and exploited agricultural workers."

Russian Revolution to the Machado Dictatorship: 1917-1925

The termination of World War I and the Russian Revolution fired the imagination of the advanced sections of the labor and radical movements around the world. Many anarchists expected an immediate revolution and the realization of the just society worldwide. In 1919 a number of Cuban anarchists, succumbing to the revolutionary euphoria, issued a manifesto in favor of joining the communist Third International, dominated by the Bolshevik Party.

But with more complete and reliable information, and a more sober objective analysis of Russian events, the Cuban anarchist movement entered a new phase. Enthusiasm for the Russian Revolution died out as the dictatorial outrages of the Bolsheviks became obvious and as critical comments from Kropotkin, Voline, Berkman and other anarchist refugees in Europe and elsewhere reached Cuba.

The years between 1917 and 1930 marked bitter and widespread class struggles: local and national strikes for more wages, the eight hour day, union recognition, campaigns against obligatory military service; tremendous demonstrations against scarcity and the high cost of living, etc. All these manifestations of popular rebellion called forth government persecution of the radical movement. Spanish anarchists were deported, halls closed down one day by the police were reopened the next; papers suspended one day, reappeared the next day under another name. In spite of the repressions, hundreds of young men and women joined the anarchist organizations.

The anarchists were feverishly active, above all in the labor unions among the tobacco workers, bricklayers and masons, gypsum workers, bakers, engineers, railroad workers, factories etc. The libertarians published the weeklies, *Nueva Aurora* and *Labor Sana*; the magazines, *El Progreso, Voz del Dependiente* (clerks), *El Productor Panadero* (bakers), *Nueva Luz* (New Light), *Proteo, El Libertario,* and other periodicals.

This agitation and strike activity resulted in the organization of the Havana Federation of Labor, and much later, the National Labor Federation of Cuba. Both these organizations adopted anarcho-syndicalist forms of struggle and organization. Here is a partial listing of the main events:

1918—Bloody strike of the Havana construction workers. Invoking the 1893 anti-anarchist law, the government tried to extirpate the anarchist influence in labor organizations by imprisoning anarchist organizers and activists on trumped-up charges of sedition and conspiracy to overthrow the state. The police opened fire on a demonstration called by workers' unions against the high cost of living.

1920—In April a national congress was called under the auspices of the Havana and Pinal del Rio Federation of Weavers, in which many anarchists held important posts. Corruption in government was rife.

(In 1921, for example, Alfredo Zayas, nicknamed "the Peseta Snatcher" by his victims, was elected President of Cuba.)

1924—A congress of anarchist groups united all the anarchist tendencies into the newly organized Federación de Grupos Anarquistas de Cuba. The tiny scattered papers were consolidated into one really adequate, well edited, well produced periodical. The new journal *Tierra!* (Land) attained a wide circulation, until forced to suspend publication by the Machado dictatorship. (*Tierra!* continued publication intermittently till the late 1930s).

One of *Tierra's* most brilliant collaborators, Paulino Díaz, took a very prominent part in a workers' congress held in Cienfuegos, which laid the basis for what later (1938) became the Confederation of Cuban Workers (CTC). But the anarchists never controlled the CTC, which became, and remains to this day, a quasi-governmental agency, dominated successively by the Grau San Martín, Batista, and Castro governments.

The first General Secretary of the National Confederation of Cuban Workers (CNOC) was the anarchist typographer, Alfredo López. There were also socialist and communist groups in the CNOC. The growth of the anarchists had been severely curtailed as a result of the struggles under the regime of President Menocal, by deportations to Spain, and by police repression. Recognizing the need for a better organized and more efficient labor movement, the anarchists reorganized the craft unions on an industrial basis—based on factories and industries—regardless of crafts.

The anarchists and anarcho-syndicalists practically controlled one of the strongest unions in Cuba, Sindicato de la Industria Fabril (Brewery Union—SIF). With the cooperation of the anarchist groups, the anarcho-syndicalists also organized sugar cane and railway workers' unions in the province of Camaguey.

1925—A vicious campaign to obliterate preponderent anarchist influence in the SIF was launched by the Machado government which accused the anarchist militants Eduardo Vivas and Luis Quiros of poisoning the beer in a strike against the Polar Brewing Company. The Subsequent scandal prepared the way for an all-out offensive against the union and the anarchist movement. All of the organizers were persecuted. Some anarchist organizers went into hiding. Others were jailed and foreign-born anarchists deported. A few were driven to commit suicide.

But in spite of all the atrocities, the great mass of workers, who during the years still retained their libertarian spirit and approach to problems, continued to organize and spread anarcho-syndicalist ideas. When in 1925, at the Congress of the Cuban National Confederation of

46

Labor (CNOC), in Camagüey, some agents of the employers proposed the expulsion of the anarcho-syndicalists, the Congress, far from approving expulsion, expelled those who made the motion for expulsion of the anarcho-syndicalists. In that same year (1925), paid assassins of the employers shot and killed the anarchist Enrique Varone, the most effective organizer of sugar and railway workers in Camaguey and Oriente provinces. The anarchists also organized the peasants and rural industrial workers into the Sindicato General de Trabajadores de San Cristóbal, Province of Pinar del Río.

The Dictatorship of Machado: 1925-1933:

On May 20th 1925, General Gerardo Machado, a semi-literate power-mad despot (later known as the notorious "Butcher of Las Villas") became President of Cuba. His election campaign was a well organized brainwashing publicity stunt. Posing as a paternalistic, benevolent democrat, he was, at first, immensely popular. Scarcely a dissenting note marred the chorus of universal acclaim. But the anarchist weekly *Tierra!* published a magnificent editorial ending with the words:

> ...We go with the common people, with the masses; but when they follow a tyrant: then we go alone! Erect! With eyes raised high toward the luminous aurora of our ideal!

In conjunction with the agitation in the University of Havana, ten people founded the Cuban Communist Party. The Party attracted intellectuals, students, and few workers. Until the mid-1930s it had little influence in labor circles. The Party was temporarily outlawed in 1927.

The Machado regime formed a government-sponsored union, Unión Federativa Obrera Nacional (United National Federation of Labor—UFON) and forced all the legitimate labor organizations underground.

The anarchist labor movement was sadistically suppressed. Alfredo López, the General Secretary of the CNOC (mentioned above) was thrown into the sea to be devoured by sharks. The long struggle for control of the CNOC ended in 1930-31, when the communists, in league with the Machado government, connived by the foulest means to seize control of the CNOC and the labor movement.

Nevertheless, throughout the many popular upheavals of the 1920s and 1930s, the anarchists and anarcho-syndicalists played a significant role. After the government suppression of the CNOC they were among the principal organizers of the independent and militant Confederación General de Trabajadores (General Confederation of Labor.)

The bloody dictatorship of Machado was overthrown by a general strike and insurrection. The strike began with the walkout of the trolley and bus unions. While the communists controlled the bus union, the trolley workers' union was strongly influenced by the anarcho-syndicalists. The Havana Federation of Labor called a meeting of all unions to organize the general strike and elected a number of anarchists to the strike committee, among them Nicosio Trujillo and Antonio Penichet.

Day by day the strike grew into a formidable threat to the government. In a last ditch attempt to stay in power and break the strike, Machado gained the support of the Communist Party and in exchange for its cooperation Machado promised to legalize the Party and allow its bureaucrats to control several labor unions. The communists accepted Machado's offer and tried to break the strike. They failed. The strike precipitated the fall of Machado in spite of the efforts of the communists and their leader Cesar Vilar, to help him stay in power.

The Federation of Anarchist Groups issued a manifesto exposing the treason of the communists and urging the workers to stand fast in their determination to overthrow the tyrant and his lieutenants. We reprint extracts from the manifesto as translated in the organ of the Industrial Workers of the World, *The Industrial Worker,* Chicago, October 3, 1933.

Manifesto to the Cuban Workers and the People in General

> The Anarchist Federation of Cuba, conscious of its responsibility in these times of confusion, feels obliged to expose before the workers—and public opinion—the base actions of the Communist Party...We believe that the truth is the most powerful weapon, and that is the weapon we use. We want everybody to know the truth. Here it is...
>
> On August 7th (1933), when the general strike against Machado and his regime had the whole island in its grip, Machado was frightened and foresaw his imminent fall...At this juncture, the so-called "Central Committee" of the communist party controlled puppet union, National Labor Confederation [CNOC]...with the full authority of its Communist leaders offered and arranged an agreement with the Machado government...
>
> The day after the machine gun massacre of unarmed people by the Machado assassins the Communist labor fakers were transported in luxurious cars provided by the military officers and Machado's Secretary of War to a banquet with Machado in the most expensive luxury restaurant in Havana—El Carmelo. At the banquet, Machado agreed to recognize the Communist Party legally, and grant other requests...

The communists made frantic appeals to the workers to go back to work because the employers granted their demands. But the workers (including even the Havana bus and transportation union, controlled by the communists) refused. They decided to obey only their own conscience and to continue resistance until the Machado regime is overthrown or forced to flee.

Machado and his communist allies retaliated. No labor union was allowed to meet. The Havana Federation of Labor [FOH, founded by the anarcho-syndicalists], to which the largest number of non-political labor unions were affiliated, could not meet because it did not have a signed authorization from the government. Only the communists, thanks to their betrayal, were allowed to meet. Armed with revolvers while all others were forbidden to hold or carry arms and constitutional rights were suspended, the communists held meetings, rode in automobiles burning gasoline supplied by the army because the filling stations were closed by the strike...

..in conclusion we want the workers and the people of Cuba to know that the rent for the offices of the communist party labor front the CNOC is paid by the Machado regime, that the furniture was forcibly taken away from the Havana Federation of Labor offices with the permission and active help of Machado's Secretary of War...

THE BATISTA ERA

On August 12, 1933, Carlos Manuel de Cespedes, former Ambassador to Washington became President of Cuba (he bore the same name as his father who the was the first President of the Provisional Republic of Cuba in 1869—see above) In spite of the all out support of the U.S., his regime collapsed after being in office only 21 days. Cespedes was overthrown by the famous "sergeants revolt" (Sept. 4, 1933) led by the then unknown Fulgencio Batista y Zaldívar.

Fulgencio Batista was born in 1902 in Oriente Province. His father was a peasant laborer on a sugar plantation. In 1921, he enlisted as a private in the Cuban army, where he learned typing and stenography. In 1932 Batista became a military court stenographer with the rank of sergeant.

Batista's Revolutionary Junta took power on the basis of a democratic program summed up in the following extract:

1) Economic reconstruction of the national government and political process on the basis of a Constitutional Convention to be held immediately.

2) Immediate elimination from public life of parasites and full pun-

51

ishment for the atrocities and corruption of the previous Machado regime.

3) Strict recognition of the debts and obligations contracted by the Republic.

4) Immediate creation of adequate courts to enforce the measures above mentioned.

5) Undertake all measures necessary...towards the creation of a new, modern, democratic Cuba.

Batista promoted himself to the rank of Colonel and Commander in Chief of the Armed forces. Batista was the de facto dictator of Cuba and ruled through a succession of puppet presidents (seven in all). The civilian, Dr. Ramón San Martín (a professor of medicine), was appointed Provisional President of Cuba by Batista's junta. His administration in line with Batista's democratic program, enacted a number of reforms (eight hour day, women's suffrage, repeal of the notorious Platt Amendment, legalizing U.S. intervention in Cuban affairs, etc.)

Batista lost the 1944 presidential election to Grau San Martin's Autentico Party and with the millions stolen from the Cuban treasury retreated to his Florida Estate in 1950. Presidential elections in Cuba were scheduled for June 1952. The favorite candidate wo win was Roberto Agramonte, Professor of Sociology in the University of Havana. Agramonte belonged to the Ortodox Party (Partido del Pueblo Ortodoxo). The Ortodoxos wanted a return to the original principles of the Autentico Party whose leaders were Presidents Grau San Martin (1944-1848) and Carlos Prio Socarras (1948-1952). [Fidel Castro was an active member of the Ortodoxo Party, whose leader, Eduardo Chibas, in despair over the failure of the reform program and the corruption of Cuban institutions—in the midst of a radio program —committed suicide, August 1951]

In the meantime Batista prepared the ground for his return to Cuba and seizure of power; he spent huge sums to get himself elected Senator from Las Villas Province; he planted his men in the mass organizations (some of them were communists who worked with him previously). He organized support in the army, the governmental bureaucracy, among the landlords, industrialists, and the bankers. He cleverly took advantage of the widespread venality and colossal corruption of former administrations and promised democratic reforms. (For example, just before President Grau San Martin was about to be tried for misappropriation of $174,000,000 in public funds during his administration, thieves broke into the Havana Court House and stole the records.) The presidential elections scheduled for June 1952 were never held. On March 10 1952, Batista staged his coup d'etat and seized power.

The Communists and Batista

In January 1940, the Comintern sent representatives to purge and Stalinize the Cuban Communist Party. Francisco Caldero, (a self-educated cobbler, who rose to prominence in the Cuban Party and in the Castro regime, under the name of Blas Roca) became the new Secretary of the Party. After the Seventh Congress of the Comintern (Third International) decreed the "popular united front" alliance with bourgeois organizations, the Cuban Communist Party established close relations with Batista.

In November 1940, the communists supported Batista's candidates in the elections to the Constituent Assembly. In return for their support, Batista allowed the communists to organize and control the government sponsored union, Cuban Confederation of Labor (CTC Confederación de Trabajadores de Cuba) The first Secretary General of the CTC was Lazáro Peña—who, ironically, enough, held the same post in the Castro regime. In exchange for these favors the communists guaranteed Batista labor peace. In line with the Communist Party's "Popular Front Against Fascism" policy, the alliance of the Communist Party with the Batista was officially consumated when the Party joined the Batista government. The Communist Party leaders Carlos Rafael Rodríguez and Juan Marinello (who now hold high posts in the Castro government) became Ministers Without Portfolio in Batista's Cabinet. To illustrate the intimate connections between the communists and Batista, we quote from a letter of Batista to Blas Roca, Secretary of the Communist Party:

June 13, 1944

Dear Blas,

With respect to your letter which our mutual friend, Dr. Carlos Rafael Rodríguez, Minister Without Portfolio, passed to me, I am happy to again express my firm unshakeable confidence in the loyal cooperation the People's Socialist Party (the then official name of the Communist Party of Cuba) its leaders and members have given and continue to give myself and my government . . . Believe me, as always,

Your very affectionate and cordial friend,

Fulgencio Batista

In the electoral campaign the Communist candidates won ten seats in the Cuban parliament and more than a hundred posts in the Municipal councils.

In line with their pro-Batista policy the communists joined Batista in condemning Fidel Castro's attack on the Moncada Barracks (July 1953—the anniversary of the attack is a national holiday in Castro Cuba).

> ...the life of the People's Socialist Party (communist)...has been to combat...and unmask the putschists and adventurous activities of the bourgeois opposition as being against the interests of the people...(reported in *Daily Worker,* U.S organ of the Communist Party, August 10, 1953)

Throughout the Batista period the communists pursued two parallel policies: overtly they criticized Batista and covertly they cooperated with him.

The Crisis of the Labor Movement and the Anarchists: 1944-1952

The anarcho-syndicalist militant Ernesto Barbieto outlined the problems of the Cuban Labor Movement and the position of the anarchists in an article, Los Libertarios Vuelvan (The Libertarians Return: *Estudios*—anarchist monthly—Havana, March, 1950;

After the bloody repression of the Machado dictatorship, the libertarian militants most active in the labor movement were severely persecuted or forced into exile, and the anarchist influence was consequently considerably weakened. Another major reason for the decline was state intervention, de facto control of the labor movement.

The exclusion of the anarchists left the field open for Stalinists, reformists and professional politicians to widen and tighten their grip on the unions. The democratic phraseology of the politicians gave the proletariat the illusion that they were actually masters of their destiny. This illusion was further fostered by granting certain immediate demands, obtained without struggle or sacrifices. The workers did not realize that a coalition of employers, the state and the labor politicians made these concessions only to stave off militant action by the workers, and above all, to strengthen their own positions and influence in the unions.

For these concessions the proletariat paid a very high price; direct interference and de facto state control of their unions; the virtual destruction of legitimate, independent labor organizations like the General Confederation of Workers [CGT]. And the vehicle for this monopoly was the state sponsored Cuban Confederation of Labor [CTC] [controlled by the Communist-Batista coalition]. It was this threat that galvanized the militants of the Libertarian Association of Cuba [ALC] and other independent labor organizations to rally the workers in defense of the autonomy and independence of the labor movement, to expel the labor politicians and arouse the revolutionary consciousness of the working class.

The Third National Libertarian Congress was called (March 11-22, 1950) to reorganize the libertarian labor movement and adopt concrete practical measures enabling its militants to again orientate and play a decisive part in the regeneration of the Cuban labor movement. The Congress approved the following resolutions:

A) fight against the control of the labor movement by bureaucrats, political parties, religious sects, and class-collaborationists
B) extend the influence of the libertarians by actively participating in the daily struggles of the urban and rural workers for better wages and working conditions.
C) encourage workers to prepare themselves culturally and professionally not only to better their present working conditions, but also to take over the technical operation and administration of the whole economy in the new libertarian society.
D) educate the workers to understand the true meaning of syndicalism, which must be apolitical, revolutionary and federalist, which will help prevent authoritarian elements to institute a tyrannical type of unionism, actually becoming an agency of the state.

On tactical problems the Congress resolves to work actively with the workers of the CGT, the only legitimate national labor organization with syndicalist tendencies, and which is most responsive to the real needs of the workers.

To warn the workers that the CTC is a state-sponsored union, supported by the Stalinite faction and allied labor fakers; that the CTC is a pseudo-proletarian organization without a trace of revolutionary ideas, spirit or practice; that the CTC is entirely dominated by dictatorial political parties and a corrupt leadership.

(signed) Ernesto Barbieto

Partial Listing of Libertarian Activities in Cuba in the 1950s
(Article in *Views and Comments,* organ of Libertarian League, New York, Spring 1965)

In the mid and later 50s, the Libertarian Association of Cuba (ALC) had functioning local groups (delegations in Havana, Pinar del Rio, San Cristobal, Artemisea, Ciego de Avila, and Manzanillo, as well as a heavy scatering of members elsewhere). Their sympathizers and influence were in complete disproportion to their actual membership. Anarcho-syndicalist groups consisted usually of a few members and a larger number of sympathizers existed in many local and regional unions as well as in other organizations. The following is s partial listing (from one exiled comrade's memory) of the libertarian activities and influence in the six provinces of Cuba. The listing is by provinces and municipalities from west to east.

Province of Pinar Del Río

> *City of Pinar del Río*—There was a delegation of the ALC that coordinated the activities in the province and which on occasion ran local radio programs. In addition, our comrades influenced and participated in the leadership of the following unions: tobacco workers, food workers, electricians, construction workers, carpenters, transport workers, bank employees and medical workers. The magazines of the tobacco, bank workers and electricians unions were edited by libertarians.

> *San Juan y Martínez*—Libertarians influenced and led the tenant farmers union which covered a large agricultural zone.

> *Viñales*—A comrade pharmacist personally influenced various activities of local civic institutions.

> *San Cristóbal*—There was a delegation of the ALC whose members influenced and led the Municipal Agrarian Association, the Sugar Workers Union and the Association of Tobacco Harvesters, exerting also some influence among metal workers and commercial employees.

> *Artemisa*—There was a delegation of the ALC. The libertarians influenced and led the Tobacco Workers Union (one of the strongest in Cuba) having also some influence in Transport, sugar and food industries as well as among high school students. The group also had occasional radio programs.

Province of La Habana

> *City of La Habana*—Seat of the National Council of the ALC, which also functioned as the Local Delegation. Edited the newspaper *El Libertario* (formerly *Solidaridad)* which had been able to appear with but few interruptions since 1944. There were occasional radio programs and some books and pamphlets were published.

There were weekly forums at the headquarters and public mass meetings were occasionally held in La Habana and other points throughout the country. Our comrades influenced and participated in the leadership of the following unions: Electricians, food workers, transport, shoemakers, fishermen, woodworkers, medicine, metal and construction. To a lesser degree their influence was felt among the dockers, slaughterhouse workers, movie industry, graphic arts, and journalists, as well as in the Naturist Association and the Spanish Republican Circle. In the food workers sector, the libertarian group published a monthly periodical *Solidaridad Gastronomica* for over eight years without interruption. Libertarians wrote regularly for the publications of the unions of other industries imparting what doctrinal orientation they could. Sporadically, it was possible to influence various professional and student organizations.

Arroyo Naranjo—In this town our comrades influenced and led the Parents, Neighbors and Teachers Association, the Progressive Cultural Association and the Consumers Cooperative.

Santiago de las Vegas—Here our members sparked the "Mas Luz" Library, and the Cultural Lyceum.

San Antonio de los Baños—Influence in the Workers Circle and among the tobacconists.

Province of Matanzas

City of Matanzas—Some influence in the textile, graphic arts and bank employees unions as well as in the Spanish Republican Circle.

Limonar—Strong influence in the Sugar Workers Union.

Cardenas—Some influence among commercial employees and in the Secondary School.

Colon—Influence in the tobacco workers union.

Itato—Influence and leadership in salt workers union.

Province of Las Villas

Santa Clara—Some influence in the electricians union.

Camajuani—Influence in the tobacco selectors union.

Zaza del Medio—Some influence in the Association of Tobacco Harvesters.

Isabela de Sagua—Some influence in the dockers union.

Sancti Spiritus—Influence in the unions of construction workers and medicine, and also in the Association of Secondary School Students.

Province of Camagüey

Camagüey—Strong influence in the Agrarian Federation and some in the railway workers union and journalists.

Jatibonico—Strong influence in the Sugar Workers Union and in the peasants' association.

Ciego de Avila—There was a delegation of the ALC which for a time maintained a daily radio hour. Influence in the peasants association, medical workers union and among the sugar workers of the Steward and Estrella Centrals.

Santa Cruz del Sur—Influence in peasant organizations and in the Santa Marta sugar central.

Morón—Influence in the sugar central Violeta. Active among the tobacco harvesters of Tamarindo and in the Agricultural Union of Florencia.

Nuevitas—Traditionally this zone has always had strong libertarian tendencies. Together with Moron it can be considered the cradle of the strong anarcho-syndicalist movement of the 20s. For decades there was no other socio-political movement in the region. In the 40s there was an active ALC delegation in Nuevitas that took the initiative in the formation of various unions and of the local peasants association which was the best known peasants' organization of the island. It seized a large extension of uncultivated farmland establishing the Cooperative of Santa Lucia. In the ensuing struggle with the landlords and the Government, there were killed and wounded on both sides including one ALC member. The peasants won and retained possession of the land.

Province of Oriente

Santiago de Cuba—Strong influence in the food workers union and

58

some in textiles and transport.

Victoria de las Tunas—Some influence in the sugar workers union.

Holguín—At one time there had been a delegation of the ALC—some influence remaining in local unions.

Bayamo—Some influence among electricians and in the Peasants Association.

Palma Soriano—Influence in the Union of Commercial Employees.

Manzanillo—Delegation of the ALC with influence among food workers and carpenters.

Contramaestre—The Miners union here had been organized and was still influenced by the libertarians.

San Luis—Some influence among bakers, commercial employees and sugar workers.

Guantánamo—Many years ago the Coffee Producers Cooperative of Monte-Rus was organized by libertarians and since then the anarchist influence has remained strong in the area, especially among the sugar workers and peasants.

During the struggle against Batista those of our comrades not then in prison or who had not been forced into exile by being too well known as enemies of the tyranny, were in the forefront of the struggle in many localities.

When Batista collapsed, there were in the Province of Pinar del Rio attempts by several peasant groups under libertarian influence to establish agricultural collectives. These were set up by the local people who seized the land they had been working. However, the Government of Fidel Castro promptly saw the danger to itself of such action and crushed the collectives by force. State farms have been established in their place. Big Brother felt he knew best!

The Role of the Libertarian Movement in the Anti-Batista Struggle

This is the title of an article published in *El Libertario* (organ of the anarcho-syndicalist Libertarian Association of Cuba [ALC] July 19, 1960. Scarcely a year later, the anarchist press and groups were suppressed by the Castro "revolutionary government."

. . . The ALC was from the very beginning in the midst of the battle against the Batista regime. On March 10, 1952, when Batista's hordes staged their 'coup d'etat' to seize Cuba, the ALC proposed the full fighting solidarity of all revolutionary organizations to reorganize armed resistance and repulse the Batista troops. But the cowardice and demoralization of the Socorras government—"It is too late. We must avoid bloodshed"—gave Batista an easy victory. Later the blood flowed in torrents! Not for an instant did the ALC relax in the struggle to topple Batista.

In 1956, the ALC published a pamphlet *Projecciones Libertarias* denouncing the disastrous policies of the Batista government and stating our position. In a speech delivered to the CTC Cuban Confederation of Labor National Council (1957) our comrade Moscu on behalf of the ALC openly attacked the top-heavy leaders who controlled the CTC, accusing them and their lieutenants of outrageous corruption. His speech was widely reported in the Cuban press. Later that year (1957) the ALC published a manifesto—50,000 copies—publicly exposing the filthy maneuvers and corruption of the labor movement, clearly explaining the position of the ALC.

The ALC at all times welcomed and made its premises available to the underground militants and rebel organizations. Thus, on December 31, 1958, we hid in our hall—in spite of the risks—a young man hunted by the police for allegedly violent acts committed in Marionao against the Batista regime.

Most of our comrades were active in the insurrectionary movement: The Directorio, Obrera Revolucionario, The Federation of University Students, etc., etc. Our hall was often the gathering place for many rebels belonging to other organizations. It was even used by the Castro 26th of July Movement to train men in the proper use of firearms. And our hall became a distribution center for mountains of anti-Batista literature.

Literally hundreds of our comrades were persecuted, tortured, driven into exile, murdered. Here are a few:

Boris Santa Coloma; killed July 26, 1953 in the celebrated Castro-led attack on the Moncada Barracks. *Aquila Iglesias;* exiled. *Álvarez y Barbieto;* exiled. *Miguel Rivas;* disappeared. *Roberto Bretau;* prison. *Manuel Gerona;* prison. *Rafael Serra;* tortured. *Modesto Barbieta, María Pinar González, Dr. Pablo Madan, Plácido Mendez, Eulegio Reloba and his sons, Abelardo Iglesias, Mario Garcia and his son:* all of them in prison, tortured and in some cases barely escaping assassination. *Isidro Moscu;* imprisoned and left for dead after brutal tortures. With Moscu, a numerous group of comrades were also imprisoned and tortured for preparing an armed insurrection in the province of Pinar del Rio.

Our hall was raided many times by the Batista police. Shootings took place. Comrades were arrested and brutally beaten. Books and organization records were confiscated. But in spite of all these atrocities, our movement, after truly heroic sacrifices, survived to carry on the struggle with undiminished dedication . . .

As Batista became more and more tyrannical, more and more people joined the opposition, until by far the bulk of all classes, (each for reasons of their own) rose against him and his corrupt regime. When Batista could no longer depend even on the armed forces which had always sustained him, his regime collapsed. On January 1st, 1959, he and his entourage fled Cuba.

The Cuban anarchists were jailed, tortured, driven into exile by successive governments. The "communists" and the corrupt politicians, powerfully backed by Machado and Batista, took advantage of the persecution of the anarchists to seize control of the labor movement. Now, again hounded and outlawed by the Castro dictatorship, the ranks of the anarcho-syndicalists have been reduced to a mere handful of dedicated militants. The Cuban anarcho-syndicalist movement has in a century of struggle written a glorious, indelible page in the history of the revolutionary movement, from which new generations of fighters will continue to draw inspiration.

(Note on sources—Aside from references noted in the text, information for this chapter was derived from a series of powerful articles by the Cuban anarchist, Justo Muriel, printed in an the organ of the Libertarian Federation of Argentina, *Reconstruir*; Buenos Aires, numbers 39-41, Dec.-April 1966; articles in various issues of *Solidaridad Gastonomica* —organ of the anarcho-syndicalist food and cafe workers union; *El Libertario*, organ of the Libertarian Association of Cuba, Havana; the anarchist papers *Ahora* and *Combat*, published in Cuba in the 1940s and 1950s; conversations with Cuban anarchists; files in the Centre International de Recherches sur l'Anarchisme, Geneva, and some data from the International Institute for Social Research, Amsterdam.)

THE REVOLUTION IN PERSPECTIVE:
THE ECONOMIC BACKGROUND

To arrive at an objective assessment of the character of the Cuban Revolution, and the validity of the claims made both for and against it, it is first necessary to examine the economic background. The information here assembled is meant to dispel widespread misconceptions and establish the facts.

Cuba, the largest of the Caribbean islands, with an area of 44,218 square miles, is greater in area than Austria, Hungary, Belgium, Israel, Israel, Iceland, or Ireland. Its population in 1961 was 6,900,000 with an annual birth rate of 2.3% as against the U.S. rate of 1.7%. By the 1970's Cuba's population reached 8,400,000. About73% of the population is white; 12% black and 15% mestizo. Density of population was 153 inhabitants per square mile in the 1960s. The island was densely populated, but because of the high proportion of arable land, was not overcrowded.

To better understand the social-economic background of the Cuban Revolution it is necessary to take into account class differences in rural Cuba. In this connection the views of Ramiro Guerra are well worth quoting:

> ...Cuba was precisely NOT a peasant country...to talk of Cuba's "peasantry" as if the population were an undifferentiated mass of impoverished peasant landowners is to miss entirely the complexity of rural Latin America. Peasants who by a swift process of sugar plantation developments have been transformed into rural

63

proletarians are no longer PEASANTS...there were, in 1953, 489,000 agricultural wage workers in Cuba and only 67,000 unpaid family laborers who were the wives and children of the small-scale land owners, the highland peasantry, Los Guajiros of Cuba...the big sugar plantations are an urbanizing force within which the rural population must concentrate itself densely...by standardizing work practices, the plantations create a factory situation—albeit a rural one. And factories in the field are urban in many ways, even though they are not in cities. A rural proletariat working on modern plantations inevitably become culturally and behaviorally distinct from the peasantry...its members have no land. Their special economic and social circumstances lead in another direction. They prefer standardized wage minimums, adequate medical and educational services, increased buying power, etc...when it is noted that there were more than 489,000 agricultural laborers in Cuba in 1953...a gross indication of the difference between peasantry and rural proletariat is provided us...(quoted by Sidney W. Mintz in the anthology *Background to Revolution*; New York, 1966, p. 182-183)

These views are confirmed by the fact that the agricultural laborers, primarily in the sugar plantations, constituted one of the strongest and most numberous federations affiliated to the Cuban Confederation of Labor (CTC)

Cuba, the "Pearl of the Antilles," though by no means a paradise, was not, as many believe, an economically backward country. Castro himself admitted that while there was poverty, there was no economic crisis and no hunger in Cuba before the Revolution. (See Maurice Halperin: *The Rise and Fall of Fidel Castro*, University of California, 1972, pgs. 24, 25, 37)

Armando Hart, a member of Castro's innermost ruling group, made the extremely significant observation that:

...it is certain that capitalism had attained high levels of organization, efficiency and production that declined after the Revolution... (*Juventud Rebelde*, November 2, 1969; quoted by René Dumont, *Is Cuba Socialist?*, p. 85)

Paul A. Baran, an ardent pro-Castroite in the equally ardent *Monthly Review* pamphlet, *Reflections on the Cuban Revolution* (1961) substantiates what every economist, as well as amateurs like Castro, has been saying:

...the Cuban Revolution was born with a silver spoon in its mouth...the world renowned French agronomist, René Dumont, has estimated that if properly cultivated as intensively as South China, Cuba could feed fifty million people...the Cuban Revolution is spared the painful, but ineluctable compulsion that has beset preceding socialist revolutions: the necessity to force tightening of people's belts in order to lay the foundations for a better tomorrow...(p. 23)

Theodore Draper quotes Anibal Escalante, (before he was purged by Castro) one of the leading communists, who admitted that:

...in reality, Cuba was not one of the countries with the lowest standard of living of the masses in America, but on the contrary, one of the highest standards of living, and it was here where the first great...democratic social revolution of the continent burst forth...If the historical development had been dictated by the false axiom [revolutions come first in poorest countries] the revolution should have been first produced in Haiti, Colombia or even Chile, countries of greater poverty for the masses than the Cuba of 1958...(quoted in Draper's *Castro's Revolution: Myths and Realities*; New York, 1962, p. 22)

The following statistics indicate the rate of production before the Revolution (Jan. 1, 1959). (Sources are two United Nations publications: *Economic Study of Latin America, 1957*, and the *Statistical Annual, 1961*. The third source is The University of Miami Cuban Studies, reported in the journal *Este y Oeste*, Caracas, Jan. 1969)

AGRICULTURAL PRODUCTION

1949-1951	1957-1958 % of increase
raw sugar	11
plantains	30
rice	120
leaf tobacco	50
potatoes	28
flour	114

65

INDUSTRIAL PRODUCTION—NON-SUGAR

%of increase

cement	55.5
fertilizer	48.8
cotton	33.6
sulfuric acid	32.3
artificial silk	18.1
rubber goods	65.5
construction	120.8
gas and electric	157.5
manufactures	118.7

(source, University of Miami Cuban Studies reported in *Este y Oeste*)

> ...according to the Food and Agricultural Organization of the United Nations, total agricultural production in 1969, 10 years after the Revolution, was 7% below that of 1958...(Carmelo Mesa-Lago, *Cuba in the 1970s*; University of New Mexico Press, 1974, p. 56)

As for sugar production, Halperin writes that while it is true that:

> ...in 1961, by harvesting uncut sugar cane left over from previous years, Cuba produced close to seven million metric tons of sugar, the largest crop in history. Production, however, fell sharply in the following eight years, averaging well below the yields in the decade preceding the Revolution [1949-1959]...per capita production of sugar in 1945 was about 30% higher than in 1963...In the 1950s, on the average, a labor force of 500,000 working three months produced 500,000,000 tons of sugar, *forty* tons per man year. In the 1970 harvest, 500,000 persons working *twelve* months producd 8.5 million tons of sugar, or only *seventeen* tons per man year...(ibid. p. 62, 241, our emphasis)

Cuba was NOT a one crop country. In 1957, sugar represented only 27% of total agricultural income. Growing crops were only PARTIALLY listed above. Cattle raising, (per 100 head) increased from 3884 to 6000 in 1958 (University of Miami Studies)

> ...before Castro, Cuba was one of the richest underdeveloped countries in the world, with Gross National Product, per-capita income in the mid 1950s of $360, Cuba was well ahead of Japan

($254 per-capita) and Spain ($254 per-capita)... (Robert Blackburn, quoted in the anthology *Fidel Castro's Personal Revolution: 1953-1973*; New York, 1975, p. 134)

—Cuba had one automobile for every 39 inhabitants, compared with Argentina's one for every 60 and Mexico's one for every 91 people.
—Cuba had one radio for every 5 people, second in Latin America only to Argentina with one for every 3 inhabitants.
—the wage rate for industrial workers in Cuba was the highest in Latin America (as of 1957) and 9th highest in the world.
—agricultural wages were the highest in Latin America
—Cuba's mortality rate of 7 per thousand was the lowest in Latin America. Its infant mortality rate was by far the lowest.
—Cuba had one doctor for every 1,000 inhabitants, exceeded only by Uruguay with one for every 800, and Argentina for every 760 people.
—Cuba ranked fifth in Latin American manufacturing.
—Though living standards were much lower than in the U.S., Canada and Western Europe, Cuba's was the third highest in Latin America, and almost as high as Italy's.
—Cuba had more railroads per square mile than any other country in the world.
—Its one telephone for 38 persons was exceeded only by the U.S. with one for every 3 and Argentina with one for every 13; way ahead of Russia's with one for every 580 people.

It must be borne in mind, however, that statistics can be misleading and conditions were by no means as rosy as implied. Favorable comparison with the already low living standards of Latin America does not mean that the Cuban unskilled workers (and far less the peasants) enjoyed a SATISFACTORY standard of living. To be a little better off than the WORST does not signify that it is the BEST. There is another, darker side to this picture. Compared to American standards, Cuba's per-capita income was 1/5 of the average U.S. income: far lower than in any of the Southern states.

The big minus sign of the Cuban economy is that it is not self-sustaining in the indispensable paraphernalia of modern life. Cuba is totally dependent for the uninterrupted flow of vital supplies; oil, coal, iron and steel, trucks and buses, cars, chemicals, sophisticated machinery etc. And it was precisely this hopeless and impossible attempt to make Cuba a highly industrialized country without these vital resources, that just about wrecked the Cuban economy. Cuba has not yet recovered from this catastrophic, totally unpardonable miscalculation, taken against the advice of qualified economic experts. Castro and his staff of fumbling amateurs, were forced to abandon this suicidal policy, but they still persist in meddling with things the know absolutely nothing about.

These serious drawbacks notwithstanding, Cuba is far from being a totally undeveloped country with a primitive economy. Given intelligent use of its natural wealth of resources, the potential for raising the living standards of its population is almost limitless. On this point there is no doubt. That the Castro "revolutionary" regime, far from developing these potentials, has not even equalled the admittedly inadequate standards attained before the revolution, is unfortunately also true.

Distribution of the national income was not balanced. The lower standard of living of the agricultural laborers was particularly atrocious, especially during the "dead season" between sugar harvests:

> ...the standard of living of the privileged classes of the cities [writes Dumont] was in violent contrast with the misery of the peasants...who were unemployed an average of 138 days a year...the unemployed numbered 250,000 even in the middle of the harvest season on the sugar plantations...(*Cuba: Socialism and Development*, p. 14)

And C. Wright Mills informs us ... "that only 3% of peasant 'Bohios' [huts] had indoor toilets. Two thirds of the children were not in any elementary school and most of those that were, dropped out ...in 1950, 180,000 children began first grade, less than 5000 reached eighth grade..." (*Listen Yankee!*; New York, 1960, p. 44-45)

It is well worth noting, as one observer remarked, "...that a substantial fraction of the town population were [like the rural proletarians] also very poor...squatters were living in shacks, and there were slum tenements. In 1953, no less than one fifth of families lived in single rooms and the average size of these families was five...taking the urban and rural population together, 62% of the economically active population had incomes of less than $75 a month..." (Dudley Sears in *Background to Revolution*, ibid. p. 213)

The Castro government is directly responsible for the awful economic situation of the Cuban people. The rising standard of living is a myth. René Dumont, the distinguished agronomist and economist, marshalls overwhelming evidence that Castro and his bumbling amateurs wrecked the economy of Cuba. There is no serious disagreement on this point:

> ...Cuba's shortages of food and other necessities are to a large extent due to the dogmatism of its leaders...in 1963, the harvests were 25% lower than in 1960 although the number of days worked had been rising rapidly...The standard of living in Cuba remained stationary in 1961, and with strict rationing, went down perhaps 15% to 20% in 1962...There are still, as I had seen in Santa Clara in 1960, no recognition of the difficulties involved in managing an economy...they were not trained and badly prepared...professors

at the Institute of Technology did not even know the names of the most common plants or their requirements...the government is increasingly calling for more effort and sacrifices as well as the acceptance of increased authority...despite constant reorganization, it is unable to put its house in order...(*Is Cuba Socialist?* pp. 100, 20, 92, 149, 29, 206.)

The economic consequences of transforming reasonably productive cattle and dairy farms and other agricultural enteprises into notoriously inefficient "people's" farms was predictably catastrophic...to the thousands of law-abiding families evicted without warning, it appeared to be an arbitrary act of brutality...
[The peasants retaliated; Halperin writes that:]
the impression obtained in usually well-informed government circles that over a period of several years, some 50,000 troops were engaged in liquidating peasant disaffection...a sizeable military effort had been under way to put down the uprising, which was not finally liquidated until well into 1964...Castro reminisced about "the uprisings that occurred mainly, but not exclusively, in the Escambray Mountains...organized groups existed all over the island...there were 1,000 bandits in the Escambray Mountains alone." (Halperin, ibid. p. 283, 284. Halperin credits the Castro quote to *Granma*, June 13, 1971)

Maurice Halperin also reports that:

"...food riots occurred in a number of towns in the western provinces, including Cárdenas, a sizeable urban center and seaport about 100 miles east of Havana. Here at a mass meeting, June 17, 1962, President of Cuba Dorticós had to be protected by tanks during a speech he made to calm the inhabitants..." (*The Rise and Decline of Fidel Castro;* Univ. of California, 1974, p. 162)

In addition to the Cárdenas riots, the Bulletin of the Cuban Libertarian Movement in Exile (Miami, June 1962) reports that:

...in El Cano, a little town in Havana Province, violence was so great that the authorities did not even try to suppress it. But afterwards, the authorities took revenge by expropriating furniture and personal belongings...Food riots also occurred in Cienfuegos...[in view of the fact that these]...sacrifices have been going on since 1961 and have been unbearable for the Cubans [Dumont asks:] To what extent has a ruling class the right to impose its singleminded conceptions of the future—and to impose it in so disorganized a manner—that the results are further aggravated? (ibid. p. 70-71)

Dumont, we are sure, will agree, in view of his own analysis, that economic disaster is not the cause, but only a symptom of the inner degeneration of the Cuban Revolution.

Anonymous Heroes of the Revolution

On a par with the vulgar display of Lenin's embalmed corpse, the deliberate deification of Castro and his tiny band of disciples in the Sierra Maestra obscures the exploits of the mass of anonymous heroes and almost forgotten resistance groups who brought about the downfall of Batista.

After Castro's deservedly celebrated, ill-fated attack on the Moncada Barracks (July 26, 1953) the Matanzas garrison was stormed by a group of heroic young militants from the Autentico Party (April 1956). All the attackers were massacred and many have not yet been identified. There were many other incidents.

Now, Castro brazenly and falsely takes credit for the daring assault of the Revolutionary Student Directorate on the Presidential Palace to kill Batista (March 13, 1957) in which all the raiders (including the leader, José Antonio Echeverria) were massacred. Herbert Matthews. the pro-Castro journalist, reveals that:

> ...Fidel was not consulted and did not approve (he heard about it indirectly). Castro called it a useless expenditure of blood...he was afraid that Echeverria would become a rival hero and revolutionary leader...the issue of Bohemia for May 28, 1957, in which Castro expressed his criticisms, would be embarassing for him if resurrected, because Echeverria and other victims became martyrs of the Revolution. March 13 is commemorated every year

71

as a glorious landmark of *Castro's revolution*...[Those who survived the attack on the palace set up an independent guerrilla force in the Escambray Mountains, the "Second Escambray Front"] (*Revolution in Cuba*; New York, 1975, p. 89; our emphasis)

One of the bloodiest battles of the anti-Batista rebellion took place on September 5, 1957. The Naval Base of Cienfuegos, 200 miles from Havana, was captured by navy mutineers and civilian underground group members. The sailors distributed weapons to the people in the area. There was supposed to be a simultaneous uprising in Havana, which miscarried probably for lack of coordination (although a dozen bombs were exploded). Air and ground reinforcement finally dispersed the rebels after bitter door-to-door fighting. An eyewitness reported that "...a common grave was dug by a bulldozer in the cemetery and I saw 52 bodies dumped into it. Officials said they were bodies of men killed in battle..." The revolt was crushed, but a second front had been opened near Sierra de Trinidad, only 60 miles from the vital communications center of Santa Clara.

The same observer graphically depicts the exploits of the spontaneously organized underground movement that blanketed Cuba with an intricate network of militant activities:

...the rebel underground stepped up its sabotage and terroristic activities throughout the country, including Havana. Homemade bombs would explode intermittently at different points in the Capital and people would be driven from motion picture theaters and other places of amusement. Fire bombs were also employed, and show windows of stores suffered from the impact of the explosions. Rebel bands harassed army outposts and even ventured into towns to capture arms. [Havana was without water for three days and the airport was completely gutted by fire.]...buses, both in cities and on highways, trucks carrying freight and merchandise, passenger and freight trains, railroad and highway bridges, public buildings and homes and businesses of "Batistianos" were blown up or burned as part of the agitation and terror designed to maintain a constant state of alarm...

Real terror was answered by the government with tenfold reprisals. Bodies of men and boys were found hanging from trees or lamposts or lying lifeless in automobiles with grenades on their persons, to convey the impression that they were caught in terrorist acts...there was hardly a communist among those detained... (Jules Dubois: *Fidel Castro*; Indianapolis, 1959, p. 182, 183)

While Castro's guerrilla group was occupied 300 miles away, the Directorio Revolucionario opened the independent Second Escambray Front in the Escambray Mountains MANY MONTHS before Batista fled Cuba (Jan. 1, 1959). The city of Cienfuegos was *this time* besieged for weeks by the Second Escambray Front. *This time* the attack succeeded. The Batista troops surrendered Cavo Loco Naval Base and the rebels took over the whole city (population 60,000).

All Cuba was in the flames of revolt. Powerfully reinforced by massive expeditionary landings of war materiel, financed and manned by exiled Cuban militants, the fall of Havana, and all of Cuba was inevitable WITHOUT the intervention of Castro's little group of rebels. Castro's campaign undoubtedly expedited the fall of Batista, but his efforts were by no means the decisive factor.

The reasons are obvious. Out of 82 Castro guerrillas who landed from the *Granma* on Dec. 2, 1956, only about 20 escaped to the Sierra Maestra mountains. Professor Maurice Halpern, an expert on Cuban affairs who spent six years in Castro's Cuba (1962-1968) sums up the situation:

> ...As Fidel himself explained on January 18, 1960, as late as June 1958 his 'army' consisted of 300 men; and when he began his final offensive in August he had 800 men...In fact what are termed 'battles' in the reminiscences of rebel leaders were skirmishes with rarely more than a score or two guerrillas involved and frequently fewer. This does not detract from the...heroism displayed by the men in combat, but does provide perspective on the [degree] of involvement... (*The Rise and Decline of Fidel Castro;* University of Calfornia, 1972, p. 37-38)

And K.S. Karol demonstrates the insignificant role of Castro's tiny band in the anti-Batista resistance as contrasted with the decisive role played by the great masses of the Cuban people:

> ...the urban front was by far the most important and the 'guerilleros'...played a subordinate part. It was the cities which supplied the 'guerilleros' with arms, money, information and provisions; and from start to finish the vast majority of 'guerilleros' were recruited in the towns. It was the towns which, in February 1957, launched a great publicity campaign in favor of the 'sierra' [mountain fighting bands] inflicting serious blows to Batista's prestige...and waged an efficient political and military campaign of their own... (*Guerrillas in Power*; New York, 1970, p. 164-165)

BEFORE Castro landed in Cuba, Dec. 2, 1956, while his boat, the *Granma*, was still at sea en route to Mexico, the 26th of July Movement led by Frank Païs, with little resistance, virtually took over Santiago de Cuba. Revolt flared all over Cuba. In April 1956, there was a Batista army uprising led by the Batista Minister of Education, Major José Fernández, a captain in the regular army, and Colonel Ramon Barquin, Military attache to Washington. Julio Comacho Aquilar and Jorge Soto assisted by three Americans, staged a foray at the eastern end of the Sierra Maestra near the U.S. Guantanamo naval base.

There were already groups of rebels scattered in the Sierra de Cristal before Raúl Castro arrived. They joined him later. Matthews tells that "...Ché Guevara had the task of imposing Castro's authority over three or four groups of Guerrillas fighting on their own in the mountains south of Havana..." The Guerrillas wre already fighting the Batista troops before Guevara "arrived to impose Castro's authority over them." In 1958, "...Roman Catholic priests and leaders were showing sympathy for Castro and opposition to Batista. The church hierarchy came out for Batista's resignation. Both Fidel and Raúl had priests and protestant ministers with them..."

Raúl Castro encountered no opposition when he came to the Sierra de Cristal in March 1958; bands of Guerrilla fighters were already there. And very effective groups from the Student Directorio were fighting in the Sierra de Trinidad. (Source: Matthews, ibid. pp. 73, 74, 76, 100, 102, 107)

Barely able to survive in the Sierra Maestra wilderness, Castro's isolated group could even with the greatest difficulty function only on the periphery of the vast popular resistance movement convulsing Cuba. Almost entirely shut off from the outside world, there could be no direct contact with the other anti-Batista organizations: not even with Castro's "own" 26th of July Movement, a fact which Castro's second-in-command Ernesto Ché Guevara repeatedly deplores:

> ...we wanted closer contact with the 26th of July Movement. Our nomad existence made it practically impossible to contact the members...(p. 35) Fidel did not have a radio then and he asked a peasant to lend him his...(p. 51) Peasants were not yet ready to join the struggle, and communication with the city bases was practically nonexistent...(p. 18—all quotes from *Episodes of the Revolutionary War;* Havana, 1967)

It is necessary to correct the erroneous impression that either Castro's 26th of July Movement or the anti-Batista organizations, constituted a unified body based upon a clearly defined program and a common ideology. The fact is that Castro did not control the rank and file membership, and certainly deserves no credit for their

74

achievements. What Theodore Draper writes about the composition of the 26th of July Movement is also true in respect to the rest of the anti-Batista opposition:

> ...The 26th of July Movement was never homogeneous, and the larger it grew in 1957 and 1968, the less homogeneous it became. It included those who merely wished to restore the bourgeois constitution of 1940 and those who demanded a 'real social-revolution.' It attracted those who admired and those who detested the United States. It took in fervent anti-communists and ardent fellow-travelers... (*Castro's Revolution*; New York, 1961, p. 75)

Guevara not only deplores "...the lack of ideological [but also] lack of moral preparation of the combatants...the men who would find the flimsiest excuses to justify their demand to be released, and if the answer was in the negative, desertion would follow...in spite of the fact that deserters [would be immediately] ...executed and desertion meant death...(p. 61)." In another place, Guevara complains that Castro's Sierra Maestra combatants "...had neither ideological awareness nor 'esprit-de-corps'..." (p. 35, 23) "...due to the lack of discipline among the new men...it was necessary to establish a rigid discipline, organize a high command and set up a Staff...(p. 91) Fidel addressed the troops urging a more strict discipline...he also announced that crimes of insubordination, desertion, and defeatism were to be punished by death..." (p. 23)

These, and similar remarks scattered throughout Guevara's book, reveal a great deal about the true nature of Castro's ARMY. We emphasize the word ARMY to demonstrate that an allegedly voluntary association of dedicated idealists, in which a member who avails himself of his right to resign is called a "deserter" and shot on sight differs in no essential respect from any other traditional army of disciplined conscripts. Castro's military conduct is wholly consistent with his domineering personality. Commandante (now General) Castro and his officers, true to form, have turned Cuba itself into a MILITARY STATE.

With the flight of Batista, Castro moved swiftly to consolidate his own power and neutralize or eliminate the other revolutionary organizations with whom he did not want to share power. The other rebel groups anticipated this and acted accordingly. Before Castro arrived in Havana from the Sierra Maestra, the Revolutionary Directorate, with 500 rifles, 5 machine guns and armored tanks taken from the San Antonio de Lós Bañas Arsenal near Havana, occupied the

University of Havana Campus and turned it into an armed camp. (See the eyewitness account of Jules Dubois, *Fidel Castro*, p. 353) Together with the fighters of the Second Escambray Front, the students also occupied the Presidential Palace—the seat of government.

When Castro and his escorting force arrived in Havana, the rebels refused to evacuate the Palace and turn it over to his newly-appointed President of the Republic, Manuel Urrutia. They were outraged because Castro had set up his own "Provisional Government" in Santiago de Cuba without consulting and without the consent of other revolutionary groups which had been fighting against Batista. They did not trust Castro. His verbal assurances that he would not seize power and would respect the rights of other anti-Batista groups and tendencies were not enough.

Castro made united front agreements when it suited his purposes, and broke them when he saw fit. In speaking of the Pact, based on the Sierra Manifesto, Guevara contends that Castro was justified in breaking it because some of the provisions were rejected by the other groups. The Pact was broken only five months after it was signed because the other organizations (which Guevara calls the enemy) "...broke the Pact when they refused to acknowledge the authority of the Sierra [of the Castro band]" (ibid. p. 88).

According to Guevara and Castro the phrase "...here in the Sierra Maestra we will know how to do justice to the confidence of the people, meant that Fidel and only Fidel knew how..." (ibid. p. 88) Guevara cynically acknowledges that Castro & Co. did not intend to honor the agreement in the first place. (p. 86)

Castro brazenly arrogated exclusive monopoly of power to his own 26th of July Movement (which Castro identified with his own person): "...let it be known, [he proclaimed] that the 26th of July Movement will never fail to guide and direct the people from the underground and the Sierra Maestra..." (Dubois, p. 206)

After he came to power, Castro liquidated all resistance groups which he could not control. He disbanded the Directorio and the Second Escambray Front by persecuting its members or mollifying some of its leaders. (Castro appoiinted Faure Chomon, one of the leaders of the Directorio, Ambassador to Russia and later other posts) He disbanded the Civic Resistance Movement, headed by his once close friend Manuel Ray, who later left his post as Minister of Public Works in Castro's Government. Through his stoqge, Rolando Cubela, Castro dominated all groups who questioned his dictatorship, accusing them of "counter-revolution."

Castro finally ended by purging "his" own party, the 26th of July Movement. One of Castro's vociferous apologists at that time, the French writer Simone de Beauvoir, explained that Castro purged his own party "...because it was petty bourgeois and could not keep pace with the Revolution after Castro took power...the party had to go, to be replaced by reliable elements..." (See Yves Guilbert: *Castro L'Infidele*; Paris, 1961, p. 170) These elements, of course, were the Communist Party and Castro's entourage of sycophants.

The mass exodus from Cuba, before emigration almost was cut off, reached the staggering figure of more than half a million and included tens of thousands of anti-Batista workers and peasants. Thousands of political prisoners who fought against Batista overflow the jails of Cuba. Absenteeism, slowdowns on the job, sporadic protests, instantly squelched, and other manifestations of popular discontent, demonstrate that the revolt of the obscure anonymous masses against tyranny cannot be permanently stamped out by Batista, or his successor, Fidel Castro.

Ingrained legends are exceedingly hard to dispel. But historic justice should still be accorded to the neglected and persecuted fighters who fought and continue to struggle so valiantly for the freedom of the Cuban people.

THE CUBAN REVOLUTION:
ANARCHIST EYEWITNESS REPORTS

The Cuban Revolution: A Direct Report by Augustin Souchy

Augustin Souchy is a veteran German Anarcho-Syndicalist. He was a delegate of the German Syndicalist Union to the Red International of Trade Unions (a Russian Communist Party front set up to dominate the world labor movement) in Moscow 1921. During the duration of the Spanish Civil War and Revolution (1936-1939) he was in charge of the International Information Bureau of the Spanish Anarcho-Syndicalist National Confederation of Labor (CNT) and in other capacities. Souchy observed at first hand the rural libertarian collectives and urban socialization and wrote extensively on this subject. He is an outstanding authority on collectivization, cooperatives and other problems of agrarian organization.

With the Franco victory in Spain and the coming of World War II, Souchy lived as a refugee in France. He came to Mexico in 1942 and for many years traveled extensively in Latin America, Israel, etc. to study at first hand rural collectivization and cooperative experiments in semi-developed countries.

In 1960, Souchy toured Cuba, gathering direct information about the Cuban Revolution, particularly agrarian cooperatives and land reform measures set up by the Castro government. Although his reports were in many respects very favorable, the authorities could not tolerate adverse criticism, however well intended. The printing of Souchy's observations was prohibited, and Souchy himself left Cuba just in time to escape arrest. His articles were published in pamphlet form, by the excellent libertarian bi-monthly Reconstruir *(Testimonias Sobre la Revolucion Cubana; Buenos Aires, December, 1960)*

This pamphlet falls into two parts. The first is Souchy's over-all evaluation of the Cuban Revolution. It was written when Castro's gradual moves toward full-fledged totalitarian rule first became apparent. While acknowledging what turned out to be the Revolution's temporary positive aspects, Souchy's observations reflected his growing concern about the authoritarian deformation of the Cuban Revolution. The second part, a direct report of his visits to various peasant "cooperatives," government "collectives," etc. is a concise critique of the disastrous consequences of Castro's Agrarian Reform program. Since "Agrarian Reform" is considered the Revolution's major achievement, Souchy's analysis takes on added significance. [S.D.]

Part One: Overall Evaluation of the Revolution

The Cuban Revolution is much more than a mere political change in the form of government. The Revolution initiated a vast economic-social transformation, which to a certain extent resembles what took place in Spain after the 19th of July, 1936 [beginning of the Civil War]. There are, nevertheless, certain important differences. While the Spanish Revolution, in the period of struggle against the existing order as well as the period of social-political reconstruction, was the work of the great masses of workers and peasants, the Cuban Revolution was propelled by a minority of self-sacrificing dedicated revolutionaries... The character of both revolutions springs from these differences.

In Cuba, the old professional army was replaced by workers' and peasants' militias [this is no longer the case]. The Revolution attacked the economic poverty of the masses, cultural backwardness and expropriated big private enterprises.

In Spain, the masses organized collectives. In Cuba, the state created and controlled cooperatives. In Cuba, as in Spain, rents were lowered in the cities, but in respect to changes in rural property, there was an important difference... While in Spain, the confiscation of the land and the organization of the collectives was initiated and carried through by the peasants themselves; in Cuba social-economic transformation was initiated not by the people, but by Castro and his comrades-in-arms. It is this distinction that accounts for the different development of the two revolutions; Spain, mass revolution from the bottom up; Cuba, revolution from the top down by decree—i.e. Agrarian Reform Law, etc.

The old motto: "The Emancipation of the Working Class is the Task of the Workers Themselves," is still eminently relevant. The Cuban Revolution will advance only with the participation of the people and only if the revolutionary spirit will penetrate all social stratums. Centralizing tendencies exist in every revolution and can be dangerous for liberty. The surest way to prevent centralization of power in the

80

hands of a few, is the initiative and action of the masses of the people.

In Cuba, the revolutionary fighters, the men of the Sierra Maestra, constituted a strong fighting force, and it was they, not the professional militants who "temporarily" constituted the new government.

The new regime came to power on a wave of popular enthusiasm and admiration for the heroic fighters...But enthusiasm comes and goes. Emotions are fickle. A power acquired by past exploits, however heroic, is not a firm base for the establishment of a permanent government. And if in the course of events, as is always the case, certain discontented popular groupings threaten or question the leadership, the "de facto" government, to remain in office, and carry out its program, resorts to threats of outright violence. The inevitable consequence of this situation is revolutionary terror, whose classical representatives are Robespierre and Stalin...

The revolutionary government of Cuba is making enormous efforts to legitimate and justify its existence by enacting deep and popular economic and social changes. The liquidation of the old corrupt administration, 50% reduction of the salaries of the new ministers, drastic reduction in rents, telephone and electric rates, construction of new hygienic housing for the masses, the installation of public beaches and recreation centers, and finally, the crowning of all these reforms by the Agrarian Reform Law, are enthusiastically applauded by the majority of the Cuban people and the whole world...

But in the radiant revolutionary springtime [Souchy wrote before the storms of winter] there are some dark clouds and shadows: censorship of the press, unilateral indoctrination by radio and television, the new foreign policy which is placing the country under the de facto domination of red imperialism, and above all, the organization of a state dominated economy, are naturally not liked by the people [in spite of propaganda to the contrary]. One has but to speak to Cubans in all walks of life, in the Capital and in the provinces, to plainly see the growing disillusionment and discontent. An infinite number of workers, thousands of people who have always fought for freedom, now oppose the policies and conduct of the government...

The Cuban Revolution achieved great social progress for the people, with a rapidity unmatched in any other Latin-American country. But all this is not the work of the people themselves. We must insist that the Revolution is rapidly turning into a dictatorship. The dictators, Mussolini, Perón, Pérez Jiménez, (and how many others!) to justify their tyrannies and glorify their names, also built houses etc. for the poor, (public works in Russia).

The social-economic agrarian revolution achieved by INRA [National Institute of Agrarian Reform] are truly remarkable. Protected by privileged legislation the INRA is the most powerful State

Monopoly, not only in Agriculture, but almost all economic activity. INRA is Cuba's number one trust.

Part Two: "We Visit the New Rural Cooperatives"

Moncada

The road to the Sierra is very rough. In certain places our jeep almost overturned and so detracted somewhat from the pleasure of viewing the beautiful panorama of hills and beautiful valley with its luxurious tropical flora. After some hours of difficult travel, we reached the shore of a stream. A group of peasants were harvesting malangas and we soon learned that they belonged to a cooperative.

'We decided ourselves to work collectively," declared one of the peasants, "Work together is so much easier than working alone. Before we worked because we were hungry, but now, we work because we really enjoy it. We share our income equally and expect good results." He beamed with joy.

We were escorted to the "Bohio" (hut) of the peasant Nicolás Pacheo. His courteous wife, with typical Cuban hospitality, served coffee...The modest "guajero" (peasant) could not give much of an explanation about the organization of the cooperative, and the other peasants, even less so. The peasants knew only about their work. For more information we had to wait for the arrival of the sergeant who represented the INRA.

The sergeant finally arrived. He made no reference to the cooperatives, but spoke only about the orders he received from his bosses, the higher executives of the district INRA. He offered no new details, but merely repeated what we already learned about other cooperatives. Though lacking positive constructive information, his remarks were interesting from a negative point of view. Cuba is the only Latin American country in which agrarian cooperatives are managed by military personnel.

If the sergeant were wearing a Russian uniform, the impression that we were conversing with a supervisor of a Sovkhoz [Russian State Farm] would have been perfect. Except for the team working on the outskirts of the village itself, we got the feeling of the standard routine procedures of an immense impersonal organization with branches all over the country, whose watchword is "Bread is more important than Freedom."

But we must never forget that there are two different freedoms! National freedom which refers to the autonomy of a nation, and *personal freedom* which is much more important. In brutally oppressed countries, with violent upheavals, and little or no experience of national sovereignty, the first national autonomy, is more valued than the second, freedom of the individual. Cuba belongs to the first. Bread there is, but we must point out on the basis of the most meticulous observation, that the rationing of human freedom has already begun. [Souchy, of course, wrote before the full impact of the disastrous economic policies of the revolutionary government brought about acute shortages and rationing of food products that before were always in plentiful supply.]

Between Bayamo and Manzanillo

The Sheltered city of Bayamo was one of the provision points for the rebels of the Sierra Maestra while they were fighting the Batista dictatorship. Situated in the fertile valley, Bayamo, the commercial center of a rich agricultural area, is today the district headquarters of the INRA. Most of the land is owned by relatively more affluent proprietors, but the creation of cooperatives by the INRA is making rapid progress. The 8 cooperatives in the district consist of 11,858 hectares (one hectare is about 2½ acres) worked by 2,700 agricultural laborers.

The administrator, Señor Carbonell, is a young man full of energy and enthusiasm for the Revolution. The army is inextricably interwoven into the whole INRA network. The army is deemed indispensable to the proper functioning of this gigantic and complex organization. The soldiers help to build houses and do other useful work. But as in all armies, a lot of time and labor is wasted on perfectly useless, even socially harmful projects.

There is also a well-equipped machine shop for the repair of agricultural machinery. The district INRA headquarters called a meeting to arrange the expansion of facilities to include the manufacture of certain agricultural tools and equipment. In addition to the workers, the meeting was also attended by the district manager, two lawyers, and two army officers.

The plans for the organization of an industrial cooperative to be managed by the INRA were presented to the meeting. When the workers asked about wages, the manager replied that wages were of secondary importance and that to speed up the industrialization of Cuba, certain sacrifices will have to be made for the sake of the revolution. The workers plainly showed that they did not like the project. Finally, the exasperated administrator laid down the law: with or without the consent of the workers, the "cooperative" project will be organized as planned. The lawyers drew up the necessary legal documents and the cooperative was officially established.

The cooperative will be patterned after the state enterprises of the "socialist countries" behind the "iron curtain." The Ministry of the Economy will organize production and distribution and manage all nationalized enterprises. And the workers will, if the "revolutionary" bosses allow it, be given a restricted share in management. The economic situation of the workers will be more or less the same as in privately owned enterprises.

Statization of Manzanillo Shoe Factories

In Manzanillo, in addition to fisheries, there are also many small shoe workshops, equipped with old machines, manufacturing shoes for the regional market. Wages were low and there were few, if any, wealthy employers.

After the Revolution conflicts broke out when the workers demanded labor laws providing minimum wages, social security and other benefits. Revolution came to the shoe industry. The employers voluntarily gave up ownership and decided to work together on equal terms with their former employees. The small workshops were consolidated into the newly organized Shoe Manufacturing Collective of Manzanillo.

A quarter century before, during the Spanish Revolution, similar collectives were established in Spain. In Catalonia, the Levante and Castille, the isolated workshop collectives later organized themselves into socialized industries. These developments were based upon the old libertarian tradition that gave the Spanish Revolution its distinctive character.

Unfortunately, this popular initiative of the Manzanillo shoe workers was soon squelched. The Manzanillo section of the Communist Party was against free cooperatives which clashed with their authoritarian ideas. They therefore urged Russian style absorption of the voluntarily collectivized workshops by the INRA. This proposal was enthusiastically endorsed by the INRA bureaucrats, and the cooperative shoe industry was taken over.

This destruction of the cooperative is not an isolated example of how a movement which began by abolishing private ownership to establish free cooperatives, was finally swallowed up by the state agency INRA, indicating the fast growing trend toward the Russian variety of state capitalism mislabeled "socialism."

The Primavera (springtime) Rice Cooperative

Cuba consumes enormous quantities of rice. To meet demand, great stocks of rice must be imported. As part of the campaign to make Cuba self-sufficient in rice by placing great new areas under cultivation the district INRA organized the Primavera rice-growing cooperative. The hundreds of new "cooperators" will be lodged in barrack-like structures equipped with two-decker beds and fed in one huge dining hall. While displaying the new accommodations, the manager went into raptures about how the new cooperative will improve production while bettering quality.

The improvements will no doubt increase production. In other parts of the world, similar projects under approximately the same conditions and procedures are in operation: there too, the workers sleep in barracks and eat in huge dining halls supplied by the companies. The only new or original feature of this semi-militarized labor army is the name "cooperative;" a description that no true cooperative anywhere will accept.

I visit an elementary school. Childrn are marching, chanting: "Una—Dos—Tres—Cuarto—Fi—Del—Castro." (one-two-three-four-etc.) The proud Principal exclaims: "Behold! Tomorrow's soldiers of The Revolution! And this beautiful rebuilt school was once an old, ugly army barracks." Alas! The Principal does not realize how little things have really changed—how the old military spirit still remains.

The Hermanos Saenz Cooperative

When the Vice Minister of the Soviet Union, Mikoyan, visited Cuba, Castro, to impress him with the achievements of the revolution, showed him the Hermanos Saenz cooperative—the pride of the new Cuba. The Hermanos Saenz cooperative, in Pinar del Rio province, is named after two brothers, 15 and 19 years old, who were tortured and murdered by Batista's executioners.

The cooperative was organized and built by the INRA. INRA advanced construction and operating finances. The complex consists of 120 elegantly landscaped houses for the tobacco workers and their families. A typical dwelling consists of three bedrooms, a dining room, tile bathroom and a fully equipped kitchen. The buildings are "functional," but the roofs are too low and the old peasant "bohios" (cottages) are better ventilated. Apart from this, we must praise the revolutionary government for its efforts to wipe out slum housing.

The cooperators make no down payment, nor are there wage deductions. Construction and maintenance costs are paid for, not by the individual cooperator, but collectively from the profits of the tobacco industry. The Hermano Sáenz debt to INRA will probably be paid quickly—about six to ten years. In other places a worker who wants to own a house would have to make monthly payments for 15 to 20 years.

The pride of the cooperative is the magnificent new school, with its spacious gardens and playgrounds, an auditorium, an immense dining hall and fully equipped kitchens where wholesome meals are prepared for the children.

San Vincente

On the day when Castro inaugurated the new School of the Hermanos Saenz cooperative a group of 20 peasants of the tiny village of San Vincente petitioned Castro to help them form a cooperative and new housing. The peasants had been tenant farmers who were forced to hand over two thirds of their crops to the landlord. They had no money, no farm machines, no fertilizers. As Castro promised, the INRA immediately began the construction of a new cooperative village for the 20 peasant families of San Vincente. With the help of the revolutionary army and the peasants themselves, construction was completed in the record time of only two months. The individual peasants do not own the property of the cooperative nor the agricultural equipment. They hold shares in the cooperative. The cooperative (like the rest of the rural economy) is not administered by the peasants, but by the INRA in accordance with a national plan. The "cooperative" is actually financed by wages, disguised as "advances" [payments for construction, maintenance and equipment furnished by INRA] paid to the peasants by their de facto employer, INRA.

My guide, the bearded revolutionist, Captain Álvarez Costa, provincial delegate of INRA, furnished me with information about the cooperatives in his district. It seems that in the Cuban cooperatives the peasants sacrifice their autonomy in exchange for economic security. Although the economic situation of the peasant "cooperator" is better than before, it is nevertheless inferior to that of the free cooperator, particularly from the moral point of view. "Is there not a danger (I asked my guide) that this situation would create a dangerous dilemma: bread without freedom or freedom without bread?"

The captain, conceding that such a dilemma is indeed possible, replied:

...our Revolution is based upon the concepts formulated by Fidel Castro. If we build cooperatives, those who benefit must accept the conditions stipulated. There are hundreds of different cooperatives in our province. Some sell their products to INRA, others in the free market etc....In general, the cooperatives are directly administered by INRA. However, in this district, the cooperative in the village of Moncada works collectively, on its own initiative. I suggest that you see how it works.

The School City: "Camilo Cienfuegos"

In the field of education the Castro regime is inordinately proud of what it considers its greatest achievement: the construction of Ciudad Escolar—School City—an immense complex named after the great hero of the Revolution Camilo Cienfuegos. The complex is being built at the foot of the Sierra Maestra Mountains, Castro's famed stronghold. This grandiose project, meant to astonish the world, was conceived while Castro's guerrilla band was still being hunted by the Batista army...

Although the construction was begun only a few months ago, many buildings have already been erected. The project is truly unique. It will accommodate 22,000 children of both sexes from 6 to 18 years of age; most of them from peasant families in the Sierra Maestra region. The complex will consist of 42 units, each with a capacity of 500 pupils, including dining rooms, class rooms, 4 athletic fields, a motion picture theater and swimming pool. The central kitchen will prepare meals for all the 22,000 students...

The project will be financed by the government and built by INRA. 9,000 hectares [about 25,000 acres] will be devoted to the growing of rice, malangas, beans and other vegetables, and the raising of cattle, poultry etc. The pupils themselves will do the work, and all this vast area will serve as a school for agriculture. It is expected that the products will pay for the education and subsistence of the students without a state subsidy. Thus, 22,000 young people will live by their own labor.

One of the officials boasted: "This will be the greatest educational project ever built." But quite a few highly qualified educators voiced serious misgivings about the educational value of the project. A well known teacher whom I interviewed declared:

> educationally speaking, to construct an educational apparatus of this magnitude is pure insanity. It would have been far better to build a school in every village in the Sierra Maestre region and the schools would at the same time constitute a local cultural center and a separate technical agricultural school could far more easily and usefully be erected in the provincial capital...

The opinion of the veteran teacher makes sense. To separate 22,000 children from their homes and parents is to deprive the children of the love, affection, and maternal care which is indispensable for their emotional and mental health. The close rapport between the old and the new generations will be loosened and perhaps irretrievably severed. The whole scheme is based on erroneous and distorted concepts. The aim of education is not only the accumulation of technical-scientific knowledge, but also to introduce the youth into the life of adults. In social life, there should be no artificial separation between old and young, but rather, an inter-penetration, a welding together, a social-personal bonding which makes possible the co-education of both the older and the younger generations.

87

Experience acquired by tradition and confirmed by modern science teaches us that family life, the rearing and education of children must constitute a truly harmonious community of love and mutual understanding.

The School City Camilo Cienfuegos resembles the military training camp of a modern Sparta; not the free community of scholars in the tradition of ancient Athens.

Revolution and Counter-Revolution in Cuba, by Abelardo Iglesias

This account of the Cuban Revolution was written by the veteran anarchist, Abelardo Iglesias, who lived through the events he describes. While still a young man Iglesias dedicated his whole life to the struggle for freedom and social justice. He was particularly active in the labor movement of his native Cuba, and much later, for many years in Spain, where he fought against Franco fascism and for the Social Revolution from the beginning to the final catastrophic defeat.

Returning to Cuba after the debacle, overcoming the pessimism which for many militants signified the end of their hopes for the realization of our ideals, Iglesias again took up the struggle against capitalist exploitation, political oppression and the monumental corruption of national life—particularly within the labor movement.

This attitude, shared by all the militants of the Libertarian Association of Cuba (ALC) led naturally to the struggle against the corrupt, dictatorial regime of Fulgencio Batista and his friends and collaborators; the very same leaders of the Communist Party, who now occupy the same high posts in the Castro-communist dictatorship.

In the crucial period preceding the downfall of Batista, the Cuban anarchists strove to defend the conquests of the workers and the independence of their organizations against the corrupt leadership of the Batista-Communist dominated Confederation of Cuban Workers (CTC).

The following articles by Iglesias were published in pamphlet form by the Argentine anarchist bi-monthly **Reconstruir** *(Buenos Aires, 1963).*

[S.D.]

Introduction

Revolution and Counter-Revolution in Cuba is a series of articles written in late 1960 and early 1961, a few months before I left Cuba. Unfortunately, subsequent events have only confirmed their contentions.

Erroneous ideas about the Cuban Revolution are to a great extent due to the lack of reliable information. Instead of the objective evaluation indispensible to an understanding of events, the views of the critics are distorted by their political prejudices and economic interests.

The reactionaries proclaim the sanctity of private property and religion as essential for the preservation of the "full dignity of man." Almost all North Americans extol the virtues of "representative democracy" and "free enterprise." In Latin-America, opinion is divided based not on the facts, but on how the critics interpret "American imperialism."

Many Cubans detest Castro, not for his totalitarian methods of government, but for the communist character of his dictatorship. Many of those who now oppose Castroism, supported his personal dictatorship from the time of the Sierra Maestra until they began to suspect that he was inclined toward Marxist remedies. For them, the totalitarian method of government was less important than its COLOR. The big landlords, the big capitalists, the heads of the church and the professional politicians fully backed Castro as long as they believed that he would be a "blue" dictator like Franco; they immediately turned against him when he became a "red" dictator like Stalin. But liberal democrats and revolutionaries from all social classes, especially in the universities, enthusiastically accepted Castro in good faith, fought in the Sierras and in the underground for the immediate restoration of the democratic regime, which had been overthrown by the Batista coup of March 10, 1952. And it is they who now constitute the most vocal opposition to Castro in Cuba and in exile. [Since this was written, most of the opposition has come from workers and peasants.]

That militant anarchists everywhere hailed the Revolution when it first began is understandable. It looked like a true social revolution, and they took the libertarian pretensions of the leaders seriously because they lacked regular and complete information about the real situation in Cuba. Another factor was psychological. With the defeat of the Spanish Revolution (1936-39) the era of popular revolutions seemed closed. Inevitably, disillusionment set in. To some extent, the Cuban Revolution rekindled the old revolutionary flame. The spectacle of a heroic handful of people struggling against seemingly insurmountable odds, disorganized, poorly armed, carrying on a guerrilla war and defeating a formidable, powerfully armed force of professional soldiers, was bound to arouse the sympathy and enthusiasm of all sincere revolutionaries.

But if these facts explain the attitudes of libertarians in 1959, the first year of the Revolution, they cannot now [1963] justify the attitude of certain individuals and groups, in several countries, who still deny the facts and obstinately maintain a position diametrically opposed to libertarian ideas and traditions.

That which compels us to fight for freedom, should also alert us to the presence of a barbaric regime, even when it hides its true nature behind revolutionary libertarian slogans.

At first sight, the expropriation of the holdings of the big landlords seems logical and correct to a movement that does not believe in private property, or recognize the validity of rights unjustly accorded to privileged minorities. But we must realize that the conversion of the expropriated land into state property creates a slavery infinitely worse than private capitalism. Libertarians should know that class privileges are subjected to the state as the supreme regulator of social relations. And we should know also that the conversion of private into state property automatically concentrates enormous political power into a reduced number of men, thereby creating a revolutionary oligarchy wielding unlimited power.

Fidel Castro has established a typical totalitarian oligarchy. In the name of liberty, he has shamelessly betrayed a politically naive people who have allowed themselves to be taken-in by the legendary "hero of the Sierra Maestra." This is no mere supposition. It is a crude, brutal, monstrous fact which libertarians will have to face in all its magnitude, if they really want to comprehend the immense tragedy now being enacted in Cuba.

Apart from byzantine discussions, there are these objective facts which no one can deny. We list briefly the main points:

1) The so-called revolutionary regime is essentially an oligarchy dominated by a handful of men accountable to no one for their actions.

2) In line with their sectarianism they have abolished all individual rights.

3) Centralized political and economic power to an extent never known before.

4) Constructed an apparatus of terror immensely more efficient than Batista's repressive agencies.

5) The land has not been distributed to the peasants, for individual, family, collective or cooperative cultivation, but has become the 'de facto' property of the state agency, the Institute for Agrarian Reform (INRA).

6) The nationalization of private enterprises has not benefited the workers. The industries are administered not by the workers' unions, but have been taken over to reinforce the power of the state, converting the former wage slaves into slaves of the state machine.

7) Public education has become a state monopoly. The state arrogates to itself the right to impose its kind of education upon the young, regardless of the opinion of the parents.

8) The legitimate necessity to prepare against counter-revolutionary aggression has been the pretext for the unnecessary militarization of children and adolescents as in Russia and other totalitarian states.

9) The right to strike has been abolished and the workers must, without complaint, obey the decrees imposed upon them in their work places. The unions have lost their independence and are actually state

90

agencies, whose sole function it is to cajole or force the workers to obey the commands of the state functionaries without protest.

10) There are no genuine judicial tribunals. Oppositionists are punished not for alleged offenses, but for their convictions and revolutionary ideas.

10) Fidel Castro's government is conducted in accordance with Mussolini's notorious dictum:

NOTHING OUTSIDE OF THE STATE!!
NOTHING AGAINST THE STATE!!
EVERYTHING FOR THE STATE!!

History of a Fraud: The "March On Havana"

The romantic aura surrounding Castro's legendary exploits must be dispelled. The myth of his alleged "March on Havana" captured the imagination of his deluded sympathizers, must once and for all be debunked. We who lived in Cuba, who witnessed, and to a certain extent participated in the events, have too much respect for the truth to remain silent in the face of such serious misconceptions.

The facts of the "March on Havana" are the following: Weeks before Batista fled Cuba, when the rebel forces advanced in Las Villas Province without meeting serious resistance from government troops, Fidel Castro, almost immobilized in Oriente province, contacted Colonel Rizo Rubido, military commander of the fortress at Santiago de Cuba, and began negotiations with this officer of the Batista army for the surrender of the city, the capital of Oriente Province.

When the negotiations reached an advanced stage, Colonel Rubido arranged a personal interview between Castro and his superior officer.

The interview took place in an abandoned sugar mill in Oriente Province. With the help of a Catholic Priest, Father Guzmán, Fidel Castro and General Cantillo reached full agreement and General Cantillo

surrendered Santiago de Cuba and the whole Province of Oriente to Castro. These events were related by Castro himself on television and reported in the first weeks of 1959 in the magazine *Bohemia,* which reproduced actual photographs of the notes exchanged between Fidel Castro and General Cantillo.

Fulgencio Batista then summoned General Cantillo to Havana and told him of his decision to abdicate and appoint him (General Cantillo) as Commander-in-Chief of the army to maintain order and return the country to normalcy. General Cantillo accepted Batista's offer and immediately contacted Fidel Castro, informing him that he was ready not only to surrender Oriente Province, but the whole country. A few hours later, Batista, together with his entourage, left Havana for Santo

Domingo in three military planes. This happened at dawn, January 1st, 1959.

With the flight of Batista, all the armed forces surrendered immediately without firing a single shot. General Cantillo transferred command of his army to Colonel Ramón Barquin who had just been released, after being sentenced to imprisonment for conspiring against the Batista government.

Upon assuming command of the armed forces, Colonel Barquin told Fidel Castro that the army and he personally was at his disposal and under his orders and that he [Barquin] would remain only as long as Castro wants him to or until he was replaced.

Fidel Castro immediately ordered his rebel troops to occupy all installations, barracks and fortresses. In line with these orders, Camilo Cienfuegos with a force of only 300 men, occupied Camp Military City after 12,000 Batista troops, including aviation, artillery and tank units, surrendered without firing a shot. Commander Ernesto Guevara took over the La Cabana Fortress. Castro's brother, Raúl, became Provisional Commander of the Marina de Guerra naval station. Faure Chamont was appointed Commander of San Antonio de lós Baños air base and of the Presidential Palace. Other appointees filled the other posts.

Fidel Castro finally entered Santiago de Cuba only after the city had been peacefully occupied by his troops, commanded by Huber Matos, the real hero of the armed struggle against Batista. [Major Huber Matos, military commander of Castro troops who blockaded Santiago de Cuba, was the Commander of Oriente and Camagüey rebel forces. Because Matos urged Castro to halt communist penetration of his government he was brought to trial with 38 other officers and sentenced to 20 years in prison. Despite international appeals for his release and the pleas of his family he has not yet been freed. His family lives in New Jersey.]

Castro's activity at this time was intense: He designated Santiago de Cuba as temporary Capital of Cuba; appointed Manuel Urrutia Lleo to be Provisional President of Cuba; ordered a general strike (which collapsed for lack of support;) appointed the list of ministers and appointed Dr. José Miró Cardona as Prime Minister; and delivered the first of his interminable harangues to a carefully staged mass rally.

Only then, when all the power was in his hands; when he was hysterically acclaimed all over Cuba; only THEN did Castro stage his massive publicity stunt, the fake "March On Havana;" a 350 kilometer parade down the Central Highway, escorted by rebel army troops, tanks and planes etc. Castro could have flown directly to Havana in a few hours at most. But he deliberately arranged this ostentatious, garish display of military power, to fool the world into the belief that he had taken by armed force, a city that voluntarily accorded him a tumultuous welcome.

On January 8, 1959, Fidel Castro entered Havana, without firing a shot, acclaimed by delirious mobs, a military spectacle which had nothing to do with a victorious assault on Havana; a vulgar imitation of Mussolini's "March on Rome."

Castro: The Anti-American Imperialist

One of the most controversial issues debated in revolutionary circles is the spurious nature of Castro's "anti-imperialism." According to his sympathizers, Castro was provoked into defying the American imperialist government which strove to perpetuate the economic interests of the capitalist monopolists in Cuba and to force the Castro regime to submit to its dictates and policies...

We need not produce too many arguments to demonstrate that the question is not quite so simple. There is evidence that while the United States did not seriously block the illegal shipment of arms to Castro's rebel army and anti-Batista resistance groups in Cuba, it slapped an embargo on arms already paid for on the Batista regime... Batista bitterly protested this policy. The most widely circulated and influential American capitalist magazines: *Time, Life, Coronet, Newsweek,* etc. as well as leading capitalist newspapers like *The New York Times,* glorified Castro and his famous "barbudos" (bearded onesl) depicting them as romantic Robin Hoods, gallantly fighting for the freedom of the Cuban people.

Another widely circulated myth cleverly concocted by the Castro propaganda mill is that the peasants enthusiastically support his 26th of July Movement and 95% of Castro's rebel "army" were peasants. The fact is, that although Castro's stronghold in the Sierra Maestra was practically encircled by cane fields and sugar factories and there are at least three million peasants in Cuba, Castro's "army" numbered only 1500 men when the fighting ended with the flight of Batista. Where were the peasant masses? The truth is that the most powerful force upon which Castro depended from the outset was the middle class. Most of the young insurgents came not from the peasantry, but from the middle class. (1)

The Catholic Church also backed Castro, mobilizing thousands of clandestine militants. The Acción Católico and its affiliated workers and student organizations spearheaded violent anti-Batista action all over Cuba. The press, the radio, and television networks provided free unlimited propaganda, stirring the masses against Batista.

In spite of its anti-Batista sentiments, the Cuban bourgeoisie was nevertheless resolved (with certain modifications) to continue the de facto subordination of Cuba to the overall interests of the United States, the "Colossus of the North."

93

The financiers and the upper clergy, hoped to seize political power by turning the pro-Castro sentiment of the masses to their account. As the first step in this direction, they gave ample aid to the Castro movement.

For all these elements, Castro became the "Lider Maximo," the "Caudillo" of a popular bourgeois revolution. Castro had at that time given them no reason to think otherwise. In 1959, only a few months after his victory, Castro vehemently denied that he was a communist, denying that he was plotting to replace military dictatorship with "revolutionary dictatorship." "...capitalism may kill a man with hunger; communism kills man by wiping out his freedom..." (2)

Scarcely a month after the revolution, Castro cautiously began to reveal his true intentions. Unleashing a violent campaign against the United States he manifested his sympathy for Soviet imperialism. Any one criticizing life in the "socialist" countries was reviled as a "counter-revolutionist." Castro's own comrades-in-arms, Manuel Urrutia Lleo, José Miró Cardona, Manuel Ray Rivero and Huber Matos who held key positions in his administration were dismissed from office, imprisoned, or driven into exile when they tried in the latter half of 1959 to oppose Castro's pro-communist policies: The mysterious death of Castro's second-in-command, Camilo Cienfuegos, was one of the tragic consequences of this fierce struggle between the top leaders of the new Cuban government. An apparently ideological dispute became in reality a war to the death for the conquest of power.

In exposing Castro's duplicity, we want to make it crystal clear that we do not in any way intend to justify American policies in Cuba, or anywhere in Latin-America. We do not for a moment overlook the age long exploitation of American imperialism and atrocities against the liberty of the peoples of Latin America. For us, who participated actively in the Revolution and know the facts, the incorporation of the Castro regime into the Russian, Chinese and "third world" imperialist bloc, was due neither to circumstances, nor the U.S. pressure. It was deliberately put into effect in accordance with treacherous Bolshevik tactics.

Fidel Castro is not an anti-imperialist. He is anti-American and pro-Soviet. He carried through a series of maneuvers to justify his total surrender to the Russian-Chinese imperialist camp. (3) To galvanize public opinion into accepting his duplicity, he not only provoked the crisis confrontation with the Washington government, but also renounced that which we libertarians consider most essential: the possibility of forging unbreakable links of solidarity between the oppressed people of Cuba and the other oppressed peoples of Latin America, the only ones who can render unselfish and effective aid to the Cuban Revolution.

The Cuban people now suffer the horrors of a totalitarian

"communist" regime, massively subsidized by thè Soviet bloc with arms, technicians, military and police experts etc. But the Cuban people have in a thousand ways demonstrated their unquenchable will to emancipate themselves from the dictatorial regime that exploits and oppresses them.

The old spirit of independence is not yet crushed. They are determined to fight for their complete freedom against both their native exploiters and the domination of their northern neighbor the United States.

Our comrades in Cuba and in exile adhere to and fight for this revolutionary policy, against both the reactionary emigre forces and the politicians in exile who would not hesitate to sell their souls to the devil himself, in order to reconquer the political and economic power they lost in the January 1st Revolution.

Note 1

In respect to the middle-class content of the first Castro Government, Theodore Draper's investigation shows:

> ...never a single one of Castro's ministers was a peasant or worker in industry. Every one of them attended a university, came from an upper or middle-class home and aspired to become a professional or intellectual...I prevailed on one of the ministers to write out in his own handwriting, on his own stationery, the professions, occupations and ages of each of the ministers...(*Castro's Revolution*...p. 43)

The list included seven lawyers, 2 university professors, 3 university students, 1 doctor, 1 engineer, 1 architect, 1 mayor and 1 captain.

note 2

The main points of the bourgeois-democratic reform constitution which Castro promised to put into effect included: full freedom of press, radio, etc.; respect for all civil, political and personal rights as guaranteed by the Constitution of 1940; democratization of the unions and promoting free elections at all levels.

In an interview early in 1958 from the Sierra Maestre, Castro pledged that his:

> ...provisional government must be as brief as possible, just time enough to convoke elections for state, provincial and municipal posts...the provisional government not to remain in power for more than two years...I want to reiterate my total lack of personal interest and I have renounced, beforehand, any post after the victory of the Revolution...these are the things we will tell the people. Will we suppress the right to strike? NO. Will we suppress the freedom of assembly? NO. We must carry this Revolution forward with all freedoms...When one newspaper is closed down, no newspaper will feel safe; when one man is persecuted for his political ideas, no one can feel safe... (quoted *Cuban Labor;* Miami, Jan. 1967)

Note 3

When Iglesias wrote this the Cuban and Chinese governments were still on good terms. To please the Russian rulers, upon whose aid the existence of the Castro regime depended, relations with China deteriorated rapidly.

[Notes by Sam Dolgoff]

How Castro's Clique Rules Cuba

Without taking into account some of the psychological characteristics of the "Lider Maximo" (as Castro likes to be known) it is impossible to explain how a regime built around the "cult of the personality" functions.

The messianic obsession which dominates Castro's personality also characterizes his official behavior. Even a brief survey of his political history leads immediately to the conclusion that we are dealing with a super-authoritarian, pathologically conceited individual, taken up with an insatiable lust for personal power.

The way he treats his friends and collaborators convincingly reveals this condition. He goes to extremes in persecuting those who dare question his orders or dissociate themselves from him; he insults collaborators in public; is enraptured to the point of hysteria by public ovations; basks in the adulation and servility of his subordinates. His ideology is, in effect, "the cult of personality." He is an unscrupulous political dilettante. If it suits his purposes, he professes any ideology. He affirms in public what he repudiates in private; deliberately falsifies known facts and constantly contradicts himself, affirming today what he denied yesterday and vice versa.

To curry favor with the peasants, Castro catered to their religious prejudices. His own religious education alerted him to the tremendous propaganda value that religious mysticism and ritual exercise over the masses. During the whole of his two-and-a-half year stay in the Sierra Maestra, Castro never once failed to display the conspicuous, colorful crucifix he wore around his neck. During his "March On Havana" escorted by the "heroes of the Revolution," the famous "Barbudos" (bearded ones) Castro ordered them to display brightly colored medallions and other religious ornaments on their uniforms.

In this and in many other ways, Castro projected a godlike image of himself, as a sort of earthly Messiah. He encouraged the illusion that only HE and his select group of "disciples" and the "heroes of the Revolution" have earned the right to wield unlimited power over the people of Cuba.

Once the undisputed right of an elite group to dominate the economic political, social and individual life of a nation has been established, the personnel of the ruling groups is of secondary importance. At the beginning, Castro's legendary "Twelve Apostles" who disembarked with him from the Granma to begin the guerrilla war against Batista constituted his government. Later, the "Commandantes of the Sierra" were allowed to join the club. Still later, Castro allowed the leaders of United Party of the Socialist Revolution—a coalition of the 26th of July Movement, the Revolutionary Directorate (mostly students) and the Popular Socialist Party (communist) to join the elite.

Castro purged, jailed, banished and tortured hundreds of his adherents, who had distinguished themselves for bravery in the Revolution, only because they were too independent; he replaced them with former enemies, who, for a few grains of power, recanted and became his fanatical disciples.

The technique employed by this little gang of dictators to dominate the people of Cuba is simple: Castro's junta appoints and discharges the President of the Republic; likewise all the ministers. It enacts or repeals all the laws. It also appoints Provincial Governors and Mayors; determines who shall administer the labor unions; the industrial federation of unions and the armed forces. The junta dictates national and foreign policy without consulting the formal, established government; appoints and discharges "revolutionary" tribunals and civilian judges; and administers the economy without being accountable to anyone. Further, it convokes "spontaneous" mass meetings to "consult" the people about government measures which have already been put into effect. It exercises exclusive and absolute control over all channels of information and communication and intervenes in all matters (including what it knows nothing about).

The top rulers aside from Fidel Castro and his brother Raúl, a member of the communist youth organization in 1952, are the late Ché Guevara, fanatical Argentine communist who was with Castro in Mexico; Osvaldo Dorticós Torrado [President of Cuba], a lawyer, in his youth a Communist Party member, later a trusted friend of Batista who rewarded his services with a high post in the municipality of Cienfuegos; Carlos Rafael Rodríguez, former Minister without Portfolio in Batista's first "constitutional" government, a former editor of the Communist Party daily *Hoy*; Blas Roca, another corrupt Stalinist bureaucrat and personal friend of Batista in whose cabinet he was also Minister without Portfolio; the late Lázaro Peña, boss of the CTC (government controlled labor organization) under Batista and at his death occupied the same post under Castro; Raúl Roa, who to win favor with Castro, became a Communist Party hack after 30 years as a virulent anti-communist; Juan Marinello, head of the Communist Party under Batista with whom he shared the electoral slate when he ran for mayor of Havana in 1940; and Armando Hart Dávalos, a lawyer and faithful Castro sycophant. [At this writing almost all of them are high officials in Castro's government.]

The absolute monopoly of power exercised by this little group can logically be called a "revolutionary oligarchy." All the functions of government, traditionally divided into legislative, judicial, and executive branches, are now concentrated in this little group. They intervene in everything. In a workers' assembly they connive to dismiss officials elected by the membership, as they also do in meetings of students, where they dictate the curriculum.

Nothing escapes their control. Everything and everybody is subject to their orders. The political parties who make up the coalition United Party of the Socialist Revolution are orientated and directed by them. The simple rank-and-file members are not given the least opportunity to question their arbitrary decisions. [All reliable reports substantiate these facts—af anything, the situation is even worse, since the dissolution of the coalition Cuba is now OFFICIALLY a one-party dictatorship, and the party is in turn subjected to the personal dictatorship of Fidel Castro.]

Cuban Labor In A Straitjacket

The Cuban labor movement was absolutely independent of governments and political parties from its foundation by the anarcho-syndicalists in the 1880s, the last days of Spanish domination, until 1938, when the communists in alliance with the Batista Government, subordinated action of the working class to the interests of the Party and the State. With the creation of the only government-sponsored union, The Cuban Confederation of Labor (CTC), the unions lost their autonomy and became totally dominated by the communist labor bureaucracy and the Batista Ministry of Labor. [Before the Revolution, the CTC consisted of 1,200,000 members, organized into 33 industrial federations and 2,490 local unions.]

In spite of repression, in spite of the fact that strikes were forbidden by law, the workers, to a certain extent, still influenced by the anarcho-syndicalist traditions of the Cuban labor movement, refused to renounce their independence as a class, and fought back with strikes and other direct action tactics, many times against the will of the leaders of their union, the CTC. In the course of years of bitter struggles, the workers defended their organizations and wrested from their employers greatly improved conditions and many other substantial gains.

With the fall of Batista, the working class expected that the injustices would be corrected and the obstacles to a free and beneficial development of the labor movement would be swept away by the triumphant revolution. But this was only "the dream of a summer night." The reality was, that the new regime also prohibited strikes, and urged the workers to wait patiently until the government would study their demands and decide whether to grant them or not. Raul

Castro tried to convince the workers that "the best union is the State— the workers don't need unions when they have a friendly government, THEIR government, to protect them."

This attitude was endorsed by the new labor leaders who after the Castro Revolution had been placed in control of the labor movement. The workers were told that in order to "defend the revolution," they must cease demanding better conditions and wages will be frozen. While the new government subordinated the needs of the workers to the plans of the government, the unions were denied the right to play their rightful part in the revolutionary transformation. Instead of allowing the labor organizations to administer the expropriated industries, which would have been correct and constructive, the Castro government, without consulting the workers, appointed state administrators. In most cases these administrators knew little or nothing about the industry and were absolutely incapable of managing them efficiently.

The 10th Congress of CTC, which took place in November, 1959, was marked by a bitter battle between the workers who had openly and freely elected their representatives who were anti-communists. But the dictators, especially Fidel and Raúl Castro, insisted on placing the unions under the control of the old-line Communist Party fakers. The workers were forced to accept hand-picked communists or communist sympathizers who control the CTC (1). This signifies that the interests of the labor movement are subordinated to the interests of the new totalitarian state and the elimination by foul means of the militant unionists who refused to accept dictatorship. Cuban labor is imprisoned in a straitjacket (2).

The communist officials are determined to liquidate all the conquests gained by the workers in 80 years of struggle. Among the list of benefits and rights eliminated by the eleventh Congress of the CTCR (the word "Revolutionary" was added to the original name) were the right to strike, job security, sick leave, 30 days paid vacations, four paid holidays, the 44 hour work week with 48 hours pay, overtime at time-and-a-half, double or triple rate, the summer work-schedules under which employees in commercial establishments and office personnel are entitled to two paid afternoons off during the hot months of June, July and August—and many other improvements.

The workers are being constantly pressured into making "voluntary" sacrifices to finance the experiments of the government:(3) The offices of the unions have been converted into recruiting centers for Militiamen and workers are threatened with the loss of their jobs if they don't join the militias. The labor officials also help to form *Committees of Vigilance for Defense of the Revolution,* who spy on the workers on the job, reporting what they say and do to the police. The reaction of almost all the workers to these provocations, is passive resistance:

non-cooperation, absence from work, absence from all meetings called by the Castro-communist bosses, etc., etc. It can be affirmed without fear of contradiction, that 80% of all the Cuban workers are against Castro.

In June 1960, the anarchists reiterated their conviction that the workers themselves, through their own union organizations, should undertake the revolutionary control and administration of all expropriated industries and enterprises, for the simple reason that no one can possibly be better or equally fitted, by reason of know-how and experience, to operate and administer the industries than those who work in them. This proposal, favorably received by the organized workers, was, of course, rejected by the "new class" who today exploit the people.

Note 1

Out of 2,963 delegates, only 247 votes were cast for the Castro backed slate. Delegates denounced the communists for their record of collaberation with Batista. Fist fights broke out on the floor and in the street. The Russian envoy, who got up to address the congress was hooted down with cries of ASSASSIN! MURDERER OF THE PEOPLE! and similar invectives.

The outrageous violation of the elemental rights of the union membership aroused the protest of the international labor movement. For example, the *News Bulletin of the International Union of Food and Allied Workers* (Geneva, June-July, 1962):

SAVE OUR MOVEMENT

David Salvador, leader of the labor section of the 26th of July Movement throughout the Cuban revolutionary struggle against Batista, was recently sentenced to 30 years in prison by Castro. Salvador was the first elected leader of the post-revolutionary CTC. He resigned his post as Secretary-General. . .in May 1960 in protest of the Communist take-over being directed by Castro.

In November, he was imprisoned without trial and remained in La Cabana Fortress, along with 700 other political prisoners. Seven others were sentenced with Salvador, including a revolutionary army commander, Jaime Vega, and two other revolutionary labor leaders.

For over a year after Salvador was arrested, the CTC had elected no leader. Finally, in November 1960, Lázaro Peña was put into the post. Peña, an old time Communist union bureaucrat, helped form the Batista controlled CTC in 1939, during the Communist-Batista coalition. [within which he was also the CTC's first Secretary-General] [S.D.]

Note 2

Labor Discipline Laws to Legalize State Domination of Labor Movement and Punish Workers Resistance.

In August 1962, a decree was issued prohibiting workers from changing their occupation or employer and making absenteeism a major crime. In September, work norms were set up and tables were worked out to compute productivity. From then on the work force was to be strictly disciplined and regulated by law. Law 647 allowed "...The Minister of Labor, through his representative, if he thinks it necessary, to take full custody of any union or federation, and is authorized to dismiss officials and appoint others to replace him..."

Correspondent Juan de Onis in a Havana dispatch to *The New York Times* (October 3, 1964) reports the enactment of a law compelling state farm workers "to put in an eight hour day and satisfy production quotas to receive full pay..." To drastically reduce absenteeism, carelessness "...and machinery breakage...stiff penalties will be provided ...the *lightest* penalties are a 15% reduction in pay...for three unjustified absences from work in a month... (our emphasis).

To supplement legal measures the government tightened its domination of the labor movement introducing greater centralization. In an article in the June 26, 1966, issue of *Granma*, the government made clear its plan for the restructuring of the labor movement. Under the headline INTERVIEW WITH BASILIO RODRÍGUEZ—MINISTER OF LABOR subtitle: Twelfth Congress of the CTC Proposes to Strengthen Unions, the article, in part, reads:

"...the call to the CTC Congress proposed the strengthening of the authority of the Central Organization...With the new structure, the activities of the CTC and the and the directors of the national unions were strictly controlled by the Central Organization."

Note 3

On "Voluntary" Labor

...the first regulations of the Socialist Emulation Program, which went into effect in 1963, set up strict controls for voluntary work. Under the program, workers were required to sign contracts withe the State, agreeing to work a determined number of hours without pay. In early 1963, the CTC decided that the Battalions of Voluntary Workers had to turn in weekly reports giving the names of workers in each battalion and the work record of each volunteer. This was one of the measures instituted to alleviate the shortage of labor and the problem of increasing absenteeism. The CTC branch in Matanzas Province had to be "hurriedly reorganized" because it failed to fulfill its "obligation to provide its quota of voluntary labor." (CMQ radio, Havana, February 5, 1963)

...in 1964 the Voluntary Labor Program was further systematized with the introduction of the Carte Laboral (Labor Identity Card). The amount of voluntary labor performed by each worker was recorded on the card. According to Arnaldo Milian, Secretary-General of the People's Socialist Party (Communist) of Las Villas, the system "guarantees discipline in each brigade, besides improving political awareness and permitting constant promotion of production and emulation...this is what enabled the Cruces (town) section to achieve such a high degree of cane cutting..." (broadcast over Radio Progresso, Santa Clara City, April 11, 1964. See also, Organization of Labor Brigades in Agriculture by Israel Talavera; *Cuba Socialista,* Havana, April 1964)

In respect to "voluntary" labor, *The Bulletin of the Cuban Libertarian Movement in Exile* (Miami, July 1967) quotes the official organ of the Communist Party of Cuba, *Granma:*

"Jose Lopez-age 88 'voluntarily' returned to work in the sugar harvest." *(Granma,* April 25, 1967)

101

"42 women in the Henequin factory Matanzas province 'voluntarily' worked *72 consecutive* hours" (*Granma,* April 26, 1967)

"Workers in the Central Workshop of the Ministry of the Armed Forces putting in a 14 to 16 hour day, 'voluntarily' worked a total of *28,000* hours" (*Granma,* April 27, 1967)

"In the Province of Oriente, 109,247 workers in three months 'voluntarily' worked a total of *1,000,000* hours." (Radio Progreso, April 29, 1967)

According to *Granma,* March 22, 1967, "the volunteer cane cutters of the Silvia Taboada Brigade, composed of members of the Revolutionary Armed Forces of Havana, worked 28 consecutive hours cutting cane in Havana Province."

In the same issue, *Granma* published an article about another brigade by Berta Cabrera, which said in part, "Today is Sunday, but it is different from other Sundays. There is no time for *paseos* [going out and having some fun]. The clock says it's almost four-thirty a.m. Everything here is work for the Ricardo Santa Brigade. 'How many hours do you work?' we asked. 'There's no limit' replies one of the cane-cutters, 'as long as one can hold out...there are a few who are ill.' Julio Robaina, another cane-cutter, says, 'How many hours do we work? No one knows. We start before six a.m. and we never know when we will finish...Sometimes, at eight, nine p.m. or after midnight...'"

According to a broadcast over Radio Progreso (Havana, March 16, 1967), "The workers of the Sakenof Factory in Santa Clara, Las Villas Province, 590 men and 350 women exceeded the goal set for production of bags and containers for fertilizer. Many workers remained on the job for 20 consecutive hours...without getting extra pay."

[Notes by Sam Dolgoff]

Baptizing Dictatorship: "Direct Democracy"

A revolutionary minority seeking to govern without the explicit endorsement of the people or the confidence of the revolutionary organizations whose militants fought to overthrow the old regime and make the Revolution, cannot consolidate its dictatorship if it does not "legitimate" its right to govern. Castro tried to justify his abuse of power by camouflaging his dictatorship as a genuine people's democracy. For these reasons he organized frequent brainwashing sessions. The sole purpose of these gigantic demonstrations was the projection of his personal power as the symbol, the perfect deification and incarnation of the popular will.

To stay in power Castro desperately sought the support of both the liberal democratic and revolutionary masses. He adopted the classical techniques used by all totalitarians from Caesar to Franco, including the manufacture of mass support by staging delirious massive demonstrations spurred on by his fanatical followers.

The man destined to baptize Castro's dictatorship was the existentialist philosopher, Jean Paul Sartre. On one of his "impartial" fact finding visits at the invitation of the "Revolutionary Government," Sartre, inspired by his reception, struck just the right note. Castro's

102

dictatorship was defined as a "direct and concrete democracy." Sartre explained: "...the revolutionary rulers converse directly with the people, thus establishing a direct and permanent bond between the will of the great majority of the people and the government minority..."

It is a fact, well-known in Cuba, that by the middle of 1959—only six months after the revolution began—more and more people were beginning to realize that they had gotten rid of one bloody dictatorship only to fall into another brutal dictatorship. The honeymoon between the Cuban people and the "revolution" proclaimed by Castro was over. And the rulers, to hide this fact, began to imitate the same procedures prevailing in the other totalitarian regimes. To insure an audience of half a million people, that he could not otherwise get, Castro resorts to the following draconic methods:

a) suspend economic activities throughout Cuba.
b) close all public entertainment; movies, theaters, cafes, etcetera.
c) command all radio and television stations to suspend all regular programs, and broadcast only publicity for the meeting.
d) suspend all public transportation leaving the city for places outside of Havana.
e) all available transport mobilized to bring people to the rally.
f) order all employees, workers, peasants, university professors and students to report to a designated official who will assign each one to the rallying point from which they will proceed to the meeting.
g) 30 days before the meeting all propaganda organs must, 24 hours a day, urge the people to attend the meeting.

And Castro boasts: "The people, the real revolutionary people, are here with us, helping by their spontaneous presence and determination to fight for the revolutionary government; this is genuine, real democracy, a direct and permanent, concrete democracy..."!

The Militarization of Cuba

The Cuban people have always been allergic to uniforms. At every opportunity, they have persistently violated rules of dress prescribed by employers of certain enterprises. For years bus drivers fought obligatory wearing of uniforms during working hours. In other industries, employees refused to wear work clothes if the garments advertised the company or its products. The average Cuban considered the wearing of uniforms degrading.

One of the strongest reasons for the popular opposition to Batista's regime was the instinctive aversion of Cubans to its overweening militarism and its vulgar display of martial finery and pomp. With the triumph of the Revolution, the masses expected a return to civilian rule, and the dismantling of the military apparatus. It seemed at first that this was being done. The rebel troops, in plain unobtrusive olive-green uniforms, numbered less than 2,000, while Batista's troops had exceeded 40,000. In his famous speech delivered on the triumphal arrival in Havana, Castro pledged an end to militarism: "Arms? What for?...The military barracks will be converted into schools."

Castro's *acts* belied his words. A few weeks later, the Cuban capital was swamped with thousands of young soldiers hastily mobilized into the new military and police forces by the "revolutionary" government. Almost all important posts in the new government were filled by officers of the Rebel Army. Many provincial executive committees of labor unions and industry-wide federations were militarized, and committee people ostentatiously displayed their uniforms and insignia of rank. All government delegates of expropriated landed estates and factories were members of the Rebel Army. When Fidel Castro appointed himself Chief of the Revolutionary Government, ("maximum leader") he gradually eliminated nearly all civilian ministers, replacing them with high-ranking officers of his army, mainly the *Commandantes de la Sierra*. All key government posts were filled by military people loyal to Castro. Castro himself intertwined his political and military functions so that it was almost impossible to differentiate one from the other.

Popular reaction against the new militarism made itself felt very quickly through practical jokes, sarcastic cartoons, etc., exposing the contradiction between what Castro had said while fighting Batista, and the military arrogance of the new government. Castro's second-in-command *Commandante* Camillo Cienfuegos, in defense of his chief, appealed to the famous slogan "the people in arms." The slogan was widely circulated in a vain attempt to justify the hated militarism of the new regime. Castro, who had promised to convert barracks into schools, was actually converting Cuba itself into one vast military camp.

The pace of militarization, which at first was justified on the pretext that the government must be ruled by "tested revolutionaries," such as the veteran "combattants of the Sierras," was accelerated by the threat of counter-revolutionary invasion from the U.S. This threat, though real enough, was nevertheless exaggerated beyond all possible limits. It served no useful military purposes but it did expedite domestic totalitarian regimentation.

The "revolutionary" government militarized the lives of men, women, adolescents, and even children. The regime created the National Revolutionary Militias, the Association of Pioneer Rebels, the Mariana Grajales Women's Batallions, the Conrado Benitez Brigades, etc., etc.—all of them decked out in colorful uniforms, similar in design to those worn in the "socialist" nations. The uniform craze was so great that the then-chief officials of the C.T.C. ordered all union officials to wear uniforms. Day and night, the streets of Cuba's cities, towns and villages resounded to the tramp of marching military trainees, to the incessant yells of drill-masters: ONE, TWO! ONE, TWO! ONE, TWO!

The anarchists watched the military policies of the government with growing apprehension. We understood perfectly the dangers threatening the Revolution, but we could not permit ourselves to be fooled by the bombastic phraseology of the new rulers. We are also convinced that to train revolutionary forces it is not necessary to resort to harsh disciplinary measures. In our *Declaration of Principles* (Havana, June 1960) we stated that, "We are unalterably opposed to the militarization of the young, the creation of professional armies and military groups for adolescents and children. Fewer soldiers and more teachers; fewer arms and more plows; fewer cannons and more bread for all."

Our anti-militarist declaration was denounced as "counter-revolutionary, reactionary, and an insult to the "glory of the Red Army." The Secretary-General of the P.S.P. (Communist Party), Blas Roca, accused us of sabotaging the "defense of the Revolution." In a letter to Blas Roca, we refuted his base accusations and slander:

> . . . libertarians maintain that the Rebel Army must not be converted into a professional army, that the militias should not become instruments for brainwashing, creating a militaristic mentality in the workers and peasants, and that it is neither necessary nor desirable that youth patrols and work brigades should transform children and adolescents into soldiers.
>
> The Secretary-General of the P.S.P. Communist Party confounds mere technical information on the use of arms and mere training in strategy with the professional militarization of the young: he confuses youth patrols and revolutionary "voluntary" work brigades with the military indoctrination of women and children. . . Blas Roca's authoritarian mentality violently rejects the ideas that a revolutionary army can possibly function without commanders and barrack discipline; that the Revolution can be successfully defended by soldiers who are not professional militarists; by soldiers who fight gallantly because they are motivated by their revolutionary convictions; an army without bemedaled generals and marshals.
>
> When Blas Roca hears the expression "army," he automatically envisions the gigantic parades in Moscow's Red Square, in brilliant uniforms adorned with gold epaulets, gilded helmets, varnished chin straps and shiny spurs. . . .

Naturally, as in all totalitarian regimes, *our reply was not published.*

The censored press and governmental control of all commercial printers prevented the libertarian voice from being heard. The regime continues its breakneck militarization of Cuba.

In the first months of the Revolution, the military forces numbered half a million. This does not mean that the Cuban people voluntarily agreed to serve the Castro dictatorship. At least 80% of those in the army were forced to join by threats ranging from outright violence to loss of jobs if they did not "volunteer." [Although Iglesias wrote before enactment of compulsory military service for all men between the ages of 17 and 45, he accurately detected the drift toward conscription.]

Regimenting Education

In contrast to the obscurantism imposed by Spain during centuries of despotism, Cuba's public education system [during the first 25 years of the Republic] provided for every child—with exemplary vigor and dedication—an ample, well-rounded, progressive education, free from all political and religious domination. To provide 300,000 children with free quality education—including food and clothing for poor children—in a country which, at that time, numbered only 1,500,000 people, was indeed a stupendous achievement.

During the Machado dictatorship [1925-33] both the quality and availability of public education declined. This was due to the dependence of jobs on political connections, the poorly trained teachers, crowded, unhealthy school buildings, the scarcity of educational equipment, and the location of school buildings far from poor neighborhoods most in need of good schools. Eventually, widespread and monumental administrative corruption, and other failures of the state, as well as rapid population growth, brought about the collapse of public education. This led to a proliferation of all kinds of parochial schools—Masonic, Catholic, Jewish, Protestant, etc.

Castro's much vaunted anti-illiteracy campaign was used to glorify his regime and to indoctrinate children, teenagers and adults with adoration of the state and the "cult of personality" a la Stalin.

The system was designated to militarize the mentality of children. For example, in teaching the alphabet, the letter "F" was introduced with "el Fusil (the gun) de Fidel Fue (was) a la Sierra." The letter "R" was treated thus: "Raúl el faRo" (Raúl Castro, beacon, bearer of light). "CH" was the pretext for constructing the following phrase: "Los MuCHaCHos y muCHaCHas quieren muCHo al CHé" [The boys and girls like Ché Guevara very much]. Similar techniques have been used in teaching other subjects. Thus, in geography, photographs of Castro and his companions were placed on maps to indicate the Sierra Maestra.

History was, and is, taught from the Marxist point of view. Before the establishment of the "Revolutionary government," Cuban parents had something to say about the kind of education their children got. Now they must accept the curriculum imposed by the state without protest. Anyone venturing even the slightest disagreement is immediately denounced as a "counter-revolutionary agent of imperialism" and treated accordingly.

Teachers are obliged to faithfully follow the official curriculum, methods, and policies meticulously worked out by the "orientators," whose indoctrination sessions they must attend. To further insure enforcement of the rules, every educational center is under the constant surveillance of the Committee for the Defense of the Revolution, which in this case serves as a sort of academic police, made up of teacher and student stool-pigeons, who faithfully obey the orders of the government.

The technical schools, the secondary schools, trade and professional schools, and the universities are subjected to the same procedures. Autonomy of the university—won after years of struggle and immense sacrifice, and of which Cuban students were justly proud—has been totally destroyed. The University of Havana is ruled by the arbitrarily imposed *Junta de Gobierno* [Administrative Council], whose membership can be revoked each year in order to guarantee the "revolutionary fidelity of the faculty."

The fake "university reform" was put into effect by intimidation and violence. The old Stalinist and Batistiano sycophants, Juan Marinello and Carlos Rafael Rodríguez, fill the most important posts in the University with their hand-picked appointees. The *Federación Estudantil Universitaria* [F.E.U.—Federation of University Students] that fought so valiantly for freedom and autonomy against all oppressive governments has lost its liberty. The students no longer have the right to elect their own officers. From his office in the Ministry of the Armed Forces, Raúl Castro dictates who shall be the president of the student organization—in flagrant violation of all the rules and regulations of the F.E.U. [For details see "How the Communists Took Over the University of Havana," below.]

An emphasis on the monstrous intervention of the state in all academic activities may appear exaggerated to readers not acquainted with the bitter reality of the Cuban tragedy; but it is a truly serious situation. It is most distressing for a man like myself, nearly 50 years of age, to be led around by a boy of 12, uniformed and shouldering a small size rifle of Czechoslovakian make. It is shocking to see boys barely 15 years of age standing guard, guns in hand, in front of public buildings. It is disgraceful to contemplate teenagers parading through streets and along highways all over Cuba, marching in step and singing martial hymns full of hate and venom...

The Propaganda Machine

The following was included in the Report of the Libertarian Association of Cuba (A.L.C.) for September 12, 1960.

At present, Communist Party people hold key posts in the government propaganda machine, which they run with the technical help of native and foreign-born Communist experts. Through the "cultural" departments created in every government ministry, in the armed forces, etc., they organize courses in so-called "revolutionary doctrine," which are actually Marxist indoctrination courses. For example, the "cultural" chief of the military camp of La Cabana [one of the most important in Cuba] is Ramón Nicalau, who for years was financial secretary of the Communist Party. Among the lecturers with him on this project are Juan Marinello, President of the Communist Party, and Carlos Rafael Rodríguez, Editor of the Communist newspaper *Hoy* [Today], organ of the Party. [Its well-equipped printing plant was donated to the Party by the Castro government after confiscation from the Batista newspaper *Alerta*]

The Cinematic Institute is the statist agency directing and controlling the movie industry. It is managed by Dr. Alfredo Guevara, another Communist Party member. Through the Film Review Board, he decides what films are acceptable for exhibition in the country. The People's Consultation Library of the National Capital is another agency which spreads only Castro Communist propaganda. All these projects are financed by the government.

The organization of Youth Patrols has been undertaken by the national police. It recruits children from the age of 7 years. They receive military training under the guise of "revolutionary indoctrination."

Official Declaration of Educational Policies

...we must orientate education according to Marxism-Leninism. Marx's CAPITAL must should be studied in all primary grades... the teachings of Marxism-Leninism in the universities is obligatory... (Armando Hart; Minister of Education, July 11, 1963)

...The Union of Young Communists and the Federation of University Students must see to it that the curriculum follows the orientation of Fidel Castro...(Ex-President of the Federation of University Students, Jaime Crómbat, speech in the University of Havana, May 26, 1965)

...the creation of Communist Party cells will facilitate the campaign of the University to eliminate counter-revolutionists and homosexuals... (Blas Roca, member of the Central Committee of the Communist Party of Cuba, speech in the University of Havana, June 14, 1965—Source for all above quotes—*Este y Oeste;* June 15 1966, Caracas)

How The Communists Took Over The University Of Havana
by Andrés Valdespino

This is the title of a revealing first hand report by Andres Valdespino which appeared in the April 1, 1962 issue of Cuba Nueva, *part of which we translate below. Veldespino was an active fighter in the anti-Batista movement. In the first months of the Castro government he served as the Under-Secretary of Finance, and later, Professor of Criminal Law in the University of Havana. He resigned from the faculty in protest of the destruction of the University as an independent center of learning, and against the regime's disrespect for human rights. [S.D.]*

Autonomy and Totalitarianism

An autonomous university not subjected to the political interests of the state, is necessarily incompatible with the conception of a totalitarian society—a society in which nothing is allowed to exist outside the control and domination of the state... autonomy of education is a genuine revolutionary conquest, and no revolution worthy of the name has the right to limit or abrogate this constitutional right granted in the Magna Carta of the Republic.

In its plans for the conquest of the University, and in order not to arouse strong mass resistance and student revolt, the Castro-communist regime decided to proceed gradually, in three stages: first, by taking administrative control of the student organization; second, by militarizing the University; and third, by replacing the legitimate governing bodies of the University with state controlled bodies.

Control of Student Adminitration

To carry out the first stage, it was necessary to find a suitable puppet as candidate for President of the Federation of University Students (F.E.U.)...The candidate selected, Rolando Cubela, was a *Commandante* of the Rebel Army who enjoyed the absolute confidence of the Commander-in-Chief of the Armed Forces, Raul Castro. [Cubela had been an early leader of the Student Revolutionary Directorate and fought with the Directorate on the Escambray Front. He was famous for having killed Batista's chief of military police in the busiest

109

intersection of Havana.]

Cubela's opponent, Pedro Boitel, was very popular with—and favored by—the students, who feared that the installation of an army officer as President of the F.E.U. would lead to the militarization of their organization.

The authorities could not risk the defeat of their candidate. On the day before the F.E.U. elections, Castro himself came to the University and addressed the students. So as not to antagonize them, he feigned impartiality and did not directly urge them to vote for Cubela, but subtly prepared the ground for the victory of his candidate by urging revision of the old electoral system: "Do away with party factional rivalries and agree on the unanimous proclamation of a single candidate." But this time the "Maximum Leader" encountered open opposition. The students, true to their traditions of democratic procedures and academic independence, rejected Castro's proposal. The decision of the students was "THERE WILL BE ELECTIONS."

But a few hours before the voting was to take place, Boitel suddenly withdrew his candidacy. The reason was not hard to find. He was forced to step aside. The confusion created by his withdrawal and above all, the fact that Cubela was the *only* candidate, automatically guaranteed his election. With Cubela as President, the capture of the FEU seemed certain. [Some months later, Boitel, falsely sentenced to 42 years imprisonment as a "counter-revolutionist" in the dreaded Castillo de Principio Penitentiary, died after a prolonged hunger strike. Castro also got rid of Rolando Cubela some time later. On March 10, 1966, he was sentenced to 25 years in prison for plotting the assassination of Castro]

Militarizing the Universities

The "election" of Cubela was followed by the creation of the University Student Militias. The government mobilized its propaganda apparatus to convince the students that it was their "heroic mission" to wear the "uniform of a militia member." But the students were not easily fooled. Out of more than 20,000 students, only 300 voluntarily joined the newly organized University Student Militia.

But, what was lacking in numbers was made up for by military fanfare. Day and night, little bands of students in uniform strutted through the University grounds, carrying pistols, rifles and machine guns. The stentorian shouts of the officers echoed with provocative insolence all over the campus, desecrating the academic community dedicated to the pursuit of knowledge and the preservation of culture. The military boot returned to profane the terrain of culture. But this time, more than before, not only did the barrack invade the University; *the University itself was converted into a barrack!*

110

Neither the fraudulent election of Cubela as President of the F.E.U., nor the militarization of the University [via the organization of the militia], sufficed to stem student rebellion. In February, 1960, the Russian leader Anastas Mikoyan, on his visit to Havana, placed a ceremonial wreath on the statue of the revered "apostle" of Cuban independence, José Martí, in Havana's Central Park [as is the custom for foreign dignitaries]. Outraged, that the representative of a tyrannical, totalitarian government should be invited to insult the memory of Martí, a group of students dramatized their indignation by placing their own wreath on Martí's statue. [They carried signs reading "Viva Fidel! Down with Communism!"]

The students were immediately arrested and branded "counterrevolutionary agents of yankee imperialism." [Among those arrested were Juan Muller, a leader of the fighting in Las Villas Province during the Revolution, and his brother Alberto Muller, Secretary of the Havana University Student Federation. See the first-hand account of Ruby Hart Philips in her book, *The Cuban Dilemma;* New York, 1962, p. 153].

The incident became the pretext for a ferocious offensive by the Communist minority in the University against those who manifested their opposition to the Castro regime. The slogan coined by the former leader of the Communist Party, Juan Marinello, Rector of the University of Havana, "To be against Communists is to be a counter-revolutionary," became the battle cry of a tiny group who publicly burned student publications critical of the Communists.

And it was the Communist, Marinello, a Minister under Batista, who declared that there is no need for autonomy under a "revolutionary regime," where the "people are the government."

When I was Under-Secretary of Finance, I wrote an article refuting Marinello's argument, which was published in the magazine *Bohemia*. Marinello replied in the [then] official organ of the Party, *Hoy*, with insults, libeling me as a "counter-revolutionary in the pay of imperialism," and "an agent of the reaction infiltrating the ranks of the revolutionary government."

Marinello's blast set off an intensified government sponsored campaign to discredit the opposition and capture the university. The University Student and Faculty Council fought back. But this only intensified the attacks not only against the autonomy of the university but also against the faculty, accusing it of sabotaging plans for university reform.

The accusation was false and unjust. After months of painstaking effort the joint Faculty and Student Commission worked out a comprehensive Reform Project which was overwhelmingly and democratically approved by the students and faculty of the while university.

In April 1960, a joint meeting of the communist dominated chapters of the universities of Havana, Oriente and Las Villas proposed that the delegates from the three universities, the Ministry of Education and the INRA (National Institute for Agrarian Reform) should jointly rule and dictate the policy of the university. This plot to capture the university was decisively rejected by the students and faculties of the three universities.

The pretext for the takeover of the university came when a few Castroite communist students, without consulting anyone, expelled two engineering professors on the false, now familiar charge that they were "counter-revolutionists." Again, without consultation the expelled professors were replaced by two non-teachers; Che Guevara's brother-in-law and an active communist. The professors protested this outrage by going on strike. The communist dominated FEU (Federation of University Students) then occupied several university buildings, and the government legalized the seizure. Recalcitrant faculty and students were purged and the freely elected administration was usurped by appointed "Revolutionary Juntas," faithful servants of the state.

The junta assumed dictatorial powers and commanded all the teachers to obey their decrees. More than 80% of the professors who refused were expelled and replaced by docile sycophants, strict followers of the "party line" . . . This spelled the end of the university as an independent entity. It turned out to be the preliminary step toward the invasion of the University by hordes of Castro-communists.

Interview With Cuban Libertarians by Roy Finch

Roy Finch resigned from the editorial board of the libertarian-pacifist magazine Liberation *because he disagreed fundamentally with its pro-Castro policy. While the editors insisted that the Cuban Revolution was taking a libertarian direction, Finch maintained, on the contrary, that Cuba was fast becoming a totalitarian state. In the ensuing debate, Finch supported his position by arranging an interview with Cuban anarchist exiles, lately arrived in New York. We extract the following excerpts from* Liberation, *March, 1961. [S.D.]*

. . . the interview took place in the present New York home of Jesús Dieguez, in Batista's day head of the Revolutionary Insurrectional Union, an old revolutionary group which worked with Castro and with which Castro was once affiliated. Mr. Dieguez is obviously a man of great courage. He threw himself whole-heartedly into the revolutionary struggle against Batista as far back as 1940. He showed me newspaper stories about the Revolutionary Insurrectional Union and newspaper clippings with photographs of himself standing beside Castro in the pre-revolutionary training days in Mexico. All members of the group I met were life-long foes of dictators, and all of them were in the underground fight against Batista...

...Most of the following interview was conducted with Jesús Dieguez and his son Floreal Dieguez. Other members of the group broke in occasionally, and it was clear that they were in substantial agreement with what was said...

Q. What is the point of view of the Cuban Libertarians about the Revolution?

A. From the outset the Libertarians supported many of the things that were done: the expropriation of private property, land and factories and taking over industries. They opposed the government's becoming the new landlord, the new capitalist. In June, 1960, A Statement of Principles of the Libertarian Syndicalist Group was issued [see below].

Q. How many libertarians left Cuba?

A. Between 20 and 30.

Q. Would it have been dangerous for you to stay in Cuba?

A. We would probably be in jail by now.

Labor Unions

Q. What is the situation in the Cuban labor movement now?

A. All the national and provincial unions have been taken over by the communists.

Q. What happened to the libertarians in the unions?

A. The libertarians were particularly strong in the Food Workers Union. When the communists came to power, they expelled the libertarians not only from the leadership, but from the union itself...the union is 100% communist controlled now.

Q. What has been the public reaction to the communists taking over the unions?

A. There has been considerable reaction of workers against the Stalinists and against the government. Many union meetings have ended in riots. Workers have demonstrated in the streets. Three men, all of whom fought against Batista, have received thirty-year jail terms for signing a declaration against the communist domination of the unions. They are Lauro Blanco, a leader of the Transport Workers Union; Salvador Estavalora, a Castro military man; and Mario Padierno, who had been very active in the anti-Batista underground. Padierno had been picked up and then turned loose. Then the secret police returned and took him away. They told him that he had been sentenced "in absentia." (Mr. Dieguez said that he had been picked up at the same time, but was released, apparently upon personal intervention of Castro himself, probably for "old times sake.")

Secret Police

Q. On the question of civil liberties—is there a secret police now in Cuba?

A. No one knows. We believe that they have a thousand people working for them in Havana. They have informants in factories, unions and schools.

Q. How does the secret police function?

A. The head is a man named Ramiro Valdés, a Communist Party member. There are two divisions under him: D.I.E.R. (Army Intelligence) and D.I.R. (Civil Intelligence.) The D.I.E.R. is run by Raúl Díaz Argelles, a man named Lavandiera, a French communist who was the right hand man of the communist Arbenz in Guatemala. The head of the D.I.R. is Ángel Valdés—also a Communist Party man—no relation to Ramiro Valdes. But the man who really runs the whole thing is a Russian agent called Fabio Crobat. He is the Communist Party's over-all control man in Cuba. He has been in and out of Cuba for thirty years now. He is never mentioned in the press. No one ever sees a photograph of him...

Q. Who are some of the democratic oppositionists (anti-Batista, anti-communists) in Castro Cuba who have been shot?

A. Plineo Orieto, one of Fidel Castro's commanders, was shot. They said that he was organizing an insurrectionary plot, but there was no proof. Porfirio Ramírez, President of the Student Federation of Santa Clara was shot because they (secret police) said he was organizing an opposition. Again there was no real proof. Gerardo Fundora, a labor leader in Matanzas, was shot.

Communists

Q. You mentioned the communists in the labor unions and the secret police. Just how important are the communists over-all in Cuba today?

A. They control education, the army, the secret police, the trade unions,...the press and mass media, the agrarian reform and the tourist industry...

Q. What about Castro himself?

A. Fidel came to a coincidence of interests with the communists from about 1956. When I was in Mexico with Fidel in the training camp of the 26th of July Movement, there was always more communist literature than any other kind. Now Castro is working completely with the Communists...

[Further questions about the communist orientation of the Cuban regime, as well as education, censorship, political prisoners, the army and militarization etc., are here omitted as they are discussed in much greater detail throughout the text]

114

Roy Finch sums up the lessons that could not be learned from the experience of the Cuban Revolution.

> Through the connivance of American blindness and Cuban Communism, the Cuban Revolution has all but been stolen from the Cuban people... [and quotes Albert Camus] "... None of the evils which totalitarianism claims to remedy is worse than totalitarianism itself..."

Other Reports

The following reports were sent from Cuba by anarchist militants active in the anti-Castro underground resistance movement who also fought against Batista. [S.D.]

...Those who organized the April 1961 invasion of Cuba misunderstood the reality of the Cuban situation. The failure of the invasion points up the need for a thorough re-evaluation of the means for the liberation of Cuba. For the moment, we shall try to describe the situation.

The invasion caught us by surprise. There was a total lack of information and the underground were not consulted or notified. The government immediately proceeded to detain anyone suspected of being opponents of the regime. Only those able to go into hiding escaped arrest. There is no way of knowing how many were seized, but we believe that in Havana alone there were over 40,000. There must have been at least half a million nationally...
In one of the phony "cooperatives" 800 workers were hauled in. Detention centers in Havana and in the provinces were surrounded by machine-gun troops. And the prisoners were warned that at the first sign of trouble, they would immediately be shot down. Nevertheless, in many places the prisoners attempted jailbreaks. In one case—the Palace of Sports—prisoners were machine gunned and a number were killed and wounded. Prisoners in the Castillo del Principe Fortress were so sadistically tortured that many became seriously ill and some had to be placed in insane asylums...
...it was the Committees for the Defense of the Revolution CDR who conducted most of the house by house raids. No one can escape their vigilance. These block and neighborhood stoolpigeons are a permanent danger...
...a people that has sent such a huge proportion of its sons, daughters and friends into exile, because they cannot tolerate the regime; a people in armed opposition to the dictatorship with over half a million imprisoned for opposing the dictatorship are decisively rejecting the tyrannical social regime which they are

being forced to endure. A detested regime maintains itself in power through terror supported by the armaments and military technicians of foreign imperialist powers. Rather than submit to such domination the people will, if necessary, die fighting to overthrow the totalitarian usurpers of the Revolution...

LIBERTY OR DEATH!
"Antonio". Cuba May 13, 1961.

(source: *Bulletin of the Cuban Libertarian Movement in Exile (MCLE)*, Miami, May-June, 1964.

...on the accusation of any stoolpigeon anyone can be imprisoned, even shot, without being given the least opportunity to defend himself or engage counsel. We know of many cases where persons detained were later murdered on the pretext that they were killed while fighting against government forces...

On July 31, 1962, inmates of Principe prison hung up a poster, "We Are Hungry!" in a corridor. The guards retaliated by opening fire on the protesters, killing some and wounding many. Some of the inmates were placed in solitary confinement, without sun, in damp cells which seriously affected their health...

In the Cabana Fortress—an ancient Spanish colonial prison— protesting prisoners were stripped naked and exposed to the tropical heat...others were locked up for months in gloomy dungeons..

"Antonio". Cuba, August 5, 1962
(source, ibid. August-September, 1962)

In addition to scarcity of food and other necessities the people are subjected to arrests and house searches at any hour of the day or night, the CDR are now invested with police powers. Shootings grow more numerous each day. In the night people are herded into concentration camps...recently more than a thousand from the little town of Paguay Grands were herded into the public square, coverted into a concentration camp seventy were shot...

Antonio. Cuba, March 18, 1963.
(source ibid., March-April, 1963)

Leaving Cuba

Salvador Garcia, a veteran Spanish anarcho-syndicalist militant, fought the Franco-fascists on the Aragon front from the beginning of the Civil War in 1936, until the fall of the Republic in 1939, when his column was interned in a French Concentration camp. During World War II, Garcia fought in the underground resistance against the Nazi

116

occupation army in France. Later he and his family emigrated to Cuba where he was active in the libertarian movement and was for years Secretary of the C.N.T. Spanish refugee organization.

When the sadistic persecution of revolutionaries, by Castro's totalitarian regime, made life unbearable, Garcia found refuge in Mexico. The following excerpts from an interview given a few days after Garcia's arrival in Mexico (Summer, 1963) depicts the emotional upheavals endured by revolutionaries forced into exile. [S.D.]

Hundreds of thousands of Cubans are risking their lives, trying desperately to leave Cuba. Embassies are swamped with individuals and families seeking refuge in foreign lands. Streets are cordoned off, heavily armed troops guard the docks, ready to open fire on the hordes of desperate Cubans frantically trying to board the first American ships, returning to the U.S. after unloading medical and other supplies to ransom prisoners taken during the aborted American invasion.

Havana International Airport is crowded with high-level bureaucrats (provided with ample funds) traveling to the "socialist" and many other countries. The most expensive restaurants and luxurious accommodations are reserved for the thousands of military "advisors," technicians, specialists and visitors from Russia, China, and other "third world socialist countries." They shop in special stores, with unrestricted access to the rarest liquors, the finest clothes and luxury products. All this, while the ordinary Cuban is forced to subsist on meager rations of coffee, rice, plantains, poultry, meat, fruits and vegetables abundantly available before Castro. Even the communists cannot deny that the Cuban standard of living was among the highest in Latin America.

It is not easy to convey the haunting feeling of despair, frustration and fear that pervades every aspect of Cuban life. . .the daily provocations, the incessant brutalities of the "revolutionary" tyrants poisons the atmosphere. One can hardly breathe. I have fought for freedom and socialism all my life. One still hopes: perhaps some miracle will yet rescue the Revolution from its usurpers? Perhaps Revolutionaries will smash the state? Perhaps Fidel Castro will change? Perhaps. . .? All in vain. The walls are closing in. . .

. . .I still hope for the eventual freedom of Cuba. But there are times when I am beset by doubts and fears. I realize how difficult, if not impossible, it is, for a people all alone to extricate themselves from the totalitarian clutches without powerful help from the outside. . .

(*Reconstruir*; anarchist bi-monthly, Buenos Aires. January-February, 1964.)

WHY THE ANARCHISTS BROKE WITH CASTRO'S REGIME

Strangling the Opposition Press

To explain why the anarchists were forced to break with Castro it is first necessary to depict the cruel, unbearable harassments which made it impossible for any of the opposition groupings to function. The situation is graphically sketched out by a consciencious eyewitness report in the following extract: (Yves Guilbert; *Castro l'Infidele,* Paris, 1961, pp. 174-180) [*S.D.*]

[Fidel Castro said on television, April 2, 1959] "When one newspaper is closed down, no newspaper will feel safe; when one man is persecuted because of his political ideas, no one can feel safe."

Officially there is still freedom of the press in Cuba. There is no law limiting the right of expression. However, Castro's dictatorship could not tolerate the existence of a press not entirely devoted to him...

Shortly after the beginning of the [January 1, 1959] Revolution, Castro requisitioned the newspapers *Alerta, Pueblo, Atajo, El Comercio de Cienfuegos, El Diario de Cuba* of Santiago, and also closed down the journal *El Camagueyano,* founded in 1902... Although Castro pretends that the press is not being shackled, there is a great deal of unofficial, but no less harmful, harassment and sabotage...

To create a subservient press, Castro subsidized *Revolución* [former organ of the July 26 Movement], *Combate, Diario Libre, La Calle* of Havana, *Sierra Maestra,* etc. Journals that he could not, for the moment, entirely suppress were neutralized by an ingenious system of camouflaged censorship. The newspaper workers' union tried to nullify the impact of articles that did not strictly echo Castro's party line by printing a *coletilla*...a sort of disclaimer warning the reader that the article is "counter-revolutionary." It usually reads, "By virtue of the freedom of expression which exists in this country, this article has been printed according to the will of the owners of this publication. But, by virtue of this same freedom of expression, we, the employees of this journal, alert the public that this article is contrary to the truth." Another tactic has been to shut down an obstreperous publication by cutting off its supply of paper or other necessary materials.

Castro was not at all pleased with *coletillas*, which had the opposite of the intended effect, leaving the government open to the accusation of censorship. Early in 1960, he therefore launched an all-out offensive to liquidate, once and for all, the independent press.

[for example]...the editors of *Prensa Libre*, savagely attacked by the Castroites, realized that it too would soon be compelled to cease publication, and sounded the alarm in a hard-hitting article titled "The Hour of Unanimity." [Guilbert here quotes from the article] "Unanimity reigns supreme in Cuba—totalitarian unanimity...there must be no discordant voices, no possibility of criticism. The control of every avenue of expression will facilitate the brain-washing of the public. Dissident voices will be bull-dozed into silence: the silence of those who CANNOT speak out or the silence of those who DARE NOT speak out...."

The great illustrated weekly magazine, *Bohemia*, of Havana, one of the most widely read Cuban magazines in Latin-America, was edited by Miguel Ángel Quevado. Under Batista, *Bohemia* constantly fought for freedom and democracy, and denounced the dictator's outrageous violations of human rights. Castro considered Quevado one of his close friends. In the columns of his magazine, Quevado [initially] backed Castro and the Revolution to the limit. But he could not tolerate the increasing totalitarianism of Castro's government. [*Bohemia,* the only non-censored magazine after 1960, was preparing its "Liberty Edition," with a painting of Castro on its cover over the inscription "Honor and Glory to the National Hero!" when] ...He closed down *Bohemia* and, on July 18, 1960, left Cuba. Quevado explained why he had to do so in a farewll message to the readers:

[Guilbert quotes] "...a diabolical, skillfully prepared plot to impose a Communist dictatorship on the American continent has been organized under the close supervision of Moscow. After listening to the declaration of Nikita Khrushchev, there can no longer be any doubt that Cuba is being used as a tool to promote the foreign policies of the U.S.S.R.... Cuba is being pictured as a weak little nation whose very existence is being safeguarded by the guns of revolutionary Russia, the greatest military power in the world. After Castro's enthusiastic pledge of solidarity with the U.S.S.R. and the "socialist countries," Castro's part in this attentat against freedom has become obvious...

..."In making our own revolution, it is not necessary to subject our people to the oppression and vassalage of Russia. To make a profound social revolution, it is not necessary to implant a system which degrades people to the lowly level of state serfdom, to wipe out the last vestige of freedom and dignity. This is not a genuine revolution...

"These lines should have appeared in the pages of *Bohemia*, but this is no longer possible. Barred from publishing this message in our own magazine, acutely conscious of its moral obligation to the people, to whom *Bohemia* has always been honest and faithful, the editor of *Bohemia* has made the only decision which these circumstances permit: to proclaim in these lines the sad truth of what is happening to Cuba, and to go into exile..."

Many other collaborators of *Bohemia* also left with Quevado. The magazine was immediately taken over by a gang of Castro Communists—while Castro hypocritically deplored "the exile of Quevado as one of the hardest blows to our Revolution."

The Anarchist Press Fights Back

Guilbert is perhaps the only witness who not only mentions the Cuban anarchists, but appreciates their unflinching dedication to the principles of freedom and justice.

...in the Cuban night some light still flickers. As far as circumstances over which they have no control permit, the little anarchist journals still valiantly defend freedom to the utmost. Their papers, *El Libertario* and *Solidaridad Gastronomica* (Organ of the Anarcho-Syndicalist food and restaurant workers union) still courageously project their gleam of hope that Castro fears. They, too, will soon be suppressed...(ibid. p. 178)

In the face of the growing oppression, the libertarian movement while constrained to modulate its criticism so as not to be confused with the counter-revolutionary reactionaries or the more liberal bourgeoisie, nevertheless succeeded in making its position unmistakably clear. For example, both papers prominently displayed provocative headline slogans:

WE ARE AGAINST ALL IMPERIALISMS!
PRIVATE PROPERTY IS THE SYMBOL OF SLAVERY!
SOCIALISM WILL BE FREE OR THERE WILL BE NO SOCIALISM!

121

THE LAND AND THE INDUSTRIES TO THE SYNDICATES!
FOR FREE COLLECTIVES AND COOPERATIVES!

The anarchist papers were compelled to cease publication about two years after the revolution. Since *Solidaridad Gastronomica* appeared monthly and *El Libertario* (organ of the Libertarian Federation of Cuba—ALC) irregularly, the following excerpts from the more important articles, though few, should nevertheless give a fair idea of how the anarchists viewed events during this short period.

The Anarchists and the Revolution

From the Libertarian Association of Cuba to the
International Anarchist Movement
Havana, June, 1959

Dear Comrades:
What follows are our first tentative impressions of the situation in Cuba on the morrow of the Revolution.

With the triumph of the Revolution, many of our comrades released from prison have been joined by ALL our exiled comrades, who have returned to participate in the revolutionary reconstruction of the new Cuba.

It is still too early to predict what orientation the Revolution may take in our country. But there can be no doubt—in view of the adequate measures taken—that the murderous Batista dictatorship will never again be restored to inflict itself upon our people.

The Revolution is preeminently a true people's revolution. The thousands of armed men fighting in the mountains, through their audacity and courage, demolished the dictatorial fortress. Our armed militants enjoyed the full moral and material backing of the masses. The widespread clandestine propaganda and militant actions and uprisings of popular movements all over Cuba, and the fighting solidarity of all groups, undermined the morale and will to fight of Batista's army and his civilian allies.

We feel that a new epoch in the life of Cuba has been opened. But we have no illusions about the character of the institutional changes now taking place. For the time being—how long nobody knows—we still possess civil rights, as well as the possibility of reorganizing our forces and making our ideas and ideals known to the people.

In a widespread revolutionary movement such as this, all sectors are represented; different groupings, often with conflicting aims, strive to exert maximum influence. And it is not always those helping libertarian conceptions who exert the greatest influence.

The doctrine of state centralization has, in Cuba as in so many other countries, had the most harmful effects. Many who sincerely desire a regeneration of society are unfortunately obsessed with the notion that a successful revolution is possible only under a rigid and authoritarian regime. Among these are the extreme nationalists and fanatical patriots—a very dangerous tendency which could facilitate degeneration of the Revolution into a sort of Nazism and Fascism, particularly here in Latin-America.

The formidable Catholic influence is equally dangerous for the Revolution. The duplicity of the top of the Church hierarchy has been amply demonstrated in recent years. In return for supporting Batista, the Church was subsidized with donations of hundreds of thousands, even millions of *pesetas*... Nevertheless, many Catholics fought heroically against Batista, and the lower "rank and file" priests and other clergy fought bravely on all fronts to topple the Batista regime. When normal life has been restored, the Church will surely take advantage of this fact to curry favor with the new regime.

The Communist Party of Cuba is just as dangerous for the Revolution as are the extreme nationalists and the upper echelons of the Church. Fortunately, their influence is limited because they are discredited by their association with Batista and their servility to the Russian totalitarian dictatorship. Hiding behind the banner of liberalism, patriotism, mutual tolerance and the coexistence of all anti-Batista forces, they have been able to infiltrate a number of organizations and some sectors of the labor movement. Though small in number, the Communists are skillful connivers, well-organized and totally unscrupulous; their counterrevolutionary potential must not be underestimated.

The role the labor movement is to play in revolutionary reconstruction is a particularly crucial problem. From the fall of the Machado dictatorship in 1933 to the present, the unions have been the tools of, and one of the main pillars supporting, the government. The fact that the new Revolutionary government is moving to consolidate the labor movement into a single rigidly dominated centralized organization has fortunately—at least for the time being—not weakened the determination of the workers to fight for the autonomy and integrity of their own organizations against dictatorship. The Communists, naturally, are striving to reconquer their controlling position in the labor movement, which they enjoyed for so many years under Batista and the others. But the circumstances are not the same; they are not favorable, and we hope that, in spite of their efforts, the Communists will not succeed in dominating the labor movement.

Despite these and other obstacles, we will continue to struggle for the maximum realization of our libertarian alternatives—in accordance with the realities of the situation and with unflagging dedication—and against Statism and the deformation of the Cuban Revolution.

Manifesto to the Workers and the People in General

As early as January 18, 1959, only a few weeks after the Revolution, the Libertarian Association of Cuba already detected the first signs of the authoritarian character of the new regime and sounded the alarm in its Manifesto to the Workers and the People in General. *The Manifesto reads in part:*

...In this historic moment of the nation and the working class, the ALC is obliged to call attention to certain fundamental problems...

...The Revolution that recently freed the people of Cuba from the bloody tyranny of Batista is a people's revolution for liberty and justice, made by the people. The labor movement of our country was captured by the tyrants, who used it to promote their own sinister purposes. The voices of the rebels and the non-conformists were stilled by the prison officer, the persecutor and the assassin. Unions which dared question the authorities were immediately taken over by the Secretary-General of the [collaborationist] Confederation of Cuban Workers (C.T.C.) and/or Ministry of Labor. Their freely elected representatives were ousted [or even arrested] and replaced by hand-picked faithful servants of the dictatorship, who were imposed upon the membership without the least semblance of democratic procedure. The workers themselves must see to it that such atrocities are never again revived in Cuba...

We are alarmed that the allegedly "temporary" administrations of the unions and their officials are being installed without consultation or agreement of the membership or of the various organizations that made the Revolution...

In the midst of the revolutionary turmoil, we do not expect everything, including the labor organizations, to function normally in so short a time. But it is our duty, and the duty of all the workers, by militant action, to see to it that the democratic procedures, the freedoms, and the rights gained by us with the triumph of the Revolution are respected...

We must immediately hold free elections in the unions, where the workers will freely chose their representatives... It is absolutely necessary that general membership meetings be called immediately to freely discuss and deal with the great and urgent problems...

It is absolutely necessary that the workers themselves elect, dismiss or reinstate their officials. To permit any other procedure would be to allow the very same dictatorial practices which we fought against under Batista...

124

We, the people who fought a bitter war against the old dictatorship, must now make sure that the Revolution will built a new social order that will guarantee liberty and justice for all, without exception...

We workers, who felt on our own bodies the blows inflicted by the old tyranny, must now, again, defend our fundamental rights.

RESOLVE NEVER AGAIN TO INSTITUTE A REGIME OF SUBMISSION AND SLAVERY!

From *Solidaridad Gastronomica*

THE WORKERS MUST BE ALERT NOT TO FALL INTO THE SAME ERRORS TWICE!

The heroic fighters who, with so much effort and sacrifice, defeated the Batista tyranny, merit the eternal gratitude of the Cuban people. Never again must the Cuban people be subjected to horrors such as the Batista tyranny.

We are tremendously disturbed to see swarms of adventurers and other phonies taking advantage of the victorious Revolution, and, by strong-arm methods, taking over control of the unions... Far from signifying a real revolutionary change, these methods only repeat the institutionalized violence of the Batista dictatorship... The Communists wait in the wings, all too anxious to repeat their betrayals of the workers—as when they collaborated with Batista to subjugate them.

Now, with the triumph of the Revolution, is precisely the time for the workers to be doubly alert and watchful not to repeat the same errors, not to allow the democratic assemblies to be destroyed by tolerating decrees from above, edicts converting the unions into agencies of the all-embracing state. The destructive power of the state is the sword of Damocles hanging over the heads of the workers.

We must avoid centralization. We must impede the surge of *new hierarchies* which are no better than the old ones. We must have free and open assemblies where the will of the majority of the workers can determine the future of our class and its organizations. (Jan. 15, 1959)

The Labor Racketeers and the Gangsters Return—Beware!

Barely two months after the Revolution overthrew the dictator Batista and his faithful lieutenant, Eusebio Mujal [fascist thug and Secretary-General of the Batista "labor front," the C.T.C.], the new dictators are already conniving to seize control of the unions, and, like their predecessors, rule the workers by decrees from above.

These tyrants are packing the union meetings with their stooges—strangers who are not even members—brought in to vote for

125

the labor racketeers. The workers are being intimidated by the presence of armed militiamen. These and other practices constitute flagrant violations of the elementary rights of the workers.

The Revolution must guarantee and defend the right of the workers to freely conduct their affairs without intimidation or interference. The fate of the Revolution is in our hands; the destiny of our class is in our own hands! (March 15, 1959)

Warning! Juan Marinello Is Moscow's Stooge and Batista's Friend!

It is reported in the press that "...yesterday afternoon, in a simple ceremony, Dr. Juan Marinello was appointed to the faculty of the Department of Languages and Literature in the Escuela Normal de la Habana [Havana School of Education], the same position from which this well-known writer and political leader had been ousted by the Batista Ministry of Education..."

This announcement deliberately gives the one hundred per cent FALSE impression that Marinello consistently fought the Batista dictatorship. The phony "comrades" [of the Communist Party] who now enjoy such great influence in the new revolutionary government were the staunchest and most faithful friends and supporters of the Batista dictatorship, and were rewarded for their services by being appointed to very good posts in Batista's corrupt government. To deny this incontestable fact is absurd.

Is there a single Cuban who does not yet know that Juan Marinello head of the Communist Party of Cuba (P.S.P.), was instructed to collaborate with Batista by his masters, the Russian Communist Party officials?

From El Libertario

The following article was published in El Libertario, June 20, 1959, shortly after the promulgation of the Agrarian Reform Law. It accurately predicted the disastrous consequences of massive seizures of land by the state, which led to the establishment of state farms (granjas) and the total domination and subjugation of the agricultural workers and peasants. [S.D.]

Plows, Tractors, and the Guajiro

Under the watchwords "Land and Liberty" and "The Land to Those Who Work It," the anarchists pioneered the organization of agricultural workers. Such men as Niceto Pérez, Sabino Pupo, Casanas and Montero were in the struggle for the emancipation of the agricultural workers and peasants.

In contrast to the Marxist bias for the urban industrial workers [based on the fatalistic theory that the realization of socialism will depend exclusively on the technical-scientific development of industry], our conviction that the will of man to create his own social structures is paramount, leads us to attach special importance to the struggles of the rural masses.

The fact that the two greatest upheavals of our century have taken place in predominantly agricultural countries, leads us to place our greatest hope for social change in the vast peasant masses. And it is precisely because it is too often forgotten that the rural masses have always been the most downtrodden victims, that we passionately encourage and sustain all measures which promote their rights.

All these considerations lead us to regard them, not as passive automatons and lifeless pawns, but on the contrary, as dynamic human beings who are capable of great revolutionary achievements when inspired by a just and noble cause.

We have been dedicated champions of agrarian reform, which we have been demanding for many years. Nevertheless, we view with increasing alarm the Agrarian Reform Law, which gives priority to the purely mechanical as opposed to the human factors. We view with alarm the government's mistrust of the peasants, the enactment of measures which inevitably lead to the creation of a state superstructure ruinous to the creative self-activity, spontaneity and initiative of the agricultural workers, and a certain tendency to dismiss the small peasant proprietor as a conservative-minded "kulak."

We must realize that for every machine and every technical blueprint to work, there must be human beings ready and willing to make the necessary sacrifices for the triumph of our cause. If we lose sight of this fact, our cause is lost.

We must realize that the worst possible danger to the Revolution is the bureaucratization induced by the deification of technology and the consequent downgrading of the peasants.

Without underestimating the importance of huge cooperative farms to meet the need for agricultural products, it must be stressed that the small peasant prpoprietors can also contribute greatly to agricultural production by organizing *themselves* into collectives for the intensive cultivation of the land in common. . .

(The reader will note how closely *El Libertario* anticipated the constructive recommendations of the agricultural scientist, René Dumont—see introduction.)

Concentration Camps

Generally speaking, those who now demand that political prisoners be tortured and locked in concentration camps became "revolutionaries" only AFTER the Revolution. Many of these "Johnny-come-latelies" were a short time ago humble lackeys of the Batista dictatorship. These vindictive sadists are far more severe than are the humane, magnanimous revolutionary veterans who fought on the Sierra Maestra and Escambray fronts.

The fact that the Revolution must defend itself against the most vicious and intractable counter-revolutionaries does not mean that it should become a blind, vindictive nemesis, totally impervious to human kindness.

The Revolution must not be sullied, corrupted and ultimately undermined by toleration of the concentration camps and the forced labor characteristic of the odious regimes of Hitler and Stalin! (June 20, 1959)

Children in Uniform

In the streets of Havana, in towns and villages, all over Cuba teenagers, and even children, are on parade: goose-stepping like Prussian soldiers, strutting, puffed up with their own conceit that they are training to "defend the country." And their commanders boast about how "revolutionary" they are. How vain their pretensions that they are really defending the Revolution! How far removed they are from the road to freedom!

These juvenile patrols remind us of Mussolini's *Fasci Combatini*, and the parades of Franco's Blue Shirts. In no way do these little boys resemble the valiant fighters of the mountains, or the brave underground fighters of the French *Maquis*. For a future of oppression and servitude they are needed: but never to forge a tomorrow of fraternity in a free and happy community. They represent the militarization of the future, the poisonous herb of the barracks—that which the Revolution must abolish forever.

It is one thing to train the masses in the use of arms for self-defense. But it is a grievous error to militarize and corrupt the minds of youth, to inhibit the unfolding of their personalities and to turn them into a herd of mindless animals.

Are professional armies really better equipped to meet the hazards of war and invasion? History demonstrates that a people determined to defend its rights has been able to defeat regular armies. Ye who boast of "military glory," remember the Germany of the Kaiser and Hitler—their pompous, corseted, goose-stepping generals committing their most odious crimes! Remember the France of Laval and Petain betrayed by the militarists! REMEMBER! (Nov. 25, 1959)

128

Is There Real Freedom Of The Press In Cuba?

More than two weeks ago the C.N.T. exile organization in Cuba received an urgent appeal from the C.N.T. underground in Spain, asking for international solidarity on behalf of 99 imprisoned anarcho-syndicalist militants now facing very heavy sentences for opposing Franco-fascism. [The C.N.T.—Confederación Nacional del Trabajo, National Confederation of Labor—was the anarcho-syndicalist confederation which fought in the Spanish Revolution and Civil War, 1936-39.] C.N.T. comrades here in Cuba personally delivered copies of the appeal to the daily newspapers of Havana, as well as the radio stations, requesting publication and announcement. But not a single word has thus far been published or broadcast. Is this freedom of the press? Isn't the nonsectarian revolutionary press maintained by the public obliged to print something of general interest, to serve all the people without discrimination? Or are the libertarians not liked by those who control the press?

Those who rightly condemn capitalist monopolizers of the press for their partisan, reactionary policies, must not sink to their level. They must not impose their own brand of "revolutionary" monopoly and go so far as to renounce all moral obligation and refuse to help those who are fighting fascist barbarism, only because they do not like their revolutionary ideas...

It would indeed be criminal to deny freedom of the press to a movement like ours, whose struggles for the emancipation of the oppressed have been unequaled in the history of the Cuban Revolutionary movement. But if this sabotage and boycott continues, we will have to ask, IS THERE REAL FREEDOM OF THE PRESS IN CUBA? (July 19, 1960)

Declaration published in the *Bulletin of the MLCE*; Miami, July-Aug. 1962.

...All militant Cuban libertarians fought for the downfall of Batista and enthusiastically hailed and assisted the Revolution. We hoped that the Revolution would bring more liberty and social justice to the men, women and children of Cuba. We tried to help the people's voluntary organizations (unions, cooperatives, cultural groups, peasant and student groups, etc.) assume a decisive part in the construction of the new Libertarian Cuba. Little by little, we saw our hopes dissipated as the new rulers became more and more arrogant, ruthless and dictatorial.

While we saw the outrages and bestialities committed daily by the members of the revolutionary oligarchy, we remained silent because we did not want the people to confuse our revolutionary criticism with the criticism of reactionary elements, who attacked the regime only to safeguard their economic and political privileges. We criticized the Castro-Communist dictatorship, not because it was TOO REVOLUTIONARY, but because it was NOT REVOLUTIONARY ENOUGH.

Between the spring and the summer of 1960, we exposed ourselves to the persecution of the regime by attempting to initiate a widespread discussion which would have given us the opportunity to expose before the Cuban people the ideological bankruptcy of the new dictatorship and present our constructive solutions to the problems of the Cuban Revolution.

The rulers made a free and open discussion of issues and principles impossible. We were accused by Blas Roca [leader of the Communist Party, ex-friend of Batista] of "hiding behind the mask of extreme revolutionism, the better to serve the interests of the American State Department." [In August, 1960, he said, "Today in Cuba we have anarcho-syndicalists who publish 'Declarations of Principles' that are of wonderful assistance to counter-revolution...they help counter-revolution from extremist positions with phraseology and arguments that look leftist."] When we wrote a fifty-page pamphlet replying to these slanders and outlining our viewpoint, the State Publishing House refused to publish it, and private publishers were strictly warned not to do so. We, and other non-conformist groups, were not allowed to print anything. Our paper *Solidaridad Gastronomica* was so hounded by the authorities that it ceased publication March 20, 1961. The best equipped print shops confiscated from the bourgeois press were opened to the Communists. A veritable flood of Marxist books and pamphlets were used to brain-wash the workers and peasants of Cuba.

This, together with appointing Communists to key posts in the government, the unions, the schools, peasant and cultural organizations, etc., convinced us that the Revolution was lost. This was the bitter end of our hopes, and from that time on our opposition to the increasingly brutal totalitarian regime began.

[The Bulletin also published the following notice dispatched from Cuba:]

Havana, August 16, 1962

Through this little note, we are letting you know that, for reasons too long and too complicated to explain at this time, the Executive Committee of the Libertarian Association of Cuba has decided to suspend publication [of its journal and other activity].

Fraternally yours,
THE SECRETARIAT

Behind these few lines of lie shattered hopes, the despair and the tragedy of the aborted Cuban Revolution.

130

Anarchists in Castro's Prisons

This is a partial list of anarchists imprisoned because they refused to serve the Castro totalitarian regime, just as they fought its predecessor the Batista tyranny, remaining always faithful to their ideals. (From Boletin Informacion Libertaria—Movimiento Libertaria de Cuba En Exilio: Miami, July-August 1962) [S.D.]

Plácido Mendez: Bus driver, delegate for routes 16, 17, and 18. For many years, fought against the Batista tyranny and at various times imprisoned and brutally tortured. In 1938 he was forced to go into exile, returning secretly to Cuba to fight in the Cuban underground movement against Batista in the Sierra Escambray. With the downfall of Batista, he resumed his union activities refusing to accept the totalitarian decrees of the so-called "revolutionary government." Comrade Mendez is serving his sentence in the National Prison on the Island of Pines, built by the bloody dictator Machado. Mendez has been condemned by Castro's "Revolutionary Tribunal" to twelve years at hard labor. His family is in desperate economic difficulties.

Antonio Degas: Militant member of the glorious National Confederation of Labor of Spain (CNT): living in Cuba since the termination of the Spanish Civil War, working in the motion picture industry. This comrade conspired against the Batista tyranny and with the triumph of the Revolution, unconditionally placed himself at the service of the new Castro regime. Because of his activities against the communist usurpers of the Revolution, he was imprisoned by the lackeys of Castro without trial. Antonio Degas is imprisoned in the dungeons of Cabana Fortress and subjected to inhuman treatment. His wife and children, under conditions of growing poverty, must also find ways of helping him in prison where he is under medical treatment.

Alberto Miguel Linsuain: Comrade Linsuain is the son of a well-known Spanish Revolutionist, who died in Alicante towards the end of the Spanish civil War. Linsuain was extremely active against the Batista dictatorship and joined the rebel forces in the Sierra Cristal, under the command of Castro's brother, Raúl Castro. For his bravery in battle he was promoted to Lieutenant in the Rebel Army. With the end of the armed struggle, he left the army and dedicated himself to the union movement of his industry. He was elected by his fellow workers as General Secretary of the Federation of Food, Hotel and Restaurant Workers of the Province of Oriente. When the communists subtly began to infiltrate and take over the organized labor movement, Comrade Linsuain fought the communist connivers. This aroused the hatred of the communist leaders in general and Raúl Castro, in particular. He had violent quarrels with Raúl Castro even when he had first met him in the Sierra Cristal while fighting against Batista. Comrade Linsuain has been in jail for over a year without trial. His family has not heard from him for months and fears for his life. (A later Bulletin reported that Linsuain was either murdered or died in jail.)

Sondalio Torres: Young sympathizer of libertarian ideas, who, inspired by our comrades, fought bravely in his native Cuba, against Batista. With the triumph of the Revolution, Torres threw himself, body and soul, into the consolidation and constructive work of the Revolution, moving to Havana on government construction projects. On the job, he openly voiced his fears that the Castro government was gradually, but surely, becoming a ferocious dictatorship. For this, the stool-pigeon members of the local Committee for the Defense of the Revolution (CDR) accused him of counter-revolutionary activities. Sondalio was sentenced to ten years imprisonment. To force him to falsely accuse other fellow-workers of counter-revolutionary acts, Sondalio was subjected to barbarous torture. Four times he was dragged out to face the firing squad and four times he was retrieved just as he was about to be shot. Torres is serving his sentence in the Provincial prison of Pinar del Río.

José Acena: Veteran libertarian militant; employed in the La Polar brewery; Professor (at one time) at the Instituto de la Vibora. For thirty years Acena carried on an uninterrupted struggle against all dictatorships, including the first as well as the second periods of Batista's tyrannical regimes. For his bravery in the underground revolutionary struggles of the 26th of July Movement, he was made treasurer of the Province of Havana. With the triumph of the Revolution, Acena collaborated fully with the new Castro regime, particularly in the labor and political movements. Acena soon realized that a totalitarian Marxist-Leninist system was being established in Cuba and quarreled violently with the new rulers, denouncing Castro personally and telling him plainly why he hated his regime. From that time on, he was hounded and persecuted by Castro's henchmen and imprisoned various times. Finally, after a year without trial, he was accused of counter-revolutionary acts and sentenced to twenty years imprisonment. This, in spite of the fact that he still bears on his body the scars of wounds inflicted on him by Batista's jailers. He is desperately ill and in need of surgery.

Alberto Garcia: Comrade Alberto Garcia, like so many other militants of our movement, fought against Batista in the ranks of Castro's 26th of July Movement. Because of his well-earned prestige earned in the course of hard underground struggles, Garcia, after the fall of Batista,

132

was elected by the workers of his industry to be Secretary of the Federation of Medical Workers. For his uncompromising opposition to the super-authoritarian conduct of the communists, he was arrested and sentenced to thirty years at hard labor, falsely accused of "counter-revolutionary" activities. Comrade Garcia is one of the most valiant young militants in the Cuban Libertarian Movement.

THE POSITION OF THE CUBAN ANARCHISTS:
SELECTED DOCUMENTS [1960-1974]

These documents spanning the course of the Cuban Revolution demonstrate the consistent approach of the Cuban anarchists toward the problems of the Cuban Revolution as summarized in the Statement of Principles (first document) and in the concluding statement, "Cuba: Revolution and Counter-Revolution." All the selected documents emphasize constructive proposals and practical libertarian alternatives to dictatorship (strikingly similar to the recommendations of the noted agronomist and economist Rene Dumont and other qualified critics. (see introduction). For the anarchists (and with them a growing number of concerned people) socialist production—socialism itself—cannot as the Statement of Principles insists. . . "be viewed as a simple technical process. . . the decisive factor is the human factor. . ." the sentiments, interests, and the aspirations of men, women, and children, considered not as mere ciphers, but as INDIVIDUAL HUMAN BEINGS. [S.D.]

Declaration Of Principles of the Libertarian Syndicalist Group of Cuba (Havana, 1960)

(1) Against the State in All its Forms

WE the Libertarian Syndicalist Group, consider that in this period of revolutionary reconstruction by the people of Cuba, it is our

135

inescapable duty to affirm our position in relation to the pressing problems of the Cuban Revolution. We oppose not only specific acts or policies of the State, but the very existence of the State itself and its right to exercise supreme and uncontested supremacy over every aspect of social life. We must therefore resist any policy that tends to increase the growing power of the State, the extension of its functions and its totalitarian tendencies.

WE, Cuban Libertarian militants, as well as our comrades in other Countries, believe that it is impossible to make a Social Revolution without eliminating the State. The social functions usurped by the State must be returned to and exercised by the grass-roots organizations of the people themselves such as labor unions, free municipalities, agricultural and industrial cooperatives, and collectives and voluntary federations of all kinds; all of them must be free to function without authoritarian interference.

Politically naive worshippers of the State believe that human society was created by the State. In reality, the State owes its origin to the rise of privileged classes and the consequent degeneration of society. In spite of all its admirers both right and left may say, the State is not only the parasitic excrescence of class society, but is also itself a generator of political and economic privilege and the creator of new privileged classes. The revolutionary transformation of bourgeois into socialist society also demands the abolition of the State.

(2)   The Unions as the Economic Organ of the Revolution

WE, Revolutionary Syndicalists maintain that the labor movement is the truest expression of the interests and the aspirations of the working class. It is therefore the historic task of the unions to effect the economic revolution by substituting the "government over men by the administration of things." The labor unions and the federations of industry, properly and rationally restructured, contain within themselves the human and technical elements needed for the most complete collective development and self-management of industry.

As against the "revolutionary" and reactionary politicians who strive only to capture power, the decisive role of the unions in this period of revolutionary organization is to become the living organisms for the direction and coordination of the economy. The subordination of the unions to the political power of the State, especially in this revolutionary period, constitutes a betrayal of the working class; a vile maneuver to assure labor's defeat, in this historic moment when it should be fulfilling its most vital socialist task; the adminstration of production and distribution in the interests of the whole of society...

(3)   The Land to Those Who Work It

WE, the men and women of the Libertarian Syndicalist Group, now, more than ever before, stand by our revolutionary watchword: "The Land To Those Who Work It." We believe that the classic cry of the peasants of all countries, "LAND AND LIBERTY," is the truest expression of the immediate aspirations of the Cuban guajiros (peasants); their own land to till and the freedom to organize themselves and to administer agricultural production.

This may be done through family cultivation in some cases, or by organizing producers' cooperatives in other cases; but ABOVE ALL [wherever possible] through the organization of COLLECTIVE FARMS. The form of cultivation must always be decided by the peasants themselves, never imposed by the State. While the representatives of the State may, in some cases, be technically capable men, they are in most cases, ignorant of and insensitive to the true sentiments, interests and aspirations of those who till the soil.

Through long experience and participation in the revolutionary struggles of the peasantry, we are convinced that the planning of agricultural production, cannot be viewed solely as a mere technical process. Although it is true that the condition of the land and machinery of cultivation are very important, the decisive factor is for us, the human factor: the peasants themselves. We therefore declare that we favor the organization of collective and cooperative work on a voluntary basis—extending to the peasant the necessary technical and cultural tools—no doubt the best means—of convincing him of the greater advantages to him of collective cultivation as distinct from and superior to individual or family cultivation.

To act otherwise, to use coercion and force, would be to lay the basis for the complete failure of the agrarian revolution—and consequently, THE REVOLUTION ITSELF.

(4)   The School Should Instruct; the Family Should Rear the Young

WE, militants of Revolutionary Syndicalism, maintain that culture must not be the exclusive property of anyone in particular, but of the whole of humanity. Culture is a right—not a privilege.

All persons regardless of class, race, religion or sex, must have complete access to the fountains of knowledge without limitations or restrictions of any kind. Education should not be monopolized by the State or any privileged group. Education at all levels must be free to all (primary and secondary schools, technical and scientific schools and the universities). The moral and political education of their children should be considered the inalienable right of the parents, with no ecclesiastical, political or statist interference. In the final analysis, the family is the basic unit of society and its supreme responsibility is the moral and physical protection of its youngest members. This responsibility implies rights that must not be taken away; that of the formation of character, and ideological orientation of new generations within the family, the home itself.

(5)   The Struggle Against Nationalism, Militarism and Imperialism

WE are opposed to all wars. The instruments of death produced in such frightening quantities by the great powers must now be converted into instruments for the abolition of hunger and the needs of impoverished peoples; to bring happiness and well-being to all mankind.

As revolutionary workers we are fervent partisans of fraternal understanding between all peoples irrespective of all national boundaries, or linguistic, racial, political and religious barriers...

WE are unalterably opposed to the military training of the young, the creation of professional armies. For us, nationalism and militarism are synonymous with fascism. Less arms and more plows! Less soldiers and more teachers! Less cannons and more bread for all!

We, Libertarian Syndicalists are against all forms of imperialism and colonialism; against the economic domination of peoples, so prevalent in the Americas; against military pressure to impose upon peoples political and economic systems foreign to their national cultures, customs and social systems—as is the case in parts of Europe, Asia and Africa.

We believe that among the nations of the world, the small are as worthy as the big. Just as we remain enemies of national states because each of them holds its own people in subjection; so also are we opposed to the super-states that utilize their political, economic and military power to impose their rapacious systems of exploitation on weaker countries. As against all forms of imperialism, we declare for revolutionary internationalism; for the creation of great confederations of free peoples for their mutual interests; for solidarity and mutual aid. We believe in an active militant pacifism that rejects the dialectic of "just wars" and "unjust wars," a pacifism that demands an end to the arms race and rejection of nuclear and all other armaments.

(6)   To Bureaucratic Centralism We Counterpose Federalism

WE are inherently opposed to all centralist tendencies; political, social, and economic. We believe that the organization of society should proceed from the simple to the complex; from the bottom upwards. It should begin in the basic organisms: the municipalities, the labor unions, the peasants' organizations, etc. coordinated into great national and international organizations based on mutual pacts between equals. These should be set up freely for common purposes without injury to any of the contracting parties, each of whom must always retain the right to withdraw from the agreement should it at any time be felt that such action would best serve its interests.

It is our understanding that these social organizations, the great national and international confederations of unions, peasants' associations, cultural groups and municipalities, will carry the representation of all without possessing any greater powers that those granted them by the component federated units at the base.

The liberty of peoples can only find adequate expression through a federalist type of organization, which will set the necessary limits to the freedom of each while guaranteeing the freedom of all. Experience demonstrates that political and economic centralization leads to the creation of monstrous totalitarian states; to aggression and war between nations; to the exploitation and misery of the great masses of the people.

(7) Without Individual Freedom There Can Be No Collective Freedom

WE, Libertarian Syndicalists are firm supporters of individual rights. There can be no freedom for the community as a whole if any of its members are deprived of their freedom. There can be no freedom for the collectivity where the individual is the victim of oppression. All human rights must be guaranteed. These include freedom of expression, the right to work, to lead a decent life. Without these guarantees there can be no civilized basis for human beings to live together in society. We believe in liberty and justice for all persons, even for those holding reactionary views.

(8) The Revolution Belongs To Us All

The Libertarian Syndicalist Group reiterates its will to support the struggle for complete liberation of our people. Affirming that the Revolution is not the exclusive property of any individual or grouping, but belongs to all the people.

Just as we have always done, we will continue to support all revolutionary measures that tend to remedy the old social ills. At the same time we shall, as always, continue our struggle against authoritarian tendencies within the Revolution itself.

We have fought against the barbarism and corruption of the past. We now oppose all deviations that attempt to undermine our Revolution by forcing it into authoritarian channels...which are destructive of human dignity. We oppose all the reactionary groups that battle desperately to reconquer their abolished privileges and we also oppose the new pseudo-revolutionary oppressive, exploiting groups that in Cuba can be already discerned on the revolutionary horizon.

We are for justice, socialism and freedom; for the well-being of all men regardless of origin, religion or race. Workers! Peasants! Students! Men and Women of Cuba! To these revolutionary concepts we will remain faithful to the end. For these principles we are willing to stake our personal freedom and if necessary our lives.

Libertarian Syndicalist Groups
La Habana, 1960

Miscellaneous Declarations 1961-1975

Statement of Cuban Libertarian Movement Addressed to its
Sister Organizations of All Countries, August, 1961

...The Cuban Libertarian Movement wishes to point out that whenever the Cuban people suffered the consequences of dictatorship, our movement joined hands with those who sincerely struggled against such dictatorships. In the various times that this has happened, it has cost our movement precious lives.

Long before the present revolutionary organizations did so, the Cuban Libertarian Movement fought by all means at its disposal, against all imperialism, especially against North American imperialism, since this was the one that most directly affected our personal liberties and our economic development. Thus, our movement cannot be accused at any time or for any reason of being indifferent to the sufferings of our people or tolerant towards any imperialism, either democratic or totalitarian. The Cuban Libertarian Movement feels that in each case it has taken the position that it should have taken as a revolutionary organization...

...Cuba is controlled by a super-statist regime based upon the most rigid Marxist school. Its planning, structure and development follow the historic pattern of similar countries, and if there is some difference between them, it is only a difference of degree.

In consequence, the Libertarian Movement of Cuba does not see in the Cuban Revolution any of the principles that can identify it with the fundamental concepts of our ideology. On the contrary, it would appear that just as in the other Marxist-Socialist countries all libertarian thought will be suppressed, man will completely lose his personality, his dignity and his rights in order to be a mere cog in the machinery of the State—a process already underway. We know that Capitalist, clerical and imperialist interests are allying themselves against the Cuban Revolution. But it is also true that great numbers of workers, peasants, intellectuals and professional people maintain a virile opposition to the totalitarian regime.

The Cuban Libertarian Movement has at no time made common cause with the representatives of reaction and will not do so in the future. Nor will we accept the selfish intervention of any imperialist country in the Cuban problem. But the peoples of the Latin American continent have every right to intervene. They have a moral obligation to defend the minimum rights that have been won at so great a cost, when these rights are usurped anywhere in Latin America [or anywhere else]. In view of all that we have said, the Cuban Libertarian Movement will maintain its ideological postulates under all circumstances and will struggle to the end for the freedom of the Cuban people and for the Social Revolution . . .

The National Executive

(Names have been omitted or changed to prevent official reprisals.)

Message of the Libertarian Movement of Cuba in Exile
To The Fifth Congress of the Libertarian Federation of Argentina
(Buenos Aires, December, 1961)

The many letters we have received from individuals and from groups indicate that the international libertarian movement is not only deeply disturbed about the present situation in Cuba, but equally concerned about our general attitude with respect to Cuba's problems and what the new situation would be, should the Castro dictatorship collapse or be overthrown.

We will support the revolutionary movement of the masses to solve the great problems of the country and abolish all special privileges and injustices. We will resolutely oppose all reactionary elements who today fight Castro-Communism, only because they yearn to recapture their political power and bring back the old order with all its greed and corruption. We fight against the Castro dictatorship because it signifies the strangulation of the Revolution, submitting our people to the exploitation and oppression of the new exploiting class, just as evil as its predecessor. We fight the new tyranny that placed our country at the service of Soviet-Chinese imperialism.

We must do our utmost to help the Cuban people recapture their freedom of action, by achieving the revolutionary transformation of their country in accordance with their own special interests, and in solidarity with their natural allies, the people of Latin America, who are fighting against their own feudal and capitalist regimes. We want a new Cuba, that will reorganize its social life with the most ample economic justice and most complete political freedom; because we are, above all, socialists and libertarians.

The concern of the international libertarian movement with our struggle against Castro-Communism should in no way benefit nor have any connection with the sinister forces of reaction is also our concern. With all the solemnity that the critical situation warrants, with all the emphasis at our command, we, the Cuban libertarians, assure our comrades of the Libertarian Federation of Argentina that we will never make political deals with anti-Castroites to barter away our independence as a movement in its fight for freedom; nor will we subordinate the freedom of the Cuban people to the interests of Russian or American imperialism or any other foreign power.

We pledge our solidarity with all sincere underground revolutionaries struggling against the Castro tyranny. We are prepared to fight with all lovers of freedom for common aims without sacrificing our libertarian principles nor our identity as a distinct revolutionary organization.

In order to counter-balance the enormous political-economic power of the reaction which fights Castroism only because it aims to replace the Cuban dictatorship with the kind of totalitarian regime which after a quarter of a century is still oppressing the Spanish people, it will be necessary to forge an equally formidable alliance.

We do not believe that we alone, with our weak forces, can possibly overthrow Castro's "revolutionary government," formidably reinforced by the technical, economic, political, and military might of the "socialist" countries. Furthermore, the Castro government has built up so monstrous an apparatus that it cannot be dislodged by the Cuban people alone. We consider that the best (though by no means the only) allies of the Cuban people in their struggle for justice and freedom, are the other Latin American peoples who are also fighting to emancipate themselves—under different circumstances—but with the same spirit and the same ideals.

To this revolutionary task we dedicate our best efforts and we urge the libertarian movements in other lands to take the initiative in uniting all libertarian forces on the basis of a general program acceptable to all.

BOLETÍN de Información Libertaria—General Delegation Libertarian Movement of Cuba—in Exile (Caracas Venezuela, July 1962)

The necessities of the war against the totalitarian regime in Cuba which has organized a political police apparatus along Soviet lines, impedes the creation of large concentrations operating openly. It makes necessary the creation of small, loosely connected, secret resistance groups carrying on a guerilla war of attrition, to wear down, exhaust and finally force the collapse of the dictatorship... The people will make the hangmen of the revolution pay for the atrocities they have committed and give them a dose of their own medicine.

We are convinced that the line of total revolutionary action is the only viable way for the Cuban people to re-conquer their lost freedom and liquidate the Castro-communist dictatorship. We do not believe that the Cuban tragedy can be resolved by military adventures, like the invasion of April 1961. We believe that other Cuban people must learn from the methods of struggle of the Irish Republicans, the Jewish secret army of Israel, the Cyprus patriots and the Algerian resistance movements. We must adapt these methods to Cuban conditions.

For us, the principal function of the exiles is to help stimulate the revolutionary action of the organizations inside Cuba, which represent the fighting will of the people. Whoever wastes time, trying to create paper organizations whose aim is to capture power, if and when the Castro-Communist dictators fall, is guilty of deceit and is delaying the liberation of the Cuban people.

As lifelong militant revolutionaries, we fight always for the freedom of the Cuban people to make their own revolution without becoming victims of foreign and domestic tyrants. Our main task is to agree on a plan of united acion which will bring about the destruction of the Castro-communist dictatorship. While we are prepared to fight with all sincere lovers of freedom for common objectives, we will remain an independent organization and will not collaborate with the power hungry politicians who are already plotting to take over and are already creating "Governments in Exile" or "Governments in the underground."

Agrarian Labor And The Land
(Abelardo Iglesias: *Revolution and Counter-Revolution in Cuba.*
Boletín de Información Libertaria—Organ of the Libertarian Movement of Cuba in Exile; Miami, June 1966)

The root cause for political and social unrest in Cuba, dating back to centuries of Spanish colonial domination is the horribly unjust distribution of the land. A predominantly rural country, with its economy almost totally dependent on agriculture and animal husbandry...must of necessity wipe out all vestiges of feudal property and place the land directly into the hands of the agricultural workers.

While the landed aristocracy allows vast areas of fertile land to remain uncultivated and great masses of peasants suffer the ravages of disease, hunger and poverty, the urban population enjoys a standard of living vastly superior to anything known in Latin-America.

For this reason the Libertarian Movement was always intensely concerned with the problem of organizing a radical, deeply rooted agricultural revolution. Following the example of the libertarian miltants who in Mexico had been inspired by the epic of Emiliano

Zapata, a group of valiant Cuban militants dedicated themselves to the emancipation of the peasants.

From the organization of a producers' coffee cooperative in Monte Ruz over a half century ago, to the organization of the *Peasant Federation of Cuba*, in which dozens of our comrades fought, the Cuban Libertarians carried on the struggle against the rich landlords, inciting the peasants to forcibly seize uncultivated property and work the land collectively by organizing themselves into voluntary revolutionary collectives or similar cooperative organizations...

With the triumph of he Revolution of 1959, the Cuban Libertarians urged the peasants to seize the land and organize agricultural cooperatives without waiting for orders from the new Castroite authorities. This policy was undertaken for two reasons: first, to involve actively the peasant masses in the construction and administration of the new agricultural economy through their own voluntary organizations; and second, because direct action of the peasants would place economic power in their own hands, thus preventing the "revolutionary state" from converting free cooperators into slaves of the totalitarian regime. After a great deal of resistance, the new dictators dislodged the peasants from the land by force and threats.

The Cuban anarchists repeatedly warned against dismissing or underestimating the vital contribution that the small peasant proprietor who works the land himself with the help of his family and does not employ hired labor can make to the Revolution (this policy also applies to artisans, small workshops, cooperatives, and the thousands of specialized services without which the economy would come to a standstill. The feasibility of this policy was amply demonstrated during the Spanish Revolution in the libertarian type rural collectives and urban socialized industry.) [To remind the reader, this extremely important point, already discussed in the article Plows, Tractors and the Guajiro (peasant) is repeated here:]

> "...without underestimating the importance of huge cooperative farms to meet the need for agricultural products, it must be stressed that the small peasant proprietors can also contribute greatly to agricultural production by organizing themselves into collectives for the intensive cultivation of the land in common.

Joint Statement Of The Libertarians Of The Americas
(published in the U.S. by the Cuban Libertarian Movement—Miami, 1968)

Whereas: Libertarian principles are unconditionally opposed to all forms of human slavery...

Whereas: Viewed objectively, the social and political course of the so-called Cuban Revolution which has led to the establishment of a Communist regime in Cuba has cynically frustrated the aspirations of the Cuban people.

Whereas: The Castro-Communist regime is able to maintain its control over the Cuban people thanks only to the military and economic support and backing of Russia which has turned the island into one more satellite of Red Imperialism through a policy of terror, imprisonment , and crime and inhibiting the resistance and struggle of the people of Cuba against tyranny.

Whereas: The so-called Cuban Revolution, after offering land to those who work it has instead taken the land away from its former owners—including peasants—given in toto to the State, thereby converting the peasants into wage-slaves of the State. In the same way, all industrial and productive centers, transport, distribution, the press and in short all social, political and economic activity of the country has been taken over, subjecting the people to the will and authority of the Totalitarian State.

Whereas: All freedom of thought and expression is forbidden in Cuba, no citizen being permitted the free expression of disagreement with the political system and the norms established by the government in power; that all communications media are totally in the hands of the State; that all publication of books and other literary material is subject to the supervision and authorization of the State, and furthermore, that any oral or written expression of opposition or criticism of the government is a *punishable offense.*

Whereas: Over 90% of the Cuban people are against the political system that has been imposed on them by force and violence, it being a fact that after nine and a half years of Communist domination there are now *100,000* persons in Cuban prisons with the number increasing. Executions and murders of fighters for freedom are daily occurrences in the prisons and the total of these is already more than ten thousand. Over half a million persons have already fled from Cuba, by every means imaginable. These have been of all social classes, but mostly workers and peasants, and their leaving Cuba is a clear demonstration of the rejection by a people of the regime that enslaves them.

Whereas: The so-called Cuban Revolution does not in the least represent the aspirations of the Cuban people which fights and always will fight for its freedom with the fullest respect for human life and safety and for continual improvement in the search for peace and the social good.

Therefore We, the organizations signing this *Joint Statement of Libertarians of the Americas,* declare:

That the Castro regime is at the service of Russia in its plans for the future domination of the peoples of the Americas: That the Cuban people have the legitimate right to combat and overthrow the political regime that now oppresses them: That the present struggle of the Cuban people against their oppressors and enslavers is just, and should, therefore, have the support and help of all libertarian organizations and individuals on the American Continent and of the World: That the undersigned organizations support the Cuban people in their struggle to wipe out the Totalitarian Communist State that now oppresses and enslaves them, and take upon themselves the task of denouncing before the World by every means at their command, the criminal savagery and slavery suffered by the Cuban people, as well as giving all the collaboration and support that they can in the struggle against Castro-Communism, until the Cuban people achieve their freedom.

MOVIMIENTO LIBERTARIO CUBANA EN EL EXILIO (MLCE)
LIBERTARIAN LEAGUE (USA)
ORGANIZACIÓNES LIBERTARIAS DEL PERU
FEDERACIÓN ANARQUISTA DEL MEXICO (FAM)
MOVIMIENTO LIBERTARIO DEL BRASIL
FEDERACIÓN LIBERTARIA ARGENTINA (FLA)

Message from the Cuban Libertarian Movement—in Exile
(Miami, October 1974)

TO OUR EXILED COUNTRYMEN
TO THOSE WHO SUFFER IN ENSLAVED CUBA
TO THE PEOPLES OF LATIN AMERICA
TO THE PEOPLE OF THE UNITED STATES

We will always remain faithful to the noble ideals which we have proclaimed and defended for so many years against all tyrants and misleaders of the people, including the "Marxist-Leninists" and the Castro-Communists. In defense of our principles we have always fought with equal determination against the equally bloody right-wing conservative totalitarians. For this, we have paid a very heavy price in persecution and lives.

While professing to hate tyranny, the Pope, in the name of Jesus who preached agains violence and slavery, bestows his benediction on dictator Castro...Fascist Spain relates well to totalitiarn-communist Cuba...Russia donates arms and supplies to its Cuban satellite...At the same time, the great American corporations surreptitiously provide Castro with ample credit to purchase autos, buses, and other equipment. In view of the "co-existence" policy between the great Soviet totalitarian empire and the American-European democracies

146

contending for the domination of Cuba, our position remains:
AGAINST BOTH POWER BLOCS!
NEITHER THE ONE NOR THE OTHER!
ALWAYS FOR FREEDOM! ALWAYS FOR HUMAN DIGNITY!

Without a clear, convincing program of full liberty, full human rights and well-being for all, the Cubans abroad cannot stir the oppressed people in Cuba to rebel, and even less, the peoples of Latin America. For, the struggle against Castroism is not only our concern. The Latin American masses, too, are also threatened with the imposition of a Castro-type dictatorship. The plight of the oppressed, downtrodden, impoverished peasants and workers renders them receptive to communist propaganda. Their well-trained, well-paid agents promise them a better life. The masses are naive, they know nothing about the kind of despotic "communism" that these agents really want to impose. They feel that they have nothing to lose, and in despair they join.

We must counteract this threat. We must reach the masses with our constructive, practical program and warn them about the real character of the phony "communists." We must tell them:

> ...you have the right to live decently. If you are a peasant, you have a right to the land you cultivate, just as you have the right to sun and air. If you are a worker, you have the right to the full product of your labor. Your children are entitled to a good education and the sick to the finest medical attention. You are a human being. You have the right to learn. To think. To act without humiliating yourself, without bowing to the will of an omnipotent, omniverous government. BEWARE! Do not follow false leaders who will enslave you, just as they enslaved your unfortunate fellow workers in Cuba...

[The appeal concludes with a ringing call to]

> ...All the peoples of our America, of all classes, who do not wish to change one tyranny for another; to the Rebel Youth of this country; to all who realize the seriousness of the hour to join the crusade for the liberation of Cuba...

Declaration of the Cuban Libertarian Movement in Exile
(published in March, 1975)

*It outlines, not the maximum, full anarchist blueprint for the future society, but a **minimum** program as the basis for a united front of all tendencies of the Cuban revolutionary movement for the immediate*

147

task of achieving the overthrow of the totalitarian regime. It sketches the first steps toward the regeneration of Cuban society. [S.D.]

Preamble: The Cuban workers are not counter-revolutionaries yearning to restore the old order. The real counter-revolutionaries are the tyrants now wielding absolute power over our country, subjecting our people to the most brutal political oppression and economic exploitation. Cuba is not a socialist society. It is a totalitarian state with a militarized economy and a militarized social system. The alleged "socialized" property actually belongs to the State, and the State is, in fact, the property of the oligarchy commanded by the "maximum leader," Fidel Castro. All political and economic power is concentrated in the hands of this minority, which constitutes the new ruling class.

Therefore, our first and most important task is to destroy the totalitarian state. Only then can we reconquer the freedom to shape our own destiny and prepare the way for a social system in which *the workers and peasants will become the real masters of all the means of production, distribution and public services.*

Our comrades now living in Cuba in totalitarian slavery are convinced that the Cuban problem is essentially a political problem, and that our strategy should be directed toward first recuperating the indispensable civil liberties necessary to initiate a process of social change leading to a more just, more cultured, happier and freer life. The following programmatic proposals accurately express the ideas and sentiments of our comrades in Cuba.

Political Structure: (a) The totalitarian State must be replaced by a political structure which will guarantee unrestricted civil liberties with the most scrupulous respect for human rights [freedom of speech, assemblage, movement, organization, worship, etc.]. (b) The political police must be abolished. (c) Entirely autonomous municipalities and their confederation into free provinces must be established. (d) A nationally federated system based on a new, decentralized order, must be organized. (e) Abolition of the army, maintaining only the absolute minimum of professional officers and minimum military training, is essential.

Economic Structure: We advocate (a) the land to those who work it, organized and planned as the peasants themselves decide—individual or family cultivation, creation of voluntary cooperatives and collectives similar to the Israeli Kibbutzim, etc.; (b) collectivization and operation of large-scale basic industries by the workers, technicians and administrators through a system of self-management, supervised by their respective unions; where necessary for the general welfare and the economy, allowance for individual or group ownership of small craft workshops and similar small-scale enterprises by artisans; (c) overall economic planning by integrated coordinated workers' organizations, technical and administrative organization...; (d) in privately-owned establishments which, because of special circumstances cannot be socialized, the system of co-management, participation by the workers, shall prevail.

Social Structure: All social services shall be rendered and administered by the unions, municipalities and other federated bodies, which will guarantee to all Cubans the following free services: maternity care, other medical and health services, unemployment benefits, access to cultural and entertainment facilities... (b) Free education shall be provided at all levels and in all areas [primary and high school, university, technical and artistic school, etc.]. (c) Free housing will be provided for all.

Conclusions: With the passage of time, and under the dictatorship, the long-suffering people of Cuba have endured profound changes in their way of life. The mentality of the young people who have come to maturity under the dictatorship differs greatly from that of the preceding generation. To try to turn back the clock to a bygone era is both utopian and absurd. If we are to succeed, we must be realistic, take into account the present situation and act accordingly: this means eliminating existing evils, retaining that which is valuable, and initiating new and progressive changes in the quality of Cuban life.

[After outlining the structure of the proposed united front of the Cuban libertarian movement of resistance in exile which would insure mutual solidarity while retaining the full independence of participating organizations, the Declaration goes on to stress that] In the new Cuba, the labor movement must be organized according to federalist principles in industrial unions totally independent of the state and of political parties. Only thus can we assure freedom of movement, initiative and creative action.

Summation: Revolution and Counter-Revolution
(Translated from *Acción Libertaria,* Organ of the Argentine Libertarian Federation, Buenos Aires, July 1961)

The heroic impetus of a people that overthrows a dictatorship and expels the tyrant and his assassins—THAT IS REVOLUTION.

But to assume absolute power in order to accomplish by dictatorial methods that which the recently liberated people should themselves do—THIS IS COUNTER-REVOLUTION.

To cleanse the country of the abuses of the regime that has been overthrown—THAT IS REVOLUTION.

But to establish terror for the shameless, pitiless extermination of those who will not conform to the new dictatorship—THIS IS COUNTER-REVOLUTION.

To assume the direct participation of the peoples in all of the new creations and accomplishments—THAT IS REVOLUTION.

But to dictate by decree how things should be done and to canalize the accomplishments under the iron control of the State—THIS IS COUNTER-REVOLUTION.

To seize the lands for those who work them, organizing them in free peasant communities—THAT IS REVOLUTION.

But to twist the Agrarian Reform, exploiting the guajiro as an employee of the National Institute of Agrarian Reform—THIS IS COUNTER-REVOLUTION.

To expropriate capitalist enterprises, turning them over to the workers and technicians—THAT IS REVOLUTION.

But to convert them into State monopolies in which the producer's only right is to obey—THIS IS COUNTER-REVOLUTION.

To eliminate the old armed forces such as the army and the police—THAT IS REVOLUTION.

But to establish obligatory militias and maintain an army subservient to the governing clique—THIS IS COUNTER-REVOLUTION.

To oppose foreign intervention in the lives of the people, and repudiate all imperialism—THAT IS REVOLUTION.

But to deliver the country to some foreign powers under the pretense of defense against others—THIS IS COUNTER-REVOLUTION.

To permit the free expression and activity of all truly revolutionary forces and tendencies—THAT IS REVOLUTION.

But to recognize only one single party, persecuting and exterminating as counter-revolutionaries, those who oppose communist infiltration and domination—THIS IS COUNTER-REVOLUTION.

To make the University a magnificent center of culture, controlled by the professors, alumni and students—THAT IS REVOLUTION.

But to convert the University into an instrument of governmental policy, expelling and persecuting those who will not submit—THIS IS COUNTER-REVOLUTION.

To raise the standard of living of the workers through their own productive efforts inspired by the general welfare—THAT IS REVOLUTION.

But to impose plans prepared by State agencies and demand obligatory tribute from those who labor—THIS IS COUNTER-REVOLUTION.

To establish schools and combat illiteracy—THAT IS REVOLUTION.

But to indoctrinate the children in the adoration of the dictator and his close associates, militarizing these children in the service of the State—THIS IS COUNTER-REVOLUTION.

To give the labor unions full freedom to organize and administer themselves as the basic organs of the new economy—THAT IS REVOLUTION.

But to stamp these with the seal of subordination to the dominant regime—THIS IS COUNTER-REVOLUTION.

To sow the countryside with new constructive people's organizations of every sort, stimulating free initiative within them—THAT IS REVOLUTION.

But to prohibit them or inhibit their action, chaining them to the doctrine and to the organisms of State power—THIS IS COUNTER-REVOLUTION.

To call on the solidarity of all peoples, of the decent men and women of the World, in support of the revolutionary people who are building a new life—THAT IS REVOLUTION.

But to identify with Russian totalitarianism as a "Socialist State" of the type acceptable to the Soviet Empire—THIS IS COUNTER-REVOLUTION.

All those forward steps that were taken by the Cuban people under the banner of liberty, which shone forth as a great hope for all the Americas and for the World, WAS THE CUBAN REVOLUTION.

The bloody dictatorship of Fidel Castro and his clique, whatever the mask it may wear or the objectives it may claim to have, IS THE REAL COUNTER-REVOLUTION.

CUBA IN THE LATE 1960s AND THE 1970s

To what extent is our assessment of the early years of the Cuban Revolution still relevant to the Cuba of the late 1960s and the 1970s? Have there been significant changes, not in minor respects, but in the general DIRECTION of the Revolution?

Forming the "New Man"

Between 1966 and 1970 the Cuban leaders attempted to steer the Revolution in another direction. In accordance with the ideas of Che Guevara, they decided to begin building the new communist society; gradually do away with money and the money economy; distribute goods and services according to the essential principle of communism, "From each according to his ability and to each according to his needs," and in the process, form the "New Man." The "New Socialist Man" is a self-sacrificing idealist who willingly and gladly works not for his private gain, but for the welfare of society. Strongly animated by moral-ethical incentives, the "New Man" does not have to be compelled to fulfill his obligations by the authoritarian decrees of a dictatorial government.

Castro declared that: "...the great task of the Revolution is basically the task of forming the New Socialist Man...the man of a truly revolutionary consciousness..." (speech in Las Villas, July 26,

153

1968) The Cuban rulers even boasted that in respect to the building of communism (distribution, revolutionary consciousness of the people, equalization of income, etc.) Cuba was far ahead of the Soviet Union.

But all attempts to institute socialism by decree, as Bakunin foresaw over a century ago, leads inevitably to the enslavement of the people by the authoritarian State. They attempt to build communism failed because the "new socialist man" can be formed only within the context of a new and free society, based not upon compulsion, but upon voluntary cooperation. The attempt failed because it was not implemented by thoroughgoing libertarian changes in the authoritarian structure of Cuban society. Communization and forming "the new man" actually camouflaged the militarization of Cuba. Castro made this clear:

"...today I can see an immense army, the army of a highly organized, disciplined and enthusiastic nation ready to fulfill whatever task is set...". In his speech of August 23, 1968, Castro announced his decision to militarize the whole island and give absolute priority to the economic battle—and to achieve this, the absolute need for a dictatorship of the proletariat exercised by the Communist Party... (see K.S. Karol; *Guerrillas in Power*; New York, 1970, p. 447-448, 528)

The "communization" turned out to be a cruel hoax. It took on the familiar characteristics of typical totalitarian regimes. This stage of the Cuban Revolution has been correctly identified as the "Mini-Stalin Era." Moulding the "New Man" according to totalitarian specifications connotes the process of training people to become obedient serfs of the state: and moral incentives becomes a device to enlist the participation of the masses in their own enslavement. To their everlasting credit the workers resisted:

"...a wave of sabotage beset the country's economy. Saboteurs burned a tannery in Las Villas Province, a leather store in Havana, a chicken-feed factory in Santiago, a chemical fertilizer depot in Manzanillo, a provincial store belonging to the Ministry of Internal Commerce in Camaguey, and so on...Castro also gave a long list of acts of sabotage in schools and on building sites..." (Karol; ibid. p. 447)

The resistance of the people in addition to the suicidal economic adventures of the dictatorship hastened the collapse of Guevara's scheme.

Relations with Russia

Since 1968, when Castro endorsed the Russian invasion of

Czechoslovakia, the USSR has increasingly dominated Cuban affairs. The Cuban economy has been even more closely integrated into the Soviet orbit since Cuba in 1972 joined the Comecon (Council for Economic Assistance—eight-nation Russian controlled economic trading bloc).

The extent of Cuba's absolute dependence on Russian economic support can be gauged by the increase of Cuba's trade with Russia which in 1972 reached 72%—about the same percentage of trade as with the United States in the 1950s. According to Vladimir Novikov, Vice-President of the USSR Council of Ministers, trade between Russia and Cuba in 1970 amounted to three billion rubles a year or about three and a half million dollars a day; an increase of 60% in four years. (see Carmelo Mesa-Lago; *Cuba in the 1970s*—University of New Mexico, 1974, pp. 9-11)

Under the terms of the economic agreement between Russia and Cuba, "...the Cubans committed themselves to accepting Russian advice and planning of key industries for three years (1973 to 1975, inclusive)...Russia agreed to construct two new textile plants, a new nickel and cobalt combine with a capacity of 30,000 tons a year, thermo-nuclear plants, a railroad line between Havana and Santiago de Cuba, a factory to make reinforced concrete, reconstruction of Cuban ports, a new television and radio factory, etc. etc...." (Herbert Matthews, *Revolution in Cuba*; New York, 1975, p. 398, 399)

Russian military aid has turned Cuba into one of the most formidable military powers in Latin America. In 1970, Cuba received "...one and a half billion dollars of direct military aid from Russia—double the amount of United States military aid to the rest of Latin America..." (Juan de Onis, report to the New York *Times*; May 10, 1970). Through a joint Soviet-Cuban Commission, the USSR not only supervises its military and economic shipments to Cuba, but also exercises de facto control of the Cuban economy.

It is this dependence which accounts for Castro's conversion to Marxism-Leninism. His brazen hypocrisy transcends all respect for truth. Even Herbert Matthews, one of Castro's staunchest admirers, is outraged!

"openly critical of the Kremlin's [policy of] 'peaceful coexistence'... by 1973 he was brazenly asserting that even the attack on the Moncada Barracks in Santiago de Cuba twenty years before (1953) was an example of Marxism-Leninism...[Matthews quotes Castro] '...without the extraordinary scientific discoveries of Marx and Engels, and without the inspired interpretation of Lenin and his prodigious historic feat [conquest of power in Russian Revolution] a 26th of July could not have been conceived of...' [Speech on the 20th anniversary of the Moncada attack]

155

"...this factually was pure nonsense. There was only one Communist in the 1953 attack and he is a political accident. None of the participants could have given a thought to Marx, Engels or Lenin, least of all Fidel. Castro was rewriting history to suit...political needs..." (ibid. p. 390)

Castro's unrestrained flattery of his Russian saviors, rivals the praise heaped upon Stalin by his idolatrous sycophants. A front page featured report of Brezhnev's visit to a new vocational school under the headline: BREZHNEV INAUGURATES V.I. LENIN VOCATIONAL SCHOOL, reads:

"Dear Comrade Brezhnev: During whole months the teachers, workers, students and students of this school and the construction workers were preparing for your visit..."

"WE WELCOME YOU WITH THE GREAT AFFECTION YOU DESERVE AS GENERAL-SECRETARY OF THE CENTRAL COMMITTEE OF THE GLORIOUS PARTY OF THE SOVIET UNION..." APPLAUSE!

"It's a great honor and a reason for deep joy and satisfaction for all of us that this school bearing LENIN'S BRIGHT AND GLORIOUS NAME should be inaugurated by you, who now occupies his distinguished place in the Communist Party of The Soviet Union. (APPLAUSE)

"ETERNAL GLORY TO VLADIMIR ILYIICH LENIN!" (APPLAUSE!) "LONG LIVE THE INDESTRUCTIBLE FRIENDSHIP BETWEEN CUBA AND THE SOVIET UNION!" (APPLAUSE AND SHOUTS OF "LONG MAY IT LIVE!)

PATRIA O MUERTE!
VENCEREMOS! (SHOUTS OF: "VENCEREMOS!")
(OVATION)   (GRANMA February 10, 1974)

It is axiomatic that relations between states are not guided by ethical-moral considerations. To promote their interests states do not hestitate to resort to the most revolting treachery and hypocricy. The conduct of the Cuban government confirms this universally acknowledged fact. Castro established friendly relations with Franco-fascist Spain. Maurice Halperin remarks that:

"...in 1963 mutual economic benefits proved stronger than ideology...and by the end of the year all references to 'fascist Spain' disappeared from the Cuban media...trade between Cuba

156

and Spain increased from eleven million dollars in 1962 to approximately one hundred and three million dollars in 1966—making Spain Cuba's third most important trading partner..." (ibid p. 304) Castro went so far as to agree in 1971 in a trade agreement with Spain to pay Spain for all expropriated Spanish owned property nationalized by Cuba. (see Matthews, p. 405)

Agriculture

The economic expert on Cuba, Carmelo Mesa-Lago, concludes that "...agriculture, especially sugar, the backbone of the Cuban economy, has had a discouragingly bad performance under the Revolution since 1961...according to the Food and Agricultural Organization of the United Nations (FAO) total agricultural output in 1969 was 7% below that of 1958 (before the Revolution). *(Cuba in the 1970s;* University of New Mexico, 1974, p.56)

Even Dumont, the distinguished agronomist, after recalling that Castro boasted that Oriente Province would be producing 1.3 million litres of milk daily by 1969 reversed this optimistic prediction and admitted in his 26th of July, 1970, speech that "...in the first half of 1970 milk production decreased by 25%. In 1968 beef deliveries were 154,000 tons—for 1970, deliveries decreased to 145,000 tons; and Castro declared that we may end up with a (further decline in livestock..." *(Is Cuba Socialist?* New York, 1972 pp. 90 - 142) (The economist Lowery Nelson calculates that yearly per-capita meat consumption fell from seventy pounds in 1958 to only 38 pounds in 1972. See Matthews, ibid p. 367.)

Cubans have been living on a severely restricted diet since rationing of foodstuffs and other necessities was introduced in 1962. Dumont severely castigates the Castro regime for this tragic situation. He deserves to be quoted at length:

"...given its fertile land, its level of technique, its tractors, its fertilizers—all infinitely superior to China's resources—there is no reason for Cuba's failure to end shortages of fruits and vegetables that have been going on since 1961...neglect of people's needs for food amounts to contempt...(ibid. p. 142)

"...instead of the green belt for Havana, I had proposed in 1960 (to make the city practically self-sustaining in fruits, vegetables, etc.) ...in 1969, the peasants forced to plant only sugar cane or coffee, who had formerly suppled the city, now became consumers instead of providers of food...the vegetable and fruit crop for Havana Province decreased from 90,000 tons in 1967 to 70,000 tons in 1970..." (ibid. p. 67)

157

"...in 1969 Castro promised: 'We'll have so many bananas, that we won't sell them to you. We'll GIVE them to you.' But I saw mile upon mile of banana plantations where the trees were dying because they were planted in poorly drained soil...the average peasant would have avoided this gross error...there were only enough bananas for ill people and children...no one could buy a single banana; and this in a land where bananas were not a luxury, but a daily staple preferred to bread... (ibid. p. 90)

"...Everywhere, from Bayamo to Havana, vegetables, fruits and clothing disappeared from the stores...shortages which had been bearable until then became shocking and dramatic..." [Dumont attributes much of the shortages and lack of services to the abolition of small shops and severe curtailment of small peasant holdings] ...when the last small shops and various services went, an important supplementary food source disappeared, because State production [nationalization] was unable to replace it. That meant that food was in short supply..." (ibid. p. 63)

According to Joe Nicholson, Jr., (*Inside Cuba:* New York, 1974, p. 33) the 1974 monthly ration for each person was 6 pounds of rice, 3 pounds of meat, 3 pounds of beans, 2 pounds of spaghetti, 1½ pounds of noodles, 1 pound of salt, 12 ounces of flour, 6 ounces of coffee, 15 eggs, 3 containers of canned milk (fresh milk only for children and the aged). Even sugar was rationed to only four pounds per month per person! (According to an announcement monitored on Miami Radio Dec. 1975, sugar is to be removed from the rationing list.)

There is no doubt that Castro together with his amateur economic adventurers are directly responsible for the continuing deterioration of the Cuban economy. Their grandiose and impossible 1970 ten million ton sugar goal turned out to be a major catastrophe. Almost the entire working population (including students and others not engaged directly in production) were mobilized in military fashion to work in the cane fields."...many essential activities" (writes Maurice Halperin) "were brought to a standstill...this economic nightmare set back the entire economy to its lowest point since the Revolution (Jan. 1, 1959)...the economy held up only because of massive Russian subsidies..." (*Rise and Decline of Fidel Castro;* University of California, 1972, p. 316)

Taking full responsibility for this debacle, Castro in a major speech (July 26, 1970) admitted that;

"...our incapacity in the overall work of the Revolution—especially mine...our apprenticeship as directors of the Revolution was too costly..." (quoted René Dumont; ibid. p. 152)

On the extent of waste, inefficiency and mismanagement there is voluminous documentation—a few examples:

158

"...50,000 tractors imported since 1959 were used for all sorts of non-productive purposes...driving to baseball games...visiting relatives, etc. Castro said, '...the former owner of a private business had a tractor. It lasted twenty years. But later, when the ownership passed to the state, a tractor lasted only two, three, or maybe four years...'"

...imported equipment lay unutilized for years...rusting on the docks because the building to house the equipment had not been constructed...in 1971, 120 million cubic yards of water were lost in Havana alone because of neglect of maintenance...of the waterpipe system...President of Cuba Dorticós reported in early 1972...that out of 300 locomotives only 134 were working...a time-loss study published in 1970 revealed that from ¼ to ½ of the workday was wasted...in late 1973, Raul Castro said that it was common in state farms that labor costs alone exceeded value of production...on one state farm the annual wage bill was $48,000 while the value of output was $8,000...

Mesa-Lago; ibid. pp. 33, 34, 37

To illustrate the bureaucratic maze choking the Cuban economy, Rene Dumont reveals: "...that in Cuba the exportation of a single case of vegetables involves authorizations for packing, refrigeration, as well as loading...this requires the coordination of thirteen government bureaus—none of them in a hurry..."(Ibid. p. 90.)

Even the pro-Castro economists, Huberman and Sweezy, deplored the bureaucratic structure of the Cuban economy, citing the major agrarian economic agency INRA (National Institute of Agrarian Reform) as an example:

...coordination was difficult, often impossible...the situation was no better industry. Having all industry under the centralized control of one agency in Havana could not be but an unwieldy and inefficient arrangement...

Socialism in Cuba; New York, 1969, pp. 82-83)

Non-Agricultural Production

According to incomplete, scanty data gathered by Mesa-Lago, industrial production declined in 1969-1970. It improved in 1972: 48% in steel; 28% in beverages; 11% in fishing; 44% in building materials; 41% in salt; *200%* in refrigeration, etc. There were also increases in the production of telephone wire, glass containers, plastics, cosmetics and great increases in nickel and copper production. Overall production increased 14% in 1972 and 15% in the first nine months of 1973.

Information about the economic situation in Cuba is, as Mesa-Lago puts it, "necessarily fragmentary...there are no accurate statistical data—and in many areas, none at all—..." Claims by Castro and official Cuban sources concerning the extent of Cuba's economic progress cannot be verified and "...must be taken very cautiously..." (All above data, Mesa-Lago; ibid. pp. 52-60) René Dumont also complains that "...the organization of Cuba's economy is such that it has become all but impossible to obtain reliable data..." (*Is Cuba Socialist?*; p. 71)

Castro is not overly optimistic about the rate of Cuba's future economic progress. He cautions the people not to expect spectacular increases in production:

...the objectives of our people in the material field cannot be very ambitious...we should work in the next ten years to advance our economy at an average annual rate of 6%...

quoted, Mesa Lago; ibid. p. 59

In view of Castro's record of fantastically exaggerated claims and broken promises, the prospects for a significant betterment of the standard of living of the Cuban masses are indeed dim.

STRUCTURE OF POWER IN CUBA

In the first phase of authoritarian revolutions, the revolutionary elite (sometimes commanded by a personal dictator) seizes and consolidates power on the pretext that it is acting in the "name of the people." But in order to govern the country and carry out the decrees of the leadership, every regime must eventually institutionalize its power by creating a permanent, legally established bureaucratic administrative apparatus.

To implement institutionalization, Castro, in 1970, launched the re-organization of his government and the drafting of a new constitution, proclaiming that the Revolution had now come of age and the people could now be trusted to more self-rule. Castro promised the enactment of measures to expedite the decentralization of his administration; expand local autonomy and workers' self-management of industry, democratize the mass organizations and create new state agencies designed to encourage more participation of the people in local and national affairs. (We list the more important changes and our comments under appropriate headings.)

161

Reorganization of the Governmental Structure

In 1973 the top governmental structure was reorganized in the following manner: 1) The division of the government into legislative, executive, and judicial sections was rejected as "bourgeois." The functions of the three branches are concentrated into the Council of Ministers, "...the supreme ...organ of State power..." In addition to the Council of Ministers, there are a number of affiliated national agencies such as Agriculture and Husbandry Development, the Fishing and Forestry Institute, the National Poultry Board and a number of cultural bodies (the Institutes of Cinema, Literature, the National Council of Culture and similar groupings).

2) Actually, the real power is exercised by the Executive Committee of the Council of Ministers (equivalent to a Cabinet) composed of ten Deputy Prime Ministers who control and coordinate their respective departments and agencies. These departments include: basic industry and energy; consumer goods industries and domestic trade; the sugar industry; non-sugar agriculture; construction; transportation and communications; education and welfare. "...The Executive Committee of the Council of Ministers was created pursuant to the orientation of the Political Bureau of the Communist Party of Cuba..."

3) At the intermediate levels, Coordinating Provincial Councils appointed by the Deputy Prime Ministers of the Executive Committee in "...coordination with the Provincial Delegates of the Political Bureau of the Communist Party will carry out...the directives issued from above...by the corresponding central authority..." (i.e., the Deputy Prime Minsters of the Executive Committee of the Council of Ministers.)

4) "...the Prime Minister of the Council of Ministers, Fidel Castro Ruz, who also presides over the Executive Committee of the Council of Ministers will be directly in charge of the following agencies: Ministry of the Revolutionary Armed Forces (FAR), Ministry of the Interior, National Institute of Agrarian Reform (INRA) and Ministry of Public Health..."

Since Castro is also the First Secretary of the Central Committee of the Communist Party of Cuba (CPC) and since every major ministry and agency head is a member of the CPC and is appointed by Castro, Herbert Matthews (a Castro sympathizer) reluctantly concludes that: "...all the organs of state power are under Castro's direct command. He is all-powerful and it is *his* Revolution...Castro does not want—or dare—to create a self-governing administration, a managerial apparatus, an autonomous political party, a powerful military elite; because any one of them could threaten his power..." (1, for continuity of the text all notes for this chapter have been placed at the end of this chapter).

Following the Stalinist pattern, the Cuban State is a structured pyramid in which absolute power is ultimately exercised by an individual (Castro) or by a collective dictatorship as in post-Stalin Russia.

The Judicial System

There is no independent judiciary. "...the courts [reads the law] receive instructions from the leadership of the Revolution which are compulsory..." The judicial system is only an agency of the Council of Ministers, which regulates and controls all courts and legal agencies. The highest judicial administrative body is the Council of Ministers of the Supreme People's Court, which transmits to the lower courts the "...instructions of the leadership of the Revolution which are compulsory..." (2) The system centralizes all four judicial branches: ordinary, military, political, and the People's Courts for minor offenses. The judges of the People's Courts are laymen. The President of the Republic, the Ministers, and the members of the Political Bureau of the CPC are exempt from the jurisdiction of the courts and can be tried only by special Party courts. (3) Private law practice is prohibited. Defendants in court cases can be represented only by state appointed lawyers even when the State itself is being sued. Judges, juries, and other judicial personnel must be ideologically reliable. (4) "...knowledge and study of Marxism-Leninism, Marxist sociology, and the materialist interpretation of history are indispensable prerequisites for the true integral education of a revolutionary judge..." (5)

The Communist Party of Cuba (CPC)

Under the name "People's Socialist Party" (PSP) the Communist Party was organized in 1925. Under Castro, it was known as Integrated Revolutionary Organizations (ORI); the United Party of the Socialist Revolution (PURS) and, since 1965, as the Communist Party of Cuba (CPC).

The Communist Party was never on good terms with Castro, not only because of its collaboration with Batista, but also because it ridiculed Castro's historic July 26th, 1953, attack on the Moncada Barracks (now commemorated as a national holiday). The communists called the attack a "bourgeois putschist adventure." Moreover, the communists took no part in the fight against Batista and sabotaged Castro's call for a general strike to unseat Batista. The communists came to Castro only a few months before the overthrow of Batista, when they saw that Castro was going to win.

The revolution was made in spite of the opposition of the Party. Since the Party did not, as in Russia, initiate revolutionary action and seize power, it was in no position to dictate terms to Castro in exchange for its collaboration. The Party was accepted only on condition that it acknowledged Castro's leadership and accepted without question all his ideological, political and economic policies.

Castro dominates the CPC, much like Stalin. The members of the Communist Party's Central Committee belong to Castro's clique. Castro himself (as already noted) is the First Secretary of the Party and his brother Raúl ranks next. There is, of course, no democracy within the Party. Thus, when Aníbal Escalante was accused of "micro-factionalism" (a crime that is not even listed in the penal code), because he tried to subordinate Castro to the discipline of the Communist party, he was sentenced to 15 years at hard labor. "...Escalante and his lawyers were deprived even of the right to address a single word in self-defense to the court and the public documents contain no defense pleas of any kind..." (6)

The CPC does not make policy. Its function is to carry out government orders, not to govern, or, as Maurice Halperin puts it: "...the function of the CPC is to mobilize the population for goals set by Castro himself..." (7)

In Cuba, the CPC fulfills the same preponderent role as in Russia and the other "socialist countries." The expanding role of the CPC in the reorganization process is manifested in its growing membership, which increased from 55,000 in 1969 to 200,000 in 1975. The estimated membership of the Union of Communist Youth is about 300,000. 85% of armed forces officers also belong to the CPC. An interesting sidelight: according to *Verde Olivio* (organ of the Armed Forces) the composition of the Central Committee of the CPC was 67% military (including 57 Majors), 26 professionals and only 7% workers. In addition to the 6 secretariats of the CPC in the provinces, there were in 1973, 60 district secretariats, 401 in the municipalities and 14,360 party cells in mass organizations, factories and rural areas.

The Communist Party governs Cuba and Castro rules the Communist Party. The Stalinist subservience of the CPC to Castro was stressed by Armando Hart (in 1969, Organizing Secretary of the CPC) in a speech at the University of Havana:

...can anyone analyze or study theoretical questions, raised, for instance, by philosophy, the roads to Communism; or any field of culture, mainly those of social science and philosophy, without taking into account the ideas and concepts of Fidel [Castro] and Che [Guevara]?...(8)

The first post-Castro Congress of the CPC (Dec., 1975) ratified the new constitution drawn up by the veteran communist leader Blas Roca and the juridical committee of the Party Central Committee. The CPC was proclaimed as the "...supreme leading force of Cuban society and the State." The national program of the Party was approved and the tentative first five year economic plan for 1976-1980 inclusive was also recommended.

Pending implementation of the new directives of the Congress, the CPC is headed by a 100 member Central Committee. Below the Provincial Committees are the Regional and Municipal Committees down to factory and farm cells. At every level of this complicated, autocratically centralized organization, the orders of the high command (Castro's clique) are faithfully carried out.

Driven by the necessity to remain on good terms with his saviors, the "socialist countries" upon whom his survival depends, Castro falsifies the history of his relations with the Cuban communists, affirming now what he vehemently denied before. His mouthpiece, *Granma* (August 16, 1975) hypocritically stressed that:

...throughout its history our nation's first communist party performed tremendous work disseminating Marxist-Leninist ideas; fought the local oligarchy and against imperialism and selflessly defended all democratic demands of the working class... (9)

People's Democracy and Decentralization

In the summer of 1974 an experiment in democracy and decentralization was initiated in Matanzas Province. Municipal, district and provincial Organizations of the People's Power (PPO) were established. 5,597 production and service units were handed over to the PPO. The PPO performs the combined functions of city council and local administration, and also takes on certain functions of the Committees for the Defense of the Revolution (CDR) etc. 90% of the people voted in the elections, but "60% of the deputies are communists and young communist members..." (10)

An interview with a high official of the PPO proves that the much publicized "decentralization," "democracy," and "people's self-management of affairs" allegedly being instituted in Cuba is a brazen fraud:

Q) Is the establishment of self-governing Organs of People's Power (PPO) to promote mass participation in local and provincial administration part of the process of reinforcing the Dictatorship of the Proletariat?
A) Actually, the establishment of the PPO—being tried out as an experiment in Matanzas—is part of the process.
Q) On what principles are the PPO based?
A) The Communist Party is the principal, the indispensable

165

organism for the construction of socialism in our country and, as such, directs as it deems best all the organizations and organisms, including of course the Organs of People's Power. (11)

This system, patterned after the fake Russian "soviets," actually reinforces the dictatorship.

The Committees for the Defense of the Revolution (CDR)

"...What [asked K.S. Karol] has become of the many rank-and-file organizations that were once so dynamic?...these organizations have ceased to exist on anything but paper. They became puppets..for example, the CDR..spring into action when it comes to tracking down bad citizens and small traders. The CDR have been reduced to mere appendages of the "Seguridad" [National Police Force]..." (12) And Herbert Matthews writing five years later in 1975 states flatly that the CDR is now completely "...under the control of the Communist Party...Besides spying the CDR also performs certain functions such as helping to organize vaccinations for polio, diptheria and measles, and sees to it that parents send their children to school, that food and other rations are fairly handled, etc...." (13)

The CDR is actually a vast, intricate network reaching into every neighborhood, every home and even into the personal life of every man, woman and child in Cuba. The following verbatim conversation with a native Cuban tells more about the operations of the Cuban Police State and the total obliteration of individual freedom than any number of abstract academic dissertations or statistical tables:

> ...I ran into a hurricane of a woman named Mrs. S. "The famous literacy campaign," she stormed, "was indoctrination. There was no dissent...It was like a new Dark Age in Cuba. These spies of the CDR know who visits me and whom I visit...Under Mr. Castro, it is suddenly my neighbor's duty to know how I live. Everybody knows that in a civilized country your home is your fortress...Here in Cuba, every jackass is knocking on your door to give you advice on who is dangerous...They want to take the lock off my front door...You think I exaggerate? Well, you don't live here...Our deepest need is to be our own selves, different, non-conformist...My motto is 'leave people alone'...It is intolerable to have only one power in the State...even a righteous power...because human beings have a perverse desire to say NO—even to righteousness—to disagree.
>
> [A medical student told the visitor:] We all know who are the self-appointed spies. Go and talk to Mrs. Blanco. [The visitor quotes her:] ...Yes, I know what everybody says about me, but I

166

have to see that people do not do certain things—like being absent from work. No absenteeism on THIS block... [An absentee who claimed sickness—"Stress" he called it—was actually, unbeknown to his wife, visiting his girl friend. When Mrs. Blanco threatened to expose him to his wife;]...he was all right for two days [she said] —I checked with his work place—Two days, and then more "stress"...He was hungry for his girl friend...I felt like following him one day and catching him out...because, after all, it IS MY BUSINESS...He is a parasite letting down my block...I wondered if I should not talk to his girl friend...warn her to keep away from him, break relations...I am not saying anything...but I am watching from here what is happening...but what a pain if his wife finds out!... (14)

René Dumont tells that in the barracks of the "machateros" (cane cutters) working away from home: "...there are sometimes little signs that read: 'Sleep quietly. The Revolution is watching over your wife.' As a matter of fact, if a 'machatero's' wife is visited by a man, the husband gets a telegram from the local CDR..." (15)

Cuban Youth Rebels

In the spring of 1972, Jaime Crombat, Secretary of the Young Communist League, complained that among the youth there was a "...backward minority who neither study nor work—or do so only under pressure—those who, permeated by the old ideology...maintain a conduct contrary to socialist morals..." (16) Mesa-Lago's painstaking research unearths the true situation. He deserves to be quoted at length:

"...in spite of the remarkable progress in education, i.e., reduction in the illiteracy rate...serious deficiencies were reported. In April, 1971, out of the number of school-age youngsters 14 to 16 years old, there were 300,00 who neither worked nor studied: 23% among 14 year olds, 44% among 15 year olds, and 60% among 16 year olds. The dropout rate was worse—more in rural areas (88%) than in urban areas (66%). In elementary schools, 69% of those who attended classes in 1965 did not finish in 1971...students showed a lack of concern for socialist property..." According to the Minister of Education, 50% of the books sent to school were lost every year due to carelessness. Castro exploded in indignation: "...there is something wrong when we have to educate our young people in the need to care for socialist property...loafers, people who don't work, criminals are the ones who destroy..."

> ...in the same speech Castro denounced the youth for wearing "extravagant" foreign fashions [Too tight pants and long hair in the case of boys. Too short mini-skirts in the case of the girls.], liking "decadent literature." In some cases, "...the youth were used by counter-revolutionaries against the Revolution..." Castro found "residual manifestations" of prostitution and homosexuality. In 1967, minors participated in 41% of all crimes committed in the nation. Four years later the percentage rises to 50%... (16)
>
> ...in 1972, Joe Nicholson, Jr., a sympathetic journalist who visited Cuba, asked Cuban officials why boys are not allowed to wear long hair. The official answered that if one boy is allowed to be different in hair, dress or behavior, the rest might request the right to be different too. This, in turn, would create controversy, something that was considered incorrect...(17)

Measures to correct his situation included compulsory military service, military units to aid production, and to work in constuction, irrigation and other projects. Nevertheless, it was reported that the number of youngsters in the 13 to 16 year bracket who committed offenses remained unchanged. Castro alleged that the high juvenile delinquency rate was due to the fact that they were exempted from criminal punishments by the courts. In May, 1973, legal liability was reduced from 18 to 16 years and tough penalties up to life imprisonment were imposed for crimes against the national economy, abnormal sexual behavior and other offenses.

> ...The drop-out problem was partially solved through the SMO (compulsory military service) and the Youth Centennial Columns. The SMO recruits numbered 300,000 in 1972 (about one third of all youngsters between 16 and 17). In 1973 both these youth organizations were merged into the Youth Army of Work (EJT)...(18)

Plight of the Workers

The promised abolition of house rents and increasing wages of the lowest paid workers was not kept. Likewise, full pay for sick and retired workers was eliminated. There was no lessening of the severe food rations in 1973. One of the main resolutions of the 13th Congress of the Cuban Confederation of Labor (CTC), Nov., 1973, restored the worst features of the capitalist wage system—payment according to output, instead of according to need. In his speech to the closing session of the Congress, Castro tried to justify this policy: "...paying the same wage for the same type of work without taking into account the effort required to do it, is an equalitarian principle we must correct...payment should be measured in physical terms according to the complexity and skill required to do the job..." In line with this policy, 132 million pesos were allotted to raise wages for technicians in order to spur them to "increase their productivity." (19) At the First Congress of the Communist Party of Cuba (Dec., 1975), the motto "From each according to his ability; to each according to his WORK." was displayed in huge red letters.

Wages are linked to work quotas. Every worker is given a quota. If the quota is not fulfilled, wages are proportionally reduced. Purchase of scarce appliances (television sets, refrigerators, washing machines, etc.) are allotted not according to the worker's need but according to his correct attitude (obeying orders, patriotism, overfulfillment of work quotas, etc.). The faithful wage slave will be allowed to spend his vacation at the better resorts and be granted first access to housing. (20)

Actually, the 13th Congress of the CTC rejected the right of the Unions to defend the interests of the workers. According to the resolutions, there are no conflicts. The State, the Communist Party, and the unions are partners cooperating always to produce "more and better products and services; to promote punctual attendance at work; to raise political consciousness; to follow the Communist Party directives..." (21)

To get a job, every worker must carry an identity card and a file with a full work record of his "merits" and "demerits." "Merits" include voluntary unpaid labor, overfulfillment of work quotas, working overtime without pay, postponing retirement to keep on working, defense of State property, and a high level of political consciousness. "Demerits" are "activities that negatively affect production, disturb discipline, lower the level of political consciousness..." (22)

In the Spring of 1971, the government proclaimed a law against "loafing," compelling all able-bodied men between the age of 17 and 60 to work. Worker absenteeism was 20% in late 1970. Penalties for the "crime of loafing" fluctuate between house arrest and one or two years at forced labor. (23)

Union "Democracy"

In September, 1970, Castro announced that we "...are going to trust the workers to hold trade union elections in every local...the elections will be absolutely free..." Castro then brazenly contradicted himself, making it clear that "...only workers who would unconditionally follow government, management and party orders would be elected..." (24)

The election procedure prohibited candidates from electioneering or advertising their candidacy. Only the election committee had the exclusive right to advertise the "merits" of the candidates. More than half the workers refused to participate in the rigged electoral farce, because they did not expect any real changes, or because there was only one candidate on the ballot. When the CTC was discussing election proceedings, some union members strongly criticised the methods of conducting the elections and the choosing of the candidates. The Minister of Labor interrupted the discussion, calling the critics "counter-revolutionists" and "demagogues" and warning them that their "negative attitude" had to be "radically changed." (25)

The 13th Congress of the CTC (Nov., 1973) was the first in seven years (1966). The Congress was attended by 2,230 delegates allegedly representing 1,200,000 workers. The main business was automatically ratifying or modifying details of the "thesis" submitted by the organizing commission (over 99% in favor). The number of national syndicates was increased from 14 to 22. (26)

Workers' Control and Self-Management

The Castro government never seriously intended to allow meaningful participation of the workers in management (to say nothing about full self-management of industry). K.S. Karol reveals that in 1968: "...Castro himself confessed to me that he saw no chance of granting the workers the right to self-management in the near future—let alone of introducing a truly socialist mode of production..." (27)

Jorge Risquet, the Minister of Labor, declared that: "...the fact that Fidel Castro and I suggested that the workers be consulted, does not mean that we are going to negate the role that the Communist Party must play...decision and responsibility fall to the management...one thing that is perfectly clear is that management should and does have all the authority to make decisions and act...management represents the organization of the State and is charged with the planning and fulfillment of production and services..." (28)

In his famous speech of July 26th, 1970, Castro made it clear that: "...we must begin to establish a collective body in each plant...but it must be headed by one man and also by representatives of the Advanced Workers Movement (The Cuban equivalent of the Russian Stakhanovites, who excelled all other workers in speed and output—model workers. Later Stakhanovism became the prototype for the Socialist Emulation Movement.), the Young Communist League, the Communist Party and the Women's Front..." (29)

A 1965 law established Labor Councils (Consejos de Trabajo). The Labor Council is composed of five workers elected for a three year term. But the Council does not manage, administer, or even partially control production. Its functions are to settle workers' grievances, expedite the orders and directives of management, enforce work

170

discipline and process transfers. The transfer of a worker must be approved by both the Ministry of Labor and the Communist Party nucleus. (30)

The unions are actually transmission belts for the administration and implementation of production. Raul Castro declared that the "...unions are supposed to be autonomous, but must be politically guided by the Party and must follow its policies..." The 13th Congress of the CTC declared that: "...the functions of the unions are to cooperate in improving management performance, strengthen labor discipline; assure attendance at work, increase production, and eradicate absenteeism, malingering and carelessness..." (31)

The union could participate in the administration of the enterprise through two institutions, Production Assemblies and Management Councils (Consejos de Dirección). These two institutions are the top administrative bodies at all work centers..." "...each Management Council is composed of an administrator, his or her top assistants, the worker elected union representative, the Communist Party nucleus and the local branch of the Communist Youth Organizations..." (33)

"...the Assembly could make recommendations but the manager could accept, reject, or modify the recommendations as he sees fit...unions are not allowed to intervene in the determination of salaries, hiring or firing, dismissal of managers, or in planning..." (34)

European, American and many Latin American workers actually exercise more workers' control than do the Cuban workers. There was, in fact, more workers' control before Castro's regime came to power.

K.S. Karol, commenting on the massive militarization of labor, which reached a high point in the 1968 "Revolutionary Offensive," tells how "...the whole country, was, in fact, reorganized on the model of the army...Command Posts were set up...in every province...Labor Brigades were turned into batallions, each divided into three squads, led by a Major and a Chief of Operations...the Che' Guevara Brigade [on the agricultural production front]...was under the direct control of the army..." (37)

Militarization of Labor

According to Gerald H. Reed who studied the Cuban educational system during his long visit to Cuba: "...the plan for the Technological Instruction Institutes converted these institutions into military centers. The students live under strict military discipline and complete their draft obligations while they study..." (35)

The Youth Army of Work (EJT) is a branch of the regular army, commanded by Commandante (equivalent to Major General) Oscar

171

Fernández Mell. Mell is also Vice Minister of the Revolutionary Army and a member of the Central Committee of the Communist Party. The EJT was founded Aug. 3, 1973, in the Province of Camagüey. On its first anniversary, a message of congratulations grandiloquently signed "Fidel Castro, First Secretary of the Communist Party and First Prime Minister of the Revolutionary Government" thanks the EJT for:

> ...your decisive help in the sugar harvests of 1974. Your formidable work in fulfilling agricultural plans, in the construction of schools, factories, housing and ferries surpasses even the extraordinary achievements of preceeding organizations...

And Castro's brother, who signs himself, "Raúl Castro Ruz, Commander of Division and Minister of the Armed Forces":

> ...sends our most fraternal greetings to all soldiers, officers, under officers [non-commissioned sergeants, corporals, etc.] and political commissars of the Youth Army of Work, and exhorts them to perfect themselves politically, and ideologically for combat...as we have already said on other occasions, we are certain that this army will become a true bastion of production and defense of the Revolution... (36)

The Armed Forces

At the Inception of the Revolution Castro was acclaimed by the people when he vowed to curb the power of the military, reduced the highest rank in the rebel army to Major and eventually to abolish the army entirely in favor of the People's Militias.

The process of compulsory military service, begun in 1963, culminated in 1973 with the abolition of the vaunted Militias, "The People in Arms." "...the Militia has been replaced by civil defense organization under direct army control. Nor is there anything of a "People's Army" about the new organization...after each exercise, the guns are safely locked away in the barracks—a far cry from the days when Fidel declared that he was prepared to distribute arms 'even to cats'..." (38)

Cuba boasts the most powerful army in Latin America. Russia and "the socialist countries" supplied Cuba with massive armaments and military technicians. Hundreds of young officers in the Revolutionary Armed Forces (FAR) were trained in Russia. (39) As early as 1963, the military expert Hanson Baldwin considered the Cuban air force to be the "most modern and potentially the most powerful in Latin America." (40)

It has been greatly strengthened since with Russian MIGs and other equipment. Cuba also has a "formidable array of anti-aircraft missles, coast artillery, radar stations," (41) long range cannons, the latest light and heavy tanks, and other modern weapons.

With the cooperation of Soviet military experts, Raul Castro transformed the Cuban armed forces into a highly disciplined, highly stratified military machine differing in no essential respect from the modern conventional armies of the great military powers.

Raúl Castro is a far more capable military organizer and strategist than is his brother Fidel. Raúl, and not Fidel, devised the strategy and organized the Guerrilla War in the Sierra Maestra and in the Sierre de Cristal, which precipitated the downfall of Batista. Raúl has since then capably commanded the Cuban army. (42) Nearly all the commanders who served under Raúl became high officers in the Cuban army and government, and became members of the Central Committee of the Communist Party.

It would be a mistake to assume that Raúl Castro is a mere figurehead in the regime. He not only shares power with his brother Fidel, but also wields considerable power on his own account. When Castro travels abroad, Raúl rules Cuba in his place until Fidel returns. And Fidel named Raúl to succeed him if he is killed or dies of other causes. Matthews emphasizes that if Fidel Castro should for any reason disappear, Raul would easily succeed him as ruler of Cuba, because he would be in a position to rally all the most formidable power blocs to support him. "...Raul would have with him a powerful military and police force, a strong administration, the governmental bureaucracy and the all-powerful Politburo of the Communist Party..." (43)

Although Raúl Castro cut the size of the Cuban army in half (from 300,000 to 150,000), it is still five times greater than Batista's 30,000-man army, navy and air force. Better organized, better trained, and better equipped with th most advanced weapons, the numerically reduced army has been reorganized into a far more formidable fighting force. So much so, that, at this writing, the Cuban government has, in collusion with Russia, been able to send thousands of troops to fight in Angola without noticeably impairing the combat power of the Cuban army.

The hierarchical ranking system of the armed forces has been reorganized to conform with the prevailing traditional ranking systems of all military powers, "capitalist" or "socialist." "...Law 1257 leaves Fidel as Chief Minister of the Armed Forces. Raúl Castro, as Minister of the Armed Forces (directly under Fidel), becomes the only Division Commander whose equivalent in other countries is Lieutenant General. (Raúl is in fact now called "Lieutenant General" in Cuba.) Four Brigade Commanders were named who are the equivalent of Major Generals..a number of First Commanders, or Colonels, were also appointed. Below the rank of Commander (Lieutenant Colonel), the titles of First Lieutenant and Sub-Lieutenant are used as in other

173

armies...Similar changes are made for the Revolutionary Navy. (Ship Commander, for Admiral, down to Corvette Captain, for the equivalent of Commander as in other navies..." (44)

In justifying counter-revolutionary militarization, Castro said that the armed forces "...had been distinguished in the past for their modesty of rank and uniform [plain, shabby olive-green, but that now the] Revolution had become more mature and so had the armed forces..." (45)

Increasing militarization signifies revolutionary progress! This remark alone signifies the degeneration of the Revolution—even without additional incontrovertible evidence.

Concluding Remarks

While Castro is at present the undisputed ruler of Cuba, institutionalization is eventually bound to undermine his personal dictatorship.

It is axiomatic that no State can possibly rule without an administrative apparatus. The reconstruction of the Cuban government therefore necessitates the creation of an enormous bureaucratic administrative machine. The Communist Party, the armed forces, the educational establishment, the economic agencies, the unions, the local, regional, provincial and national governmental branches, etc., relentlessly compete for more power. As these formidable power blocs expand and become more firmly entrenched, Castro's machine will increasingly be obliged to share power with them. Personal rule will give way to a collective dictatorship and tyranny will be perpetuated.

The institutionalization of the Cuban Revolution is, however, still in its early stages. Thus far, the first attempts in this direction indicate that the institutionalization of the Revolution serves only to re-inforce the personal dictatorship of Fidel Castro and his faithful lieutenants.

Powerfully abetted by the massive support of the Soviet bloc of "socialist countries" and its own massive internal apparatus, the Castro regime is still powerfully entrenched. The Cuban people, unable to revolt by force of arms, are waging a relentless guerrilla war of passive resistance against the Police State. They have, in the course of their struggles, developed ingenious ways of harassing and even seriously frustrating the plans of their tyrants (loafing, slowdowns, evading laws, sabotage, sporadic acts of violence, ridicule, etcetera).

The rebellion could provide a solid base for a mass underground movement comparable to the anti-Batista resistance movements. On the other hand, the ability of modern totalitarian regimes—both "right" and "left"—to survive mass discontent indefinitely for generations—must not be underestimated. Many hard battles will have to be fought, many lives lost, before victory will have at last been achieved.

NOTES

There were so many notes in this chapter that we felt it would read best if we included them here.

1) Herbert Matthews, *Cuba In Revolution;* New York, 1975, p. 379
2) Carmelo Mesa-Lago, *Cuba in the 1970s;* University of New Mexico, 1974, p. 68
3) *ibid.* p. 68 (unless otherwise noted, Mesa-Lago's sources are from *Granma,* the official organ of the Communist Party of Cuba)
4) Mesa-Lago; *ibid.* p. 68
5) *Granma;* Jan. 6, 1974
6) K.S. Karol, *Guerrillas in Power;* New York, 1970, p. 472
7) *The Rise and Decline of Fidel Castro;* University of California, 1974, p. 133
8) *Granma,* Sept. 28, 1969-quoted, Halperin, *ibid.* p. 17
9) *International Affairs Monthly;* Moscow, Nov. 1975, p. 17
10) *ibid.* p. 17
11) *Granma,* May 28, 1974
12) Karol, *ibid.* p. 457
13) Matthews, *ibid.* p. 15
14) Barry Reckord, *Does Fidel Eat More Than Your Father?;* New York, 1971, pgs. 60-69
15) René Dumont, *Is Cuba Socialist?* New York, 1974, p. 137
16) Mesa-Lago, *ibid.* pgs. 93-96
17) Mesa-Lago, *ibid.* p. 97
18) Mesa-Lago, *ibid.* p. 96
19) Mesa-Lago, *ibid.* p. 43
20) Mesa-Lago, *ibid.* pgs. 44-45
21) Mesa-Lago, *ibid.* pg. 3
22) Mesa-Lago, *ibid.* p. 87, 88
23) *Granma,* Jan. 17, 1971
24) *Resumen Granma Seminal,* Oct. 10, 1970
25-26) Mesa-Lago, *ibid.* p. 77-88
27) Karol, *ibid.* p. 546
28) Speech to closing session of the 13th Congress of the CTC
29) quoted by Andrew Zimbalist, paper presented to 2nd annual Conference on Workers' Self-Management; Cornell University, June, 1975
30) Zimbalist, *ibid.*
31) Mesa-Lago, *ibid.* P. 82, 83
32) Mesa-Lago, *ibid.* p. 84
33) Zimbalist, *ibid.*
34) Mesa-Lago, *ibid.* p. 84
35) *Comparative Education Review;* June 1970, pgs. 136, 143
36) *Granma,* Aug. 18, 1974
37) Karol, *ibid.* p. 444-445
38) Karol, *ibid.* p. 457; also *Granma,* April 22, 1973
39) Matthews, *ibid.* p. 187
40-41) Matthews, *ibid.* p. 102
42) Matthews, *ibid.* p. 102
43) Matthews, *ibid.* p. 407
44) Matthews, *ibid.* p. 407
45) *Granma,* April 22, 1973

APPENDICES

On the Constitution of the Republic of Cuba

Since the text of the *Constitution of the Republic of Cuba* arrived after the completion of this book, comment is included in the appendix. (English Translation, Center for Cuban Studies, N.Y. 1976)

Although Article 4 of the constitution proclaims that "...all power belongs to the working people who exercise it directly or through the Assemblies of People's Power..." the constitution actually institutionalizes and perpetuates the dictatorship in much the same manner as the Constitution of the Soviet Union promulgated by Stalin. A few examples:

> [Article 66:] ...State organs are based...upon the principles of...unity of power [and the totalitarian Lenin-Stalin principle of] democratic centralism...
> [Article 5:] ...the socialist State...consolidates the ideology and rules of living together and of proper conduct in Cuban society... directs the national economy...assures the educational, scientific, technical and cultural progress of the country...
> [Article 38:] ...education is a function of the state...educational institutions belong to the state...[which promotes] communist education and training of children, young people and adults...
> [Article 52:] ...citizens have the freedom of speech and the press [in keeping with] socialist society [but the exercise of that right is vested in the state]...press, radio, television, movies and other organs of the mass media are exclusively state property...
> [Article 19:] The wage system of Cuba is based upon the...socialist principle of 'From each according to his ability, to each according to his work...'

Following the Russian pattern, the Constitution of Cuba "...basing ourselves on the...proletarian internationalism...of the Soviet Union..." (Preamble) is a hierarchically structured pyramid in which the absolute power of the state, through its chain-of-command is imposed from the top down over every level of Cuban society (homes, neighborhoods, municipalities, provinces etc.) "...decisions of superior state organs are compulsory for inferior ones..."

> [Article 66:] Starting from the local, municipal and provincial Assemblies of People's Power, the Council of Ministers and the Council of State, supreme power is ultimately personified in a

176

single dictator: The President of the Council of State.
[Article 105:] [Decisions of Local Assemblies of People's Power can be] ...revoked, suspended or modified...by the...Municipal and Provincial Assemblies of People's Power.
[Article 96:] [The Council of Ministers can] ...revoke or annul provisions issued by...heads of central agencies and the administrative bodies of the local organs [Municipal and Provincial Assemblies] of People's Power...
[Article 88:] [The Council of State can, in turn,] ...suspend the provisions of the Council of Ministers and [even the] Local Assemblies of People's Power which in its opinion run counter to the Constitution...or the general interest of the country..."

The prerogatives of the President of the Council of State match the absolute power exercised by Stalin:

[Article 91:] ...The President of the Council of State is Head of the Government and is invested with the power to:
...organize, conduct the activities of, call for the holding of and preside over the sessions of the Council of State and the Council of Ministers...control and supervise...the activities of the ministries and central agencies of the administration...assume the leadership of any ministry or central agency of the administration ...replace...the members of the Council of Ministers [Article 88] ...represent the state and the government and conduct their general policy...

The totalitarian character of the constitution is best summarized in this extract from its Preamble:

WE adopt the following Constitution...to carry forward the triumphant Revolution [initiated]...under the leadership of Fidel Castro [who] established the revolutionary power...and started the construction of socialism under the direction of the Communist Party...

Chronology 1959-1975

Jan. 1, 1959   Batista flees Cuba: Revolution begins.

Jan. 4   Manuel Urrutia Lleo appointed President of Cuba. Armed Student Directorio seizes and refuses to evacuate the Presidential Palace, the seat of government and the University of Havana campus because Castro unilaterally appointed his "Provisional Government" without consulting allied anti-Batista fighting groups.

Jan. 10	Habeas corpus suspended. Capital punishment decreed.
Jan. 28	People's Socialist Party (PSP-Communists) pledges allegiance to Castro.
Feb. 16	Miró Cardona resigns and Castro appoints himself Premier.
April 5	Censorship of press, radio, television etc. begins. Strikes prohibited.
May 8	Castro government assumes unlimited power. Council of Ministers can decree laws and change constitution at will.
May 17	Agrarian Reform Law (National Institute of Agrarian Reform—INRA) makes illegal ownership of more than 5 caballerias (1 caballeria = 33½ acres) of land. INRA institutes state farms on Russian model. Law 43 giving INRA dictatorial powers reads: "...the INRA will appoint administrators and the workers will accept all orders and decrees dictated by INRA..."
June 3	Pedro Luis Diaz, Commander of the Air Force and close friend of Castro, protests growing influence of Communists and leaves Cuba.
June 9	Resolution 6, gives Castro unlimited power to spend public funds without being accountable to anyone.
July 7	Article 25 of Fundamental Law further extends death penalty for "acts hostile to the regime"
July 18	Urrutia resigns. The Communist Dorticós appointed new President of Cuba
July 26	The day after he resigns, Castro before a delirious mass demonstration of 500,000 people withdraws his resignation as self appointed Premier of Cuba. The carefully staged proceeding was a cheap publicity hoax.

178

Sept. 30	Cuba sells 3,300,000 tons of sugar to Russia
Oct. 13	Article 149, regulating private schools and education, prohibits teaching of subjects not taught in public schools, state dictates curriculum.
Oct. 20	Castro's close friend and second-in-command, Major Hubor Matos, Military Commander of Province of Camagüey, resigns in protest of communist infiltration of Cuban government. Arrested by order of Castro and after fake "trial", sentenced Dec. 14 to 20 years imprisonment. Sentence stirred dormant resentment in armed forces and also civilians who revered Matos, as hero of the Revolution.
Oct. 27	Nationalization of oil property begins.
Nov. 30	10th Congress of Cuban Confederation of Labor (CTC). Communist candidates endorsed by Castro are defeated. A little later, officials freely elected by rank-and-file are dismissed by order of Castro and replaced by Castro's appointees. The democratically elected Secretary, David Salvador, is sentenced to 30 year prison term.
Nov. 26	Ernesto Che Guevara (who knows nothing about finance) appointed President of the Bank of Cuba.
Dec. 27	Law 680 tightens press, radio, television, etc., censorship.
Jan. 1, 1960	Vice-President of Council of Ministers of the Soviet Union, Anastas Mikoyan, inaugurates Soviet exhibition in Palace of Fine Arts
Feb. 13	Commercial treaty signed by Mikoyan and Castro grants credit of $100,000,000 and exchanges Cuban sugar for Soviet armaments.
March 16	Establishment of Central Planning Body (JUCEPLAN) to manage economy. Blas Roca, veteran communist leader appointed Director of JUCEPLAN.
April 20	Instituto Superior de Educacion established to indoctrinate teachers with Marxist-Leninist principles.

April 22	Gala Celebration of Lenin's birthday.
May 7	Formal diplomatic relations with Russia established.
May 8	Commandante Rolando Cubela (later mortal enemy of Castro) President of the Federation of University Students (FEU) orders expulsion of anti-communist students from the University of Havana.
June 3	Death Penalty decreed for misappropriation of funds.
June 6	Law 851 decrees nationalization of property. In successive months the property of the Cuban Telephone Co., Cuban Electric Co., three oil companies (Standard, Shell and Texaco) and 21 sugar refineries are nationalized. (By the end of 1960, the state expropriated 11,287 companies, equal to two-thirds of Cuban industry. By March 1961, nationalization totalled 88% of industrial production and 55% of agricultural production.
July 15	Most of the faculty of Havana University resigns in protest over communist party takeover.
Sept. 28	Organization of the Committees for the Defense of the Revolution (CDR) to spy on citizens even in their homes.
October	"...a strike is a counter-revolutionary act in a socialist republic..." (Castro). "...The destiny of the unions is to disappear..." (Guevara). "...the Minister of Labor can take control of any union or federation of unions, dismiss officials and appoint others..." (law 647)
Oct. 13	With nationalization of 376 additional firms and Urban Reform Law (including housing) Castro proclaims the completion of the first phase of the Revolution.
Nov. 7	Gala parade in celebration of anniversary of Russian Revolution with participation of thousands of Russian, Chinese and "socialist" countries' technicians and "advisors."

Nov. 22	Cuban Government predicts that in 1961, production of potatoes, beans, poultry, eggs, corn, and cotton "will have quintupled." Actually, "production between 1958-1963 decreased by 50% (Rene Dumont)
Nov. 30	Cuba and China sign trade agreement. China buys 1,000,000 tons of sugar and extends $50,000,000 credit to Cuba.
Dec. 31	Castro creates Higher Council of Universities headed by Minister of Education to rule universities.
Jan. 1, 1961	2nd anniversary of the Cuban Revolution.
Jan. 3	U.S. severs relations with Cuba.
Jan. 4	"...any counter-revolutionary activity (as defined by the dictators) by any worker, either in the public or private sector, will be sufficient cause for immediate dismissal and additional punishment for criminal acts under the law..." (law 934)
Jan. 21	6 complete factories arrive from Yugoslavia. 100 due to be delivered by Russia. Cuba sends 1000 children to Russia to learn how to become obedient communists. Educational collaboration with Soviet ambassador to Havana, Yuri Gavrilov, and Czechoslovak Vice-Minister of Education, Vaslav Pelishek, to teach Cuban educators methods used in communist lands.
Jan. 29	Cuban Ministry of Education will train teachers in Minar del Frío, a communist school, how to become good Marxist-Leninists.
Feb. 10	Stepped up campaign to mobilize hundreds of thousands of "volunteers" to cut cane and do other important work.
Feb. 23	Guevara appointed Minister of Industry (which he knows nothing about)
April 17	"Bay of Pigs" invasion by unofficial U.S.-sponsored forces.

May 1	Castro proclaims that Cuba has become the first Socialist Republic in Latin America. Thousands parade carrying huge portraits of Castro, José Martí, Khrushchev, Mao, Lenin, Marx and Engels. On being awarded the Lenin peace prize, Castro exults: "GLORY TO THE GREAT JOSÉ MARTÍ!" "GLORY TO THE GREAT VLADIMIR ILYICH LENIN!"
Dec. 2	Castro delivers his "I am a Marxist-Leninist Communist" speech.
March 8, 1962	A forerunner of the Communist Party of Cuba, the Integrated Revolutionary Organizations (ORI) is organized.
March 12	Law 1015 decrees rationing of most foods and other necessities.
July	To combat absenteeism and enforce work discipline the government announces plans to issue in August and September, identification cards which all workers must show as condition for employment... "...thereby guaranteeing full compliance with directives established by the Revolutionary Government as far as labor is concerned..." Ministry of Labor institutes forced labor in Province of Pinar del Río for "...employees who committed transgressions in fulfillment of their functions..."
Aug.-Sept.	Drive against political and social dissenters stepped up. *El Libertario*, organ of the Liberation Association of Cuba (anarcho-syndicalist) forced to suspend publication. Workers threatened with loss of jobs if they do not "volunteer" to work without pay. Students, housewives and others told they will lose benefits if they do not "volunteer" their services. Agricultural cooperatives transformed into state farms.
Spring, 1963	Compulsory service for 15 to 17 year-old "delinquents" decreed to provide a labor force for a wide range of agricultural and civic projects. Formation of the United Party of the Socialist Revolution (PURS)

another version of the future post-Castro Communist Party of Cuba (CPC)

Oct. 4   Second Agrarian Reform restricts ownership of land to five caballerias.

Nov.   For the first time in Cuba compulsory military service is decreed in preference to volunteer service in militia.

Feb. 14, 1964   Castro takes personal charge of INRA.

Summer, 1965   The much vaunted militia, "The People in Arms" is practically liquidated as an independent force. Nationwide disarmament of the militia is decreed. Militia officers and civilians are commanded to turn their weapons in by Sept. 1st or face severe penalties. Members of the military reserve and communities for the Defense of the Revolution must also comply.

July 4   Havana Longshoremen refuse to load meat for Italy because of meat shortage in Cuba. 200 arrested and later released with only stern warnings for fear of further complications.

Oct. 3   Militarily organized labor camps established to rehabilitate "delinquents."
Havana University is again purged. Writers and artists sent to penal camps, ostensibly to "purify the Revolution."

March, 1966   Rolando Cubela (former favorite of Castro) sentenced to 25 years at hard labor for conspiracy to assassinate Castro because he betrayed the Revolution.

Aug. 22-26   12th Congress of the CTC adopts resolution stating that: "...the labor movement directed and guided by the Communist Party, must effectively contribute to the mobilization of the masses in fulfilling of the tasks assigned by the Revolution and strengthening Marxist-Leninist theory..."

1967	Organization of the Vanguard Workers Movement. Like the Stakhanovites in Russia, the Vanguard Workers are expected to set the pace and initiate speedup of their fellow workers. In exchange, Vanguard Workers get special privileges.
	A program of Youth Reeducation Centers established for youngsters under 16 found guilty of minor offenses. They are to perform "a full day's work" and get military training.
Oct. 8	Ché Guevara killed in Bolivia guerrilla campaign.
Jan. 28, 1968	Castro asserts his domination over the Communist Party. Aníbal Escalante, a prominent communist, is sentenced to 15 years at hard labor for plotting to subordinate Castro to the discipline of the Party. He was accused of the typical Stalinist crime of "microfactionalism."
March 13	Castro introduces the "Great Revolutionary Offensive" by nationalizing 58,000 trades, shops and services. Young people are mobilized, military fashion, for agriculture and sugar production.
Aug. 2	Castro defends the Soviet invasion of Czechoslovakia.
Aug. 17	The Minister of Labor, Jorge Risquet, announces introduction of "labor card" recording acts of indiscipline, work record, etc.
Oct. 22	A "social-security law" providing incentives for workers who demonstrate "exemplary" behavior is decreed. Those who exhibit "communist work attitudes," renounce overtime pay, are not absent without authorization, exceed work quotas and enthusiastically perform "voluntary" labor become eligible for special benefits.
Jan. 2, 1969	Castro introduces rationing of sugar!
July 9	Castro praises "revolutionary achievements" of the military totalitarian Junta that seized power in Peru.

Sept. 24	Armando Hart (prominent member of Casto's ruling junta) praises Soviet achievements under Stalin and urges Cubans to follow Stalin's example.
1970	The whole labor force is mobilized (military fashion) for harvesting the 10 million ton sugar crop while the rest of the economy is neglected. The campaign fails and Castro himself takes the blame for setting back the rest of the economy to the lowest levels since the Revolution, declaring that: "...I want to speak of our own incapacity in the overall work of the Revolution...our responsibility to must be noted...especially *mine*...Our apprenticeship as directors of the Revolution has been too costly..."
Sept.	A series of drastic measures to strengthen weak labor discipline enacted by the Labor Ministry and CTC bureaucracy. Sanctions against absentees include denial of right to purchase goods in short supply (new housing, repairs, loss of vacations and other privileges. In extreme cases offenders can be sent to labor camps etc. There is a dossier for each worker which every worker is obliged to show, detailing his work record. Less than half of the workers participate in rigged union elections. Castro's henchmen screen all candidates. In some locals there was only one candidate on the ballot.
March 1971	Dissident poet Herberto Padilla arrested on trumped up charges of "counter-revolution" for writing critical poetry and articles about Cuban dictatorship. Later, in true Stalinist fashion Padilla "repents his sins" and is "rehabilitated." The case aroused world-wide protests.
Dec. 1972	Creation of the super-centralized Executive Committee of the Council of Ministers. Between 1972 and 1975 the institutionalization and

185

	reorganization of the Revolution was being implemented.
Mid-1973	Reform of the judicial system. Courts and all legal bodies dominated and completely responsible to the Executive Committee of the Council of Ministers. There is no independent judiciary. The Prime Minister, the President of the Republic, other ministers, and the members of the Political Bureau of the Communist Party of Cuba are exempt from the jurisdiction of the regular courts.
April	Militias ("People in Arms") abolished.
May	Liability of 18 year olds for "crimes" against the economy, abnormal sexual behavior, etc., etc., applied to 16 year old "offenders."
Aug. 2	Creation of the Youth Army of Work (AYW), a paramilitary organization controlled by the Revolutionary Armed Forces (FAR).
November	13th Congress of the CTC endorses and promises to carry out the dictatorial policies of the Regime.
December	Law 1257 decrees creation of regular, conventional army complete with ranking system and discipline of great military powers.
May 8, 1974	With the establishment of the People's Organization of Popular Control (PCP) an experiment in "decentralization" and "direct democracy" designed to promote mass participation in Local, Regional administration is initiated in Matanzas Province (to be extended to rest of Cuba in 1976). The system patterned after the fake Russian "soviets" actually reinforces the dictatorship.
July 2	Castro proclaims 3 days of mourning for the death of the fascist dictator of Argentina Juan Perón. With Congress of the Communist Party of Cuba (Dec. 1975) the institutionalization of the Revolution was substantially completed. The permanent, legally sanctioned, totalitarian apparatus inflicts itself on future generations.

Glossary

ALC	Libertarian Federation of Cuba
MLCE	Libertarian Movement of Cuba in Exile
CNT	National Confederation of Labor (Spanish Anarcho-Syndicalist)
IWMA	International Workingmen's Association

(Abbreviations of Cuban organizations with date of founding)

CDR	Committees for the Defense of the Revolution, 1960
CTC	Confederation of Cuban Workers, 1939
EJT	Youth Army of Work, 1973
FAR	Revolutionary Armed Forces, 1961
INRA	National Institute of Agrarian Reform, 1959
JUCEPLAN	Central Planning Board, 1960
OPP	Organs of Popular Power, 1974
ORI	Integrated Revolutionary Organizations, 1961-1963
PCC	Communist Party of Cuba, 1965
PSP	Socialist Popular Party, 1925-1961
PURS	United Party of the Socialist Revolution, 1963-1965
SMO	Compulsory Military Service, 1963
SS	Compulsory Social Service, 1973
UMAP	Military Units to Aid Production, 1964-1973
UNEAC	National Union of Writers and Artists of Cuba, 1961
UJC	Young Communist League, 1962

Bibliographical Notes

A full bibliography of writings on the background of the Cuban Revolution and the Revolution itself would easily fill several volumes. It is therefore necessary to list such works in English as seems best for the general reader.

Interestingly enough, the sources are the speeches and writings of Castro and members of his inner circle (official government publications, periodicals, newspapers etc.) Another excellent source is the works of the pro-Castro friendly critics. Both the Cuban officials in the process of justifying their dictatorial measures and the friendly critics in trying to account for the degeneration of the Revolution inadvertently supply valuable information about the nature of the Cuban Revolution.

Official Sources

Castro's speeches and writings are easily available—a convenient compilation is *The Selected Works of Fidel Castro: Revolutionary Struggle;* Rolando Bonachea and Nelson P. Valdes (M.I.T. Press, Cambridge, 1971—First of three volumes.)

John Gerassi, *Venceremos! The Speeches and Writings of Ché Guervara* (New York, 1968.)

Ché Guevara, *Episodes of the Revolutionary Struggle* (Book Institute, Havana, 1967.) An invaluable, intimate first-hand account of the early struggles of Castro's guerrilla band in the Sierra Maestra.

Granma Weekly Review (English Language Edition)—official organ of the Communist Party of Cuba. Good for current events, official notices, proclamations, etc.

Other Background and Source Materials

Cuban Studies Newsletter; published twice yearly by the Center for Latin American Studies; University of Pittsburgh. Contains many informative articles, theses and other writings.

The University of Miami's *Center for Research on Caribbean Studies;* also the *Cuban Economic Research Project*, an excellent research staff manned by Cuban specialists.

Yale University's *Antilles Program.*

Center for Cuban Studies, New York.

United Nations publications.

Background to Revolution; a collection of essays on Cuban history leading to the Cuban Revolution. A good general survey by competent authorities (Edited by Robert F. Smith, New York, 1966).

Jaime Suchlicki, *From Columbus to Castro*, New York, 1974; also his excellent collection of essays by ten specialists; (University of Miami, 1972). Suchlicki's works are particularly important because he participated in the Revolutionary Students' Movement in his native Cuba.

Although Hugh Thomas' massive history *The Pursuit of Freedom* has been widely acclaimed, his atrocious work on the Spanish Civil War (1936-1939) should be borne in mind when reading his Cuban volume.

Personal Accounts

Jules Dubois' *Fidel Castro;* (Indianapolis, 1959). Dubois, late correspondent for the Chicago Tribune, interviewed and was on very cordial terms with Fidel Castro and associates. An excellent account of events from Castro's landing in Cuba, to the fall of Batista, plus interesting biographical data.

Herbert Matthews, New York Times correspondent who first interviewed Castro in the Sierra Maestre, was welcomed to Cuba several times since then. Matthews has written extensively on the Cuban Revolution. Among his writings are: *Fidel Castro;* (New York, 1959) and *Cuba in Revolution;* (New York, 1975). Though strongly biased in favor of Castro, the latter work contains valuable information.

Rufo López Fresquet: *My First Fourteen Months With Castro;* (New York, 1966) and Andrés Suarez, *Castroism and Communism: 1959-1966;* (MIT Press, Cambridge, 1967). Both Fresquet, former Minister of the Treasury in Castro's cabinet, and Suárez, the Assistant Minister of the Treasury, broke with Castro because they disagreed with his pro-communist policies. Their revelations contribute greatly to an understanding of the Cuban Revolution.

Under the intriguing title, *Does Your Father Eat More Than Castro?* (New York, 1971), Barry Reckord, a Jamaica dramatist, describes the daily life of ordinary Cubans, and in so doing, tells more about the effects of the Cuban Revolution than any number of abstract statistical studies. The same is true of the journalist, Joe Nicholson Junior's *Inside Cuba* (New York, 1974.)

Critical Studies

Fidel Castro's Personal Revolution: 1959-1973 (New York, 1975); an anthology edited by James Nelson Goodsell, is a good general survey.

Adolfo Gilly's *Inside the Cuban Revolution* (New York, 1964), although passionately pro-Castro, is nevertheless a penetrating critique.

In his *Castro's Revolution: Myths and Realities* (New York, 1962), Theodor Draper dispels the euphoria surrounding both the character and achievements of the Cuban Revolution. A realistic analysis. His *Castroism: Theory and Practice* (New York, 1965) develops his themes more fully.

K.S. Karol's *Guerrillas in Power* (New York, 1970)—Karol, a Marxist-Leninist writer who was welcomed to Cuba by Castro, was later excommunicated for his critical insights and revelations about the unfavorable features of the Cuban Revolution. His work constitutes an able political history of the Cuban Revolution, far superior to Huberman and Sweezy's *Socialism in Cuba* (New York, 1969).

Maurice Halperin's *The Rise and Decline of Fidel Castro* (University of California Press, 1972) deals primarily with the complex relations between Castro and the Soviet Union and foreign affairs. His observations on the situation in Cuba itself enhance the work. Halperin taught at the University of Havana for six years and in Russia for three years. His is one of the better works.

The analytic books of Rene' Dumont: *Cuba: Socialism and*

Development (New York, 1970) and *Is Cuba Socialist?* (New York, 1974), and the painstakingly researched work of Carmelo Mesa-Lago, *Cuba in the 1970s* (University of New Mexico, 1974) have already been discussed and need no further comment.

Education
  anarcho-syndicalist program for,
    137-38
  before Castro, 68, 106
  under Castro, 85-88, 90, 106-12, 128,
    167, 176, 181
EJT (Youth Army of Work), 168, 171-72
Emigration from Cuba under Castro, 77,
  117
Engels, Friedrich, 155, 156
Ensayo Obrera (periodical), 3
Escalante, Anibal, 65, 164, 184
Estavalora, Salvador, 113
Esteve, Pedro, 39
Estrada Palma, Tomás, 42
Estudios (periodical), 54
Executions under Castro, 11-12

Family, anarcho-syndicalists on, 137-38
Federación Anarquista del Mexico
  (FAM), 46
Federación de Grupos Anarquistas de
  Cuba, 46, 48
Federación Estudantil Universitaria
  (F.E.U.), 60, 107, 108, 109-12
Federación Libertario Argentina (FLA),
  141-42, 146, 149-52
Federación Local de La Paz, 2
Federación Obrera Regional Argentina
  (FORA), 1, 2
Federación Obrera Regional Paraguaya, 1
Federación Regional Obrera (Puerto
  Rico), 3
Federalism
  vs. bureaucratic centralism, 138-39
  in Spanish anarcho-syndicalism, 32-33
Federation of Anarchist Groups (Federa-
  ción de Grupos Anarquistas de
  Cuba), 46, 48
Federation of Food, Hotel and Restaurant
  Workers of the Province of
  Oriente, 131
Federation of Medical Workers, 133
Federation of University Students, *see*
  Federación Estudantil Universitaria
Fernández, José, 74
Ferrer y Ferrer, José, 3
Finch, Roy, 112-115
First International, 1, 3, 31
FOH, *see* Havana Federation of Labor
Food and Agricultural Organization
  (FAO), 66, 157
Food rationing, 157, 158, 168, 182

Food riots, 69
Food Workers Union, 113, 121
FORA, *see* Federación Obrera Regional
  Argentina
Franco, Francisco, 12, 79, 116-17
Frank, Waldo, 5-7
Freedom, individual and collective, 139
Freedom of speech, 176
Fresquet, Rufo López, 189
Fundora, Gerardo, 114

Gadea, Hilda, 27
Garciá, Alberto, 132-33
Garciá, Mario, 60
Garciá, Rafael, 41
Garciá, Salvador, 116-17
Gastronomica (periodical), 43
Gavrilov, Yuri, 181
General strikes, 39, 43, 48
  Castro's call for, 92
General Confederation of Labor (Work-
  ers), *see* Confederación General de
  Trabajadores (Cuba)
Gerona, Manuel, 60
Gilly, Adolfo, 7-8, 189
Gómez, José Miguel, 42, 43
Gómez, Maximo, 40
González, Eduardo, 38
Government, Castro's
  Constitution of, 176-77
  1973 reorganization of, 161-63
  as oligarchic, 96-98, 148, 174
Granma (newspaper), 15-16, 69, 101-2,
  165
Grau San Martin, Ramón, 46, 51, 52
Great Revolutionary Offensive (Castro's),
  184
"Grito Yara, El," 40
Guantánamo Bay naval base, 42
Guatemala, anarcho-syndicalists in, 2
Guerra, Ramiro, 63-64
Guevara, Alfredo, 108
Guevara, Ernesto Ché, 11, 97, 106, 112,
  164
  death of, 184
  economic rule of, 12, 179-81
  as guerrilla in Cuba, 74-76, 92
  "New Man" of, 153-54
  Perón and, 27
Guilbert, Yves, 77, 119-21
Guzmán, Father, 91

Hacia la Libertad, 2

Long hair, 168
López, Alfredo, 46, 47
Lorenzo, Anselmo, 33
Lozana, Gonzales, 43
Luz y Libertad, 2

Maceo, Antonio, 40
Machado, Gerardo, 46-49, 52, 106, 131
Madan, Pablo, 60
Malatesta, Errico, 42-43
Management Councils, 171
Mao Tse-tung, 21
"March on Havana," 91-93
Mariana Grajales Women's Battalions,
    104
Marinello, Juan, 53, 97, 107, 108, 111,
    126
Marks, Herman, 11
Martí, José, 25, 38, 111
Marx, Karl, 15, 37, 108, 155, 156
"Mas Luz" Library, 57
Massetti, Jorge, 27
Matthews, Herbert, 9-13, 27, 71, 74,
    155-57, 166, 173, 187
Matos, Huber, 12, 92, 94, 179
MCLE, see Cuban Libertarian Movement
    in Exile
Mell, Oscar Fernández, 171-72
Mendez, Plácido, 60, 131
Menocal, Mario García, 46
Mesa-Lago, Carmelo, 27, 66, 155, 157,
    159-60, 167-68
Messinier, Enrique, 37, 39
Mexico, anarcho-syndicalism in, 2, 146
"Micro-factionalism," 164, 184
Mikoyan, Anastas, 85, 111, 179
Milian, Arnaldo, 101
Militarism
    anarcho-syndicalists on, 138
    by Castro, 27-28, 75, 104-6, 172-74
    State and, 26, 27
Militarization, 17, 75, 90, 103-6, 154
    of agriculture, 17-18, 82
    of education, 86-88, 106-12, 128
    of labor, 105, 171-72
    of youth, 186
Militia, 104, 172, 183, 186
Mills, C. Wright, 68
Miners Union, 59
Miró Cardona, José, 92, 94, 178
"Mini-Stalin Era," 154
Monati Sugar Company, 44
Moncada Barracks assault, 54, 60, 71,

155-56, 163
Moncada cooperative, 82-83
Moneda General Strike, 43
Montero y Sarria (anarchist), 43, 126
Monthly Review (journal), 7, 8, 18
Moscu, Isidro, 60
Movimiento Libertario Cubana en el
    Exilio, see Cuban Libertarian Move-
    ment in Exile
Movimiento Libertario de Brasil, 144-46
Mujal, Eusebio, 125
Muller, Alberto, 111
Muller, Juan, 111
Mundo Ideal, El (periodical), 42
Municipal Agrarian Association, 56
Muriel, Justo, 61
Mussolini, Benito, 81, 91, 92

National Institute of Agrarian Reform
    (INRI), 17, 81-86, 90, 112, 162, 178
    183
National Confederation of Cuban Work-
    ers (CNOC), 45-49
National Confederation of Labor, see
    Confederación Nacional del Trabajo
National Institute of Social Security, 26
Nationalism, anarcho-syndicalists on, 138
Nationalization, 6, 84, 90, 179, 180
    socialism vs., 23
Naturist Association, 57
Naval Base at Cienfuegos, 72, 73
Navy, Castro's, 174
Nelson, Lowery, 157
Nettlau, Max, 2, 31
New Left Review (journal), 18
"New Man," 153-54
New York Times (newspaper), 9-10, 101,
    155
News Bulletin of the International Union
    of Food and Allied Workers, 100
Newspapers
    anarchist, 121-33
    Castro and, 119-22, 129, 176
    See also Censorship
Nicalau, Ramón, 108
Nicaragua, 2
Nicholson, Joe, Jr., 158, 168, 189
Nikirov, Boris, 3
Novikov, Vladimir, 155
Nueva Aurora (periodical), 45
Nueva Luz (magazine), 45

Obrera Revolucionario, 60

196

ACKNOWLEDGMENTS

Although I am solely responsible for the contents of this work, I gratefully acknowledge the cooperation of the Cuban Libertarian Movement-In-Exile, Miami; The International Institute Of Social History, Amsterdam; The International Center For Research On Anarchism, Geneva; all of whom supplied invaluable data.

I wish to express my deep appreciation to my friends Chuck Hamilton, Free Life Editions; Dimitri Roussopoulos, Black Rose Books; for their unstinting cooperation in the production and distribution of this book; and both Bob Palmer and Bruce Elwell who volunteered to compose the index.

This book could not have been published without the generous financial aid of Arthur Bartell; The Libertarian Book Club; The Groupo Libertario of Detroit; the fellow workers of Portland, Oregon and the many friends and comrades as well as the encouragement of my wife Esther. All of them have earned my undying gratitude.

I am also indebted to my friend, Dr. Paul Avrich, who read the manuscript and made valuable suggestions.

WORKING IN CANADA

edited by
Walter Johnson

Walter Johnson has been working since he was seventeen years of age. During the last seven years he was working on the assembly-line at General Motors, in St. Therese. He came to certain conclusions about the workplace and Canadian society. Having received a Canada Council to put together a book of his experience, he sought out other young workers to see whether there was some commonality to his feelings and thoughts.

Working in Canada is a collection of experiences written or interviews of young working people about what they do and feel on a day to day basis and what they think needs to be done to change their condition and that of other working people.

Walter Johnson has had articles published in *Canadian Forum*, and *Our Generation*.

225 pages / Hardcover $10.95 / Paperback $3.95
ISBN : 0-919618-64-2 / ISBN : 0-919618-63-4

Contains: Canadian Shared Cataloguing in Publication Data

BLACK ROSE BOOKS No E 25

THE BOLSHEVIKS AND WORKERS' CONTROL 1917-1921

by Maurice Brinton

Workers' control is again widely discussed and widely researched. This book has two main aims. It seeks to contribute new factual material to the current discussion on workers' control. And it attempts a new kind of analysis of the fate of the Russian Revolution. The two objectives, as will be shown, are inter-related.

An impressive array of documentation is brought to bear on how the Bolshevik State related to the whole question of self-management in revolutionary Russia. Sources are used which have never before been so inter-related and interpreted within such a profound and original analysis. This book has great significance today especially for those who are interested in a historical understanding of the question of a democracy of participation and popular control.

100 pages | Hardcover $10.95 | Paper back $2.95
ISBN: 0-919618-70-7 / ISBN: 0-919618-69-3

Contains: Canadian Shared Cataloguing in Publication Data

BLACK ROSE BOOKS No. E 23

THE UNKNOWN REVOLUTION 1917-1921

by Voline

Introduction by Rudolph Rocker

This famous history of the revolution in Russia and its aftermath has been long out of print. The present edition combined the previous two-volume English-language edition plus omitted material from later editions. It is a complete translation of La revolution inconnue, first published in French in 1947, and re-published in Paris in 1969 by Editions Pierre Belfond.

Voline was both a social historian and educator during this period as well as an active revolutionary. He writes and researches this history from a point of view which covers the achievements of ordinary people and not of this political party or other. It is a libertarian analysis written by a famous anarchist, and a kind of history not read in our schools.

717 pages, illustrated /Hardcover $16.95/Paperback $4.95

ISBN : 0-919618-26-X/ISBN : 0-919618-25-1

BLACK ROSE BOOKS No. E 29

DURRUTI :
THE PEOPLE
ARMED

by Abel Paz

translated by
Nancy MacDonald

Forty years of fighting, of exile, of jailings, of living underground, of strikes, and of insurrection, Buenaventura Durruti, the legendary Spanish revolutionary (1896-1936) lived many lives.

Uncompromising anarchist, intransigent revolutionary, he travelled a long road from rebellious young worker to the man who refused all bureaucratic positions, honours, awards, and who at death was mourned by millions of women and men. Durruti believed and lived his belief that revolution and freedom were inseparable.

This book is the story of Durruti and also a history of the Spanish revolution. It is more than theoretical, it is a rich and passionate documentary, of a man and an epoch.

551 pages | Hardcover $12.95 | Paperback $4.95
ISBN: 0-919618-73-1 / ISBN: 0-919618-74-X

Date of Publication: Fall 1976

Contains: Canadian Shared Cataloguing in Publication Data

BLACK ROSE BOOKS No. F 28

THE ANARCHIST COLLECTIVES

Workers' Self-Management in Spain 1936-39

edited by
Sam Dolgoff

"Although there is a vast literature on the Spanish Civil War, this is the first book in English that is devoted to the experiments in workers' self-management, both urban and rural, which constituted one of the most remarkable social revolutions in modern history."

— Prof. Paul Avrich, Princeton University

"The eyewitness reports and commentary presented in this highly important study reveal a very different understanding of the nature of socialism and the means for achieving it."

— Prof. Noam Chomsky, M.I.T. University

194 pages with illustrations | Hardcover $10.95 | Paperback $3.95   ISBN: 0-919618-20-0
ISBN: 0-919618-21-9

BLACK ROSE BOOKS C. 14

QUEBEC AND RADICAL SOCIAL CHANGE

edited by
Dimitrios
Roussopoulos

This collection of essays drawn from the Canadian quarterly journal, OUR GENERATION which was founded in 1961 covers a wide range of social questions. The journal is well-known for its outstanding contribution to the publication of important material on the evolution of Québec society. These essays have not appeared elsewhere in English when published over the years in the journal, and are brought all together in this volume for the first time.

The essays deal with nationalism, the role of intellectuals in society, the trade union movement, an analysis of various important elections, the contribution of students and youth, the question of class, and related questions.

Among the contributors are included: Marcel Rioux, Hélène David, Louis Maheu, Adèle Lauzon, Robert Favreau, Mario Dumais, Serge Carlos, Jean Laliberté, and others.

225 pages / Hardcover $10.95 / Paperback $3.95
ISBN 0-919618-52-9 / ISBN: 0-919618-51-0

Contains: Canadian Shared Cataloguing in Publication Data

BLACK ROSE BOOKS No. E 17

THE KRONSTADT UPRISING

by Ida Mett
with a preface by
Murray Bookchin

The full story at last of the monumental 1921 events: the first workers' uprising against the Soviet bureaucracy. This book contains hitherto unavailable documents and a bibliography.

The book is in effect a different kind of history. It is written from a perspective that is concerned with the *people* as the primary social force in changing society and not leaders, conventions, manifestos and the like.

Murray Bookchin puts this recently translated book from the French into its contemporary setting.

2nd Edition

100 pages | Paperback $1.45 | Hardcover $5.45
ISBN: 0-919618-13-8 / ISBN: 0-919618-19-7

BLACK ROSE BOOKS No. B 3

LUCY PARSONS
American Revolutionary
BY CAROLYN ASHBAUGH

Lucy Parson, 1853 to 1942, was called "the tramp's friend." From her Black and Mexican-Indian heritage she forged a commitment to advance the rights of the disinherited — the workers, the unemployed and the targets of racial and sexual oppression. This important new work about a central figure in the Haymarket affair and in the development of Chicago was published in cooperation with the Illinois Labour History Society.

041 / 225 pages / Hardcover $12.00 / $4.95 Paperback

MAN — AN ANTHOLOGY OF ANARCHIST IDEAS, ESSAYS, POETRY AND COMMENTARIES
EDITED BY MARCUS GRAHAM

Drawn from the magazine MAN which appeared for seven and a half years in the USA between the wars. It was a milestone in the history of anarchist thought and ideas. Graham who worked as a garment worker was arrested many times, threatened with deportation and beaten by police. As this collection shows, MAN maintained a high quality of political journalism throughout its history.

042 / 637 pages / Paperback $7.95

Printed by
the workers of
Éditions Marquis, Montmagny, Qué.
for
Black Rose Books Ltd.

Behavioural Studies for Marketing and Business

FRANK SPOONCER

HUTCHINSON

London Melbourne Auckland Johannesburg

Hutchinson Education

An imprint of Century Hutchinson Ltd
62–65 Chandos Place, London WC2N 4NW

Century Hutchinson, Australia Pty Ltd
89–91 Albion Street, Surry Hills,
New South Wales 2010

Century Hutchinson New Zealand Limited
PO Box 40-086, Glenfield, Auckland 10,
New Zealand

Century Hutchinson South Africa (Pty) Ltd
PO Box 337, Bergvlei, 2012 South Africa

First published in 1989
© F. Spooncer 1989
Set in
by Activity Ltd., Salisbury, Wiltshire
Printed in Great Britain by Scotprint, Musselburgh

British Library Cataloguing in Publication Data
Spooncer, Frank A.
  Behavioural studies for marketing and
  business.
  1. marketing. Psychological aspects
  I. Title
  658.8′001′9

ISBN 0–09–172973–4

Dear Student...

With courses becoming more and more intensive there is a greater need for students to have *precise study information* available so that they can study more efficiently and speedily.

At the same time this enables *tutors* to devote more effort towards the understanding and analysis of the subject. Rather than give up valuable time dictating and providing notes, they can concentrate more on actively involving students in the learning process.

In this text the authors have covered all aspects of coursework providing:

- A comprehensive text on the subject
- Study and exam tips on each topic
- Self assessment tests
- Past examination questions
- Specimen answers to selected questions
- Answers to self assessment tests

The combination of these elements will greatly improve your confidence and performance in the examinations.

Frank Spooner

Contents

General study and exam tips

"In many situations information is so great a part of effectiveness that without information a really clever person cannot get started. With information a much less clever person can get very far." Dr Edward De Bono.

Being successful on a course does not simply result from listening to lectures or reading a textbook. You must become actively involved in the learning process in order to acquire knowledge and skills and perform well in assessments.

There is no reason why you cannot achieve this aim. After all you are on a course of study because an examining authority believes that you have the necessary ability to complete the course successfully. If you are prepared to become actively involved and do the work required, you have every right to feel confident that you can succeed in the final examinations.

These notes are designed to make your study more efficient, to ensure that you use this manual to best advantage and to help you improve both your coursework and your examination techniques. They have been divided into four parts:

1 general study tips
2 improving the quality of your work
3 examination technique
4 studying with this text

■ 1 GENERAL STUDY TIPS

An eminent physicist once said: 'Thinking is 99 per cent perspiration and 1 per cent inspiration'. Take his advice and that of most of us who have had the benefit of a good education. Ignore the advice of those who believe you can prepare yourself for the examination in one or two weeks. Knowledge and skills of any value are not easily learned. For most of us it takes time to understand and permanently remember the content of a subject; instead of forgetting everything immediately the examinations are over. Therefore start working at studying right at the very start of your course and continue at a steady pace until the examinations. Do all the work expected of you by your tutor including homework and mock/mid term examinations. Homework is good practice and the mock exams simulate aspects of the final examination. Doing them as best as you can makes your tutor more willing to help you, as he or she will see that you are playing your part in the learning process.

The knowledge and skills you will gain on your course of study are precisely the kind needed by professional business people. So approach the study of each subject as if you were in real life a business man or woman, or a person following a profession such as accountancy or law. In this way the subject should come alive for you, and your motivation to learn should increase.

To help realise this objective, read a quality daily and Sunday newspaper that has a good business section. By doing this you will discover what is happening on a day-to-day basis and be in a better position to understand the topics you are studying on the course. You will also broaden and deepen your knowledge of the subject. Professional people at work usually read a quality newspaper and monthly or quarterly periodical related directly to their discipline in order to keep abreast of the latest developments. You will probably wish to do the same when you commence work, so why not start now?

Carry a pocket dictionary with you and look up words you hear or read but do not understand. None of us has a complete vocabulary but we can improve it if we really want to be able to read and study more effectively. In the case of students it is even more important because words used in lectures, textbooks or newspapers often become misused in examinations. Some words which cause problems with their meaning or spelling are:

aggregate	disseminate	heterogeneous
antithesis	distinguish	homogeneous
constituent	evaluate	panacea
discipline	facsimile	prognosis

Do you fully understand how these words may be used in the context of your subject? Use a dictionary.

As soon as you start your course, find out if you are going to be given past examination reports for your subject, examiners reports, specimen answers to previous examination questions and a work scheme. It is probable that they will not all be available at your school, college or university or even from the examining authority. You should, however, obtain as much information about your course of study and the examinations as possible so you know exactly what amount of work lies ahead of you and the academic standard you are expected to reach. This will help in planning your personal workload for the period of your course.

If you do not understand something ask your tutor. Do not assume that you are inadequate because you did not understand something that other students seemed to appreciate. They may be having difficulties too or your lecturer may simply not have explained the point to everyone's satisfaction. If something is overlooked by the tutor, don't be afraid to bring it to his/her attention.

Personal health is something that many students dismiss with comments such as: 'what has health got to do with ability to think?' Studies on the topic have now clearly indicated that general health and mental performance are statistically related. Within four weeks of being given multi vitamin and mineral tablets students in two separate controlled studies improved upon their written performance in intelligence tests by approximately ten points. Your common-sense alone should tell you that you cannot perform at your best if you continually feel tired or have flu or a heavy cold in an examination. Eat a varied diet that includes protein foods, vegetables and fruit, and get some daily exercise even if it is only a good brisk walk home after your day's study.

Contrary to the belief of many students, the best academic work is not done at night-time. Once again research shows that students perform better in the early part of the week, in the daytime – particularly mornings – and in a place where there is natural daylight to read and write by. Therefore plan your study schedule so that it is completed in the day. This will also leave you the evenings and weekends free to relax and enjoy yourself.

■ 2 IMPROVING THE QUALITY OF YOUR WORK

The earlier in the course you bring your work to a satisfactory standard the more likely you are to exhibit a good standard of work in the examinations. Obviously, academic standards do relate to the thinking abilities of the student but they also depend on motivation, and a logical approach to one's work if effective presentation at the appropriate academic standard is to be achieved. Here are three tips that will help you develop a logical approach to the presentation of your work.

Read the question carefully

When undertaking essay or numerical work make sure you read the question very carefully. Underline the key words in the question so that your mind is concentrated on the essential aspects. For example, distinguish between the two main types of question.

DESCRIPTIVE QUESTIONS
A descriptive question is one in which you will be expected to describe or explain something and possibly distinguish it from alternative or similar items or ideas. Two examples are:

(a) *Describe* and *distinguish above-the-line advertising* from other forms of *advertising*.
(b) *Explain* with the *aid of graphs, how the price* of a product is *determined* in a highly *competitive economy*.

Some of the key words have been emphasised in italics to give you an idea of which words are at the heart of the question. Always underline or highlight the key words yourself before attempting to answer.

ANALYTICAL QUESTIONS

These include the purely analytical question, or the analytical question that requires you to evaluate a statement (indicate your level of support for an idea/give it a value) or only to present your own ideas. Examples of these are:

(a) *Solely analytical*: Analyse the contention that there is no such thing as fixed costs.

(b) *Analytical and Evaluative*: How far do you support the idea that adult behaviour is predominantly related to one's early childhood experiences?

If you have been presented with a minicase (short story) or case study (extended story) detailing opposing opinions regarding a problem a company is faced with, you may be requested to offer your own solution. In this event your answer should analyse the value of all the opinions offered in the case as well as possibly suggesting your own.

Consider also the way a question is structured. If it is in two or more parts give equal time to each if equal marks are awarded to each part. If more marks are awarded to one part than another, allocate your time in the same proportions as the marks awarded. For example, if a Question has marks awarded: part (a) 5 marks, part (b) 15 marks (total 20 marks), you should spend a quarter (5/20) of your time answering (a) and three quarters (15/20) on (b).

Sometimes the time you should allocate to a part of a question is indicated by the implied requirements of the question, rather than by marks. For example

Q1 (a) Briefly outline 'actual' and 'ostensible' authority.

(b) Brown and Brown Ltd contracted with a married woman for the laying of new carpets. After the work had been done, the woman's husband refuted the contract and refused to pay for the carpets. Advise Brown and Brown Ltd and the woman on their legal position.

By using the words 'briefly outline' the examiner is indicating that much less time should be spent on answering part (a). The question requires more marks to be awarded to part (b) as the analytical and applied nature of this part indicates that it is more difficult to answer.

With numerical type questions, such as in accountancy and statistics, do not assume that all you have to do is arrive at the right answer. Your tutor – or an examiner – will expect you to explain what you are doing as you introduce each set of workings, graphs, illustrations or tables. After all, how is your tutor to know how you arrived at the right answer if you do not explain? Even more importantly, even if you give the wrong answer, at least you will be given some marks for those parts of your calculation which are correct. Such subjects involve a large element of communication and if you do not communicate effectively in your answer what you are doing you will lose marks.

Construct an essay plan

Always spend a few minutes constructing an essay plan before answering a question. This only requires jotting down a few notes for each paragraph which indicates the approach you will take to your answer and the points you will include. This will make sure that you construct your essay in a logical manner and that you keep to a target when writing your answer.

Follow up with your tutor

To understand fully what is required when answering questions, ask your tutor about the work you have handed in and had marked if he or she has not commented sufficiently on your script, informing you of where you were right and wrong and why.

■ 3 EXAMINATION TECHNIQUE

If you are studying at college you can start improving your examination technique in the mock/mid term examination which will help you in the coursework assessment during the second half of the course as well as in the final examination. Here are a few tips on improving your presentation.

- *Always do rough workings*. Use essay plans and/or numerical workings to plan your answer, but on a page other than the one on which you start your answer to the question. Cross through your rough working before starting to answer the question.
- Select the questions you intend to answer and *start with the one you think you will find the easiest* to answer. In this way you may gain your highest marks early in the exam which is very important in case you do not complete the examination.
- *Keep an eye on the clock* so that you allow about the same amount of time for answering each question (unless one is a more difficult, compulsory question). Noting the time in order to complete all the questions you are required to answer gives you a better chance of achieving high marks.
- Allow at least a third to half a page for illustrations or diagrams. In this way they look like illustrations rather than scribblings and you have sufficient space available if you have to return to your illustration to add more detail later in the examination. Always explain what your illustration is supposed to illustrate.
- Unless otherwise instructed, use a complete page of graph paper for presenting graphs and make sure that you provide a title for any entries you have made. Explain what your graph illustrates.
- Do not present workings for numerical subjects such as accounts and statistics without explaining what you are doing and why.

If you would like a deeper understanding of study skills and exam techniques a useful book containing a wealth of tips and examples that will help you to succeed in examinations is *How To Pass Exams* by W. G. Leader, also published by Hutchinson.

4 STUDYING WITH THIS TEXT

Hutchinson's student texts have been specifically designed to act as study aids for students while on a course, as well as present the contents of a subject in a way that is both interesting and informative.

Use this text as part of your study activities, adding your own or your tutor's notes at appropriate points. Study your textbook in great detail, making notes on the chief points in each chapter so that the ideas have gone through your own head and down onto the paper in your own words – though perhaps with key quotations from the text.

Don't get bogged down in any one chapter. If you really can't follow the chapter leave it and go on to the next, returning at a later date. What seems difficult at the start of your course in September will be easier by December and child's play by March! You are going to develop as you do the course – so don't give up too early. Perseverance is everything in acquiring professional status.

Do not just read the specimen answers provided at the end of certain sections. Study their content and structure in the light of what you learned earlier in the particular section and what you learned in this section. In this way your skill in answering questions set by your tutor and/or the examination should improve.

At the end of each section there are examples of past examination questions. Where the answer is to be in essay form jot down beside the question the major points that you think should have been highlighted when answering. Then check back with the appropriate text of the particular section to see if your answer would have been correct. If you are still uncertain, discuss the problem with your tutor.

Talking with the tutor and fellow students is essential for developing the ability to analyse problems.

Always complete the self assessment part of each chapter as they are designed to reinforce what you have learned and improve your recall of the topics. Check your answers with those provided in the manual. As repetition of a process improves one's memory, it is very useful to re-test yourself every few weeks or let someone else read the questions to you and tell you if you got them right.

If the subject covered by the particular manual involves value judgements do not assume that what is mentioned in the manual is the only correct version. Your tutor may have other opinions which are just as valid. What matters is that you have sufficient knowledge of the subject to illustrate a firm understanding of the topic in the examinations.

One of the best ways to study is to buy a lever arch file and make dividing pages from brown paper for each subject or chapter. File your notes, and your essays and any newspaper cuttings, articles, etc. that are relevant in the appropriate topic position. You will then have an easy to revise and lively set of notes. If you find it a bit bulky to carry, use a ring binder instead and then at the end of every week or two weeks transfer the notes you have made to the lever arch file, keeping it at home for safety.

Now that you have read these Study and Exam Tips you should feel confident to continue with your studies and succeed in the examinations. It just remains for ourselves and Hutchinson to wish you every success on your course.

1 Behavioural studies and marketing

In order to become a bullfighter, it is first necessary to become a bull. Old Spanish proverb.

■ INTRODUCTION

Glance into a supermarket after closing time, and you will see a complex picture of rows of packages on shelves, checkout tills lying idle, advertisements on walls, endless trolleys stacked together, but no movement, no action.

Return when the store is open, and you will see it full of people, and full of action. Lorries are arriving with new supplies, employees are filling gaps on shelves, customers are considering and selecting. By the cereal shelves, a customer is looking for a particular brand recommended by a friend and demanded by her children while another moves purposefully forward, selects the brand her family have eaten for years and goes determinedly on her way.

At the checkouts the operators are hard at work, sometimes taking cash, sometimes cheques, sometimes credit cards, as the customer chooses. One operator's queue is rapidly getting longer as she struggles with the technology around her. A supervisor sees the difficulty, opens up a relief checkout, and gives a few words of advice. Meanwhile, she wonders how to solve the long term problem of supplying better checkout service for the customers.

Away from the store, at the central headquarters, there is also plenty of action. A new promotion is being planned for an own-brand product, and copy and illustrations are being examined. The search is on for the best form of presentation for the type of customer the store attracts. Buyers and buying groups are coming to decisions, sometimes routine, as for fresh supplies of a well-tried product, sometimes exceptional, perhaps for lifts to be installed at a new outlet.

Products without people are lifeless. It is people who bring them to life. People produce products, people present, sell and distribute products, and people buy and consume products. It makes sense therefore for marketers to be aware of how and why people behave as they do as individuals, in groups and as members of organisations.

These topics are amongst the subject matter of the sciences which study human behaviour: the **behavioural sciences**. Though they may examine much more general issues than those involved in marketing, they can illuminate the everyday scenes described above.

The people-product relation outlined has been aptly summarised by the statement that *marketing is about people, not products*.[1] If we look at such events as an American Presidential election, or Bob Geldof's work for Live Aid and famine relief, it will remind us that the products involved in this interchange are not only objects, but include people, ideas and services. With that in mind, we can use the definition as a good start to our behavioural studies.

Modern marketing demands a sound knowledge of how people behave not only as customers – **consumer behaviour** – but also as members of organisations – **organisational behaviour**. This book will introduce you to some of the behavioural studies and theories most relevant to marketing. You should not expect them to provide an instant solution to all marketing problems. Rather, they will provide a framework which, with experience, you will adjust to fit your own needs.

In this first section, the nature of the behavioural sciences and the contributions they can make to marketing will be the major theme.

■ WHAT ARE THE BEHAVIOURAL SCIENCES?

As an introduction to behavioural studies, let's first look at one or two simple experiments.

EXAMPLE 1.1   NOW YOU SEE IT, NOW YOU DON'T

Have a glance at Fig. 1.1. What do you see?

Fig. 1.1

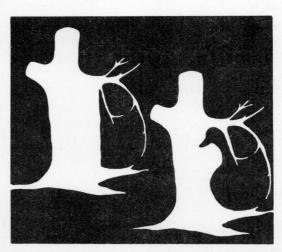

Probably you see two trees. Look again. There's something else there. Got it? Try the right hand side of the right hand tree. There's a creature hiding there. (If you still haven't found it, the answer is a duck.)

This may not seem at first to have much to do with marketing. But what the 'experiment' shows is in fact of considerable relevance. It demonstrates that we select part of a visual presentation, and see that as a figure standing out from a background. But under other circumstances, a different part can be the prominent figure and hold our attention. Marketers want to be sure that the image or message they intend stands out for the viewer and doesn't become part of the background. They therefore need to know what makes part of a picture or message stand out, and whether everyone will interpret it in the same way. If there *are* individual differences in selection and understanding, it would help to know what causes them. These points are examined in Chapter 2.

Glance back at the drawing. It is probably difficult *not* to see the duck once you have recognised it. Familiarity with something makes it easy to pick out. This small test was part of a larger investigation: half the subjects tested were shown only the left hand tree (no duck) and half the right hand tree (with hidden duck) for three brief exposures. They were then asked to relax, imagine a nature scene and draw it, labelling the parts. Judges then rated the drawings for 'duck-related' content – feathers, birds, water and so on. It was found that a higher proportion of subjects who had seen the right hand tree had duck-related images than those seeing only the left hand tree. But even when the right hand tree was shown for as long as 30 seconds with the clue 'There is a duck somewhere in the picture – find it', over half of *both* groups failed to find it. The implication was that stimuli which we have failed to register consciously can influence our imagery and thinking. This part of the experiment is related to a considerable argument in marketing theory, about whether brief or very faint messages or pictures inserted into commercials can affect our behaviour, without our having consciously registered them. More consideration to this topic of **subliminal perception** is given in Chapter 2, and the idea of unconscious motives for our behaviour will be examined in Chapter 7.

EXAMPLE 1.2 'NO-ONE CAN CHANGE *MY* OPINION' – OR CAN THEY?

You are sitting in a room with seven other people. A group of four lines is being presented, as shown in Fig. 1.2.

Fig. 1.2

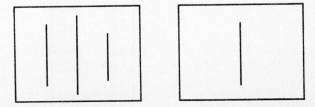

Each person has to say in turn which of the three lines on the right is equal to that on the left. You listen to the others and give your answer last or next to last. What you don't know is that the others have been told to give wrong answers. Do you follow their lead, either consciously or unconsciously? The general answer from this sort of experiment is that you probably do. In other words, you **conform** to the pressure of the group around you.

The relevance of this example for marketing is that we do not necessarily take purchasing decisions entirely alone – whether or not we have anyone with us. Mr Robbins goes to buy a new hat. What will his wife and children think of it? Is it stylish enough to impress the neighbours? Appropriate for work? Will his friends at the pub make fun of him if he wears it there? Group influences – from family, his social class, even casual friendship groups – will affect his decision-making. Consequently a study of how such groups may produce conformity, or otherwise influence individual decisions is of importance. (See Chapter 5.)

EXAMPLE 1.3   ECONOMICS AND THE RAT

1 A rat is in an apparatus where he can press a bar either to produce food pellets, or a small electric shock to the brain, which appears to give some pleasure to him.

2 The apparatus is arranged so that the number of presses to get one pellet or one small shock can be varied – rather as the cost of commodities can be varied in human exchange.

3 It is found that as the 'cost' of getting pleasure from the electrical stimulation increases, the 'consumption' of the rat decreases. But as the 'cost' of the food increases, the rat continues to 'buy' the same amount, even though he must use more of his 'resources' (his bar presses) to do so.

This experiment imitates the way that people use their resources (e.g. money) to purchase goods. It is thus related to economic behaviour, and shows a parallel between humans and animals. You probably know that for some goods, such as chocolates, increase in price tends to reduce demand. But for others, demand remains fairly steady in spite of cost increases. The rat appears to follow similar principles in his economic management!

Some behavioural scientists believe that studying 'lower' animals may help us understand our own behaviour: Chapter 3 looks at the work of Pavlov and Skinner, and the application of their research with animals, which can be seen in many promotional campaigns, though the relevance of their work to the complexities of human life is far from unchallenged.

EXAMPLE 1.4   BUMPER STICKERS AND THE COPS

1 Members of a party known as the Black Panthers claimed the police discriminated against them by picking on them for traffic offences. Their membership of the party was shown by a bumper sticker on their cars.

2 Fifteen students with clean driving records agreed to put stickers on their cars. They were of varied race, sex and appearance, and the cars had only the orange and black sticker on the rear bumper in common. They had agreed to drive in an entirely normal manner.

3 Within two hours, the first ticket was given. Next day five more were received. In 17 days, 23 were handed out, and some students had to withdraw from the experiment in case they lost their licence.

The experiment in Example 1.3 was carried out in laboratory conditions whereas this one is a **field** experiment, carried out in everyday conditions. It shows many important points.

1 A slight change in one part of a whole (the sticker) can completely change people's reactions. In marketing experiments, ratings of a peanut butter were markedly higher when its package carried the label 'Jif' than when it had a 'Superman' label, illustrating the importance of choosing the 'right' name and packaging.
2 It draws attention to the value of working in real-life situations. Merely asking the policemen their opinion of the group might not have produced such dramatic results. Statements about behaviour and actual behaviour do not always tie up.
3 It shows how a 'hunch' (that the stickers were the important element) can be investigated in a careful and controlled way. The essentials of good scientific method will be examined later.

Taken together, these four experiments cover some points from **psychology**, **sociology** and **economics**. Obviously there are many other subjects which study humans, but these are the most relevant of the behavioural sciences for marketing. The specialists who work in these fields tend to stick within them. Marketers, however, have to integrate their findings into a form most appropriate for their own needs, and adopt a **multi-disciplinary approach**.

We will look next at the three **disciplines** of psychology, sociology and economics in more detail.

Psychology

A very concise definition of psychology would be simply

the science of behaviour.

Notice that the word 'human' is omitted. Psychologists, as we saw from the rat experiment, study animals other than humans, and we shall be examining how far evidence from animal research can be helpful in explaining human behaviour.

To the strict **behaviourist** school, the behaviour to be examined is only that which is capable of being observed externally, i.e. **responses**, which are associated with **stimuli**, the 'signals' from people, events and things in the outside world. For this reason, behaviourism has sometimes been called **stimulus response** psychology. One of its benefits is that its theories rest on soundly observed and measured events which therefore reduces personal opinion and speculation.

Using this approach, marketers would be interested in what customers bought, what outlets they used, what preferences they showed, rather than in the internal processes which might lie behind these outward behaviours. Marketing would then develop and use theories relating the information and influences directed at the consumer (the stimuli such as packaging, store layout, appearance of a presenter in a commercial) to their buying behaviour (the responses).

Recently, however, psychology has put increasing emphasis on what might be going on *inside* humans, as well as how they behave outwardly. Thus a more recent definition is somewhat wider than the first one given:

the scientific study of behaviour
and mental processes[2]

These mental processes are often referred to as cognitive processes and include how we come to interpret information from the outside world (**perception**), how we store such information (**memory**) and how we use it in problem-solving and decision-making (**reasoning**).

In addition, humans have feelings or emotions and have drives or urges to do some things more than others (part of the study of **motivation**). These may also be considered as part of humans' internal processes.

Finally, some psychologists feel that the totality of thought, emotion and behaviour can be brought together as the **personality** of a person – the qualities which make them unique as an individual human being.

The implications for marketing of these inner and outer directed approaches are compared in diagram form in Fig. 1.3.

Fig. 1.3   The black box: open or closed?

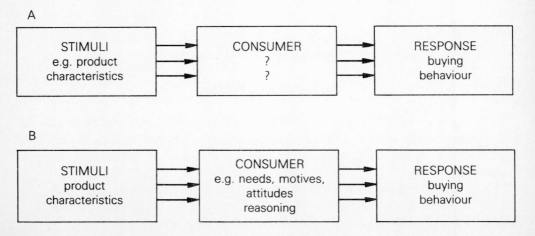

In A, the consumer is regarded as a sealed black box and study must therefore be confined only to what can be observed outside it.

In B, attention is given to the processes which might be going on in the box. These are not themselves directly observable, but can perhaps be inferred from outward behaviour. This enables a more detailed picture to be built up, but also results in more complex explanations being generated. So to the stimulus and response variables, we can add a third class, which come between and mediate the effects of input on output. These are known as **intervening variables**.

The behaviour studied in psychology may include that of the individual on his own or that of a group, as in **social psychology**, or in a formal **organisation**, studied by **organisational psychology** – all are very relevant to marketing:

1 Consumers are individuals, and an understanding of their individual behaviour is therefore vital.
2 They are also members of groups, and therefore the effect of group membership on behaviour widens the ideas gained from individual psychology.
3 Organisational theory can help us towards efficient practices within marketing institutions, and with the important aspect of **organisational buying behaviour** and its differences from individual **consumer behaviour**.

You will see in subsequent chapters – particularly when we consider the 'models' proposed for individual and organisational buying behaviour – how much marketing has relied on psychology to form its own specialised approaches to human behaviour. A recent paper, *Marketing and Exchange*, commented:

Our disciplinary focus is not the investigation of markets, but the study of customers. Hence marketing emphasises consumer behaviour, drawing heavily on psychology for its insights.[3]

Sociology

Whilst psychology tends to concentrate on the individual, even when studied as a member of a group, sociology takes the group as a unit. It studies **institutions** such as the family, and educational and political organisations. It also considers the relations between them, for example, the effects of social class membership on voting behaviour.

Sociology also studies the influence of society as a whole on groups and individuals, and, very relevant for marketing, the **culture** of societies and groups. The way in which children are prepared for the culture of adult society is examined under the topic of **socialisation**. Clearly the extent to which later consumer behaviour is shaped by early experiences is well worth investigating since children are the adult consumers of the future.

Allied to sociology is **anthropology**, which applies the process of cultural analysis to primitive rather than modern, advanced, groups. It also makes cross-cultural comparisons of how, for instance, customs such as betrothal and marriage are handled by different societies.

A similar type of analysis and comparison is made by sociologists when studying groups within the same society (**sub-cultural groups**). Awareness of how the 'same' material can be regarded quite differently by members of different cultural groups can be particularly useful where products will reach a range of societies. Mistakes can be avoided, and products can be presented in a way which is 'in tune' with local thinking, feeling and values. (See Chapter 5.)

Economics

At first sight economics might seem to be too concerned with facts, figures and finance to qualify as a behavioural science. But it is people who try to *make* money, people who *exchange* money for goods, and people who try to get '*value* for money'. Thus any science which deals with exchange systems, whether involving payment or not, is likely to be of benefit to marketing.

The 'economic domain' has been described as

*constituted by human **action** directed towards the satisfaction of **wants** by the power of **choice**.*[4]

It is important, however, to realise that humans are not always rational beings, and not always completely guided by purely economic considerations. To regard them in that way is to ignore the complex non-economic influences at work in both individual and organisational buying decisions. They have been described as the 'imperfections of the market place' which muddy the tidy picture presented of economic man. In other words, a purely economic view might close our eyes to the contents of the black box, and the help that considerations of its working might give.

Nevertheless, a knowledge of the relations between 'input' and 'output' (e.g. how the stimulus of a change in price affects the response of demand) is undoubtedly useful in forecasting likely consumer behaviour, and in guiding the strategies of the individual firm – **microeconomics**. **Macroeconomics** is similarly of value in understanding the larger-scale, total marketing mechanism, and enables the individual marketer to look beyond his own organisation and its dealings with consumers.

Other 'human' disciplines

GEOGRAPHY

Geography offers a spatial backcloth to human activity, with a static aspect (where people live, and how, in the widest sense, they communicate) and a dynamic aspect (how patterns of living and communication change). The 'gentrification' of run-down urban areas illustrates the need to be aware how the population of a district, and therefore the marketing possibilities, can fairly quickly change, as shown by the sudden invasion of working-class Dockland in London by executive and middle-class people.

HISTORY

History offers a time perspective. Looking back can also help us to look forward, and anticipate future trends. The direct assistance of history may be, for instance, to show how trade union organisation and purposes have changed over time – an important perspective to have when considering management-worker relations, and preparing for change. But besides direct assistance, an historical approach can be valuable. The manager or marketer who operates in a 'time vacuum' may fail to recognise the lessons from the past in his field, may fail to recognise change, and may thus remain fixed in a present which is already past. In other words, marketing needs to develop a theory which extends beyond today.

Some of the complex influences at work on the consumer are summarised in Fig. 1.4, which also introduces topics to be considered later in more detail.

Fig. 1.4   Influences on consumer behaviour

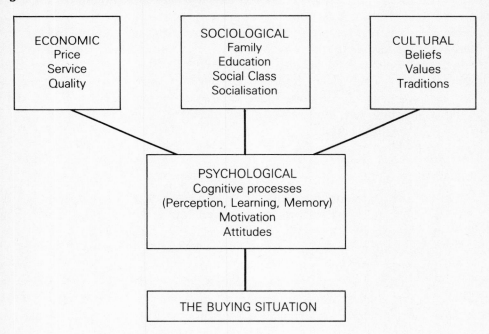

■ THE SCIENTIFIC STUDY OF BEHAVIOUR

Information about behaviour is all around us. Newspapers report the activities of people of all levels and occupations. Magazines and radio/TV 'phone-ins' give advice about children's behaviour, girl/boyfriend's behaviour, and even offer to predict behaviour in features such as horoscopes.

Such information is interesting, and often useful. But these informal studies of behaviour do not fully meet the conditions required of good scientific method. For convenience these conditions can be divided into **aims** and **methods**.

Aims

It is usually held that science should aim at four main functions. These are **description**, **explanation**, **prediction**, and **control**.

DESCRIPTION

Ask two supporters from rival clubs for their views on an incident at a football match. It is likely you will get two quite different versions. Personal opinion and feelings have coloured their interpretations of the 'same' event. Science could not operate effectively if its descriptions depended more on factors within the observer than on the facts themselves. It aims therefore at **objective** description, which is as free as possible from personal bias or interpretation.

Description in science often includes **measurements**. This in turn involves measuring instruments such as tests and questionnaires. But these also can produce problems of description. If you took two different intelligence tests on the same day, it is unlikely that the assessment of your ability would be exactly the same on each. This is because human qualities such as intelligence and emotion are far harder to measure than physical ones such as height and weight. Nevertheless behavioural scientists continually strive for accuracy in their measurements.

As part of the search for shared, accurate descriptions, scientists try to share **specialist vocabularies**. These are the technical words of their discipline, which have special meanings attached to them. *Science aims at descriptions which are as accurate and objective as possible.*

EXPLANATION

From childhood onwards, humans like to know the 'why' of things, as well as the 'how'. I sit at my word processor, and I know how to work it, without understanding exactly why. At a superficial level, I could explain how to make certain things happen to someone unfamiliar with it. But I certainly could not repair it, or suggest changes in the parts to make it more efficient. For deeper understanding I would need the help of an expert, who could assess what had gone wrong, or suggest internal changes to improve performance. In a similar way, everyday, practical experience of behaviour can be given fuller insight by drawing on the expertise of specialists in the behavioural fields. *Science aims towards deeper understanding and explanation of the information obtained by accurate and objective description.*

PREDICTION

Explanation gives an understanding of what has happened so far. Prediction aims at forecasting what may happen in the future, or in different circumstances. It answers questions such as 'What will happen next? What will happen if ... ?' Prediction is thus more powerful than explanation. It enables events to be anticipated, and is held to be a good test of any scientific theory. *Prediction moves from explanation of present events to forecasting of events in the future or in changed circumstances.*

CONTROL

If events can be anticipated, then they may perhaps be controlled. We may believe, for instance, that goods at eye level tend to draw consumers' attention (the stage of description). This may then lead to the prediction that heightened attention may produce increased purchase. Thus we may be able to control consumer buying behaviour by placing certain goods, rather than others, at eye level.

In a paper on the application of learning theory to marketing, the authors wrote:

In marketing, the desired end is appropriate behaviour manipulation and control to further the goals of the organisation.[5]

Many people are anxious about the extent to which science can be used to control behaviour; the ethical consideration of whether humans have the *right* to manipulate and control the behaviour of others has been levelled at marketing. But control of other people's behaviour is a fact of everyday life, and provided there is some restraint on techniques which are considered unethical, marketing itself simply reflects this aspect of human life.

Gordon Allport has summarised the aims of science as

understanding, prediction and control above the levels achieved by unaided common sense.[6]

Once more we have the suggestion that the practical, common sense and experience of the marketer can be supplemented, but not of course replaced, by knowledge of the behavioural sciences.

Methods and measurements

Description cannot exist if there is nothing to describe. So science needs **data** or facts for its operations. These facts may be collected as **primary** or **secondary** data.

PRIMARY DATA

This is material which is specially gathered by an individual or organisation, and thus might be termed original or first-hand.

SECONDARY DATA

This comes from already existing sources such as government surveys, census information, published reports by other individuals and organisations. Its benefit is that the information is already available, and thus time, money and effort are saved. But it must of course be accurate, for otherwise those relying on it will have unknowingly imported errors into their work. *Scientific conclusions can never be more accurate than the data on which they are based*. The methods used in collecting primary data in the behavioural sciences include **surveys, interviews, observation** and, of especial importance, **experiments**.

1 Observation This sounds quite easy. Simply go out and watch what happens! But to be accurate and objective, certain principles are necessary:

(a) observers on the same project should be looking for similar things – if the attention of one is drawn by some incident which another ignores, agreement will be small;

(b) observers should use common methods of recording and reporting their observations, including the use of a common vocabulary;

(c) observers should not allow personal opinion to colour their observations or their descriptions of them;

(d) observers need to be unobtrusive. Human beings, unlike physical objects, are sensitive to being observed, and their behaviour may therefore change as a result, so that what is observed is not their 'true' behaviour.

A simple example of observation would be to record the number of customers at checkouts at different times of day. This would be the **descriptive** level, but could lead to changes in checkout provision if queues were particularly long at certain times. The hunch of casual observation could thus be confirmed by more systematic study.

Often there may be no substitute for observation. Customers are unlikely to recall how long they spent in any particular section, what order they visited sections, how long they spent deliberating over an item before selecting or moving on, how often a 'jam' occurred from too many shoppers converging on one area.

Observation of this kind is much more difficult than in a simple head count, and might require the assistance of a trained researcher. But such a study could supply accurate information which in turn could lead to better store layout and design, and therefore greater customer satisfaction.

Modern techniques can now supplement person-person observation with detail no human observer could produce.

EXAMPLE 1.5   KEEPING TRACK OF EYES

1 Photo-slides are taken of supermarket shelving, displaying a product whose packaging is to be assessed in terms of consumer attention.

2 Competitive brands are shown, the relative position of package and competitors being changed to avoid position effects.

3 The series of slides imitates a walk through a store.

4 The viewer can control the time of exposure of the slide. Meanwhile, a record of eye movements is taken. This will show:

- order of looking at packages
- number of times a package is looked at
- how quickly a package gains attention
- total time spent viewing an individual display.

Such a detailed assessment of attention and interest is clearly beyond the unaided eye. Other forms of 'mechanical' observation include measurement of emotional responses by the psychogalvanometer, which measures rate of perspiration, and the pupilometer which measures changes in pupil size.[7]

2 **Surveys** The nature and purpose of a survey has been defined as:

A form of planned collection of data for the purpose of description or prediction as a guide to action.[8]

Questionnaires and **interviews** are the most frequently used methods for collecting data. The questionnaire can be used to gain information from a large number of people who are responding to the same list of questions. This is a good step towards objectivity, but even with the 'same' list care must be taken:

(a) to avoid ambiguity in the questions;
(b) to avoid giving offence by the questions;
(c) to be aware that people may sometimes give the answers they think are expected of them, rather than their true opinions.

Multiple choice formats may be used in an attempt to standardise responses as well as questions, as in this item from a survey of people who visit racecourses.

EXAMPLE 1.6

Which of the following phrases below best describes your feelings about Sunday racing?

I would definitely go racing on Sunday	1
I would probably go racing on Sunday	2
I am not sure whether I would go racing on Sunday	3
I would probably not go racing on Sunday	4
I would definitely not go racing on Sunday	5

This is a **closed** item, with the advantage of easy recording of response. The same questionnaire also contains **open** questions where the respondent replies more freely.

EXAMPLE 1.7

Which racecourse do you like best? _
Why is that? _
_ _

In the one case, the respondent **selects** his response. In the other, he **constructs** it. Selected responses are easy to score, but restrict the information to the alternatives offered. Constructed responses may show a wider range of opinions, but are more difficult to assess objectively.

Interviews obviously involve person-to-person contact, and thus have advantages and disadvantages over questionnaires sent by post (mail question-naires). Interviews range from straightforward explanation and presentation of a fully structured questionnaire, to situations where considerable discretion is given to the interviewer in handling the topics discussed. In such cases, there is considerable flexibility to suit the discussion to the client. Against this is a possible lack of objectivity since the course and content of the interview are no longer so well controlled. Where several interviewers are involved, there are also dangers that differences in personality, sex, social class and so on may influence responses.

The group on which information is needed may often be far too big for the time, information and expertise available. A **sample** is therefore taken from the whole group (technically known as the **population**). It is vital that this sample reflects the characteristics of the population in relevant aspects. Using a sample from the population of primary school teachers in England which failed to reflect the high proportion of women and the low proportion of black teachers could easily produce a false impression of the overall group.

3 Experiments Everyday life is full of 'hunches' about what might happen if a change of some sort was made. A supermarket manager might consider whether a certain line would sell better if placed higher on the shelves. In a sense, he is predicting what would happen if a certain change were made in existing conditions.

Science puts such predictive statements, known as **hypotheses**, to the test by **experiment**. *An experiment frequently tests out a hypothesis concerning the relationship between two variables*. The **independent** variable is one which the experimenter can systematically alter to test whether any change results in a second, or **dependent** variable.

A classic experiment from the study of work conditions will show how this testing is done, and some of the pitfalls involved. In the 1920s, experiments were carried out at a large electrical plant in America, initially to investigate the effect of changes in level of lighting (the independent variable) on productivity, the dependent variable. To cope with the fact that influences other than changes in lighting might be causing any changes observed in productivity, a **control** group was selected. This group was similar in number, experience and had an average production rate at the start of the experiment, to the **experimental** group. Both groups were composed of women. The control group worked at the same level of lighting as normal – there was no change in the independent variable. At the end of the experimental period, the level of production was again measured. The experiment can be summarised diagrammatically (Fig. 1.5).

The results were somewhat surprising. Although, as expected, productivity increased as lighting increased in the experimental group, it also increased in the control group – where lighting wasn't changed! As a check on this, the lighting was then decreased for the experimental group. Productivity still went up, even

Fig. 1.5

Before	*Experimental period*	*After*
Pre-test by measuring dependent variable (productivity)	**Control group**: no change in independent variable (lighting) **Experimental group**: lighting changed	Post test by remeasuring dependent variable

when the light was very poor indeed. The lessons to be learned from this include:

(a) always be aware of the possibility of variables other than the chosen independent one being at work;

(b) in particular, in work with humans, be on the lookout for **social factors**. The relations between the workers themselves and with their supervisors proved to be of great importance in follow-up studies;

(c) be aware that the novelty and interest of being involved in an experiment, of being rather 'special', may in itself affect motivation and therefore performance. This finding from the experiments was so important that it has been called the **Hawthorne effect**, after the Western Electric plant in which they were done.

Hypotheses are often produced from **theories** which in the behavioural sciences aim at explaining rather wide areas of behaviour. Thus, in the 'duck' experiment, the hypothesis was that subjects who were given the hidden-duck picture (the experimental group) would have different subsequent imagery than those given the tree-only picture (the control group). This hypothesis was derived from Freud's theory of personality which includes the idea that behaviour can be modified by unconscious influences.

If the results of an experiment are in line with the hypothesis then it, and the theory giving rise to it, can be said to be **supported** rather than **proved**. This is to ensure that the possibility of new evidence coming forward to contradict the theory is always kept in mind.

If support is not found, then the hypothesis and theory will be examined with a view to possible revision, as shown in Fig. 1.6.

The Hawthorne experiments, many of which failed to support the expected relation between working conditions and output, produced a considerable re-think in theories about the behaviour of workers in organisations, as will be seen in Chapter 9.

Finally, a word of caution. Even if there seems to be a clear relationship between independent and dependent variable (e.g. as one increases, so does the other) this does not **prove** that one directly affects the other. When people put more clothes on in England, they take them off in Australia. This could be verified many many times – but there is no direct causal link between the two!

Fig. 1.6

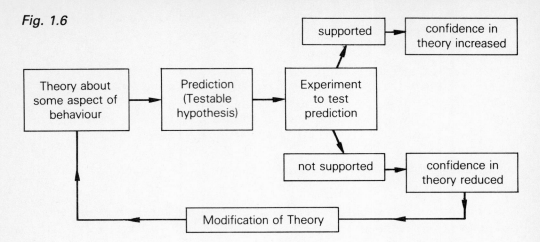

Measurement

The scales used in the behavioural sciences fall into four groups: **nominal**, **ordinal**, **interval** and **ratio**.

NOMINAL
People or things are grouped together for the purposes of **identification** and **classification**. A shopkeeper might classify his jogging shoes by brand name, therefore giving a clearer picture of his holdings (Fig. 1.7a). A survey might allocate coded numbers to commuters to indicate the area from which they began their journey. But no comparisons are made between the classes, other than numbers in each.

ORDINAL
The nominal scale tells us how many of what, but it does not, for instance, enable us to tell whether Nikes are more long-lasting than Adidas or Brookes; it gives no sense of order. In Fig. 1.7b the runners are shown in order of finishing, but we have no idea of the precise time-intervals between them. The ordinal scale literally puts things **in order** on some quality or qualities, but the **intervals** of the scale are not known.

INTERVAL
This scale does take account of intervals between units. The runners might be asked to give the shoes a figure out of ten to indicate their preference apparently giving more detailed measurement. But there are problems:

1 One person's '8' might not match up to another's: people are using a subjective rather than objective scale;
2 The intervals between scale units might not be equal. The change in preference between 7 and 8 might be different from that between 8 and 9;

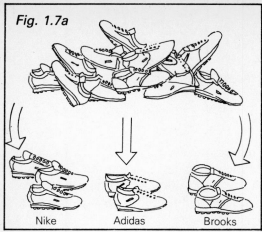

Fig. 1.7a

Nike   Adidas   Brooks

Nominal

Units of the scale are categories. Objects are measured by determining the category to which they belong. There is no magnitude relationship between the categories. Can only determine whether A = B or A ≠ B.

Fig. 1.7b

Ordinal

Possesses the property of magnitude. Can rank-order the objects according to whether they possess more, less, or the same amount of the variable being measured. Thus, can determine whether A > B, A = B, or A < B. Cannot determine how much greater or less A is than B in the attribute being measured.

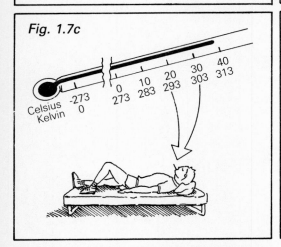

Fig. 1.7c

Celsius -273   0   10   20   30   40
Kelvin   0   273 283 293 303 313

Interval and Ratio

Interval: Possesses the properties of magnitude and equal intervals between adjacent units. Can do same determinations as with an ordinal scale, plus can determine if A − B = C − D, A − B > C − D, or A − B < C − D.

Ratio: Possesses the properties of magnitude, equal interval between adjacent units, and an absolute zero point. Can do all the mathematical operations usually associated with numbers, including ratios.

3 Because of this, and because the scale has no zero point we cannot assume that a score of 8 indicates a preference twice as strong as a score of 4.

In an **equal interval** scale, problems **1** and **2** are avoided. Temperature is an equal-interval scale, because a change of temperature on the Celsius scale from 20 to 30 is equivalent to that between 10 and 20. But we still cannot say that a day when 40 degrees is recorded is twice as hot as one when the temperature is 20 degrees. We cannot make **ratio** statements unless there is a proper **zero point** to the scale. 0°C is not the true zero, since you can have temperatures below zero.

RATIO
If, however, we measure our runner's temperature on the Kelvin scale, which has a true zero (Fig. 1.7c), we can make ratio statements. 200 on the Kelvin scale is twice as great a temperature as 100 on that scale. Ratio scales have a true zero and their intervals are equal. True ratio scales are difficult to produce in studies of behaviour.

■ USE OF OBJECTIVE TESTS

1 The short tests at the end of each section can be used in several ways:
   (a) as a check on what you have learned soon after reading a chapter or considering the topic in class;
   (b) as a revision aid during your course of study: re-work the tests to check your knowledge isn't fading;
   (c) as a final check in the run-up to the final exam.
2 If you score below 16, note your errors and re-read the relevant sections.
3 Words from which to select your answer are sometimes provided in a box beneath the question. For other questions, you may have to supply your own answer.

■ SELF ASSESSMENT QUESTIONS

Marks

1 List **three** of the functions any soundly-based scientific theory should be able to perform.
   (a) _____
   (b) _____
   (c) _____   (3)

(D.... E..... P..... C.......)

2 (a) Personal views of events are often _ _ _ _ _ _ _ _ _ _ _ _ _ _

(b) Science aims at an approach which is _ _ _ _ _ _ _ _ _ _ _ _ _   (2)

(O......... S...........)

3 List **three** ways of collecting **primary** data:

(a) _

(b) _

(c) _   (3)

(S.... E..... I........ O........)

4 Eatwell Foods PLC sponsor several competitions.

(a) in the general knowledge quiz Aberdeen came first, Blackpool second, and Cardiff third. Such a scale is called _ _ _ _ _ _ _ _ _ _ _ _

(b) In the Eatwell mile, the results were:

J. Runwell   3 m 50 s

S.O. Nearly   3 m 50.2 s

N. Also-Ran   3 m 54 s

The times are an example of a(n) _ _ _ _ _ _ _ _ _ _ _ _ _ _ scale   (2)

Choose from: | ordinal;   ratio;   interval;   nominal |

5 Eatwell's Research Department tried out two versions of a video, both identical except that one had a male presenter, the other a female. One group of women rated the 'male' version. A second, similar group of women rated the 'female' version. Both groups used a 5-point scale.

(a) the sex of the presenter is the _ _ _ _ _ _ _ _ _ _ _ _ _ _ _ _ _ _ variable.

(b) the ratings are the _ variable.

(c) if Ms Liberty gave the female version 4, but Mrs Trad gave it 2, can we say that Ms L. liked it twice as much as Mrs T.? _ _ _ _ _ _ _   (3)

6 The researchers were hoping that the results of the study would indicate the likely responses to the video of all unmarried females aged from 20–35, living in Greater London.

(a) this large group is the _

(b) each female group is a _

(c) the rating scales are a source of _ _ _ _ _ _ _ _ _ _ _ _ _ data.

Choose from: | primary;   sample;   secondary;   population |

(d) would the London telephone directories be an adequate source for the two groups of women? _ _ _ _ _ _ _ _ _ _ _ _ _ _ _ _ _   (4)

7 To assess the possible long-term effects of the video, the researchers compared the ratings of the advertised product both before the viewing, and again two weeks later. They also did this for a group, similar to the viewing group, who did not see the video:

    (a) the groups who saw the videos are the _ _ _ _ _ _ _ groups.
    (b) the group who did not see it is the _ _ _ _ _ _ _ _ _ _ _ group.
    (c) ratings taken a fortnight after a viewing form the _ _ _ _ _ _ _   (3)

Choose from: | pre-test; control; post-test; experimental |

(Total 20)

(Answers are on page 219)

■ STUDY AND EXAMINATION TIPS

Planning

1 Many readers of this manual will be studying principally to take an examination. For such readers, planning is very important:

    (a) during the study period, so that the material you have learned is well-organised and readily available;

    (b) during the examination, so that you present your material in a way which is easy for the examiner to read, and which impresses him or her by its clarity.

2 The various 'Focus' items at the end of chapters will guide you towards which particular points you could concentrate on, and how to apply these to particular questions.

3 To answer questions on the behavioural sciences and marketing, you need to consider at least the following:

    (a) the nature of science and scientific method;
    (b) why a scientific approach may be helpful to marketing;
    (c) what constitute the behavioural sciences;
    (d) the special relevance of these to marketing;
    (e) marketing's need to take an **interdisciplinary** approach, combining material from several fields.

4 Most importantly, have examples ready. Examiners want to see that you can put theory to practical use. Keep your eye on the marketing scene for illustrations of theoretical points. A file into which you put interesting material (e.g. advertisements, mail-shots, articles) is very useful to dip into from time to time.

5 Make sure you understand the technical terms. It's worth making a small dictionary of such words.

6 Questions on 'black box' models occur in some papers. Here you need to understand different viewpoints on consumer behaviour:

(a) viewing consumer behaviour as simply a set of responses or output, resulting from a set of stimuli, or input;

(b) acknowledging the possibility of intervening variables, mediating between stimulus and response;

(c) focusing on these 'inner' variables, in the belief that these are the true key to understanding consumer behaviour.

7 Fuller consideration of the black box approach is given in Chapter 8. This raises an important point. Do not learn your material in such rigid chunks that you can only answer one type of question. While these chapters are designed to point you towards different sections of the papers, on many issues it is quite possible to form a perfectly sound answer by combining material. Therefore be **flexible** in your study. Then, if your 'banker' does not appear, you can still make use of your material – but make sure it **is** relevant to the question.

■ EXAMINATION QUESTIONS

1 'The black box approach provides merely a broad picture of marketing phenomena which can only be completed through knowledge provided by the other behavioural sciences.' Explain this statement.

2 What contribution does behavioural science make to the marketing of consumer goods? Illustrate your answer by reference to three specific areas.

3 Are 'black box' models of consumer behaviour too simplistic to be of practical value to marketing?

4 Discuss the ways in which a knowledge of the behavioural sciences can help a marketing manager have a better understanding of consumer choices and purchasing behaviour.

5 Explain the relevance of the behavioural sciences for marketing, using specific examples from the behavioural theories you have studied.

6 Describe ways in which the behavioural sciences can help resolve marketing problems, illustrating your answer from the theories and techniques you have studied.

2 Information processing I – sensation, attention and perception

There's more in seeing than meets the eyeball

■ INTRODUCTION

Our first topic in the behavioural sciences is taken largely from psychology. It concerns how we receive, attend to, and interpret, information from the world about us. Imagine, if you can, that you see nothing at all, hear nothing at all. You are now in the world of Helen Keller, who was both blind and deaf. Your idea of the world outside you would come only from touch, taste and smell. Contrast that with the richness of sensation available to most of us. Patterns of coloured light meet our eyes wherever we look; sounds great and small surround us. Information rushes into our eyes and ears through books, television, radio, and simply from looking and listening. We are immersed in **signals** from the world outside us.

■ SIGNALS AND THE MARKETER

What the marketer wants to do, of course, is to ensure that his 'signals' (his products and information about them) stand out from other elements in such a way that the customer acts positively towards them – by seeking further information, by trying them, by repeat buying or by recommending them. The process can be divided, perhaps a little artificially, into four elements, as shown in Fig. 2.1.

Fig. 2.1

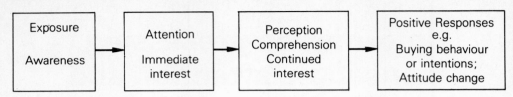

1 Exposure and awareness. Clearly, people are not going to buy anything if they never see it, or receive any information about it. The product must therefore be exposed, be it material, person, idea or service, in such a way that potential consumers have a chance to become aware of it.

2 Attention and interest. There is no point in an elaborate display if in fact no-one takes any notice of it. Then there is only potential, but not real, awareness. If an ad is flipped over casually, or the coffee is made during a commercial, the message has been lost. The intention is for the product or message to be picked out (preferably in preference to that of the competitors' products). But remember, this is only the first stage. *Getting attention and interest is not the same as holding attention and interest.*

3 Perception and comprehension. It would again be pointless to make a video which captured attention but was not understood by the viewers, or delivered a message quite different from the one intended. Ideally, the 'receivers' should take from presentations the messages marketers intend – the characteristics or attributes of the product, and its advantages over competitors, for instance.

4 Positive response. Hopefully, because of the first three elements, the consumer's responses will change in a positive direction, or, if already positive, will be maintained or heightened. Such responses could include actual buying behaviour, or heightened interest, or a more positive attitude.

Consumer sets

According to Howard and Sheth[1] the consequences of the exposure-response process will result in a product or brand being placed into a 'set'. In all, five possibilities have been suggested.[2]

1 The **awareness set**: brands of which the consumer is to a greater or lesser extent aware.

2 The **unawareness set**: brands of which he is not aware at all.

3 The **evoked set**: those brands towards which he has a positive response (e.g. he would consider buying).

4 The **inert set**: those for which he has insufficient information, or an insufficiently strong attitude, to make a decision to buy.

5 The **inept set**: brands which are negatively evaluated because of past experience, comments from other users, or other associations.

A hypothetical example of the sets in operation is given in Example 2.1.

EXAMPLE 2.1   A TREE OF CONSUMER SETS

Fig. 2A

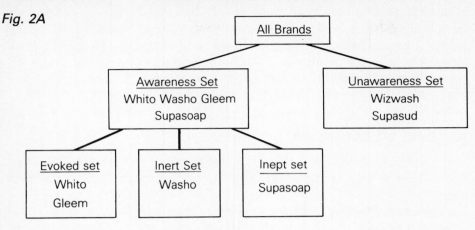

The implications from this diagram are:

1 Unawareness set: greater exposure is needed for Wizwash and Supasud.

2 Evoked set: intermittent backup featuring positive attributes will help maintain the position of Whito and Gleem.

3 Inert set: more information, especially about positive features, may move Washo into the evoked set.

4 Inept set: why is Supasoap seen unfavourably? Do product characteristics need changing, or is it the way information about the product is presented?

We can now examine the psychological foundations for the formation of these sets and the implications for the marketer.

■ FIRST SIGNALS FROM OUTSIDE – SENSATION

A customer approaches a display in a supermarket – the **exposure** element. There is perhaps a 'titbits' table near the entrance where he can taste a new brand of cheese. He will 'see' a gaily decorated table with a smart attendant, 'hear' a pleasant voice inviting him to try little biscuits and cheese, 'smell', happily or not, the cheese itself, 'feel' the texture of the biscuits in his hand, and finally 'taste' the combination in his mouth.

Psychologically, what is happening is that various physical signals are coming from the display and being translated by the sense organs or receptors of the customer. Conventionally, the overall process is divided into **sensation**, the first arrival and registration of the signals, and **perception**, the interpretation of those signals into meaningful information. In practice, of course, the two blend so rapidly that we are not aware of any separation except in very unusual circumstances.

Human beings are equipped with sense organs which can 'code' the physical signals around us into messages which our brains can then handle. Our eyes convert a limited range of electromagnetic waves into electrical messages, and our ears do the same for sound signals. These are distance receptors, which can sometimes give us information from miles away, say from a fire or explosion. Our noses operate at smaller distances, but touch, pain and taste are close or near receptors, since they can only register events on or in our bodies.

Limitations on sensation

For many types of signal, then, there is an appropriate receptor. But although these senses give us a great deal of information, our sensory apparatus has many limitations.

1 Some signals are too weak for us to register them. They are then described as below our **threshold**. As an example, the average lowest level of illumination we can register is equivalent to the light of a candle seen from a distance of 30 miles away on a dark, clear night. Pretty impressive! But even so, light at a lower intensity would simply not exist for us at all: it would have dropped below our **absolute threshold**. *The absolute threshold marks the transition between no experience and some experience.*

Besides these absolute thresholds, which vary from person to person, and from time to time, there are also **difference** thresholds. These indicate the smallest amount of difference there must be between two stimuli for us to register that there really *is* a difference. Thus, an average person can tell that two weights are different if one is 100 grams and the other is 102 grams. The difference threshold (also called the **just noticeable difference** or **jnd**) is then 2 grams. *The difference threshold marks the transition between awareness of difference and no awareness of difference.*

An interesting fact emerges when we compare the size of difference needed to detect change with the size of the original stimulus. Roughly, the amount of change needed before a change is actually noted is a constant fraction of the original stimulus. Thus if a 2 gram difference is noticed between weights of 100 and 102 grams, then a 4 gram difference would be needed if the first weight were 200 grams. This relationship is known as **Weber's Law** and can be expressed as follows:

$$\frac{\Delta I}{I} = \text{constant}$$

where I is the stimulus intensity, and ΔI is the increase needed to produce awareness of change, or: *the difference threshold for any stimulus is approximately proportional to the intensity or size of the stimulus.*

For pitch, the constant is quite low. We can detect a difference between notes when the frequency of one is only 0.3% higher than that of another. But for their loudness, we have to increase the intensity of one by 20% before a difference is heard.

The law is not precise in its application but suggests, for instance, that the increase in size of a cereal packet needed to impress the customer with increased volume is proportional to the volume of the original packet – the bigger the packet, the more we need to increase the volume before a change is significantly noticed. A second consequence is held to be that the gain in attention is in proportion to the *square root* of the increase in size. To gain **twice** as much attention, size needs to be increased **four-fold**.

The law has also been extended to price, but may need some care in its application. The purely objective factors (such as a decrease from £2000 to £1900) will obviously be *noticed* if both appear on a sales label. But whether the change will affect consumer behaviour or attitude may depend on the relation of the change to the last price paid, or an estimate of the range of fair prices for the product. If Weber's law can be applied to price, it would imply that a reduction of £1 on £20 might appear to be just as significant to the customer as a reduction of £100 on £2000. Further, there would be no point in a reduction if it lay below the just noticeable difference of the consumer. The rather complex issues involved are examined by Williams.[3]

2 We cannot possibly register *all* the signals around us. For example, our eyes are sensitive to a wide range of frequencies, but do not react to infra-red waves. Our ears cease to hear sounds of very high frequency.

Some people, like Helen Keller, have faulty sensory equipment, and must rely on other senses in an attempt to compensate for the missing information. Others have equipment which functions, but does not give complete information, like the 6% of men who are colour-blind, and partially deaf people who cannot hear high frequency sounds, leading to difficulties in distinguishing words like 'chin', 'shin' and 'thin'.

On both commercial and ethical grounds, it may be worthwhile for marketers to consider the special needs of these and other sense-disadvantaged groups. Large-print books, sub-titles, 'signing' on television and talking newspapers are all useful ways of by-passing sensory difficulties.

3 We lack the equipment entirely for some signals. No way can we watch television without a set! Yet the waves must be around us, ready for the receiver to re-code them into sound and light waves which we *can* receive and interpret. We are thus, by means of these amplifiers of human sensory capacity, able to see and hear, as they happen, events thousands of miles away from us. In this respect, the marketer of today has at his disposal an information distribution system far in advance of that available even 30 years ago.

4 If we are exposed repeatedly to the same type of signal, our sensitivity to it is reduced. We become habituated to it and may eventually fail to register it, as with the clock whose monotonous tick we 'tune out' – only to 'tune in' again when it stops! Material, therefore, should not be *over*-exposed to potential consumers or they may well tune it out.

■ MAKING SENSE OF SENSATIONS: PERCEPTION

Sensation may be thought of as providing the raw material of information, the building bricks, whereas **perception** gets to work constructively, making coherent patterns from the raw material. Nothing could be more mistaken than to suppose that our sense organs act just like cameras or tape recorders. Certainly our eyes admit light and our ears sound but there the similarity ends. Humans ignore, distort, emphasise aspects of the incoming information to produce their own **individual** perceptions. The copy theory, which suggests that our sense organs work to produce exact replicas of the things 'out there' is far from the truth. Certainly there are some basic principles, to which we will shortly turn, which will help marketers produce desired impressions. But we can never guarantee that the same type of presentation will produce similar interpretations by all people. Humans are not passive copiers of information. They use it *constructively*, fitting it into their own world pattern.

Selective perception and attention

Even though the cheese display may offer stimulating colours and interesting smells there is no guarantee that the customer will pay much, or indeed any, attention to it. There are endless competing display elements externally, and various needs and motives internally, which may not be related to cheese-buying at all. From the enormous range of signals rushing at us at any moment we only register some, not because of any fault in our senses but because of **selective attention**. Certain features of the environment 'catch our attention', while the remainder fade into the background or are ignored.

The main factors which cause us to attend selectively to some things rather than others are generally divided into two groups: **external** and **internal**. Alternatively, we can think of them as causing **involuntary** attention, as when we turn towards a sudden loud noise, or **voluntary**, when we investigate further out of interest. It is important to remember that there is no magic blueprint which can automatically catch people's attention over and above other competing stimuli. Attention is usually the result of the interaction of several factors operating at once, rather than of one single, dominant, factor.

External factors affecting attention

INTENSITY OR SIZE
While loud sounds and bright lights undoubtedly do catch our attention, there are dangers in the overuse of intense signals. In the first place, habituation and monotony will reduce impact. Secondly, continued 'full volume' may cause irritation rather than interest. Lastly, and probably most importantly, there is no point in attracting attention if the message is lost. A good example is election time, when the loudspeaker vans of candidates certainly make heads turn, but

often fail to deliver their message because of distortion. Attention has been obtained, but not comprehension.

Size is often a relative rather than an absolute matter. The quarter-page advert in a newspaper, surrounded by smaller notices, catches the eye, but would be insignificant in a street display; for example, the impact of advertisements in *Reader's Digest*, a relatively small magazine, is as effective as in much larger publications.[4] The **absolute** size may be small, but the **relative** effect of a full-page display may be considerable.

CONTRAST
Because of habituation, contrast can be effective. Having seen several pages of close print in a paper, we may well be attracted to a small notice tucked into the corner of an otherwise blank page. Clearly marketers feel this has some effect or they wouldn't pay for blank paper!

NOVELTY
Related to contrast, and humans' liking for change in stimulation, is novelty. Advertising by captive balloon, for instance, is still sufficiently unusual to gain attention, but sometimes the message is lost because the actual text is too small to be discriminated at a distance. The size factor has offset the novelty effect.

Novelty may only be novel for a very few times. The attention-gaining gimmick of today is often the boredom of tomorrow.

REPEATED EXPOSURE
Repetition may be helpful in gaining initial attention, but then runs the risk of habituation. However, in spite of habituation, repetition can sometimes act positively on attention. A useful technique is to take an old but well-liked presentation, rest it, and then bring it back. The old pleasure is revived, and there has been an opportunity for 'spontaneous recovery' from the effects of habituation. In England, the 'surfing' advert for Old Spice, and the 'story' adverts for John Smith's Bitter make welcome returns from time to time.

POSITION
Long-standing suggestions have included:

1 Left or right side of page? The advantage is held to depend on the reading habits of the culture (England: left side advantage. Arab countries: right side). Why?
2 Left or right page? No significant advantage was found.
3 Early or late? In a magazine early is better – somewhere in the first 10%, with little advantage thereafter.
4 Placement near to compatible editorial features helps attention.

MOVEMENT
Perhaps as a biological feature, humans are very sensitive to movement, so that displays involving movement may have the advantage over static presentations.

With the development of computer graphics, quite amazing motion sequences are possible.

A well-known employment agency uses a commercial which very rapidly superimposes pictures of people: the rapid changes catch attention, and the succession of images underlines the wide range of people considered by the agency – a good example of both gaining attention *and* delivering the message in a very brief presentation. Movement is also arousing, and thus helps to maintain attention and prevent boredom. Even the flashing of a telephone number in a display can catch attention more effectively than a constant stimulus would.

Internal factors

Two customers might approach the cheese display at the same time yet another might quickly pass on, the other stop and taste. At a motor show, one visitor makes rapidly for a particular model on display, another moves about idly from stand to stand. The stimuli for both visitors are similar, yet their behaviour is different. Clearly there are influences at work from within the individual as well as from outside. The marketer who relies solely on externally produced attention is ignoring a very important set of personal forces which will now be considered.

INTEREST

Common knowledge suggests that when we have an interest in anything, we are likely to pay attention to it or things to do with it. However, different forms of interest can be distinguished:

1 Long-term interest, from a hobby or from work. Here the consumer does not want jazzy, arousing presentations to catch his attention. Rather, it is the other way round – his interest causes him to select material relevant to it. The first visitor to the motor show probably already had an interest in the model, and simply scanned the scene before moving directly to it. The other was waiting for interest and attention to be aroused.

Psychologically one visitor has a **set** towards one class of material, while the other is neutral towards it. Such a set can of course operate on ideas as well as material products. A politically interested viewer will tend to select political programmes for viewing, will attend to political items in news broadcasts and may, as we shall see later, even distort information because of his own attitudes.

People usually have several long-term interests, and these may fluctuate, particularly between work and leisure. The manager who has a set towards work-related material during the week may be far more responsive to leisure-orientated matters by the weekend.

2 Short-term interest. Examples of this are a brief glance at a lively display in a store, a passing interest in a product mentioned to a friend or a short, possibly intense, interest in an activity, followed by burnout and decay. The common factor in these is that short-term interest is not converted to long-term interest. The gimmicky display attracts attention, but does not sustain it. The friend's

recommendation kindles interest and selective attention, but the product itself does not carry it through. Perhaps worst of all, the intense kind of interest shown, for example, in skateboarding and, to a lesser extent, small home computers, may collapse and leave producers with large stocks on their hands and damage to their reputation.

NEEDS AND MOTIVES

These terms are used differently by different writers. For simplicity, they will be used interchangeably here, with further consideration being given in the next chapter.

We can distinguish between long-term, universal needs such as hunger and thirst, and needs in the popular sense, as in saying, 'I need some washing powder'. Certain essentials are basic to human life, and will be sought regularly. But while someone might say, 'We need bread', they are less likely to say 'We need White Chief bread'. Thus the marketer must convert this basic need into attention and positive behaviour towards his own particular product.

This could be done, for initial interest, by the external factors above, or appeal could be made to internal needs or motives. The use of young children and mischievous puppies in commercials may appeal to caring motives, draw interest to the product, and perhaps by association, link the caring feeling with it. The product need not be directly related to the motive, as shown in Example 2.2.

EXAMPLE 2.2   TWINS? YOU MUST BE JOKING!

A car company used a double-page colour spread, with a picture of a nurse holding two twins occupying over three-quarters of the pages. One twin looks directly at the reader, both have hands appealingly raised. The copy then leads on to the need for family cars, and from there to the merits of a particular model.

The factors here include:

- large, colourful, 'first attention getter' at the head of the page, relying on infant-family-caring appeal
- then product-related information (second stage of attention).

While there are these lifelong needs and motives, it may also be necessary to *establish* a need, in the ordinary sense of the word. A dishwasher is not an essential need for survival, and families could manage without (though some might doubt it). Yet if the idea that the quality of life will be improved with one can be effectively presented, a family member may say 'We really *do* need a dishwasher'. But unless attention and interest are aroused towards a particular brand or model, all that will have happened is that *general* interest has been aroused – not at all what the marketer intended.

FEAR

This emotion needs careful handling in presentations. One effect may be to make some people more sensitive to material about, say, AIDS. They will then voluntarily seek out information, and attend to it if they encounter it accidentally. Others will be so painfully afraid that they actively avoid exposure to material about it (**selective exposure**). If they do encounter the topic, they may tune out or distort aspects which are particularly frightening to them. The persuasive aspects of fear arousal will be examined in Chapter 6.

THE POST-PURCHASE EFFECT

Have you ever bought a car and then noticed how many of 'your' model are on the road? This suggests that post-purchase interest may make consumers quite attentive to their chosen product, and to further information about it. There may thus be, for non-routine purchases, a sensitive period to be taken advantage of by marketers.

■ PERCEPTION AND COMPREHENSION

When we interpret the sensations aroused by external signals, we are entering the first stage of **comprehending**, or understanding, the input. We *see* a table, rather than a collection of visual signals, *hear* a dog rather than sounds of a certain frequency. There are however many factors which may either ease or hinder this passage from exposure to understanding.

Selective exposure

Selective exposure occurs when the individual chooses to avoid material. Thus, a Labour supporter may switch off either physically or psychologically during the Conservative Party broadcast, but maintain attention throughout the Labour Party's offering. This effect was well documented during the Kennedy-Nixon television presentations for the 1960 election. Both candidates appeared together, which should have been a corrective for selective exposure, but observers found that when the 'opposition' candidate spoke, he was tuned out by conversation, beer-drinking and other distractions. Merely presenting a message does not ensure attention, and without attention there can hardly be comprehension.

Set

Set (or expectancy) in relation to attention, has already been considered. But sets can also lead us to expect something, and to 'recognise' it when in fact something different has been presented.

Experiments done at Yale Univarsity

Stop, and read the sentence again. Have you spotted the error? This set has come from previous experiences of the association between 'Yale' and 'University'. *Previous experiences can be an important determinant of perception.*

The effect of set and expectancy in marketing has been demonstrated many times by the so-called 'blind trials'. In these, consumers are asked to recognise or rate different unlabelled brands of the same product, or the same product in different packages.

EXAMPLE 2.3   WHAT'S IN A NAME? WHAT'S IN A PACKAGE?

1 Beer drinkers were asked to rate three unlabelled brands of beer, one being their favourite.

2 Ratings showed little ability to distinguish one brand from another.

3 The same procedure repeated a week later with labels attached showed an overall improvement in rating for both favoured *and* non-favoured brands, but with a clear advantage for the favourite.

4 Similar results have been found using *identical* soft drinks, labelled as 'Diet' or 'Regular': Regular rated as better.

5 Bread wrapped in cellophane was rated 'fresher' than the same bread in waxed paper.

Packaging and labelling can establish positive sets and expectations towards products.[5,6,7]

Other studies have shown that price may be used by consumers as an indication of quality – the higher the price, the better the assumed quality.

Consumers therefore do *not* rely solely on the purely physical attributes of a product. They use various **surrogate indicators** as guides to the assumed product qualities. Marketers can thus supplement the basic attributes of their product by developing the best 'mix' of these secondary, but very important, indicators.

The old saying, 'never judge a book by its cover' could be a useful caution to consumers – and a useful reminder to marketers.

Motivated perception

Frequent demonstrations have shown the effect of *needs* on perception. An early and often-quoted one is that disadvantaged children tend to over-estimate the size of coins shown briefly to them when compared with the estimates of better-off children. More personally, an urgent need for relief makes us very sensitive to signs for toilet facilities!

It has also been found that the exposure time needed to recognise some types of words is longer than that for others, even when they are of similar length and exposed at the same level of illumination. Obscene four-letter words for instance are responded to more slowly than neutral four-letter words. Although it has been argued that it is uttering, rather than recognising, the words which is the barrier, such findings do suggest that a defensive screen may be erected against offensive or upsetting material. This **perceptual defence** may thus boomerang on presentations which include sexual or aggressive overtones. Instead of providing a focus for attention they may in fact be screened out.[8]

Sub-threshold or subliminal perception

It has been claimed that we may be able to react to stimuli which we do not consciously register.

This suggests that in some way our behaviour may be affected without our conscious knowledge. In the 1950s controversy raged over claims that very brief or very faint stimuli could be presented during a presentation – say of a commercial. Consumers could not recall any such message, but sales figures for the product 'advertised', if that is the word, subsequently increased. It is very difficult to control all other variables in investigating these effects, and the general opinion is that the technique is less effective than first thought. But Vance Packard, who drew early popular attention to it in 1957, claimed in his 1981 edition of *The Hidden Persuaders* that it was still in use then.[9]

Many ethical criticisms can be made of the technique, if indeed it can be used effectively. The *New Yorker* of 1957 claimed that minds had been 'broken and entered'. It is thought more ethical to allow people conscious awareness of factors which might affect their decisions, and not to 'hide' such factors. Packard did however report a pro-social use. The message, 'I am honest. I do not steal' mixed at low volume with background music in a store is said to have been associated with a 37% reduction in theft over a period of nine months.

The methods used have included:

1 Very brief or very faint visual messages.
2 Faint sound messages (e.g. a Seattle radio station carried a faint message 'TVs a bore').
3 Faint accelerated speech, at about 2300 words per minute, producing great distortion, but allowing a message to be repeated thousands of times per hour.
4 Sexual imagery or words embedded skilfully in product or promotional material.[10]

It seems unlikely that distorted or minimal influences should be able to compete effectively with major demands on attention. A cautious, or perhaps cynical summary has been:

all things considered, secret attempts to manipulate people's minds have yielded results as sub-liminal as the stimuli used.[11]

■ THE ORGANISATION OF PERCEPTION

An early, but still important, examination of how our perceptions tend to be organised was made by a group of German psychologists, known as the **Gestalt**

School. The word 'gestalt' can be translated as 'pattern' or 'form', and suggests that we perceive things and events as organised patterns rather than as collections of separate parts. A famous slogan of the group was

the whole is more than the sum of the parts.

They put forward a number of general principles of perceptual organisation.

Figure and ground

As pointed out in Chapter 1, we tend to organise inputs into two parts, one of which becomes more prominent than another. Sometimes this figure-ground relation can be reversed, as in Fig. 2.2.

Fig. 2.2

This division can occur visually, as in the illustration, or in sound, when we follow the singer's line as a figure against the background of the backing group, or the smell of newly-mown grass might stand out against the background of city odours.

It is a very important effect for marketing, since marketers obviously want their brand name and their message to stand out as a figure and command attention. But sometimes this may not work out quite as planned. While attractive presenters may command attention, it may be to such an extent that the product name becomes submerged and lost.[12]

EXAMPLE 2.4   WHAT'S IN A DRESS?

1 An attractive presenter appears with a product. She is wearing a 'conservative dress'.

2 Eye tracking studies show substantial attention to the product. Three days later, there was reasonable brand-name recall.

3 Another attractive presenter appears with a product, but in a 'revealing' dress. Eye tracking showed most attention on the presenter. Brand-name recall was low.

Thus the wrong feature has become figure. Note also that recall is affected by attention. Can you remember things you haven't 'seen'?

Fortunately, the Gestalt school provided some basic principles which can serve as initial guides to producing 'good gestalts' from presentations. These are the factors of **proximity, similarity, closure, continuation** and **pragnanz**.

Proximity

Things or events which are close together in space or time tend to be grouped together. In Fig. 2.3a there is a tendency to see a group of two people, with a grouping of bottle-and-table separate from them. In Fig. 2.3b we are more likely to see the person-bottle-table as a group, with an isolated figure to the right.

Fig. 2.3

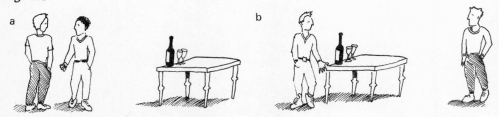

The message for marketing here is that if we want a grouping to be perceived, proximity or nearness will help. Presenter-product-proximity would be a simple guide.

Similarity

Things which are similar are likely to be seen as groups. In Fig. 2.4a you probably see a cross of 'triangle trees' as a group against a ground of 'bushy trees'. But in 2.4b although there are the same number of each kind of tree, different figures can be seen.

Fig. 2.4

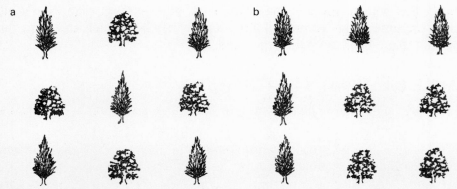

Closure

Whisper 'Schhhhhw........' to many people, and the name of a well-known brand of drinks will probably pop into their mind. We tend to fill out incomplete information, both in sound and vision, as shown in Fig. 2.5.

Fig. 2.5

You probably 'saw' the name 'Washo' even though in terms of sensation there are just 15 separate lines.

Related to closure is the **Zeigarnik effect**. Zeigarnik showed that people prevented from completing tasks returned to them more frequently than those allowed to complete them, as if there were a built-in drive towards closure. The effect has been shown in one study of complete and incomplete commercials where the incomplete one stimulated greater interest and recall.

Some commercials provide closure of an otherwise ambiguous situation. The Milk Tray story sequences show a quick series of James Bond type adventures, closed by the slogan 'And all because the lady loves Milk Tray'. Next time we see one, there will be a tendency to leap to the end: 'And all because....'. In such presentations, the product or brand name may only be exposed for a fraction of the total time, yet placed effectively, it acts as a satisfying last piece of a jig-saw, filling out the complete picture.

Continuation or 'good curve'

When patterns flow smoothly in a particular direction, we tend to follow that direction, and see the elements as a group. In Fig. 2.6 we are unlikely to see picture b, although it is certainly part of the whole.

Fig. 2.6

This 'pointing' effect can be used to lead the eye towards a message or brand name, as in Fig. 2.7.

Fig. 2.7

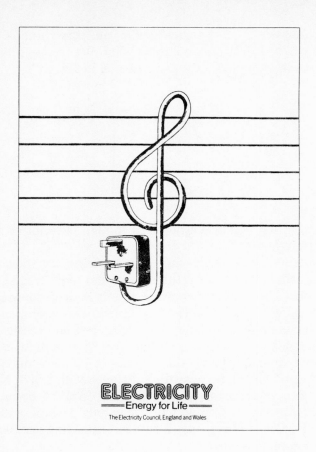

Pragnanz or the good gestalt

Reduction to simplicity and the formation of good patterns lie behind the previous principles. Figure 2.8b is embedded in the whole, but tends to be rejected, because there is a 'better' organisation possible.

Fig. 2.8

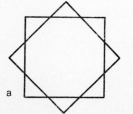

a   b

■ SELF ASSESSMENT QUESTIONS

Marks

1 According to Weber's Law, if someone can **just** tell the difference between 50 and 51 gm weights, what weight should they **just** be able to distinguish from a 100 gm weight? _ _ _ _ _ _ _ _ _ _ _ _ _   (1)

2 (a) Too long exposure to similar material may result in _ _ _ _ _ _
  (b) Trials of the new perfume showed it was far too weak. The smell was lost beyond five feet. By then it was below everyone's _ threshold.
  (c) Mrs Smiley says, 'I really *can't* tell marge from butter.' This suggests the distinction is below her _ _ _ _ _ _ _ _ threshold.   (3)

> closure   absolute   habituation   difference

3 Each of the following corresponds to a 'consumer set'.
  (a) 'Never heard of that brand.' _ _ _ _ _ _ _ _ _ _ _ _ _ _ _ _ _ _
  (b) 'Wouldn't use it if they gave it away.' _ _ _ _ _ _ _ _ _ _ _ _ _
  (c) 'That's the one for me!' _ _ _ _ _ _ _ _ _ _ _ _ _ _ _ _ _ _
  (d) 'Don't know enough about that one.' _ _ _ _ _ _ _ _ _ _ _ _ _   (4)

> unawareness   evoked   inert   inept

4 Put these factors affecting attention under the headings

        INTERNAL   or   EXTERNAL
(a) _ _ _ _ _ _ _ _ _ _ _ _ _ _   (c) _ _ _ _ _ _ _ _ _ _ _ _ _ _
(b) _ _ _ _ _ _ _ _ _ _ _ _ _ _   (d) _ _ _ _ _ _ _ _ _ _ _ _ _ _   (4)

> repetition   motives   novelty   interest

5 What Gestalt principles are at work here:

        fast   RELIABLE   fast

    RELIABLE | SONA | RELIABLE

        fast   RELIABLE   fast

  (a) _

(b) _____ (2)

Choose the best answers from:

> proximity   similarity   figure/ground   contrast

6 What process is shown by the following statements:

(a) 'How strange we noticed such different things in that film.' __

(b) Sexual words take longer to recognise than neutral words. __

(c) 'I never listen to Labour Party broadcasts.' _____

(d) 'You mean they tried to influence consumers by flashing words on the screen so fast they weren't noticed?' _____ (4)

> perceptual defence   selective attention
> selective exposure   subliminal perception

7 Write 'True' or 'False' by the following:

(a) Small advertisements will never attract attention. _____

(b) 'The louder you shout, the more they will hear.' _____ (2)

(Total: 20)

(Answers are on page 219)

■ STUDY AND EXAMINATION TIPS

Selecting your questions

1 Finding the right 'mix' of questions to allow you to show your ability and knowledge is an important part of examination technique. Take a little time to assess the whole paper, and **don't** leap in too fast. You might regret it when the question turns out to be not quite what you thought.

2 Let's take the questions below (p. 41) as an example.
Which seems to you the most straightforward?
Which seems the most complex?

3 My own choice would be for No. 4 as the most direct. It lays out very clearly what is required, and almost gives you the essay plan in its wording. Here's how it might work out:

(a) Introduction. Briefly describe the origins of the sets, and how they fit into the pattern from awareness to decision.

(b) Main division into awareness and unawareness sets.

(c) Subdivisions of the awareness set.

(d) Implications for the marketer.

(e) Short conclusion evaluating the usefulness of the concept of consumer sets.

Approach A	Approach B
(Repeated Theory–Example) Awareness/Unawareness: Example Evoked set: Example Inert set: Example Inept set: Example	(All Theory – All Example) Consumer set Theory Examples and relevance to marketing.

4 In this, as in many other questions, you have two choices in placing your marketing examples.

(a) Place your examples close by each theoretical point.

(b) Develop your theory in a block, then give the marketing relevance in a block.

The Table below shows how the two approaches would work for this question. The first approach allows you to punch home your practical points close by the theory, but could interrupt the theoretical argument. The second method gives you a good run at theory, but perhaps makes the relevance of your illustrations less obvious. The more complex the theory, the more effective approach B might be, since it will allow your theory to 'flow' more effectively.

5 Question 2 appears to be the most complex, though this may only be because of the quotation at the beginning. It may be one of the questions used by examining bodies to 'stretch' students, by allowing them to show their abilities with less straightforward material. It certainly gives great scope, and the problem might be what to leave out. Here's one possibility.

(a) Everyone, including consumers, is bombarded by stimuli ('the landscape of awareness').

(b) But we cannot, and do not, focus on all the stimuli. We select (the 'handful of sand').

(c) The factors affecting this selection are external and internal.

(d) The principal external factors are: (Check your memory by listing them, and then consulting the chapter. Remember to refer to the Gestalt school, especially figure-and-ground.)

(e) The principal internal factors are: (Check again.)

(f) The selection itself will be interpreted by the process of perception. Here mention can be made of familiarity, expectation, and the use of 'surrogate indicators'.

(g) The ways in which marketing could use these points. Here you could take a particular product, and show how the principles could be applied to make your chosen product the 'core' of the handful of sand. This would make a well-organised presentation, preferable to using different examples for different points.

Whatever approach you use, *get your examples in*. Examining bodies allocate as much as 50% of marks for practical illustrations, so: *get your examples ready now, not when the paper is in front of you.*

■ EXAMINATION QUESTIONS

1 'Our attention … is voluntarily influenced by our interests, needs, activities and expectations.' (Williams). How do these internal factors operate and what significance do they have for the approaches and techniques employed by marketers?

2 'We take a handful of sand from the endless landscape of awareness around us and call that handful of sand the world.' (Zen and the Art of Motorcycle Maintenance.) What factors encourage us to perceive some features of our environment as opposed to others, and what can marketing do to manipulate those factors?

3 Attention is an important determinant of what is perceived. What are the external factors governing attention, and how may these be used in promotional campaigns to gain consumers' attention?

4 Define the concepts of awareness set, evoked set, inert set, and inept set, and discuss the implications of these concepts for marketing strategy.

5 Discuss the interaction between perception and motivation. What are the implications of this relationship for the design of an advertising campaign?

3 Information processing II – learning and memory

We forget more clearly as time goes by. Student essay.

■ INTRODUCTION

A young child is by himself in a room. The television is off. He has watched his parents work the television, but so far has not turned it on by himself. He twiddles with the knobs, and finds that it comes on. A new behaviour has been learned!

A customer, unused to the layout of a new store, asks where the bedding section is. She follows the directions, buys her goods, and goes home. On the next visit she needs no telling. She has remembered where the section is, and probably the route there as well. A new behaviour has been acquired, *and* retained.

Throughout our lives we acquire new behaviours. In learning to swim, we acquire a new skill. In learning that Paris is the capital of France, a new fact is learned. Learning how to introduce a friend to someone else is a social skill. Emotionally, we can learn when it is appropriate to show anger, and when it should be concealed. Learning is of course not always positive in nature. We can learn a 'bad' golf swing, learn how to use drugs, or learn how to cheat and get away with it.

Taken together, these cover a wide range of behaviour, but do not include what might be called 'internal learning': learning which has changed the individual in some way which is not necessarily noticeable in his outward behaviour.

Suppose you see someone reading a book of Shakespeare's sonnets. It would not be possible to tell whether they had learned any without getting them to recite aloud. Yet the person might well have learned a poem, thereby acquiring new 'behaviour' which was not externally observable. Although the youngster might appear to have 'learned' to switch on TV quite suddenly, it is likely that earlier, internal, changes occurred as a result of observing his parents, thus paving the way for his own efforts.

For this reason, recent definitions of learning include the possibility of internal changes, as well as those in observable, outward, behaviour. So learning can be defined as:

Relatively permanent changes in behaviour and response tendencies that result from experience.[1]

Note that the learning must be more than temporary. If the youngster could not remember next day how to switch on the television, we could hardly say he had truly learned the skill.

Some of our behaviours are not due to experience. The pupils of our eyes get smaller in strong light, but we do not have to 'learn' how to do this as it is in-built. Such behaviours are not usually considered as learning.

In this section, we will consider two major themes in learning, coming from the **behaviourist** and **cognitive** approaches. In addition, as we can hardly consider anything as 'learned' if we immediately forget it, we will be looking at the concept of **memory**.

■ ASSOCIATIONIST OR CONNECTIONIST THEORIES

Much of our learning consists of linking one thing with another. Say 'Fish and …' to an English person, and 'chips' will be the response. Say 'Laurel and …' to a film buff, and 'Hardy' will be the reply. And what about 'Beanz meanz …'? In these cases, there seems to be a link or **connection** between words, so that the appearance of one triggers the other. But we can also associate **actions** with **situations**. Mother lifts the baby, and makes for the door of Gran's house. Baby waves a hand. Gran is delighted, and says, 'She's waving bye-bye.' The child has connected handwaving with being picked up and carried through the door.

Even as early as the 18th century 'Laws of Association' were being proposed. Amongst these was the law of **contiguity**, which stated that things close together in time or space will become connected, so that later the presence of one 'releases' the idea of the other. The law of **frequency** suggested that the more frequently two things are paired, the more easily the presence of one will evoke the idea of the other.

Besides these laws, others connecting the needs, interests, and past experience of the individual with the kinds of associations formed were proposed, so that many of the ideas explored by scientists in the 20th century (and applied by marketers) were in existence nearly 200 years ago.

Thorndike's connectionism

Thorndike[2] studied how animals come to learn associations, or connections, which lead to rewards, or satisfying situations. Typically, he used a puzzle-box from which a cat could escape by operating a mechanism whose workings were concealed. By a process of trial-and-error, false moves which did not produce release were *gradually* replaced by movements which produced the reward of release. The successful movements were 'stamped in' or reinforced as connections between the stimuli from the puzzle-box and the satisfaction of escape.

Thorndike thus drew attention to three points:

1 Learning. Where the elements of a problem are not obvious, slow, trial-and-error learning will occur.
2 Reinforcement. Those responses which lead to a desired goal will become more likely in the future. They are 'stamped in'. But in his view, the consequences act directly, and need not be mediated by 'ideas' or central processes. Note that in Thorndike's learning, an action *must* occur before reinforcement can result.
3 Motivation. Although behaviour itself may be trial and error, the cats appear to work towards a definite goal. So behaviour is more likely when the need to reach a goal motivates the learner.

Associationism or connectionism has formed the basis for two other major approaches to learning. These are the **classical conditioning** of **Pavlov** and the **instrumental** or **operant conditioning** of **Skinner**. Both involve environmental events, or stimuli, and responses which become connected with those stimuli. The relationships between stimulus and response are however somewhat different in the two theories.

■ CLASSICAL CONDITIONING

Ivan Petrovitch Pavlov was a physiologist who won a Nobel Prize for his work on the digestive system. In his report on this work in 1897 he noted that the dogs he studied quite naturally salivated when meat was presented. But he also noticed that salivation began when, for instance, they heard the footsteps of the man who brought their food. Were they, perhaps, expecting to eat the man?

Fig. 3.1 Pavlov's conditioning apparatus. A light can appear in the window, and meat powder can be delivered automatically to the food bowl

To study this puzzle more carefully, he built an apparatus in which there was no 'signal' from the experimenter's footsteps – the dog was in a separate room, and food could be given automatically. In place of the footsteps, various stimuli such as a bell, a light, or a metronome could be presented. To measure the flow of any saliva, he took a thin tube from the salivary gland in the dog's cheek, and led it down to the measuring apparatus (*see* Fig. 3.1).

He presented a light, and naturally found that the dogs did not salivate. In later trials, meat was presented very soon after the light appeared, and salivation began. After a number of pairings of light-and-meat, the meat could be left out, and the sight of the light *alone* would produce salivation. These three stages are shown in Fig. 3.2.

Fig. 3.2   Stages in classical conditioning

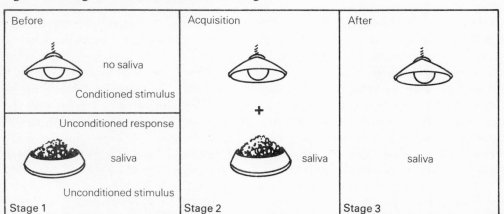

A comparison of Stages 1 and 3 will show that a connection which did not exist before has been formed between light and salivation, because of its association with a stimulus which *already* produces saliva.

Pavlov developed the idea of connections by suggesting that the process was rather like a telephone system. Some connections were made permanently, so that they occurred automatically (meat — saliva). Others had to be plugged in via a central switchboard (light — [meat] — saliva). More technically, he used the following terms to indicate how the connections were made:

1 Unconditioned stimulus (US). A stimulus which is already well-connected to a definite response (e.g. the meat produces saliva).
2 Unconditioned response (UR) which already is connected to the unconditioned stimulus (saliva automatically produced by meat).
3 Conditioned stimulus (CS) which at the start is not connected to the unconditioned response (e.g. the light, which does not produce salivation initially).
4 Conditioned response (CR) which, after the acquisition stage comes to be connected with the conditioned stimulus (e.g. salivation produced by light alone). This conditioned response is likely to be similar, but not necessarily identical, to the unconditioned response.

From Pavlov's and other work, further details of the classical conditioning process emerged.

Generalisation

A small child is badly frightened by a large dog which bounds up and barks furiously. Afterwards, the child shows fear, though to a lesser extent, when other dogs come near. The fear response has become generalised. *Generalisation occurs when a response to one stimulus is also brought out by other, similar stimuli.* The same brand name for a range of products can encourage generalisation. The associations with successful trial of one product may be carried over to other, possibly untried, products carrying the same name.

Discrimination

The child may gradually learn that while one particular dog is wild and noisy, others are quite calm and friendly. He has learned to discriminate and his responses towards them will be different accordingly.

Pavlov tested discrimination in dogs by always following one stimulus, such as a circle, with meat but never presenting meat after another, such as an ellipse. This strengthening of one connection (circle — meat) rather than another is **selective reinforcement**. *Discrimination occurs when the class of stimuli producing a given response is narrowed, often by selective reinforcement.*

Comparative advertising can be used to discriminate a brand from its competitors by naming other brands, but making clear the (advantageous) characteristics of the brand advertised. Care must be taken, however, or the consumer may make the 'wrong' association – with the competitors' brand!

Extinction

In the acquisition stage, repeated pairing of the light and meat eventually produced salivation to the light alone. But if the light is never followed by meat again, salivation gets less and less with each appearance of the light by itself. *Extinction of the conditioned response occurs when the conditioned stimulus is no longer followed by the unconditioned stimulus.* But if there is a rest from presentation of the conditioned stimulus, then the response may revive, a process known as **spontaneous recovery**.

Higher order conditioning

Once a stimulus has been connected with a response, as when a light is paired with meat to produce salivation, it can be paired with another stimulus, such as a bell. After pairings of the light and bell, the bell on its own produces salivation. But the bell has never been paired with the meat! This is called higher-order conditioning, where the response-producing properties of one stimulus are transferable to another, often quite different, one.

Pavlov did not suppose that the animal necessarily understood or worked out the situation. ('Aha, light. Food must be on the way. Better get the salivary glands ready.') What he said was:

In our 'psychical' experiments on the salivary glands, at first we honestly endeavoured to explain our results by fancying the subjective condition of the animal. But nothing came of it except unsuccessful controversies, and individual, personal, unco-ordinated opinions. We had no alternative but to place the investigation on a purely objective basis.[3]

This emphasis on objective, externally verifiable evidence, lay at the heart of the behaviourist approach, which was a strong thread in psychology for the first half of this century.

Applications to marketing

While we should not try to force Pavlovian conditioning onto marketing situations, it is possible to see its relevance and application in several ways.

EXAMPLE 3.1   MUSIC AND PREFERENCE FOR PENS

An experimental study of the effect of music on the choice of two similar pens (one beige and one blue) showed that when one was paired with favourable music it was chosen more often than the other which was paired with unfavourable music. But when the pairings were changed, so was the preference.[4] How this may have worked is shown in Fig. 3.3.

Fig. 3.3

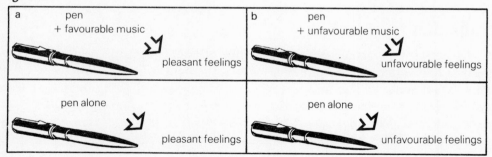

EXAMPLE 3.2   HOLIDAYS AND WINE

A well-known and attractive presenter appears in a commercial, on a golden beach, not a cloud in the sky, crisp-white breakers in the sea. Under her sunshade, she is smiling as she raises her glass of ice-cool Seashine, a new white wine. The camera closes in to a full-screen shot of her with the wine as she gives the final message. Now there is a possibility that the pairing of the presenter (the US) with the wine (the

CS) will result in a new association: sight of Seashine in supermarket: good feelings (the CR).

Fig. 3.4

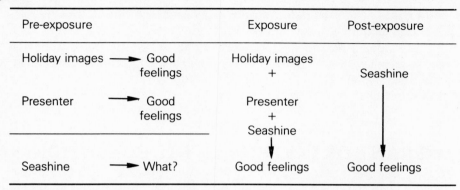

Pre-exposure	Exposure	Post-exposure
Holiday images ⟶ Good feelings	Holiday images +	Seashine
Presenter ⟶ Good feelings	Presenter + Seashine	
Seashine ⟶ What?	Good feelings	Good feelings

There are, however, one or two extra points to be noted. Firstly, all the other aspects of the setting – sea, sky etc. – are, by association with the pleasure of good holidays, themselves signals for good feelings.

Secondly, consumers are by no means unaware of what the marketer is doing. They are not simply passive, being worked on by careful arrangement of stimuli. Laboratory experiments have shown that conditioning effects with humans may depend on what the subjects think the experimenter is testing out.

Thirdly, if the stimuli associated with the wine itself (name, label, design etc.) are not sufficiently distinctive, then problems of **generalisation** may occur. Similar sounding names, similar labels, may evoke the same sort of feelings – and we have raised competing brands' sales! Of course, if the product is new to the field, it may be an advantage to use generalisation by having some similarity to a well-known brand with a good reputation.

Generalisation has been called a two-edged sword. By similarity we may draw from competitors' markets; but they might also draw from us. Some straightforward advice is:

- when competitors are high in market share, generalise
- when competitors are low in market share, discriminate.[5]

EXAMPLE 3.3 COLOUR-BLINDNESS? (A HYPOTHETICAL EXAMPLE)

A well-known company markets an established product for removing colour which has run into white articles. It is called 'Colouraway'. Near to it on the household shelves is a similar package from a less known company. It bears the label 'Colourgo'.

- how do you think this might affect consumers?
- what technical points from conditioning theory are involved?
- what might the lesser known company be trying to do?

EXAMPLE 3.4 'AN EXCELLENT TEAM SPIRIT'

Sponsorship is another example of using an existing, positive, situation to derive good associations for a brand name or product. In September 1987, the European Golf Team made history by defeating the Americans in America, thereby retaining the Ryder Cup. Johnny Walker, the whisky manufacturers, sponsored the team.

Next day, under a picture of Tony Jacklin and Seve Ballesteros appeared the caption 'An excellent team spirit'. The brand name then becomes associated with the famous victory, and with two celebrated golfers, while the slogan unites the two sets of associations of 'spirit'.

■ OPERANT OR INSTRUMENTAL CONDITIONING

In Pavlov's experiments, the animal was passive. Food arrived when the experimenter decided, and the dog's response of salivation was **elicited**, or brought out, by the stimulus. It was not **emitted** as a voluntary action.

B F Skinner arranged a somewhat different situation in which food was delivered *only* if a certain response was made. The animal or human must then **operate** in some way, and its response is **instrumental** in obtaining food. In a typical experiment a rat, new to the situation, explores a cage until by chance he presses a bar. This is followed by the sound of a food pellet falling into a food tray. The rat finds the food and eats it. He has emitted the response of bar-pressing, and been reinforced by food. As a result, pressing the bar becomes more probable in future. A number of important issues have arisen from work on operant conditioning.

Reinforcement

The association of food with light in Pavlovian conditioning can be said to 'reinforce' or strengthen the SR connection. But in Skinnerian conditioning, reinforcement only occurs when a definite response is made. A child puts his hand up in class, gives a correct answer to a question, and is reinforced by the approval of the teacher. This is **positive reinforcement**, which makes it more probable that the child will behave similarly in a similar situation in future. A customer tries a new washing powder. It works brilliantly so she is more likely to repeat-purchase it. Buying that product has risen up the **response hierarchy**.

There can also be **negative reinforcement**. A customer tries a new brand of yoghurt, opens it in the expectation of a great taste, but finds it most unpleasant. He spits it out and has some milk to wash the taste away. These actions bring to an end the unpleasant condition. Negative reinforcers, then, are those from which we try to escape. Our 'escape' responses are, in a sense, positively reinforced – they become more likely in the future. There may be a second effect of a negative reinforcer, for the customer once having escaped from the unpleasant taste may avoid it in future, by not buying the flavour or even, by generalisation, by not buying the brand. *Positive reinforcement occurs when an action becomes more likely in the future as a result of its consequences. Negative reinforcement occurs when behaviour which ends or avoids unpleasant situations becomes more probable.*

Secondary or **conditioned** reinforcers can occur in Skinnerian conditioning, parallel to the higher order conditioning in Pavlovian work. A rat presses a bar, a tone sounds briefly, and food follows. The food is a **primary reinforcer** since it satisfies a bodily need, but initially the tone has no particular reinforcement value. After the acquisition period, the rat will press the bar to produce the tone, even though no food arrives. The tone has acquired reinforcing possibilities by pairing with the food.

Skinner claimed that approval by others was a generalised secondary reinforcer, and this can certainly be seen at work in for instance the world of fashion, where the social approval of others is a strong motive in buying clothes. Money is a highly general secondary reinforcer. We can't eat it, or drink it, or indeed do anything very interesting with it but we are willing to work for it because it can be exchanged for things which *are* personally reinforcing to us.

Schedules of reinforcement

Continuous reinforcement occurs when a response is reinforced every time. A particular brand of cereal may have a toy in every packet. This may establish an early buying response, but if the toy incentive is withdrawn, and nothing is found in the packet, the response of buying that particular cereal may quickly be extinguished.

Continuous schedules are useful in establishing a response, as in the rat's acquisition of bar-pressing, or the promotion of a new product. But there are also schedules where reinforcement is not given for every appropriate response. These are termed **partial** or **intermittent**. They can be based on a ratio, so that the rat is reinforced for every fifth bar-press, for instance, or they can be interval based, when it will only be reinforced say two minutes after the last reinforced response. Anyone offering products or services on a house-to-house basis is certain to be on a partial schedule, since not every knock on a door will produce a reinforcing response! Both ratio and interval schedules can be either **fixed** or **variable**.

Partial reinforcement schedules

- fixed ratio, e.g. reinforcement every fifth response
- variable ratio, e.g. reinforcement occurs *on average* every fifth response, but exactly which responses will be reinforced is not predictable
- fixed interval, e.g. reinforcement occurs at intervals of one minute, provided at least one appropriate response is made
- variable interval, e.g. on average reinforcement is available one minute after the last reinforcement was available, but actual intervals are not predictable.

In fixed schedules there is thus a definite pattern of reinforcement, whereas in variable ones there is an *average* overall ratio or interval.

Behaviour can be maintained very effectively by a variable, or **random ratio** schedule, as can be shown by any gambling machine. On average, players must lose, yet because there is an occasional jackpot, their behaviour is maintained. Similarly, the sales representative is kept going in his door-to-door work by the occasional reinforcement of a big order!

Fixed ratio schedules are shown in 'piece work', when so much is paid per unit produced, and by promotions which offer a present for so many tops collected from cartons. In such incentive schemes, Skinner's ideas of a **token economy** and a **reinforcement menu** can be helpful. Some petrol voucher (or token) schemes allow the customer to decide what gift they will have from a range of alternatives. This reinforcement menu allows him to choose something he really wants, instead of having to take something decided in advance by the promoter. This is an important point to bear in mind both for customers and employees. What may seem highly reinforcing to one person may be unimportant to another, so the opportunity for self-selected reinforcement can be well worth offering.

Fixed interval schedules are often seen in organisations. Students tend to work to a fixed interval of examinations, and their behaviour may be at a low level until exam time comes round, when high levels of activity will be shown, only to die down again until the following exam raises response level again. Tutors would maintain a much steadier work level if they came in with spot quizzes on a random interval schedule!

EXAMPLE 3.5   COMBINING SCHEDULES

A neat combination of fixed-interval and random reinforcement was used by an evening paper. A magazine supplement was offered every fourth Friday (fixed interval). By itself, this might have produced increased sales only at four-week intervals. The paper therefore put individual numbers on the spines of the magazines. If these corresponded to any of the numbers printed in the preceding four-week period, a substantial prize was available. Thus the benefits of fixed interval and random schedules were combined.

Generalisation and discrimination

Both can occur with operant as well as classical conditioning. Reinforcement by a good meal at one of a chain of restaurants may make more probable eating in another of the same chain (generalisation). But a customer may find that although he enjoys most of Bestfood's products, he is not fond of their lasagne, whereas the lasagne offered by Fillupwell is very good. Discrimination on the basis of selective reinforcement has occurred, and will affect buying behaviour.

Extinction

The rat may continue to press the bar even when no food comes, particularly if it has been on an intermittent schedule, but eventually the response will decay and die. Similarly a product which has once been reinforcing will lose its response-producing qualities if it ceases to be positively reinforcing to the customer.

Shaping

This is specific to operant conditioning, and was used by Skinner to teach pigeons quite complex behaviours such as playing a kind of table tennis. Actions which are on the way to the desired performance (e.g. pecking a ball) are reinforced, but then reinforcement is withheld until a further step is taken (such as knocking it in a certain direction). Behaviour is then shaped in small steps, or **successive approximations** towards the final, target, behaviour. The technique has been used, in more sinister vein, to teach otherwise peaceful doves to attack each other.

EXAMPLE 3.6   FROM DOUGHNUTS TO DAIMLER

1 A car salesroom offers free coffee and doughnuts to people browsing amongst the cars on display.

2 A voucher for five dollars is offered to anyone having a 'no obligation' test drive of a model of their choice.

3 A five-hundred dollar discount is offered on purchase.
(Adapted from Peter and Nord[6])

■ MARKETING MESSAGES FROM CONNECTIONIST THEORIES

The application of association-based theories can be illustrated by dividing consumer behaviour into three phases: **pre-purchase behaviour**, **purchase decision** and **post-purchase consequences**.

Pre-purchase

In the pre-purchase phase, the consumer will already be aware of, or have his attention drawn to, a range of products in the area he is considering (Howard and Sheth's awareness set). Marketers will have used Pavlovian type situations to produce favourable associations towards their particular brand. They may have also used Skinnerian-based techniques such as discounts, vouchers or gifts as incentives towards buying.

Promotional copy can *promise* positive reinforcement – 'Reliable', 'the most effective', 'the smoothest you've ever handled' – thus affecting the pre-purchase response hierarchy, or the expectancy of the consumer. But if these promised reinforcements are not delivered, the post-purchase expectancy of the customer will be lowered, and the product's place in the repeat-purchase hierarchy will fall.

Purchase decision

At the stage of purchase decision secondary reinforcement may be used, for instance by approval of the decision. The retailer might say something like 'I'm sure you've made a very sound choice, bearing in mind the high standards you require from your system.'

Post-purchase

After the decision, there will be consequences – perhaps good, perhaps bad, perhaps mixed. If the consequences are positive, the customer will be likely to repeat-buy the brand or product ('I always buy Hitachi systems. They've always satisfied me').

If reinforcement is negative (failure to live up to promised performance, poor after-service etc.) then he may escape ('I'm cutting my losses. I'll sell and buy a different make'). Or he may avoid future problems ('You won't catch me buying that make again. Once bitten, twice shy').

Where the product or service is expensive, post-purchase reinforcement (and re-assurance) can be provided by a follow up letter or call, thanking the consumer for his choice, assuring him of its wisdom, and indicating that after-service, help and further advice, information on new developments, will be available from specified agencies or individuals should any be needed.

A large chain of High Street electrical shops has used this three-fold division as a basis for customer encouragement and re-assurance. They offer security and satisfaction

- before you buy
- as you buy
- after you buy

If we think in terms of response hierarchies, the pre-purchase stage will produce a certain ranking of likely purchase decisions, affected by Pavlovian type associations. These in turn will interact with factors such as availability and price and may result in an actual purchase.

The consequences of purchase may be:

1 The product maintains a high position in the hierarchy through positive reinforcement. Repeat purchase is likely.
2 It may lose position in the hierarchy (or even disappear into the inept set) because of negative reinforcement.

3 It may leapfrog another, perhaps temporarily unavailable brand, because of positive reinforcement.

These effects are shown in Fig. 3.5 for some (imaginary) washing powders.

Fig. 3.5   (a) Whito maintains position through good performance
(b) Whito loses ground through poor performance, Washo gains ground. Alternatively, Washo gains ground through good performance when Whito is temporarily unavailable

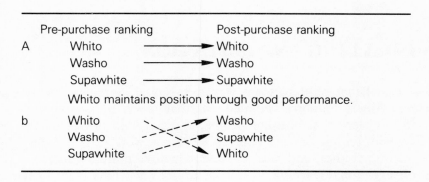

COMPARISON OF CLASSICAL AND OPERANT CONDITIONING

While close examination of the examples above may show that it is sometimes difficult to decide whether a situation is classical or operant in nature, certain general similarities and differences can be seen:

1 In classical conditioning, things 'happen' to the organism, and they happen on the terms of the experimenter. Learning is essentially passive. *Response depends upon reinforcement.*

2 In operant conditioning, the organism is more active: a response must be made before reinforcement will be given. *Reinforcement depends on response.* In a sense, there is an element of choice. Skinner himself, however, would dismiss this 'choice' element, and with it, internal states, as unworthy of scientific treatment:

We do not need to try to discover what personalities, states of mind, feelings, traits of character, plans, purposes, intentions or the other prerequisites of autonomous man really are in order to get on with a scientific analysis of behaviour.[7]

3 In classical conditioning, infrequent reinforcement may lead to extinction. In operant conditioning, intermittent reinforcement may strengthen response tendencies.

4 Both Pavlov and Skinner assume that evidence from lower-order organisms (rats, dogs, pigeons) can inform our knowledge of human behaviour:

Whereas the traditional view supports Hamlet's exclamation 'How like a god!', Pavlov, the behavioural scientist, emphasized 'How like a dog!' But that was a step forward...Man is much more than a dog, but like a dog he is within range of a scientific analysis. (Skinner)[8]

■ MODELLING AND IMITATION

Skinner argued that reinforcement was an essential ingredient for learning to take place. Albert Bandura[9] pointed out that much human learning occurs simply from observation of other people, and the tendency to imitate others, with or without reinforcement. This can be seen at work early on when children wear grown-up clothes, and 'use' the telephone like mummy does.

This **observational learning**, as it is called, may also have played a part in the young child's learning how to put the television on. The parents provided a **model** of successful behaviour which the child later imitated.

Bandura also added to the concept of reinforcement by saying it could be **vicarious**. *Vicarious reinforcement occurs when the consequences to someone else have an effect on our own behaviour.* Someone at a Weight-watchers club sees another person praised and applauded for losing weight the previous week. This will increase the observer's tendency to try to lose weight also. On the other hand, a TV portrayal of a patient in hospital, swathed in bandages, after going through a windscreen through not wearing a seat belt should decrease careless use of seat belts by the observer.

Modelling and observational learning can be seen in many marketing situations. Seeing other shoppers trying out a glass of wine at a supermarket display may increase the tendency of others to follow suit. High-prestige personalities (found by Bandura to be particularly likely to be imitated) are frequently used in commercials. TV in general, both in its commercial and non-commercial aspects, offers a wide range of models for both young and old to imitate. The power of such modelling can easily be seen when wide-scale availability of TV comes to a country. Suddenly clothing and life-styles move towards the 'benefits' of advanced civilisation and we all come closer to McLuhan's 'global village'.

A summary of possible applications of the three types of learning theory so far considered is given in Table 3.1.

Table 3.1   Marketing applications of learning theories

1 *Classical conditioning*	
Existing stimulus	New stimulus
Patriotic music	Political personality
Patriotic feelings become associated with politician	
Christmas music	Supermarket
'Christmas spirit' becomes associated with store	
2 *Operant conditioning*	
Desired response	Reinforcement
Product purchase	Trading stamps for each purchase
Product purchase	Competition offering prizes on a random basis
Opening credit account	Gift or prize (target behaviour is spending money!)
3 *Modelling*	
Modelling situation	Desired response
Models in commercials receiving positive reinforcement for product use	Increase of product purchase and use
Model receiving negative reinforcement (e.g. smoking – social disapproval)	Extinction or reduction of undesirable behaviours

Adapted from Nord and Peter[10]

■ COGNITIVE APPROACHES

Strict behaviourists were not interested in the inner mechanisms, if any, of human decision-making. But even within the behaviourist tradition alternative views were being advanced, and other, much more 'mentalistic' ideas were being proposed from outside it. As an example of the modified behaviourist position we will look at Tolman's **purposive behaviourism** and as an example of a reasoning approach we will examine Kohler's concept of **insight**.

Tolman's purposive behaviourism

The behaviourist Tolman believed in the need for human behaviour to be investigated using rigorous, objective methods. But as early as 1932 he introduced the idea of intervening variables into his purposive behaviourism.[11] These included a 'demand', indicated by an animal persisting towards a definite goal, and an 'expectancy' which is the information an animal collects about a distant goal. Three new aspects of learning were introduced: the **sign-gestalt** view, **cognitive maps** and **latent learning**.

STIMULUS-RESPONSE OR SIGN-GESTALT?
We have seen how the Gestalt school believed in the organisation of perception into good patterns. Tolman, though not a member of the Gestalt school himself, suggested that animals (or humans) do not simply learn muscular movements in relation to stimuli (the assumption of the so-called 'muscle-twitch' psychologists). He claimed that they learn that one pattern of stimuli (the sign) is related to another (the significate). Because of this emphasis on pattern, his theory is often referred to as a sign-Gestalt view.

FIXED ROUTES OR COGNITIVE MAPS?
Tolman argued that instead of learning a series of stimulus-response connections, we build up a cognitive map, in which a series of alternative patterns, rather than one rigid one, is possible. For instance, strict SR interpretations would suggest that the customer mentioned in the introduction would learn just the one route from entrance to household section. She would be at a loss if her usual lift was out of action. But in practice, as her experience of the store increased, she would develop a complex set of routes according to her needs – and some of these would not actually have been used, or reinforced, before. Her cognitive map enables her to plan in advance, according to her **present needs**, rather than because of satisfaction of **past needs**.

LATENT LEARNING
Sometimes this map will result in action, but at others it will be learned in the absence of any overt behaviour. Thus rats allowed to find their own way, quite casually, through a maze to the food box will, when deprived of food, take the fastest route from start to goal. It is as if a 'demand' or need had energised an already developing pattern of responses. Tolman gave the name **latent learning** to this inner learning in the absence of immediate need.

The examples given so far have been spatial. But cognitive maps can also be formed for more abstract qualities. A consumer might, at the exposure–and–attention stage casually explore some information about different brands of a product. Later, the cognitive map he had developed about the various qualities of the brands might be used in making a decision when a purchase was necessary.

Tolman is saying that reinforcement is not always necessary for learning to occur, and that organisms, whether human or animal **organise** input into patterns which suit their purposes. We are not passive collectors of stimulus-response connections. We *are* capable of developing our own organisational patterns.

Perceptual maps and multi-dimensional scaling

Although not derived directly from Tolman's work, the techniques of perceptual mapping and multi-dimensional scaling show how customers 'see' products on various dimensions. They may be asked to take a series of items – perhaps supermarkets – and rate them, two at a time, in terms of similarity, using a 10 or 12 point scale. A computer program is then used to produce a 'map' which indicates, in a kind of psychological space, where different supermarkets are placed by consumers. A hypothetical example is given in Fig. 3.6, using two dimensions only, though more can be generated if better information is thereby obtained.

Fig. 3.6   Two-dimensional MDS for supermarkets

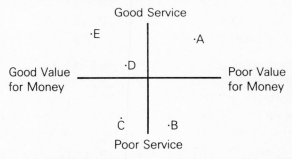

An illustration combining associationist strategies with perceptual mapping is given in Example 3.7.

EXAMPLE 3.7   IMITATION IS THE SINCEREST FORM OF FLATTERY

1 Promotional material for a fictitious toothpaste was given to students. The material 'mimicked' a number of attributes of the leader (e.g. 'A toothpaste with the same effectiveness as ... '). Format and colouring of presentations were similar to that of the top brand.

2 Perceptual maps using MDS were used for the leader, other pastes, and the fictitious brand. The 'challenger' was found to be positioned close to the leader.

3 The authors conclude that presentations that mimic the attributes of the dominant brand may elicit desired associations in the consumer's mind, and anchor the new brand close to the position of the dominant brand in the consumer's perceptual space. (Droge and Darman[12])

The Gestalt school

The building bricks approach of the connectionist groups was considered inadequate by the Gestalt school. Their emphasis was on **wholeness**. Behaviour cannot be broken down into little bits of stimulus and response, and then re-assembled, without losing something of its essential quality. It must be considered in total.

A typical worker of the Gestalt school was Kohler, who in the Great War was interned on the island of Tenerife, but allowed to continue his work on apes there. He felt that, given access to all the relevant elements of a problem, they could solve it by insight. As an example, Sultan, his most intelligent ape, used one stick to rake another from outside the cage, and joined the two to reach a banana which was otherwise beyond the reach of either. This behaviour occurred suddenly (though not necessarily quickly), rather than by the slow process of trial-and-error shown by the cats in Thorndike's studies. Placed in a similar situation again, Sultan immediately repeated the solution, which is not typical of early learning by the rat in the Skinner box. Further, the nature of the solution could be transferred to different situations, such as piling boxes to reach food too high to be reached from any one box alone.

CHARACTERISTICS OF INSIGHTFUL LEARNING
The characteristics of insightful learning are summarised as follows:

- availability and organisation of relevant information
- relative suddenness of solution
- transferability to other situations
- easy availability on future occasions.

■ MARKETING MESSAGES FROM THE COGNITIVE THEORIES

1 The cognitive view widens our conceptions of consumers. They are not passive organisms, responding inevitably to stimuli. They organise these stimuli into patterns, storing them as cognitive maps which can later be used in decision-making. The model applies strongly to the pre-purchase and purchase-decision phases noted above. The consumer responds to a pattern of stimuli (the **sign-gestalt**) either by a purchase soon after, having solved his problem, or by storing the organised information as a cognitive map to guide future planning. If the information is stored for future use, it is called **latent learning**.
2 Insightful learning will not occur easily if information is poorly presented. Good cognitive maps will be established in consumers' minds by the presentation of information as good gestalts. Poorly presented information will result in trial and error and very possibly, frustration.

3 There is a great difference between showing an attractive, well-known figure brushing their teeth with a certain paste (an associationist approach), and laying bare the problems involved in preventing decay and gum disease by the use of pastes. In one, the customer is really buying blind, on extrinsic persuasion; in the other, he is shown a problem and a possible solution. Of course, if you want to back both horses, you show an attractive, credible presenter who outlines the problem, and suggests that Brushwell is the perfect answer to it!

■ MEMORY

Life would be rather difficult if we had no means of storing what we had learned. Imagine the shopper asking for the household section, walking a few steps, forgetting the directions, asking again, walking a few steps … Impossible! But with memory, he will be able not only to find his way the first time, but also when he visits the store again – say in a month's time.

This simple illustration contains within it the three main phases of the memory process, shown in Fig. 3.7.

Fig. 3.7

In the acquisition phase, the shopper hears some sounds, which are attended to, and **encoded** into a meaningful message. This message may be **stored** for later use, to be brought back or **retrieved** when needed.

The example also shows the two systems which are held to be at work in human memory. When the shopper holds onto the information given him for a short period, we speak of **short term memory (STM)** and when information is brought back after a longer period, it is called **long term memory (LTM)**. The time limits of the two are not precise, but correspond roughly to the difference between holding onto a telephone number from directory to dialling, and recalling the address of a person we haven't contacted for several months.

A simplified but well supported model of the memory process is given in Fig. 3.8. Because of the division into short and long term memory, it is called the **dual-memory** theory.

We will work through this model to show the different fates awaiting information reaching us from outside, using the two main divisions of short term and long term memory.

Short term memory

ATTENTION AND SELECTION
In the previous chapter it was shown that we do not attend to all the information around us. There is a filter which screens out unwanted information and allows

Fig. 3.8   Dual-memory theory (Adapted from Atkinson and Shiffrin, Scientific American, 1971)

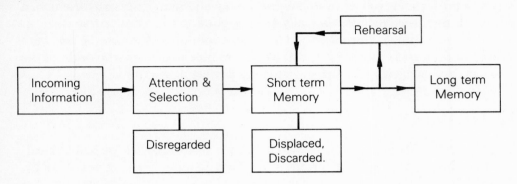

through other information. It is important therefore that the marketing message commands sufficient attention and interest for it to be processed through the filter. This is particularly true of television commercials, where the watcher is not deliberately trying to acquire information, but is simply exposed to it. The situation is different where a customer has asked for a specialist catalogue – a selective filter has already been applied.

Once through the attentional filter, the information will face the limitations of short term memory.

LIMITED STORAGE

1 The Magic Number Seven. It has been found that the average limit for separate items – say a string of unrelated numbers – is about seven. After that, many people are unable to repeat the items even immediately. Perhaps for this reason, local telephone numbers are often seven in length. They may also be **chunked** by being displayed or read in groups: 637-0942. This reduces the strain on STM, since there are now only two items to process, both below the memory limit.

Presentations which fling too much information at the consumer may fail because they produce **information overload**. To accept new information, we may have to empty out previous material, which is then lost. Students at complex lectures may be very familiar with this effect! Recent work has however shown that while consumers remember less from high-information material, they feel more satisfied with the decisions they have made.

2 Rapid decay of information. The short term memory is only a temporary storage system, and information rapidly decays from it as is shown by tests of consumer ability to remember brand names and promotional points even from recently seen commercials. The situation can be improved by **rehearsal**. We may well repeat an unfamiliar number to ourselves while moving from directory to phone. This rehearsing process keeps the information from decaying until it has been used. It is unlikely that consumers would use this technique when watching a commercial. Repetition can however be built in as a form of imposed rehearsal. Since this repetition might produce habituation, repetition with modification is often used. See Example 3.10.

DUAL-ENCODING: SUPPORT FOR MEMORY

The information which is filtered through is encoded either acoustically, as sounds when repeating a number to ourselves, or visually, as a visual image. Sometimes, however, both sound and visual codes can be used. We can add a name to a picture of an object, or we can make a visual image corresponding to a word. This is dual encoding.

Since television offers both visual and auditory channels, the same message can be encoded in both, thus offering support to memory.

EXAMPLE 3.8

Brooke Bond used the brand name 'Red Mountain' against a background of a red mountain, with the 'M' of the mountain itself also peaked. The picture of the mountain may be encoded visually, the words acoustically, supported by the presenter using the words 'Red Mountain'.

Where there is *no* clear link between verbal and pictorial messages, there may be channel rivalry, with the watcher switching from one to the other, and failing to receive and retain a coherent message. Advertising research has shown that 'framed' presentations in which the message relates brand and picture are remembered better than those in which the connection is not clear. Simply adding a picture does not necessarily increase retention.

It has also been shown that 'interactive' relation of pictures to product name helps memory. Thus, for a delivery firm called 'Rocket', the picture might be of a messenger astride a rocket.[13] Concrete words such as 'house' are easily translated into an imagery code, thus backing up the memory trace. But abstract words such as 'freedom' are not easily encoded visually. Hence image-arousing copy is likely to give more effective support to memory than material with a heavy abstract content.

Long term memory

While short term memory uses visual and auditory encoding, and generally, though by no means always, preserves the incoming information as it is, long term memory works somewhat differently.

SEMANTIC ENCODING: GETTING THE MEANING

Even in short term memory, it is not always the exact form of the information which is retained, but rather its meaning. This is especially true of long term memory. Tutors do not particularly want students to reproduce precisely pages from a textbook or notes. They would prefer the meaning to be retained. Marketers similarly may often want the message rather than its exact form to be remembered. This can be helped by using **elaboration** in which details are added which support the main message, and increase depth of processing.

One technique used to cause consumers to construct a wider network of memory links (i.e. to use elaboration) is given in Example 3.9.

EXAMPLE 3.9   INTERACTIVE PICTURES OR NOT?

1 Interactive picture-brand name presentations were developed, using *either* copy which supported the attributes of the picture, or which emphasised a different attribute.

2 Using an interactive picture to convey one attribute alongside copy discussing a different attribute produced better recall of copy material. Presumably the 'attribute map' developed is more complex and elaborated than when picture and message carry the same meaning.[14]

Semantic encoding will obviously be poor if meaning is not clear. Long, involved mail shot letters may defeat their object if transfer from short to long term memory is hindered by obscure vocabulary, over-complex sentence structure and of course information overload. For this reason the KISS principle (Keep It Short and Simple) may be a useful guide!

Where the specific details of an incident are retained, there is **episodic** memory. But if the watcher simply recalls the specific details of what happened on a commercial, without having retained the essential point, time and money have been wasted.

STORAGE

Short term memory stores for a limited time, with limited capacity. Long term memory can hold items from earliest childhood, as any talk with an old person will show, and it seems almost unlimited in its capacity. But most theorists argue that information does not enter LTM directly. It is temporarily held in STM, and then transferred via rehearsal to LTM. Students revising for exams are very familiar with this point. They go over and over material until it 'sticks' and is available at least until the exam is over.

EXAMPLE 3.10   REPETITION AS AN AID TO TRANSFER TO LTM

A motor company used no less than six television presentations on one evening. The uniting slogan of these was 'Once driven, forever smitten' – a nice, short, easy to remember message. But each presentation had a story line different from the remainder. The novelty and change produce attention, and prevent habituation, while the repetition makes for imposed rehearsal and consolidation. Once 'fixed', the slogan can be built on and form the focus of later material.

Simply using repetition (rote memory) may not however be the best method. Long term memory seems to use **organisation** as a major principle. For instance, lists which are well-organised are remembered better than those which are randomly put together (see Fig. 3.9).

Fig. 3.9   (a) Organised list
(b) Random list

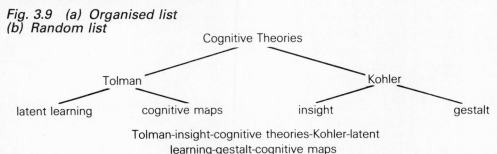

Tolman-insight-cognitive theories-Kohler-latent
learning-gestalt-cognitive maps

A message which shows good organisation, whether in written or audio-visual form, stands a better chance of reaching LTM than a less well organised one. But since organisation, like perception, is a personal thing, it is important for marketers to know how consumers classify information, so that their presentation can be compatible with the consumer's own principles. Research has, for instance, investigated whether consumers tend to organise information around brand information or product attributes.

RETRIEVAL
The context, or situation, in which information is acquired may affect ability to recall it. A familiar experience is to 'recognise' someone in the street, without quite being able to place who they are. Marketers must therefore beware. The supermarket is a different context from the home and its TV commercial, so that a bridging cue (e.g. the same picture on package and commercial) may be helpful to retrieval. This is an example of **recognition**, or knowing one has seen something before, and is generally far easier than **recall** which is unaided retrieval of information.

FORGETTING
This may be due to several causes. The **decay** theory simply assumes that items fade with the passage of time, while the **interference** theory suggests that material learned either before or after a specific learning experience may interfere with it. **Proactive** interference results from earlier material, and **retroactive** interference from later information.

This may become relevant when adverts for different brands of the same product occur close together, or when a consumer is bombarded frequently with appeals to take out insurance, or apply for a credit card. One set of information interferes with the other.

Inability to retrieve may not mean that the information is completely lost. Freud argued that some 'memories' are **repressed**, held below conscious level, and not normally available, but returning in dreams and the famous 'Freudian slips'.

■ SELF ASSESSMENT QUESTIONS

1 Put the most likely name against the following statements:
(a) Learning depends entirely on reinforcement. _ _ _ _ _ _ _ _ _
(b) Observational learning can occur without reinforcement. _ _ _
(c) Latent learning can occur without reinforcement. _ _ _ _ _ _ _
(d) Insightful learning can occur when all aspects of a problem are clearly recognised. _

(4)

> Kohler   Skinner   Tolman   Bandura

2 Choose the right technical term to go with each of the following items:
(a) When reinforcement is given every time _ _ _ _ _ _ _ _ _ _ _
(b) When reinforcement occurs only part of the time _ _ _ _ _ _ _
(c) 'You get a lovely coffee spoon for every five vouchers' _ _ _ _
(d) 'I shall be around *about* once a fortnight to see how you are settling in.' _

(4)

> variable ratio;   fixed interval;   continuous;   fixed ratio;
> variable interval;   intermittent.

3 Choose the most appropriate word from the list to fit the situations described.
(a) 'I knew a red-headed guy once. He was great. I still feel pretty good whenever a red-headed man goes by.' _ _ _ _ _ _ _ _ _ _ _ _
(b) 'I kept taking her Black Tray chocolates, but she stopped smiling at me like she used to. So I stopped taking them.' _ _ _ _ _ _
(c) 'At last, I've learned the difference between Suddsy and Sudso.' _

(3)

> generalisation;   discrimination;   extinction

4 Fit the right term to these statements:
(a) 'I found out how to use my electric meat knife properly by watching the demonstrator in the supermarket.' _ _ _ _ _ _ _ _ _ _
(b) 'The real thing that made me always use my safety belt was seeing Mary in hospital after going through the windscreen.' _ _ _ _
(c) 'At the start, I was just fiddling around with my DIY cupboard, trying this piece with that. It was pretty slow.' _ _ _ _ _ _ _ _ _ _ _
(d) 'Then I read the manual, looked at the pictures, and bingo, it was obvious how to do it.' _

(4)

> insight;   vicarious reinforcement;   trial and error;
> observational learning

5 Name the two systems of the 'dual-memory' theory.
(a) _
(b) _

6 Mrs Jannet sees a new hair shampoo advertised in a magazine. Next time she visits the chemist, she asks if they have that brand.

What are the three stages of memory involved here?

(a) _____

(b) _____

(c) _____   (5)

(Answers are on page 219)   (Total: 20)

■ STUDY AND EXAMINATION TIPS

The balance of theory and practice

1 For questions on learning you should have available:

(a) a definition of learning, which preferably allows you to talk about intervening variables;

(b) a clear awareness of Pavlov and Skinner, including technical terms, and the differences between the two;

(c) ready-prepared examples to show you know how each applies to marketing situations;

(d) criticisms of the strict behavioural approach. The approaches of Tolman and the Gestalt school;

(e) how these may affect the marketer's view of consumer behaviour, and therefore his marketing strategy.

Note very carefully whether mention is made of *cognitive* learning theory, as in Question 2.

2 For questions specifically on memory, make sure of:

(a) the stages and kinds of memory;

(b) factors assisting and hindering memory;

(c) relevant examples from marketing situations.

3 Learning is a particularly technical subject. But marketing is a practical activity. You have to balance carefully the theory and the practice. Let's compare the first two questions. They are both about learning, but what differences can you see?

4 On the theory side, No. 1 asks generally about 'learning theory' while No. 2 specially mentions cognitive theory, and appears to ask for one only. Thus No. 1 could include the whole range from Thorndike to Gestalt. Would this be wise?

5 Probably not! On the practical side there is again a difference. No. 1 asks specifically for applications, which are simply implied in No. 2. So if you went charging into your well-prepared theory on No. 1, you might not have time to score points on relevance to marketing. Take a breath before you start, and plan just how much theory you will include. Something like this would be suitable when tackling a question like No. 1.

(a) A brief definition of learning.

(b) A statement about major approaches: the connectionist/associationist and the cognitive.

(c) Take an example of the connectionist approach. *Make it clear to the examiner that you are aware of other material.* Outline its major principles.

(d) Develop a clear application of as many points as you can from the chosen example (e.g. Pavlov or Skinner).

(e) Give an example of a cognitive theory, and outline it.

(f) Show its relevance.

(g) Summarise, showing the differences in approach and application between each.

If you are a fast writer and thinker, you may well be able to get more in. If not, better to be cautious and show good knowledge of a limited range than be over-ambitious and fall apart through lack of time.

6 In No. 1 the balance is undoubtedly practical. In No. 2, a specific theoretical point, that of intervening variables, is involved. Which theory gives you the best chance to discuss these? (Check the Section on cognitive theories on page 57 if you're not sure.)

(a) Tolman is probably best. You can then talk about stimulus variables, response variables, and intervening variables mediating between them.

(b) Next, compare strict SR approaches with the S-O-R approach.

(c) You can also mention the 'closed black box' approaches and show the problems in applying them to the complexities of consumer behaviour.

But this is an examination about a practical subject, so always show by practical examples:

(a) the general difference in viewing consumers as passive pawns manipulated into stimulus-response connections;

(b) *or* as active searchers for solutions, making use of cognitive maps from sign-gestalt connections, and capable of latent learning in the absence of immediate reinforcement. Choose your examples to illustrate clearly the different types of situation.

■ EXAMINATION QUESTIONS

1 Explain how an understanding of learning theory can aid the marketer to plan more effectively product and promotional strategies.

2 With reference to any cognitive learning theory, discuss the importance of intervening variables in the learning situation.

3 What do you understand by the term 'learning'? Briefly outline any two theories of learning and discuss their practical usefulness to marketing.

4 What effect does learning have on purchasing decisions?

5 How do learning and memory influence consumer purchasing behaviour and what is their relevance for advertising?

6 How do people learn? Of what relevance is learning theory to consumer marketing?

$\boxed{4}$ **Motivation**

What a man can be, that he must be. Abraham Maslow.

■ INTRODUCTION

Mrs Johnson decides it is time to go shopping. She opens up the garage, starts the car and drives off. As petrol seems rather low, she stops at a petrol station, and fills up. She parks the car in the supermarket car park, and goes into the store.

Inside, she buys some of her usual purchases – things the family always seems to need – and picks up a new hair shampoo she's been wanting to try. She also decides to stop using a coffee with high caffeine content, and switches to another, low caffeine, brand.

After her shopping, she feels a little hungry and thirsty, so she goes into the coffee shop and has a coffee and croissant. That soothes her hunger and thirst, and she feels better as she goes out to the car park. There her car is waiting for her, ready to take her wherever she wishes.

If we compare Mrs Johnson and the car, we can find several similarities, but also a number of differences.

1 Both reach the same destination – the supermarket. But Mrs J seems to have **chosen** to go there, while the car can only respond to its driver's **control**.
2 Both need an external source of energy. The car 'needs' petrol, Mrs J needs food. But again, Mrs J chooses when, where, and what, to buy, both for herself and the car.
3 Both seem able to change direction – but Mrs J is doing the steering. She can also change direction in her purchases, by moving from one brand of coffee to another.

It looks as though Mrs J is actively pursuing some **goals** of her own choice. But how far does her behaviour come from inside – 'pushed' into being by forces within her – and how far is it 'pulled' from her, by outside factors, such as the appetising smell of the croissants, or the special discounts available at the store that week? Maybe she *is* partly like the car, started and steered by forces outside her.

This section will consider some of the questions raised by the story, such as:

1 What gets behaviour started? Why *did* Mrs J go shopping?
2 What steers it in one direction rather than another? (Why did she choose one store rather than another?)
3 What stops behaviour? (Why did she stop buying the high caffeine coffee?)
4 How far are we 'pushed' from within ourselves, and how far is behaviour 'pulled' from us by external forces?

The story uses a number of words such as 'need', 'want', 'goal', 'wishes'. These form part of the vocabulary of motivation, that is, of what causes people to behave in the way they do.

■ THE NATURE OF MOTIVATION

Motivation has been more precisely defined as

the set of processes that energises a person's behaviour and directs it to some goal[1]

Within this description can be seen two functions: the **arousal** function – the starter – and the **directive**, or steering, aspect.

Many views on motivation emphasise its cyclic, or 'start-stop' nature. At a very simple level, this is obviously true. We feel hungry, seek out food, and thereby reduce our hunger. In more technical terms, there is a physiological **need**. This in turn produces a **drive** or pattern of behaviour towards a **goal**. In the case of hunger, the goal will be finding and eating food. This pattern of behaviour aimed at satisfying or reducing the need can be called **goal-seeking behaviour**.

When the need is reduced (e.g. by eating) the associated drive will be reduced, and so will our goal-seeking behaviour, until the need arises again, as shown in Fig. 4.1. For this reason, theories of this type are often called **need-reduction** theories.

Fig. 4.1

Homeostasis

Many systems of the body have what might be called an **ideal state** – a condition of equilibrium which is maintained whenever possible, and returned to after being disturbed. Our body temperature remains around 98.4° Fahrenheit whether the outside temperature is around freezing, or above 100°. Often, this steady state is achieved by a feedback mechanism, rather like the thermostat which controls room temperature by switching a boiler on and off – we automatically sweat or shiver, though of course we help to maintain the internal equilibrium by taking off or putting on clothes. Homeostasis is the body's tendency to maintain a constant internal environment in the face of a changing external environment.

The idea has been incorporated into some theories of motivation. The drive-reduction view outlined above suggests that when some disturbance of equilibrium takes place (such as Mrs Johnson's feeling hungry) we are motivated to remove the disequilibrium, and behaviour ceases when the ideal state is regained. This cyclic repetition applies well to our basic needs. Marketers have no problems with the purely physical aspects of food and drink. We all must eat and we all must drink. But does such a model also apply to other motives?

Are basic needs the only motivators?

CURIOSITY AND EXPLORATION
Observation of a young child at play will show active and lengthy spells of behaviour which seem to have no other purpose than that of the activity itself. No food is given, no drinks are offered, because of the activity. Experiments with monkeys have shown them willing to work with wire puzzles not, as in a Skinnerian situation, for any external reinforcement, but apparently for the 'satisfaction' of the activity itself.

Some motives therefore do not rely on reinforcement from outside to get started or to continue. This has led to the widening of motives to include such factors as curiosity, investigation, and the desire to master situations whether or not we are externally rewarded for doing so. Such motives seem to occur in higher animals and humans alike, in adults as well as children, and in general throughout the human species.

SAFETY AND SECURITY
In a well-known experiment, Harlow[2] arranged for monkeys to be 'mothered' by artificial models. In one case, a bare, wire-framed, model supplied milk, while a second model covered with cloth did not supply milk. On any theory emphasising basic and bodily needs, the baby monkey should surely become 'attached' to the wire model, spending time on it, running to it in time of danger. But in fact the reverse was true. Certainly the baby would use the food-giving model to satisfy basic needs, but after that it spent more time with the cloth

model, and ran to it when any frightening situation arose. Clearly, then some other motives – proximity, 'belonging', security and comfort – may be involved here. It looks as though a level of motives beyond the purely physical is needed.

Do humans always seek an 'ideal state'?

Research suggests that a steady state may be far from ideal for humans. In one experiment, students were paid to be in a situation where the temperature was optimal, they were given food and drink, and the body was thus in a steady state. They were however wearing goggles which prevented them seeing any patterned light, and wore muffs on their hands to prevent touch stimulation. Within days, they were restless, some complaining of hallucinations, some refusing to carry on. Clearly, satisfaction of elementary needs is not sufficient for humans to function properly.[3]

Other evidence shows that many people actively seek out an increase in tension. The 'SSS' or Sensation Seeking Scale of Zuckerman compares people's preference for situations involving return to a peaceful state with those which break out of a steady state (Table 4.1).

Table 4.1   Adapted from Zuckerman's Sensation Seeking Scale[4]

Steady state	Stimulation state
• I would prefer living in an ideal society in which everyone is safe, secure and happy.	• I would have preferred living in the unsettled days of history.
• I would prefer a job in one location.	• When I go on a vacation, I prefer the change of camping out.
• The most important goal of life is to find peace and happiness.	• The most important goal of life is to live to the full and experience as much as possible.

There are obviously implications here for the marketing of adventure and safari holidays or courses. Some people appear to want to be uncomfortable and a shade anxious! They want life to be a thrilling experience, even if risks are involved. It is, for instance, particularly interesting that those with a high sensation-seeking score said they would drive well above the official speed limit, while those with low scores gave estimates much closer to the legal limit.

EXAMPLE 4.1   SAFETY VERSUS SECURITY IN PLACING YOUR MONEY

Building societies are well-known as secure, but maybe not exciting, places to deposit money. A famous British group used a commercial showing a team parachuting safely to earth, the chutes bearing messages about the company. The landing emphasises safety, but the parachute jump may make the company image more stimulating. But how might a person low on sensation-seeking react?

When the 'Big Bang' came to the London Stock Exchange in 1986, small investors were more able to buy and sell shares. Magazines and leaflets giving advice on investment multiplied. Large numbers of ordinary folk 'had a flutter'. The Stock Market crashed in October 1987, meaning heavy losses for some of them. But they had had the excitement and interest of playing the market.

Which direction would you go? Safe and secure, maybe not too high returns, or exciting and higher risk, with maybe higher gains?

Is external reinforcement always necessary?

INTRINSIC AND EXTRINSIC MOTIVATION

The child playing with a toy gets satisfaction simply from the activity itself. No one has to persuade him or reward him to start, or continue, playing. His satisfaction, or reinforcement, is intrinsic, arising from the activity itself, rather than extrinsic, when reinforcement comes as a *consequence* of the activity.

This is an important distinction, both for consumer behaviour and for the satisfaction of workers in organisations. The employee who works only to get money which in turn buys satisfaction of his needs is tied to his work by extrinsic motivation. In contrast, the one who finds interest in the work itself has intrinsic motivation as well to sustain him. The student who works simply to pass his exam and get his certificate, diploma or degree has only hoped-for external reward to keep him going. How much easier if the intrinsic motivation of interest and curiosity could be aroused!

The consumer who buys a blender mainly because it is on special offer is responding to an external incentive. The one who selects and buys the blender to increase the satisfaction obtained from cooking shows intrinsic motivation. To find the chosen appliance is on special offer is a bonus, but it is not the principal motivation.

The danger with purely extrinsic motivation is that the behaviour it starts may end when the reinforcement is no longer available. The special offer stops; buying decreases.

Different kinds of motives

There is no unique way to classify motives. The classification given below does however reflect the main points of the previous discussion.

BASIC, PHYSIOLOGICAL OR BIOGENIC DRIVES

These arise from bodily needs such as hunger and thirst, essential for individual survival, and sex, essential for the survival of the species. For this reason they are sometimes called **survival needs**.

PRIMARY DRIVES

These are also inbuilt, or unlearned, but cover such motives as **proximity seeking**, as shown by Harlow's monkeys, **stimulus seeking**, as investigated by Zuckerman, and **curiosity**, brought out by novelty.

LEARNED OR SECONDARY DRIVES

A young child is being fed. While she feeds him, the mother smiles and says, 'Good boy'. By association with the reinforcement of food, the approval of the mother itself acquires secondary reinforcing qualities, and a secondary motive of seeking approval may be established. In turn, this approval may become a general reinforcer, which can be used in Skinnerian fashion to shape behaviour.

Approval is used in all societies, but the specific behaviours which gain approval differ from society to society. A motive to compete brings approval in many communities; respect for private property exists in most, while others place co-operation and sympathy high on the list.

The models about the child will also shape the development of motives. Bandura's theory suggests that a youngster may well imitate the competitive behaviour of his father, while the schoolgirl doing voluntary work in hospital can be influenced by observing the care and sympathy of the nursing staff.

SOCIAL MOTIVES

None of us lives in a social vacuum. We are embedded in a social context. Therefore many of our motives go beyond purely individual ones such as easing our own hunger or thirst. We may, for instance, serve an elaborate meal to impress guests, work hard on a project to gain the approval of our supervisor, or show off our detailed knowledge of wines to exhibit our superiority over others in that field. More specifically, we seem to develop motives such as co-operation, competition, sympathy and dependence.

Besides getting our behaviour started, the social situation also has a steering effect. Whether or not aggression is an inbuilt drive, it is wide-spread from childhood to so-called maturity in most cultures. But the form of aggression is modified according to the situation. The temper tantrum of the three-year old would be completely inappropriate in a manager of 40, who may show his aggression in a strongly-worded note to his rival. But if he goes to war, it will be perfectly acceptable for him to kill and maim his opponents.

The 'marketing of aggression', if it may be called that, will thus have a different basis when recruiting for a wartime army than when appealing to a need to feel superiority over others.

■ THEORIES OF MOTIVATION

A comprehensive theory of human motives, that of **Maslow**, will be discussed first, followed by an examination of one specific motive, the **need for achievement**.

Maslow's hierarchy of motives

In his book *Motivation and Personality*[5] Abraham Maslow proposed a **hierarchy** of motives. By this he meant that when humans have satisfied lower order needs, such as hunger and thirst, there is an inbuilt motivation to move towards satisfaction of the next layers. This is an optimistic view of man, suggesting that we are not simply at the mercy of basic, animal needs. Rather, there is an upward and positive striving towards higher levels. A simplified version of the hierarchy is shown in Fig. 4.2.

Fig. 4.2

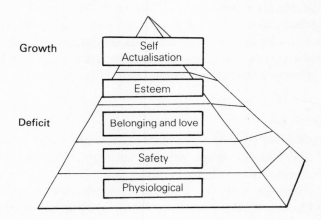

PHYSIOLOGICAL NEEDS

Firstly, in order to exist at all, we must satisfy the physiological or bodily needs. If this calls for all the energy we have, say in a famine-stricken country, there will be little motivation towards other levels. Indeed, cross-cultural studies of societies where food gathering and storage is habitually difficult have found that art forms, folk tales and mythology are poorly developed. A wartime study in America on volunteer subjects kept semi-starved for six months produced disappointment for a visiting girl-friend. As the experimenters put it, 'his reservoir of affectional responses was drying up.' In Maslow's terms, the physiological needs were prepotent or more powerful when compared with the belonging needs.

An even more startling example was an air crash in Peru, where the passengers, who included a Catholic priest, were driven to break social and moral taboos by eating the flesh of their dead fellow-passengers.

As Maslow said:

Freedom, love, community feeling, respect, philosophy may all be waved aside as fripperies that are useless, since they fail to fill the stomach.[5]

SAFETY AND SECURITY

These arise not only in the physical sense but also in terms of order in one's life, and the ability to rely on others. A job may be chosen because it provides 'security of tenure', thereby satisfying this level. On the other hand, fears of redundancy emphasise the need and make it more prepotent. Religions can bring order and the thought of protection for the faithful. Savings and insurance help to fulfil the safety needs in many people's lives.

BELONGING AND LOVE

The social needs of belonging, love and affiliation follow, with the desire to give and receive affection, to have friends and to be wanted. The reverse of this is the feeling of isolation, for the person who finds difficulty in making friends, or whose loved ones are far away. British Telecom ran into problems with a service which put together groups of young people for phone conversations. Parents received enormous telephone bills due to this service, and the apparent drive to make contact with others. The conversations were monitored, and no addresses or telephone numbers could be exchanged, thus reducing other possible motives.

SELF-ESTEEM

Besides wanting to feel part of a group, we also want to be thought well of by those around us, **esteem from others**, and to think well of ourselves, **self-respect**. Esteem from others includes prestige, status, recognition and reputation. Self-respect includes a sense of achievement and adequacy, of competence and being worthwhile as a person. Frustration of self-esteem brings feelings of inferiority, helplessness and weakness. This in turn may affect performance, so that a discouraging cycle of low self-esteem–poor performance– even lower self-esteem develops.

SELF-ACTUALISATION

At the top of the 'pyramid' is self-actualisation. This is not an easy notion to grasp. It suggests that when lower order needs are satisfied, there is a positive striving within us to use the highest potentials we have within us. Each of us has something valuable to release, and humans are motivated towards that end. Maslow said:

What a man can be, he must be. He must be true to his own nature.[5]

Unfortunately, the pressure from lower order needs may conflict with these upward strivings – they may become prepotent over higher needs. The mortgage must be paid, the old associations pull at us, so that we do not venture from safety and the companionship of old friends towards the risks of self-realisation.

Although Maslow felt that the upward movement was an inevitable general trend, he did not insist rigidly that each level must be fully satisfied before the next can be entered. Creative people in particular seem able to exist with only partial satisfaction of physical and social needs. He suggested that an average person might be thought of as 80% satisfied in basic needs, 70% in safety needs, and so in descending satisfaction to say 10% in self-actualisation. Perhaps that is why the hierarchy is often shown as a pyramid.

Maslow called the lower levels of his model **deficit** needs. By this he meant that all we do when satisfying these is to fill a hole within ourselves – literally in the case of physiological needs, psychologically as when we seek out friends to fill our craving for affection and belonging. If we are constantly making up these deficits, we have no motivation towards the higher growth needs. Satisfaction of these enhances us. We become more than we were before, we grow towards the realisation of our potential. As an example, taking a course in painting because it brings us into contact with others shows predominantly deficit motivation. Taking a course for its own sake, for the pleasure of improving our abilities and perhaps releasing some talent within us is a form of growth motivation.

Marketing messages from Maslow's hierarchy

MARKETERS AND THE PUBLIC

Within a developed community, the basic needs are relatively easy to satisfy. Nevertheless, for those moving towards higher needs, convenience in obtaining, preparing and cooking food may be important. More energy is left for higher levels. The esteem level can be combined with basic satisfaction in promotions emphasising the discernment and expertise of members of a wine club, with belonging appealed to by club trips to the vineyards.

Safety needs are often appealed to by building societies, who frequently use a protection image such as an umbrella in their material. Indeed, the building societies are almost synonymous with security in the small investment field. Such security needs are also appealed to by insurance companies.

EXAMPLE 4.2

1 Use of safety and protection images by building societies and insurance companies:

2 Appeal to prepotency of safety needs:
'Would your family be able to cope financially if you were disabled or seriously injured in an accident? Give yourself peace of mind now!'
A free smoke detector is offered as an incentive for taking out a policy.
(Letter from insurance company)

Belonging needs are appealed to by organisations with slogans like 'the listening bank', and Coke adverts frequently portray groups of happy people.

A predominant need in developed Western communities seems to be that of high esteem. Marketing which appeals to the prestige attached to a product, or which fosters a feeling that a consumer's opinion is worthy of respect is making use of this motive.

EXAMPLE 4.3 GOING FOR GOLD

'There is an exclusive club which goes to great pains to serve its membership. The key to its door is the Gold Card. Although Cardmembers might already have tried unsuccessfully to become a Gold Cardmember, they are nonetheless welcome to apply for membership again, since their circumstances might now be different.'
(Part of promotional material for the American Express Gold Card.)

The copy emphasises the prestige element, and appeals to upward-moving motives.

'Have you ever thought how your knowledge as a motorist could show today's car manufacturers the way to providing a better service in the future?
It's **your knowledge** we're seeking'
(Part of material from Ford Motor Company aimed at establishing a Ford Motorfile of information.)

With shorter working weeks, earlier retirement, and, less fortunately, unemployment, there is ample time and, in Maslow's view, a healthy purpose, for courses which allow people to explore their own latent possibilities. In Britain, the success of theme camps attests to the size of the market in self-development and self-realisation.

ORGANISATIONS

Work is the main means by which people get the wherewithal for satisfying the lower needs of food and shelter. Management can however also cater for other needs. Besides fostering a general feeling of belonging to the company, as the Japanese do, they can provide social and recreational facilities, while the esteem level suggests that mutual respect should be developed, and adequate recognition given for effective work.

The level of self-actualisation is less easy to satisfy. The majority of jobs scarcely offer wide possibilities for self-realisation, and it may well be that many workers prefer a safe, routine job which leaves them free to seek other satisfactions outside work. Nevertheless, the theory does suggest that some people may welcome opportunities for self-development at work, to the mutual benefit of themselves and the organisation. Specific ways of arranging this will be discussed in Chapter 9.

The need for achievement

MURRAY AND THE THEORY OF NEEDS AND PRESSES

The American psychologist Murray thought of people as subject to the interaction of forces both from within and outside the person. The outside forces are presses, which may be described as the power of a situation to affect the well-being of a person in one way or another. Thus p-Recognition represents pressure from the environment to compete for honours or awards. The forces from within he called needs, urging us towards behaviour which would satisfy them. Some of these are **viscerogenic**, derived from the body, and thus similar to Maslow's lower level. Others are **psychogenic**, such as the need for dependence, and are like the later levels of the Maslow hierarchy. One particular need has been studied intensively, and applied within the business field. This is the need for achievement, usually abbreviated to **n-ach**. Murray described it in these words:

To accomplish something difficult. To master, manipulate or organise physical objects, human beings or ideas as rapidly and independently as possible. To overcome obstacles and attain a high standard. To improve oneself and excel. To rival and surpass others.[6]

A useful need to have in Western competitive society! There are some similarities with Maslow's self-actualisation, but here the emphasis is on external comparison rather than on the release of internal potential.

McLELLAND AND THE NEED FOR ACHIEVEMENT

McLelland investigated this particular need and concluded that those high on n-ach tend to be task or production orientated, rather than concerned with good relations. They need feedback on their performance to monitor their efforts and adjust their goals, and they prefer to feel in control themselves, and personally responsible.

He found that those involved in sales and marketing tended to have higher need for achievement than those in engineering or finance. He also studied the relation of economic performance and level of n-ach in different countries, finding a positive relation between them. Protestant countries tended to show higher levels of both than Catholic.[7]

There is a problem in the management situation for the high achiever. Evidence shows that such people do move upwards quickly, but, because of their need for 'internal control' find it difficult to delegate. They may thus reach a position where they are exposing themselves to too many demands, and overstraining their personal resources.

McLelland has more recently worked on the motive for power. He described a **Leadership Motive Pattern** which consists of a moderate need for power, coupled with high self-control, but a low need for affiliation with others. In the non-technical field, such people rise to power, partly because of their need to achieve it, partly because their relative lack of interest in social relations (low **need for affiliation**) enables them to discount possibly adverse feedback from colleagues on their decisions.[8]

ATKINSON AND FEAR OF FAILURE

While difficult tasks are motivating for the high achiever, and draw him towards them, there are of course the negative aspects of the risks involved. Atkinson therefore added a second factor which might be called fear of failure, and suggested that motivation was the result of the positive element deriving from n-ach and the negative elements from fear of failure. This suggests different patterns of motivation in those high in n-ach, but low in fear of failure when compared with those with low n-ach but high fear of failure[9] (see Table 4.2).

Table 4.2

Difficulty level of task	High n-ach/low fear of failure	Low n-ach/high fear of failure
High	Avoid: expectancy of success low	Choose: blame attached to failure low
Low	Avoid: incentive of success low	Choose: expectancy of success high
Medium	Choose	Avoid

■ THE INTERACTION OF MOTIVES

It is too simple to suppose that behaviour at any one time is governed by a single motive, that shoppers go shopping to satisfy a single need, motivated only by economic considerations. A study of why people shop suggested eleven possible motives beyond the obvious product-related ones. Each shopper might combine these motives into a unique pattern, so that marketers face a considerable problem in finding which particular motives are important for any individual.

Where more than one motive seems to be involved, we can speak of **multi-determined** actions. Thus Murray uses the term **fusion** to describe situations where two needs are satisfied by the same behaviour. A statement such as 'Learn new skills in a companiable environment' then appeals both to the need for achievement, and that for affiliation and belonging. Where research suggests that clusters of needs exist, marketing strategies can make use of this fusion of motives by making such multiple appeals.

Sometimes, however, instead of co-existing profitably, motives may be in **conflict**. Here, satisfaction of one need interferes with or prevents satisfaction of another. A typical contemporary conflict situation exists for the 'working wife and mother' who may well find her needs for achievement at odds with her need to give affection and help to her family. The situation will be worsened by a press, in Murray's terms, from husband and children for greater attention than is easily available. Both sets of needs are not completely fulfilled, and may be described as **frustrated**.

Frustration

When a motive cannot be satisfied, when progress towards a desired goal is blocked, there is frustration. This is part of all our lives, from the small irritation of the cancelled train to the blocking of promotion because the desired position is firmly held by a not-too-old person who shows no sign of moving.

One of the most frequent responses to frustration is **aggression**. Indeed, Freud originally felt that frustration of our drives was the sole source of aggression. This aggression need not of course be physical. The four-year-old may resort to hitting to recover a toy, but the customers in overlong checkout queues will hopefully restrict themselves only to verbal abuse of inefficient management.

Opportunities for frustration abound in marketing. Products may not be available, or require a long wait; after-service may be poor; performance may not be as claimed. All of these are sources of negative feelings, if not of outright aggression. But where a goal is facilitated, frustration becomes an ally of the marketer. The electric carver which produces smooth, succulent slices of meat instead of the jagged bits previously served will be a source of satisfaction and, as shown in Chapter 3, a source of positive feeling towards the supplier. Audi cars ran a commercial showing a family enjoying the pool at their holiday villa while other families were still suffering the frustrations of their journey. Audi, satisfaction; others, frustration!

Frustration as arousal

While a frequent response to frustration is aggression, it may also be a **stimulus to problem solving**. It then energises our behaviour towards the goal, and is thus constructive. But one of the oldest laws in psychology, the **Yerkes-Dodson law**, states that there is an optimal level for arousal. Too little, and we are scarcely motivated. Too much, and performance drops through excess arousal and in the extreme, panic or unproductive temper. Thus workers who have no problems have little arousal from frustration; where frustration is extreme, extreme reactions may occur. But a problem-solving situation which presents challenge (but with it of course the possibility of frustration) can be very motivating.

Other reactions to frustration

Where frustration is considerable or prolonged, we may simply give up the immediate goal and 'leave the field'. The enterprising executive whose ideas are never taken up will go elsewhere. Where there is less extreme frustration, we may take 'time out' to recover aplomb and re-charge. Here products can be offered as relaxers as in the portrayal of cigars and pipes as soothing ways of coping with the pressures of difficult situations. Holidays and get-away weekends can be presented as giving a break from the stress and frustration of working life.

Less importantly for marketing, there may be **regression**. Frustrated in our forward attempts, we may drop backwards in level of behaviour, and for instance throw a temper tantrum like a child.

■ MOTIVATION RESEARCH

The questionnaire, administered to large numbers of people, is a familiar part of market research. It offers **quantitative** data obtained under relatively structured conditions from large samples. It is not however usually possible to go to any great depth with large numbers involved because of the time and expense. **Motivation research**, originating in the 1950s, aimed at a more **qualitative**, less structured approach, which could give fuller insight into the consumers' motives in choosing and purchasing. Much criticism has since been directed at some of the techniques involved, but individual or idiographic studies of consumer's motives remain an important area of research. The main methods used are interviews and projective techniques.

Interviews

Interviews may be carried out in a one-to-one situation, the personal interview, or in a group. They may be called **depth** or **focus** interviews, since their purpose is to probe towards underlying motives of consumer behaviour. The word 'depth' is perhaps unfortunate, since it suggests a definite association with the depth psychology of Freud and others. Dichter, one of the pioneers, was orientated towards Freud, and was criticised as seeing Freudian symbolism everywhere. But an interview certainly does allow exploration beyond straight 'yes' and 'no' answers. Against this is the possibility that bias may be introduced by the interviewer because of prior opinions, because of the topics introduced, and because of the interpretation of responses. Interviewers therefore need to be carefully trained.

PERSONAL INTERVIEWS
These offer considerable flexibility, but since only small samples can be handled, selection of a group representative of the target population is vital. While the course of the interview is guided by the interviewer, he must be clear what his brief is, e.g.

- what is the purpose of the interview?
- is it exploratory, or to investigate further a specific hypothesis about product characteristics and consumer response?
- what topics are to be covered?

In the absence of clear direction, there is a danger that different interviewers will bring out different responses, and an undesirable subjective element will have been introduced.

Personal or one-to-one interviews are indicated where:

1 detailed investigation of individual behaviour, attitudes or needs is required;
2 personal, confidential or delicate material is to be discussed;
3 where society holds strong norms;
4 where a decision process needs to be broken down into a series of clear steps.

They do of course require far more time than group interviews, so a cost-benefit assessment is desirable before embarking on an intensive programme.[10]

GROUP INTERVIEWS
These perhaps lose the intensity of the individual approach, but do allow for the interchange of ideas amongst a small group of about ten people, and, since social motives are an important element in buying behaviour, can be of value in showing in miniature the social forces on consumers. The task of the interviewer is to act as a **moderator**, keeping the group within reasonable limits without imposing his own views, and restricting the tendency for strong individuals to act as **opinion leaders**, whose contributions may sway those of others, thus biassing the discussion.

The leader may use a **focussing** or **funnelling** approach, where general discussion is followed by successively more specific exploration. The use of pens and biros might be initially introduced, followed by focussing down to ink pens, finally focussing down to what particular characteristics of pens are important to consumers.

Focus group interviews may be used for:

1 exploring consumer reaction to ideas for new products;
2 exploring consumer reaction to existing or projected advertisements;
3 generation of ideas for new products;
4 tuning in to the vocabulary and language of a consumer segment to assist in the design of questionnaires or advertising copy.

Nowadays, to assist in the analysis of discussions, video-tape recording may be used.[11]

Projective techniques

When we are faced with direct questions, especially on a sensitive subject, we may well be a little on our guard and cautious in our responses. A number of methods, largely derived from clinical psychology, have been used to lessen this 'censorship' which exists in our day-to-day responses. The common element is that they present an unstructured or ambiguous stimulus such as a person sitting, head in hands, on a settee. In the absence of any clear indication as to how this came about, the respondent is forced into their own inner resources to explain or comment on the stimulus, thereby perhaps revealing more of their deeper motivation than would be discovered by direct methods. The materials used may be visual as in the **Thematic Apperception Test** and the **Rorschach inkblot** tests, or verbal, as in **word-association** and **story completion** tests.

THEMATIC APPERCEPTION TEST (TAT)

This test was designed by Murray to bring out **themas**, which are the interactions of needs and presses in an episode. The pictures of the series aim to present episodes which can tap such needs as affiliation, dependency and, in particular, achievement. Equally, the presses from the environment may be more easily shown in this indirect way. All the subject has to do is to tell a story setting the picture in a context of what happened previously, what is happening now, and what will happen in the future.

The test is widely used in clinical work and in counselling, but is probably too general to be valuable in its official form for specific marketing use. It has also been criticised as being over-subjective in its reliance on the personal interpretation of the tester.

Adaptations of the format can however be made. Well-chosen pictures from newspapers bring out surprisingly detailed themes, and subjects appear to enjoy the 'story' element. The 'bubble' technique, where a situation is presented (say two people having a glass of wine together) with bubbles to fill in what they say can also help to bring out underlying themes aroused by advertising material.

EXAMPLE 4.4

Fig. 4A

THE RORSCHACH INKBLOTS

The stimulus in this case is even more ambiguous – one of the series of inkblots devised by Rorschach. The subject simply tells what he sees, and the responses are analysed to give a view of underlying motives. In spite of the apparent simplicity, training to use the test is rigorous, and many books have been written on its scoring. But once more, there is a fear that subjectivity of interpretation lessens its use as a scientific instrument. It is a 'restricted' test, available only to those with adequate qualifications.

WORD ASSOCIATION TECHNIQUES

These date back at least to the psychologist Jung, at the beginning of the century. A word is presented, and the subject responds as quickly as possible with the first word that comes to him. Some words, like 'grass' are likely to bring common associations, such as 'green'. Others, such as 'smoke' or 'smell' may bring very varied and personally revealing responses. Some may produce long hesitation before replying, or even complete blocking, suggesting that a kind of defence is operating. Brand names, types of product can be mixed in with neutral words to probe consumer associations. What is your first response to the words in Example 4.5?

EXAMPLE 4.5

red	sales	fair
marketing	ground	high
small	profit	study

SENTENCE AND STORY COMPLETION TECHNIQUES
An incomplete sentence, or the start of a story is given, and the subject completes it as he wishes. Again there is high opportunity for a variety of individual responses, but also the risk of subjectivity in interpretation. Try the items in Example 4.6.

EXAMPLE 4.6 TYPES OF COMPLETION ITEM

1 The salesman approached the customer and ....

2 The family had nearly decided on their choice of holiday, but father was worried about whether he could afford to take three whole weeks off work. What happened next?

The current assessment of projective methods in marketing is less positive than in the 1950s. There is a certain 'face validity' in that we seem to be tapping underlying, perhaps unconscious, motives, but they are probably best thought of as exploratory approaches which can provide pointers for larger-scale, quantitative, research.

■ SELF ASSESSMENT QUESTIONS

Marks

1 Re-arrange the words on the right to fit the descriptions on the left:

(a) Physiological balance	Curiosity	_ _ _ _ _ _ _ _ _ _
(b) Primary drive	Approval	_ _ _ _ _ _ _ _ _
(c) Secondary drive	Homeostasis	_ _ _ _ _ _ _ _ _

(3)

2 Put in the four missing words from Maslow's hierarchy in the correct position.

(4)

Fig. 4B

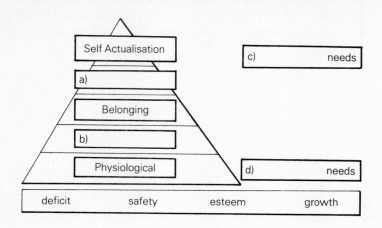

deficit   safety   esteem   growth

3 Put true or false against the following.
   (a) Young Ms A is rising quickly in the firm, so she probably ranks high on n-ach. _____
   (b) People high on n-ach do not require feedback on their performance. _____
   (c) People high on n-ach generally take impossible risks. _____   (3)

4 Choose the right words to fit the situations below:
   (a) Mrs Fanting wanted raspberry yoghurt, but there was none in the shop. _____
   (b) She shouted angrily at the manager. _____
   (c) He said, 'Madam, that's not very ...' _____
   (d) Mrs Fanting, still angry, shouted at the children, who were really quite well-behaved. _____
   (e) 'Mum,' said her oldest son, 'You're behaving just like a little child.' _____   (5)

---

aggression   frustration   constructive   regression
repressive   displacement

---

5 Put true or false against the following:
   (a) To have opinion leaders in a group discussion is always helpful. _____
   (b) Delicate topics are best handled in group interviews. _____
   (c) The TAT is a completely objective technique. _____   (3)

6 Put 'intrinsic' or 'extrinsic' against these statements, to indicate the type of motivation involved.

(a) 'I only bought that DIY kit because there was 25% off. I've hardly ever used it.' _____

(b) 'I'm so glad I bought that new set of artists' brushes. I'm so much more confident with them, and I can really express myself.'
_____   (2)
(Total: 20)

(Answers are on pages 219–20)

■ STUDY AND EXAMINATION TIPS

Don't waffle!

1 In case you don't know what 'waffle' is, it means trying to convince the examiner that you must know a lot because you have written a lot. Unfortunately, contrary to popular opinion, examiners do not weigh scripts. They are more impressed by clearly presented points than by long passages containing little hard fact.

2 Here's how *not* to do it, taking Question 3 as an example. 'Needs are very important in the study of consumer behaviour. They must be studied by the marketer if he is to understand the motivation behind purchase behaviour. Needs are of various kinds, but are always involved when a consumer makes a purchase. (etc.)'

3 The passage does not indicate what needs are, what *kinds* of needs there are, and makes no clear relation between particular kinds of needs and particular kinds of purchase behaviour.

4 If you are the sort of person whose pen tends to run away on its own, some kind of focus is important. This will keep you on the rails. A plan is one obvious method. Other suggestions are:

(a) use a relevant quotation or definition to commence your answer. This will set the scene both for you and the examiner;

(b) indicate clearly how you intend to tackle the question: 'I intend to answer this question in two main sections. Firstly, I shall discuss the concept of "needs", and secondly, I shall examine what influence they have on consumer buying behaviour, particularly in directing it towards one type of purchase rather than another.'

Now you yourself are clearly directed towards your answer! Do not simply repeat the question – the examiner already knows what it is;

(c) paragraph clearly. An answer which falls into clear blocks, each making a particular group of points, is easy to read, and makes a good impression. Some boards have said they have no objection to students using paragraph headings (e.g. by underlining). Again, this will force you to think what you are saying, and give the examiner a clear indication of what to expect. If you are a fast writer, you may need to think more in terms of sections, each of which might have more than one paragraph in it.

5 For Question 3, a paragraph (or section) approach could be:

(a) *motivation and needs* (An explanation/definition of motivation emphasising the directive function, and the internal 'push' of needs.)

(b) *types of need* (A brief classification, e.g. distinguishing primary from secondary motives, with examples. Maslow's hierarchy is a good 'package' – but will you have time to explain it *and* answer the question adequately? Be sure, however, to include the social aspects of needs.)

(c) *consumer needs* (An examination of how the needs outlined in (b) apply in practical buying situations. Use plenty of examples!)

(d) *are needs the only directive force?* (The 'pull' influences of advertising, incentives, discounts, competitions. The 'steering' exercised by these when a need already exists, e.g. for bread: why one loaf rather than another?)

(e) *can marketers establish needs?* (A discussion of whether marketing must simply build on existing needs, or whether consumers can be brought to recognise needs within themselves they were not previously aware of (e.g. self-actualisation), or whether, perhaps, a need can be created.)

(f) *conclusion* (Evaluating the concept of need in relation to marketing. Examiners will be glad to see a reasoned appreciation of the concept – but avoid purely personal phrases such as 'I think that ... '. Give an objective summary based on the points you have made.)

■ EXAMINATION QUESTIONS

1 How adequate is it to argue that a consumer's motivation to purchase a product is determined by his need for that product? Give relevant examples to illustrate your answer.

2 Explain briefly how you would research consumer motivations to purchase either:

(a) alcohol free lager, or
(b) the Sinclair C5 electric car.

3 What role do needs play in directing consumer buying behaviour?

4 'The problem with motivation research is the difficulty of interpreting with any clarity the results of such research, and the ease with which bias can affect the results.' Discuss.

5 Can advertising change individual motives?

6 Why is an understanding of the process of motivation of such fundamental importance to the marketer?

5 The consumer in society

No man is an island. John Donne.

■ INTRODUCTION

John Donne's statement is very true for the majority of people. We are not isolated individuals at all. We could not survive in infancy unless there was some group of people, usually our family, ready to look after us. At school most youngsters settle into informal friendship groups, starting in the playground, perhaps, but remaining over several years. Later, there will be more formal clubs and associations we will join for social or professional purposes.

Most of us think of ourselves as belonging also to larger groups – being British, Spanish, or American. We cannot possibly see all the members of those groups, yet are conscious that we belong within them.

Such groups may produce two effects on individuals. Firstly, we draw the benefits of support from many groups. The family supports us when young. The professional association helps to develop our career. The friendship group can be turned to when the going gets rough. There is a 'we-feeling' amongst the members which produces mutual support and **cohesiveness**.

The second effect, however, may be that in order to maintain support from the group, to feel part of it, we have to keep within certain rules, not necessarily laid down in writing, about how we should behave. The doctor who breaks the rules of his professional association will be 'struck off the register' and even within a family, extreme behaviour may result in rejection and loss of support. Groups therefore tend to produce **conformity** in their members.

Some of our groups are thrust upon us. By birth and passport, we receive a certain nationality group. By our age we are placed in a certain age bracket. By our skin, we can be identified as 'black' or 'white'. But we may have to work hard to be accepted into other groups. Many professional associations require examinations to be passed before the coveted letters can be placed after our name. We may aspire to become members, but must wait until we have shown the appropriate level of achievement.

In this section, we will look, drawing particularly on social psychology and sociology, at the groups, large and small, which can influence us.

■ DIFFERENT KINDS OF GROUPS

You may ask, 'What exactly *is* a group?' A typical answer from social psychology would be:

two or more interacting individuals with a stable pattern of relations between them who share common goals and who perceive themselves as a group[1]

So a collection of people staring into space as they patiently wait for the 54 bus to appear is not a group. Even a collection of people chatting in the checkout queue is not a group unless they perceive themselves as interacting towards a common goal, such as the downfall of the inefficient manager. But a collection of commuters who habitually make a foursome at cards on the 7.37 to town, and refer to themselves as the 'am' club can be considered as a group.

Groups can be classified in many ways, though any one group might fit into several categories.

Primary and secondary groups

The business people on the train are a primary group because their interaction is **face to face**. Their families are also primary groups. But they may also belong to professional associations, which seldom, if ever, meet face to face, and have much more distant and impersonal communication. These are secondary groups.

Formal and informal groups

The card-players also form a relatively informal group in that there are no written laws or formulations to guide behaviour. But they may also belong to official bridge clubs, which *will* have a definite and clearly-defined structure, and are thus formal.

Membership

While people may already form part of some groups – i.e. be members – there may also be groups to which they do not belong, but which nevertheless are relevant to their behaviour:

1 aspirational groups are those of which we are not yet a member, but to which we would like to belong;

2 dissociative groups are groups from which we stand apart. We would not wish to be seen as a member of such groups, and reject their values and behaviour. So a member of the quiet, non-smoking card group might dissociate himself from the noisy, smoky, group next door.

Reference groups

These can be described as the kinds of group used by individuals as a point of reference for their own judgements, values and behaviour. In consumer terms, they are those which exert an influence, directly or indirectly, on choice and decision-making. If consumers are already members of a group, they may consider what behaviours, what purchases, will maintain and perhaps enhance their position in the group. What squash racquets should be bought to impress the group? What squash clubs will be seen as poor or cheap choices?

If the individual aspires to membership, then he may use the group of which he does not yet feel a member as reference. What suit, what car, what car-phone, what brief-case, would help him feel, and be accepted as, 'an executive'?

Since consumers belong to many groups, their points of reference for different activities and purchases may be different, so marketers need to face the difficult task of finding the groups which are the strongest reference points in a given buying situation.

■ COMMON FEATURES OF GROUPS

Although the card-school may have arisen largely through chance, it will probably exhibit many of the features common to most groups, including norms and roles.

Norms

Norms tell group members how to behave, or how *not* to behave in various situations.

They therefore suggest what is considered 'normal' as distinct from deviant in that situation. In the card group, it may be a norm that soon after they meet, someone offers cigarettes all round, whereas smoking might be quite against the norms of a group in the next carriage.

TYPES OF NORM
Some norms are **prescriptive**, suggesting or laying down what we *should* do (e.g. wearing formal clothes when visiting a certain restaurant) while others are **proscriptive**, suggesting what should *not* be done (such as swearing when children are present).

HOW NORMS DEVELOP

The norms of a group may simply arise over time – Joe has the corner seat, Jane sits by him and so on. They may be perpetuated by associations such as the medical profession, which are organised for specific purposes. A doctor transferring from one hospital to another then has a set of norms to give continuity to his behaviour in professional situations.

Many important life-situations are covered by norms arising from institutions such as that of marriage. But though the institution of marriage may exist in many communities the specific rules of expected behaviour in courtship and marriage will vary not only from society to society, but also from group to group within societies.

WHEN NORMS ARE BROKEN

Some norms may be considered so important by a society they become crystallised into laws, such as that against homosexual activity between males under the age of 21 in England. There will then be penalties, or **sanctions** against those who break the laws.

But informal norms also carry sanctions which a group may use when a norm is violated, and which will tend to maintain conformity within the group. During a strike, considerable pressure may be put on those who insist on working, though there is no law to say they shouldn't. On the other hand, those who turn back after meeting a picket line are usually given a cheer and round of applause.

Consumers are not, of course, usually subject to such pressures, but nevertheless will be members of different groups, each with their own expectations. City business men and women are expected to wear suits for work – jeans would be frowned upon, but the yacht club would be astonished at anyone venturing to sea in a suit!

EXAMPLE 5.1   WHERE *DID* YOU GET SUCH BEAUTIFUL COFFEE?

1 In certain social groups, it is the norm that ground and percolated coffee should be served after dinner.

2 A commercial shows a hostess apparently complying with the norm by serving well-appreciated coffee.

3 In reality, she has used instant, but made the appropriate bubbly noises to imitate the reference group's expectation.

Norms represent the expected type of behaviour in a given social situation.

Roles

While norms tends to produce similarity of behaviour amongst members of a group, roles involve differentiation of task and behaviour. A bridge club may have a treasurer, secretary, president and so on. These are positions to be filled by individuals, who will also take on the role. In doing so, they have certain expectations of what tasks they will perform, and how they will behave. Perhaps next year the position of president of the club will be filled by someone else. The role-incumbent has changed, but the role and its associated expectations continue. *What a typical occupant of a given position is expected to do constitutes the role associated with that position.*

Roles may be **ascribed**, such as that of a son, which comes about automatically, or **achieved**, as when someone successfully studies to become a doctor. They may simply emerge, so that a student becomes the joker of his lecture group, and from then on is expected to supply the humour.

We all of us fill many roles – son, father, club member, senior executive – at the same time. But sometimes these roles do not fit easily with one another, and may produce conflict.

INTER-ROLE CONFLICT

Where someone is involved in several roles, the expectations of one may cut across those from another. We have already seen this in the working mother situation. Another example would be where a sales manager becomes over-friendly with his sales staff. The expectations of his role as a member of a friendship group may conflict with the expectations of his role as a manager, in the field of discipline, for instance.

INTRA-ROLE CONFLICT

Even when only one role is involved, conflict may arise, this time because the expectations of the role may be viewed differently by different people.

Senior management may see the role of a mid-level executive as simply organising staff to produce high productivity. The workers themselves may see the role of their supervisor as mediating on their behalf with senior staff. There is then conflict between the expectations of different groups of **role senders**.

Further conflict may occur when an individual sees his role differently from others around him. Thus a tutor may feel that wide discussion is valuable for his students, but they are simply hoping to be given precise guidance on how to pass the examination.

Such conflicts result in a form of frustration, and as such may lead to stress and loss of job satisfaction within organisations. But they can also be of value to marketing. If the consumer is faced with a problem, say of conflicting demands from the different roles he undertakes, he may be motivated towards finding a solution of the problem, and thus sensitive to presentations which suggest such a solution.

CONFLICT FROM CHANGES IN ROLES

Within a rapidly changing society, the behaviour required for a particular role may also change rapidly. An older manager in a modern organisation has at his command a breadth and speed of communication well beyond his early experience. He therefore has to adjust to new conceptions of his role. If he does not, there will be conflict and dissatisfaction with his performance.

Some people are not only able to adjust to such changes, but may also be described as **role innovators**. They are able either to find a role where none was previously, or to change radically conceptions of an existing role. Thus Bob Geldof with his Live Aid crusade originated role behaviour within the 'caring' field the scale and impact of which was previously unknown.

■ THE INFLUENCE OF GROUPS ON INDIVIDUALS

Several classic researches have shown the extent to which groups can produce conformity in individual behaviour. In his study of the **autokinetic effect** in which a spot of light in a dark room appears to move (but in fact stays still) **Sherif**[2] found that individual judgements of the extent of movement tended to settle down around a group norm over successive trials, and that this effect lasted after the individual was no longer judging in a group situation.

Venkatesan[3] researched the influence of group judgement on ratings of men's suits.

EXAMPLE 5.2 EXPERIMENT ON CONFORMITY TO GROUP NORMS

1 University students were asked to choose the best suit from three apparently identical suits, having been told that clothing experts could do so.

2 They did this individually (pre-test).

3 They then chose in groups of four. But three were confederates of the experimenter, and all gave one particular suit as the best, before the fourth gave his judgement.

4 In the individual situation, choice of best suit was randomly distributed. But in the group situation, individuals moved their judgement to the group norm.

(Note the similarity to the line experiment described in Chapter 1.)

This tendency to conformity may arise from two sources: **social** and **informational**.

1 Social conformity. Early analysis of conformity experiments suggested that factors affecting the individual included

- the value or attraction of the group
- his desire to be liked by the group
- the possible sanctions for going against the group.

2 Informational conformity. Other factors which need to be considered are more cognitive, such as

- the degree of ambiguity in the task
- the degree of agreement amongst others
- the supposed level of expertise of the others.

In social conformity, the individual acts to obtain the best social and emotional outcome. In informational conformity, he seeks the best cognitive outcome, though both of course may operate at one time.

■ CULTURE

So far, the discussion has centred mainly on small groups. But individuals also exist within a particular psychological and social 'climate' which governs much of their behaviour. This we may call the culture of a society. It has been described as a 'design for living' or more formally as:

social characteristics, including behaviour, ideas or beliefs that are shared within a group and transmitted by the socialisation process.

Within this overall description can be distinguished two forms: **explicit** culture, the typical and distinctive patterns of behaviour of those forming the culture, and **implicit** culture which is the set of cultural beliefs, values and norms underlying the behaviour shown by the explicit culture.

Explicit culture

The regularities of this behaviour will be controlled by a number of 'rules' of varying degree of scope, importance and sanction.

INSTITUTIONALISED WAYS
These are the 'patterns' or templates which regulate some of the major problems of living. For instance, mating regulations exist in most communities, but are different from one to another. Anthropology provides endless examples of this similarity-with-difference. Thus the betrothal aspect of marriage may occur in childhood, arranged by parents, in one society, but be in adulthood, arranged by the couple themselves in another.

The smaller elements of these major patterns are, in ascending order of importance:

1 Folkways These regulate relatively minor behavioural events, and carry only slight penalty if broken within a particular society, though they may be of greater importance in another. Thus, kissing on both cheeks when greeting is common in Continental Europe while single-cheek kissing (or even absence of kissing) is typical of greeting in England. An embrace-and-kiss as a greeting between males is typical of some Middle Eastern societies but is a direct violation of English folkways, and might give rise to derision and distinctly adverse comments.

2 Conventions These are best considered as organised collections of folkways around a specific event. Thus, a dinner party may involve greetings, an expectation that one will engage one's neighbour in conversation, rules for use of cutlery, serving of wine and so on. Again, these will vary from culture to culture. A Japanese tea-taking will involve quite different behaviours from a cream tea in Cornwall.

3 Mores These embody important values of a community, and are subject to heavy, even legal, sanctions. Many are derived from religious institutions, and tend to reflect the moral attitudes of society. In England, it was generally expected that a man who got a woman pregnant would marry her, or at least make provision. With the increase in women choosing to be single-parents, this expectation is declining. In some other societies there always has been much lower expectation that bachelors should marry the mother of their child. Thus mores change from time to time, and vary from culture to culture.

4 Laws Where transgression of mores results in legal sanctions, there are laws. The relation with mores is not simple. Getting a parking ticket carries a legal penalty, but little moral comeback. On the other hand, 'grassing' or informing in a Northern Ireland community may carry devastating, but legally unsanctioned, consequences.

ARTEFACTS
A simple explanation of these would be products made by humans. They thus cover as wide a range as that from the cave-paintings of Lascaux to the latest micro-processor. But just as the folkways and mores indicate the underlying values of a group, so do its artefacts. The stark, rectangular edifices of the present reflect a different view from the spired and turretted churches of the past.

Besides reflecting the general values of a community, material things can indicate, or seem to indicate, a person's standing in the culture. We have seen that in choice of cars, for instance. Perhaps more subtly, the choice of books to have around, the right magazines to take and display indicate, or appear to indicate, our personal cultural values – an obvious opportunity for marketing.

Implicit culture

This has two main strands:

1 Beliefs. This is the **cognitive** element behind the outward behaviour in a culture. It covers elements such as myths and legends, as well as the latest scientific theories.

2 Values may be thought of as standards which are commonly held. Thus a society may place a high value on cleanliness, as something 'good' while another may place high value on helping others.

The relations between these different concepts are summarised in Fig. 5.1.

Fig. 5.1

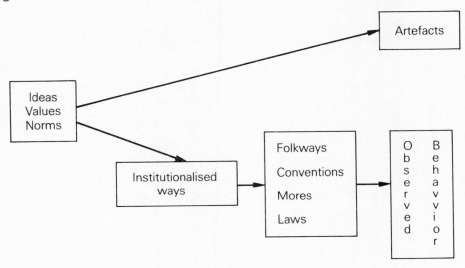

Messages for marketing

On the theoretical side, the following points are of importance:

1 Culture is not static. Its manifestations vary from place to place so that what is acceptable in one society is rejected by another. Within any one group, it changes with time, and is adaptive to the needs of the group.
2 It is wrong to think of a country as 'having a culture'. We may summarise some basic elements of, say, English culture, but within that, as we shall see, exist many sub-groupings whose values and behaviour may conflict with the dominant culture.
3 The relation between individual and culture is two-way. Although individuals are socialised into the ways of their society, some may be able to change the culture, either in minor ways, as in the invention of the mini-skirt, or in major ways, as the CND group have tried to do in relation to nuclear weapons and the values associated with them.
4 Culture exists to solve problems, and must adapt to do so. But cultural values may also *produce* problems, as is the case with pollution. Here a **counterculture** may arise – such as Greenpeace – whose values, aims and behaviour run counter to those of the dominant group.

It follows from this that the marketer must, in Engel and Blackwell's term, become **culturally competent**.[4]

EXAMPLE 5.3   ELEMENTS OF CULTURAL COMPETENCE

1 Sensitivity to cultural differences, especially between groups to which products may be marketed.

2 Cultural empathy or the ability to understand other ways of life without judging them as inferior because they are different.

3 When in a 'foreign' culture, the ability to accept cultural shock, and the need for some adaptation to the changed demands on behaviour, and the implicit values lying behind it.

When competence slips:

1 One attempt to introduce filter cigarettes, attuned to the fear of lung cancer and the generally held value of cleanliness in the West, failed completely in an Asian country.

  There, life expectancy was such that people would die before getting lung cancer, and cleanliness was not a core value.

2 Language may distort presentation, as when the brand name 'Big John' was translated into French as 'Gros Jos', whose meaning implies a large-bosomed woman! And don't ever try 'Cue' as a brand name there. (Ask your French friends why.)

Groupings within cultures

It is possible to sub-divide any culture into almost limitless smaller groups. The following are particularly relevant to marketing:

NATIONALITY GROUPS
Any country is likely to have several groups of different national origins within it. America, for instance, has at least 50 different origins for groups of 100 000 people or more. Where a minority group has been **acculturated** into the patterns of the dominant culture, marketing can use a standard approach. But where a group, whether recently immigrant or not, has retained much of its own culture, more specific approaches must be made.

1 Language may have been retained, especially amongst older members. It has been estimated that 81% of Chinese resident in America speak Chinese at home.

  Such groups may be more receptive to media using their language, and therefore appropriate newspapers and journals should be used if the segment is sufficiently large.

  Salesmen who are bi-lingual may be particularly helpful where there is a heavy concentration of a language in one area. Where material is translated into the minority language, care must be taken as noted above to avoid comic or even offensive renderings. One method to avoid this involves 'back-translation':

- a first translation is made into the second language
- that translation is then turned back (by someone else) into the first language
- a check can then be made whether the second version genuinely reflects the first.

2 Values. Certain values, such as the modesty of women, may be quite different within the minority group, making some items quite unpresentable, while the promotion of others may need to be considerably modified. The consumption of some products, such as alcohol, may be illegal, making the market almost impenetrable.

Nevertheless, where the market segment is considerable it may well be worth looking for products and presentations which are in tune with the needs and values of the group.

RELIGIOUS GROUPS

A major feature of religious groups is the existence of strong norms which control acceptable and unacceptable behaviour. While such groups may be typical of a particular nationality (e.g. England – Protestant, Spain – Catholic) they do of course embrace different nationalities. On the defensive side, care must be taken not to transgress the proscribed norms if the market segment is considerable; on the positive side, as with all groups, products and advertising which are in line with religious values are likely to be well received.

In some countries, such as Britain, the proportion of *active* religious members is decreasing, so that appeals involving religious values may only be effective at certain important religious times, such as Christmas, and then may form only a small part of promotional activities.

GEOGRAPHICAL GROUPINGS

Even when the population is largely homogeneous in racial origin, strong cultural differences may exist in different parts of the same country. The North of England has, for instance, its own form of rugby, its own form of bowls. Offal products such as tripe are far more popular than in the South. Northern values and behaviour are generally held to be 'harder' than in the South, and attitudes towards 'the others' are likely to be strongly held! And though English is the 'common' language, the accent and dialect of the North-Eastern Geordie miner may be quite incomprehensible to the South-Western Cornish farmer. On the other hand, some rural dialects and accents can be used to add authenticity to product presentation: a Somerset accent is often used in connection with advertisements for cider, a product associated with that area.

Differences may exist even between groups in the same town. People of similar values tend to live in similar areas, so that the cultural climate of one part of London may be quite different from another only a mile or two away.

The marketer must therefore consider whether he can make an appeal for his product which will be generally acceptable (i.e. a standard presentation) or whether different emphases need to be made for different areas.

The diffusion of culture

In recent years, a certain osmosis, or diffusion, of culture has taken place, partly from easier and cheaper travel, partly from television exposure of other countries, and sometimes from immigration, as in the increase in Indian and other Eastern restaurants in Britain. Greater awareness and sampling of other cultures therefore gives the possibility of 'cross-national' presentation where the products typical of one nationality are offered to another.

An illustration of osmosis between European and Japanese culture is given in Example 5.4.

EXAMPLE 5.4

A Canned poetry

1 A researcher collected large numbers of drink cans in Japan, and found many carried poetic messages, reflecting the greater emphasis on emotional and social, rather than cognitive, appeals in Japan.

2 But these messages were in *English*, as in this one, for mild coffee, based on the traditional Japanese three-line haiku:
Welcome to heaven,
As Time brings softness
Found in this can.

3 The use of English looks to modernity and progress. The message itself reflects more traditional values.[5]

B Japanese-American approaches

1 A comparison of the types of appeal made in comparable American and Japanese magazines with comparable spread and for comparable products was made.

2 This showed Japanese using 'soft sell' approaches four times as much as American, with almost ten times as much reference to the elderly, whereas American material made product points twice as much.

3 However, the researcher comments, in line with the study above, that the use of *English* in copy suggests high status.

4 She concludes: *Advertising reflects cultural values – but only when it is profitable to do so.*[6]

AGE

While the purely demographic aspects of age distribution are useful, an awareness of the typical values and behaviour of different age groups is particularly helpful. To know the trends in children's interests, the amount of money they typically handle, and the part they play in decision-making, enables a more focussed attack to be mounted on this sector.

At the other end of the scale, the so-called 'grey power' may be important.

Senior citizens may respond to incentives to shop off-peak; token promotions may be seen as helping with their difficulties in husbanding small financial resources.

■ SOCIAL CLASS

It would be of enormous help to the marketer if he could apply a small range of 'labels' to consumers which would enable predictions to be made about their incomes, occupations, sources of information and general life-styles. He would then have a set of groups or segments. Individuals within any segment would be similar to each other in characteristics relevant to the product, but different from members of other segments. Thus products and promotions could be well matched to the needs and expectations of different sets of consumers.

The concept of social class is one possibility for such a classification. Since a class society is one in which typically there is a high degree of movement, we will first compare societies having low and higher degrees of social movement.

Open and closed societies

CLOSED SOCIETIES

In the **estate** system of medieval Europe, position in society and life-chances were determined largely by birth. Fixed rankings such as nobleman, peasant and serf existed, and those born into a family at one level by and large remained within that level. At the lowest level, the slaves of some societies were regarded as little better than animals, and could be bought and sold. The traditional **caste** system of India was based on religion, but also showed the relatively fixed layering of society, and the prohibitions on mixing of the castes.

In both these types of society, there was relative similarity or **homogeneity** within each level, and relative **lack of mobility** between them. They were closed societies, though perhaps not as rigid as the brief descriptions suggest.

OPEN SOCIETIES

After Mrs Thatcher became the first woman Prime Minister of Great Britain, she often pointed out that her father was a grocer. In doing so, she drew attention to the lower rigidity within levels of society, and the greater possibility of movement between levels typical of a more open society.

Everyday observation shows that 'layers' remain, even in a democracy. But there are at least possibilities of aspiring to a higher level by one's own efforts, rather than by accident of birth or favouritism. Layers exist and persist, but individuals, to a lesser or greater degree, move through them. The question now is, what sort of layers exist in a modern society? *Can* we classify the members of an open society?

What is social class?

Example 5.5 may show the problems involved in comparing individuals within a flexible society.

EXAMPLE 5.5   MR C AND DR D

Mr C left school at fifteen, and ever since then has worked in the wholesale vegetable trade, getting up at 3 in the morning to catch the best bargains. He has worked so hard that he now has an imposing five-bedroom house, is about to retire early, and is applying to do an Open University degree course.

Dr D is 28, and has been studying in one way or another since he was six. He could not get a job last year in spite of obtaining a Doctorate of Philosophy. Fortunately his wife earns a very good salary as a computer consultant, which enables them to pay the mortgage on a pleasant, if small, apartment.

Looking at these descriptions, we can pick out several possibilities for forming a classificatory system.

1 Income. Does higher income mean higher social class?
2 Education. Do lower educational qualifications mean you are of a lower social class?
3 Occupation. Should we rank a computer consultant above a vegetable salesman?
4 Head of household. If we classify on the basis of occupation and salary of head of the household, Dr D and his wife would come rather low down. But they are comfortably off because of Mrs D's earnings.
5 Area and type of residence. Where people live may give an idea of what money they are likely to have. But will it tell us, for instance, what cultural values and interests they have?

How can we achieve a coherent system of classification? A well-known sociologist has made the following claim:

A sociologist worth his salt, if given two basic indices of class such as income and occupation, can make a long list of predictions about the individual even if no further information has been given.[7]

It is further claimed that details such as the likely interior decorating of the house, the music listened to, the size of vocabulary, and even whether sex is had with the lights on or off, can be predicted.

Such predictions will however deal in **probabilities**. They will say that any given behaviour is more likely in one class than another, not that classes will differ completely in their behaviour.

A classification based on occupation, used by the Joint Industry Committee for National Readership Surveys is given in Table 5.1.

Table 5.1   JICNARS definition of social status

Social grade	Social status	Occupation
A	Upper middle class	Higher managerial or professional
B	Middle class	Middle managerial, administrative or professional
C1	Lower middle class	Supervisory, clerical; junior managerial, administrative or professional
C2	Skilled working class	Skilled manual worker
D	Working class	Semi- and un-skilled manual workers
E	Subsistence level	e.g. Casual or lowest grade workers

Unfortunately, this tidy sort of scheme has several drawbacks.

1 Occupation may not give a true indication of disposable income. Plumbers can command incomes far higher than teachers, especially in bad weather.
2 Household incomes may be mis-represented if only that of head of household is taken into account.
3 Upward-mobile people may be more receptive to the values and beliefs of a higher group than the one where they currently fit.
4 But having made the upward step, they may retain some of the values of their earlier group.

These criticisms show that classifications using only one index (single-item) may be too crude, though occupation has been claimed as the best single indicator. For this reason, multiple-item methods have been developed.

Coleman's Computerised Status Index (CSI) takes account of education, occupational prestige level, area of residence, and total family income per year. This then produces 'layers' such as Upper American, Middle Class, Working Class and Lower American.

Clearly such techniques are likely to give a more refined picture. But objective measures alone do not tell us just how any family or individual actually lives their life. For that reason, marketers have turned to **psychographics** and the study of life-styles (see Chapter 7).

■ STATUS

There is no doubt that some people, some occupations, and some possessions are regarded as in some way higher than others, however they are officially classified. They have high **status**.

How does status come about?

Some features of status are, as with roles, ascribed. The Duke of Devonshire inherits the title and its status; a new-born girl immediately acquires feminine status.

Status may be achieved by obtaining qualifications or by outstanding personal achievement, as with Mother Theresa. Status may also come from wealth, in many societies simply from one's sex, in others from age, or from one's job.

Status symbols

Associated with status are many symbols. The Queen of England carried an orb and sceptre at her Coronation; the PhD can wear special robes. These are directly linked with the role and its status. But other 'extras' have no such formal associations. An executive will get to his London office only marginally quicker in a Porsche as compared with an Austin, but the Porsche is 'up market' and suggests higher status. He may want to show off his Porsche, to make his status conspicuous to other people. This has been called **conspicuous consumption**.

Marketing thus has a considerable opportunity in the area of status. If certain products, journals, activities are seen to be associated with high-status roles, then two results may follow:

1 Those who have status may be persuaded that products are essential for the maintenance of status. Fashion status may require that certain labels are purchased rather than others. At one time executive toys to stand on desks were part of the 'role-apparatus' of the executive. Now they are little seen.

Words such as executive acquire high status, so executive briefcases, executive flights are advertised. The word 'gold' and the colour are used in many promotions.

EXAMPLE 5.6   GOLD APPEALS!

1 GO FOR GOLD! (American Express Gold Card)

2 GO FOR GOLD! (Body Plus, a catalogue for exercise equipment and accessories.) An incentive of a Gold Prize draw, with a ticket to the 1988 Olympic Games, is offered.

3 GOING FOR GOLD! (Television: European Quiz show, again with incentive of attendance at the Games.)

4 Network Gold Card. (British Rail, South Eastern Region.)

2 Those who aspire to status may enhance theirs, in part, by displaying the apparatus of status. The rash of look-alike wedding dresses when a 'Royal' gets married shows this. Sometimes this has unfortunate results, as when

unscrupulous people set up agencies to sell fake 'degrees' to people with ambitions, but no qualifications.

A sort of inverted status may occur, when people are deliberately **unostenta-tious**. This has also been called 'parody display'.

EXAMPLE 5.7   THE PAUL SMITH MAN

To anyone in the business, the Paul Smith look is unmistakable. It is the expensive jacket in curiously rumpled worsted, the £400 cashmere blazer worn with blue jeans, the featherweight cotton raincoat that doesn't seem up to the lightest shower.

The Paul Smith man, in short, has taken the most meticulous care to look as if he hasn't given his clothes a moment's thought. He looks comfortably underdressed on every occasion, making the rest of us feel uncomfortably overdressed.

■ THE FAMILY

The family is a primary or face-to-face group, and is the first group for most people, and thus has a powerful influence on the majority of people's lives. The **nuclear family** consists of mother, father and any children who are living together, and should be distinguished from **household**, which refers to all the people, both related and unrelated, who occupy a given housing unit.

Families help to pass on and thus preserve selected aspects of culture by means of **socialisation** which helps children towards adult membership of their society. But society is not static, and changes in family size, structure and responsibilities occur. The family is also an important decision-making unit, responsible for a large share of the consumer market.

Socialisation

Socialisation has been described as

the process by which a child learns to be a participant member of society.[8]

In this process, the family will play an important part, reinforcing and rewarding some aspects of behaviour, perhaps punishing others, and acting as models which may be imitated by the children. It will thus be a filter, allowing through, and even emphasising, some aspects of the surrounding cultural influences but screening the child from others.

The methods by which this process of preparation is carried out can be related to the learning theories discussed in Chapter 3. As a sample theme, we can look at the question, 'How do girls come to behave like girls?'

1 From associationist theories. The selective reinforcement of behaviour is often used in families. Playing with members of another racial group may bring disapproval. Negative statements by the child about such groups may bring approval, setting the scene for later discrimination. Similarly, boys may be reinforced for activities which if done by girls would bring disapproval, and vice versa.

2 From observational learning. The child has near-at-hand models which can be observed, such as mother cooking, father going off to work. Together with selective reinforcement, this can produce in a girl an expectation of what the role of a girl is.

3 Cognitive learning. From the various situations to which 'being a girl' is relevant, the girl may develop a cognitive map, or set of patterns about feminine behaviour. In Bandura's terms, there is cognitive mediation which can guide her responses to situations where 'girlhood' is appropriate. She is not tied to specific experiences, but has an overall understanding of what being a girl is within that particular culture. This view leaves open the possibility that she might reject the expected pattern and move towards her own definition of womanhood.

4 Role-playing. Children do not only observe the role-behaviour of others. They try it out for themselves, being the postman, the milkman, playing doctors and nurses. To some extent they are feeling their way into adult situations, but their conception of the adult role is of course rather superficial. Nevertheless, outfits which allow the child to play 'pretend' roles are extremely popular, and show the strength of this 'trying-out' behaviour. Again, girls will probably be expected to be the nurse in such play, and discouraged from being the whooping Red Indian.

5 Identification. This can be thought of as somewhat deeper than imitation, though it certainly involves behaving like a model. The difference is that values and standards as well as behaviour patterns may be incorporated into the child's personality. Freud's explanation of why boys become boys involved identification, but perhaps typically, his explanation of why girls become girls was weaker.

The family is not by any means the only shaping force on the child. School will bring information, attitudes and behaviour beyond those observed at home, both from teachers and pupils. In particular, the peer group will begin to exert a stronger and stronger influence. And parallel with these, exerting its own influence, providing its own models for behaviour, will be the mass media, especially television, the constant companion of many children.

These forces will then interplay in the child's development, as shown in Fig. 5.2.

Life does not, however, stand still. The child becomes an adult, perhaps marries, and has children who in their turn will be socialised into the patterns of their society and culture. We can thus think of the family as having a cyclic pattern: the child is dependent, becomes independent, has his own dependents, and finally loses those dependents, who begin a new cycle.

THE TRADITIONAL FAMILY LIFE CYCLE

1 **Single stage**. Income may be low, but so are essential outlays, so cash is available for discretionary purchases. These may include a car, fittings for their

Fig. 5.2

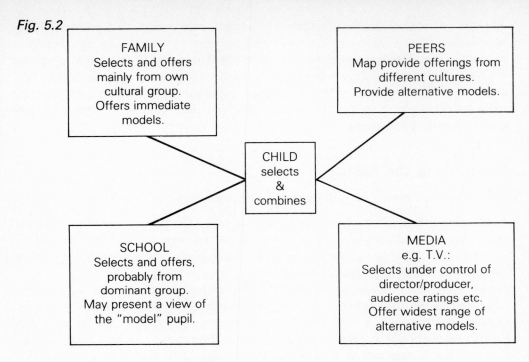

first non-family home. Interests may include fashion, recreations, and finding a mate.

2 Newly Marrieds. Probably good income as wife may work. Money is spent on cars, clothing, recreation and holidays. Durables (e.g. furniture and appliances) rank high on purchase preferences. Quite susceptible to advertising.

3 Full Nest I. First child! Income may decline if wife stops work. Arrival of child obviously alters spending pattern to a 'child-centred' approach. A more permanent home may be sought and thus, overall, discretionary income is likely to be lower than previously.

4 Full Nest II. Youngest child over six. Husband's income rising, wife may return to outside work. Financial position improves, but expenditure is still heavily child-related. Consumables of 'family' size may be attractive.

5 Full Nest III. Older children may bring in income, husband's income improves, wife may work. Financial position allows for replacement of furniture/car, purchase of luxury items. Care and education of children may weigh heavily in budget.

6 Empty Nest I. Head of household still working. The children have left home, no longer financially dependent. Good financial position, allowing for home improvements, luxury items, good holidays, travel and recreation.

7 Empty Nest II. Household head retired, so income drops. Health expenditure becomes important. Maybe a move to a smaller home, or retirement facility.

8 Solitary Survivor. If still in work, financial position is good. Home may be sold and provide for vacations, recreation, and care for possibly failing health.[9]

9 Retired Solitary Survivor. Similar pattern to the solitary survivor, but of course on lower income. May have special security and belonging needs.

Because of the changes outlined later, this traditional cycle may not always apply nowadays. The addition of socio-economic variables, especially money, has been suggested as an improvement. Nevertheless the 'FLC' remains a useful framework for considering what types of product and what approaches are best suited to different phases of the developmental cycle. Think for yourself how the cycle might apply to mortgages, endowment policies, expensive holidays, estate cars or medical insurance.

Changes in the family

In the Western world, several important changes have taken place in the family.

1 The proportion of people marrying is dropping. The percentage of households including married couples is expected to drop in America from 70% in 1970 to 54% by 1995. The age of which marriage takes place is also increasing, with a consequent rise in the 'young singles' market.

2 The number of children per family is decreasing, in some cases close to the rate needed for maintenance of the population (Zero Population Growth or ZPG). This may occur in America in the next century, but this trend is not happening everywhere, so that population distribution has changed. Europe had 20% of world population in 1800 but now has only half that. The size of international markets is thus changing.

3 The tendency to smaller families has changed the possible distribution of resources within a family. The proportion of first-borns has increased, and, since first-borns account for larger expenditure than later-born, this changes the importance of birth-order effects for manufacturers and marketers. It may also mean that the family have a greater disposable income to spend on a smaller number of children, or on items not directly related to children.

Women and the family

Although in some countries women are still held in low esteem, play little part in decision-making, and have little opportunity for personal development, the modern Western woman has much greater freedom of choice than previously.

She may choose whether or not to pursue a career as an alternative to marriage. If married, she may choose to continue her career, making arrangements for the children. In some situations, this may involve the man staying at home, acting as a 'househusband', or he may well share in domestic and caring activities which would not have been thought part of his role thirty or so years ago.

These changes have implications for marketing presentations. For the woman, appeals to the plural or double role may be effective. For men, appeals to the caring aspects of fatherhood are no longer so impossible to consider as previously. 'Men do care'! The old view was that men performed the **instrumental** functions, such as deciding on major expenditure in buying a new house. Women were expected to fulfil the **expressive**, caring role, providing the domestic, supporting, atmosphere within the house. Now these functions are much less clearly separated. We see adverts of an attractive woman, deciding that she must forgo her new car because she has just seen the house of her dreams. We see commercials of men hurriedly preparing a convenience food meal, just in time for the arrival of the girlfriend carrying flowers.

Such considerations have increased the importance of **sex-role orientation** in both men and women, and indeed a specific measure called the Sex Role Orientation instrument has been developed.[10]

The argument whether children are born 'programmed' towards masculine or feminine behaviour, or whether they are shaped into such behaviour by socialisation is difficult to answer. It has produced demands that media should not project an automatic image of male and female behaviour – girls playing with dolls, women doing the cooking, while boys play with construction kits and men make decisions. Such images may be thought by some to *cause* rather than *reflect* differences in behaviour of the sexes. Care must be taken not to run foul of the charge of sexism. On the other hand, since the large majority of consumers are probably still traditionally orientated, it would be a brave marketer who consistently reversed the images!

The family as a decision-making unit

Much domestic buying is done by individuals. But very often they are buying products which will be used or consumed by other members of the family. Because of this the family is often referred to as a **buying centre** or **decision-making unit**. An illustration of the influences at work is given in Example 5.8.

EXAMPLE 5.8   THE CASE OF THE COMPUTER

Teenager Theodore thinks it's time the family had a home computer. He could use it for games and his computer studies homework. Mum and Dad could do household accounts and keep files of dates, birthdays and telephone numbers on it.

Theodore's older sister Ann already works in the computer field, and is rather knowledgeable about the performance of different types and models. She brings home leaflets, explains them and gives advice.

After much discussion, Mum and Dad, who have a joint account, agree to pay for one, and on Saturday, Ann goes to the shop to buy the recommended model.

Marketers need therefore to consider at least five possible functions:

- **users** – those who will use the product (all the family)
- **deciders** – those who take the final decision, and in this case also pay for the purchase (Mum and Dad)
- **the gatekeeper** – those who know something about the product and can filter information through to those involved in the decision (principally Ann)

- **influencers** – those who can bring pressure to bear on the decision (probably everyone in their different ways)
- **buyer** – perhaps less importantly in domestic buying, who will actually go and make the purchase (Ann)

Several people may be involved in one function, and of course the functions of different people will vary with the product or service.

In the smaller decision-making unit of husband and wife, it was previously thought possible to divide purchase decisions into four groups, according to the product.

1 Syncratic where most decisions are jointly made.
2 Autonomic where numbers of decisions are equal, but individual decisions are made by either husband and wife.
3 Wife dominant areas.
4 Husband dominant areas.

Furnishings were traditionally woman dominated, insurance within the man's domain, and holidays were syncratic or joint. However, more recent work has suggested, as would be expected, a move towards a much higher proportion of joint decisions.[11]

■ SELF ASSESSMENT QUESTIONS

Marks

1 Put the most suitable word against these descriptions:
   (a) expected behaviour in a given social situation _ _ _ _ _ _ _ _ _
   (b) the expected behaviour of an individual occupying a certain position (e.g. Club Secretary). _ _ _ _ _ _ _ _ _ _ _ _ _ _ _ _ _ _
   (c) tension between different roles _ _ _ _ _ _ _ _ _ _ _ _ _ _ _ _ _
   (d) tension arising within a role _ _ _ _ _ _ _ _ _ _ _ _ _ _ _ _ _ _   (4)
Choose from:

inter-role conflict	intra-role conflict
norm	role

2 (a) When mores are given legal sanctions they become _ _ _ _ _
   (b) Shaking hands on greeting is one example of _ _ _ _ _ _ _ _ _
   (c) Material products of a culture may be called _ _ _ _ _ _ _ _ _   (3)
Choose from:

laws	artefacts	folkways

3 Put the right 'group' word against these statements:
  (a) 'Don't you dare class me with that lot.' _ _ _ _ _ _ _ _ _ _ _ _
  (b) 'I do wish I could get into that club.' _ _ _ _ _ _ _ _ _ _ _ _ _ _
  (c) 'Ladies and Gentlemen, welcome to the Annual General Meeting of the Profitalot Company.' _ _ _ _ _ _ _ _ _ _ _ _ _ _ _ _   (3)
Choose from:

┌──┐
│ aspirational group   dissociative group   formal group   │
└──┘

4 Put True or False against the following:
  (a) A secondary group always meets face to face. _ _ _ _ _ _ _ _
  (b) The class structure of a closed society is very fluid. _ _ _ _ _ _
  (c) Many decisions taken previously by husband alone now tend to be taken jointly. _   (3)

5 (a) List three of the agencies principally involved in socialisation in a developed country.

_ _ _ _ _ _ _ _ _ _   _ _ _ _ _ _ _ _ _ _   _ _ _ _ _ _ _ _ _ _   (3)

┌──┐
│ (F......   S......   P.G......   M...M...) │
└──┘

6 Write the socialisation process most involved in each of these situations:
  (a) Children playing with doctors'-and-nurses' outfits. _ _ _ _ _ _
  (b) Dad grumbles at Jim because he sometimes plays with dolls, but he joins in the play when Jim gets his soldier kit out. _ _ _ _ _ _   (2)
Choose from:

┌──┐
│ identification   role-playing   selective reinforcement │
└──┘

7 Put the right stage of the Family Life Cycle against these statements:
  (a) Youngest child over 6; wife may be returning to work _ _ _ _
  (b) Older couples; children left home; head of house working _ _   (2)
                                                                  (Total: 20)

(Answers are on page 220)

■ STUDY AND EXAMINATION TIPS

1 As you can see from the questions below, the contents of this section are well-represented in examination papers.

2 Be careful, however, which selection of your material you offer. Compare questions 4 and 5. Both include 'cultural differences'. But look again. One mentions international brands, and the other the domestic market. What difference would that make to your answer?

3 In one case, the product may be going to societies whose beliefs and values are very different from each other. In the other, it can be assumed that a significant 'core culture' of shared values and beliefs is typical of the majority, but that different segments, or 'specific cultures' exist within it. The possibility of a 'standard' approach is therefore less likely in the first case.

4 In preparing for questions such as No. 4, a checklist such as that below may be helpful. You may be able to add to it. Those students from overseas, or who are part of a multi-cultural group are at an advantage here because ideas and examples can be exchanged to give a 'portfolio' of material.

The following points should be considered:

(a) Important motivations: What needs might the product fill, as perceived by the society? Are these needs currently filled? Could new needs be established?

(b) Important behaviour characteristics, such as purchasing patterns. Language will be involved here. Can a non-verbal, pictorial approach be used generally? If language is used, what problems of translation may exist?

(c) Important cultural values. This is most important, both in a positive direction, to indicate what advantage can be gained by emphasising these, and negatively, to avoid giving offence.

(d) For new products, what is the attitude to innovation? What sources of information are largely relied upon?

(e) What promotion methods are typical and valued? What part does advertising play? What types of sales people are accepted by the culture?

(f) What distribution outlets are used and valued by the culture? Are these suitable and available for the product?

(g) What particular points about the culture do marketing representatives from other countries need to understand and appreciate?

5 A similar, but adapted, checklist could then be applied for questions such as No. 5, bearing in mind the need for any segment to be sufficiently sizeable for an economic return.

Actual products or product types should be considered against the checklist (e.g. those in the questions) to give a product-culture matrix which will pinpoint areas of particular importance both offensively and defensively.

■ EXAMINATION QUESTIONS

1 'The family is probably the most important group... in practice, however, marketers have often failed to consider fully the importance of the family as a decision-making unit.' (Williams)
What is the justification for these propositions?

2 Discuss (a) the importance of the family unit as a focus for the study of consumer behaviour, (b) the usefulness of family life cycles as a market segmentation variable.

3 Why do group influences have such an important impact on consumer behaviour?

4 What is the significance of cultural differences for the marketing strategy associated with international brands (such as toothpaste, motor cars or canned foods)?

5 You are a marketer, respectively, of
   (a) cola-type soft drinks
   (b) hand-held, electric hair-curling tongs.
To what extent would a knowledge of cultural differences *within your domestic market* help you to segment that market more effectively?

6 Describe and critically evaluate any one method of classifying consumers by social class. Explain how such methods could be improved.

6 Attitudes

No other single psychological construct has permeated consumer research as has the construct of attitude. J. Jacoby.

■ INTRODUCTION

Ms James, a sales representative, calls for the first time on a retailer. They chat, discuss orders, and she leaves, promising to call again.

By that time the retailer will have formed an attitude towards the visitor. This might involve

- beliefs ('Knows what she's talking about')
- feelings ('I like her already')
- behaviour or behavioural intentions ('I'll ask her advice next time on what stocks to build up')

So the next time Ms James calls, the retailer will not have to start all over again to form his view of her. He will have some idea of what to expect and how the caller will behave. But perhaps more importantly, he will have a set, or predisposition, to think, feel and act in certain ways towards her. He will have formed an attitude towards Ms James.

If his attitude is positive, he will probably be friendly, open to advice, not anxious to end the conversation when she returns. But if his attitude is negative, he may appear unwelcoming, reject advice, and bring the conversation to a quick end.

Besides having attitudes towards people, we can have attitudes towards things, such as a Ferrari car, or to groups of people, such as the Labour Party, or to ideas, such as Communism. They can be favourable, and positive, or unfavourable and negative, and they can have an intensity or strength in either direction. Prejudice, for instance, is sometimes described as an extreme unfavourable or negative attitude.

We do not come into the world with attitudes ready made. They are learned as a result of experience. They are also adaptive since they help to bring a measure of order and predictability into our world. Each individual's set of attitudes represents his own unique way of viewing important aspects of his world.

■ THE NATURE OF ATTITUDES

Although the analysis of the simple incident described above may seem straightforward enough, the concept of attitude, central for much of social psychology, has been a rather complicated issue which we must look at before turning to more practical issues.

The three-component view

It has been usual to consider an attitude as having three elements, as suggested by the visit of Ms James:

1 a **cognitive**, or belief component
2 an **affective** or emotional component, and
3 a **conative** or behavioural component.

A typical definition summarising this would be:

A learned predisposition to think, feel and act in a particular way towards a given object or class of objects,[1]

the 'object' of the attitude being a thing, person, group or idea.

Rosenberg's model, for instance, treats attitude as an intervening variable, with subdivisions of affect, cognition and behaviour. These in turn are connected with observable, and measurable, behaviours (see Fig. 6.1).[2]

Fig. 6.1

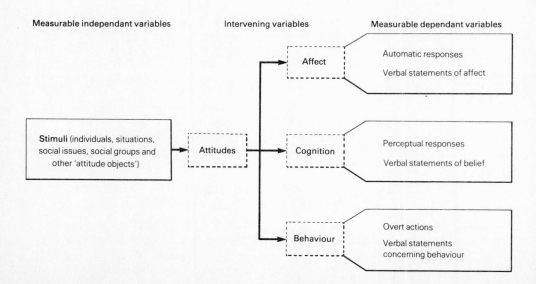

This is a version of an S-O-R model (see Chapter 3) with stimuli reaching the consumer, being organised and interpreted via the attitude system, and producing internal and external response. A number of problems can however arise.

Problems of the three-component view

1 Attitudes and behaviour. It seems to follow from such models that if we can change the attitude as a whole, we can change the sub-systems. Of especial interest to the marketer is the changing of behaviour. It would appear that a marketer who can produce a more positive attitude towards a product will also produce greater likelihood of its being bought. But much evidence has shown that knowledge of an attitude does not always help to predict behaviour, and that change in attitude does not always produce the expected change in behaviour.

2 The term 'attitude' is used both for external, measurable variables, and for inner, or intervening, variables. As we shall see, attitudes are usually measured by some form of verbal behaviour.

We cannot peer inside the person to 'see' his attitude, so we have to use observable behaviour. But the response the person gives to our questions may or may not represent his 'true' opinion. So we are not necessarily getting at the 'true' attitude when we use an attitude scale.

3 The specificity of attitudes. Although we may be able to summarise an overall attitude towards someone or something ('I like her') there are likely to be several factors on which our overall summing up depends. We probably don't like every aspect of a person, for instance. In the case of a product, our attitude might depend on the circumstances in which it is to be used: 'Great for town; hopeless for holidays'. We might like the easy handling of a car, but regret its styling.

4 Behaviour and behavioural intentions. The behavioural component is perhaps the most confusing. It appears 'within' the organism as part of the attitude system, but also outside as overt or observable action. What marketers want is change in, or maintenance of, the overt action – buying, recommending etc. A statement of behavioural intention ('I'll ask her advice on what stocks to build up') may or may not, however, produce actual behaviour. There may not be time on the next visit; advice from another quarter may have resolved the problem; the retailer may have forgotten his earlier idea.

La Piere found over 50 years ago that statements about behaviour do not always correspond with actual behaviour. His findings have been repeated several times since, but similar results would be less likely after the enactment of laws against discrimination.

EXAMPLE 6.1 TO SERVE OR NOT TO SERVE?

1 The experimenter writes or phones to several restaurants, asking for reservations for a party which includes nationalities towards whom there might be a negative attitude.

2 A high proportion of refusals and excuses is received.
3 The party, including the experimenter, visit the restaurants, and in many cases are accepted! (In some studies the visits were before the request, in some after.)
4 Thus a statement about behaviour, e.g. 'We don't serve Chinese' does not tie up with actual behaviour.
5 Has the restaurant owner changed his attitude? Or is he, perhaps, just accepting the group to avoid a fuss, while maintaining his own private opinion?[3]

We thus must remember that situational factors may affect the conversion of statements of intention to actual behaviour. These might include lack of financial or personal resources, and the felt pressure of the norms of groups which are important to us.

How then can we avoid some of these problems?

Other approaches

INTERCONNECTEDNESS

Instead of seeing the three aspects as separate dependents of an overall attitude, we could think of them as an interconnected, dynamic set, change in one being capable of producing change in the others (see Fig. 6.2).

Fig. 6.2

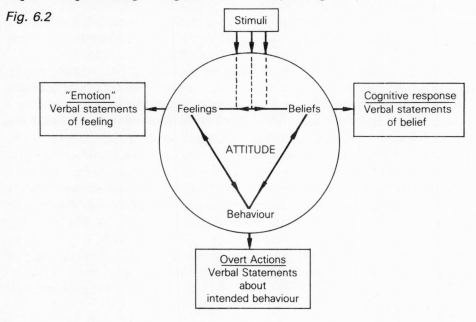

In particular, this suggests that the belief and feeling components could be affected by a change in behaviour – the reverse of the earlier views. We might therefore, by persuading a customer to try a product (i.e. change his behaviour towards it), produce a change in his attitude towards it. *Change in behaviour would come before change in attitude.*

SEPARATE DEFINITION
Some views are inclusive or multi-attribute, in that all three components are included, as in the definition given earlier. Others can be exclusive, focussing on one main component. Thus Engel Blackwell and Miniard offer the following definition to marketers:

a positive or negative evaluation of the consequences of buying and using a particular product or brand.[4]

Here there is clear separation of components, and an indication of the direction of influence between them. The use comes first, the evaluation follows.

OMIT INTERVENING VARIABLES
The view illustrated in Fig. 6.1 has been called the **latent process** view by De Fleur and Westie since it suggests some inner factor at work making for consistency.[5]

The **probability** view however concentrates on consistency or inconsistency between the observed measures, such as verbalised statements of behavioural intent and actual behaviour towards the same object. Customers would be asked about their intentions towards a product, and these would be compared with actual buying behaviour. We do not have to consider the 'inner' processes.

Relations between the components

The 'power' relations within the triangle of forces are important for the marketer. The main point of interest is the balance between behaviour and the other components. Is it better to try to create a positive feeling towards a product, on the assumption that this will produce a positive change in buying behaviour or at least in buying intention? Or can we, by incentives, 'on approval' techniques, or sampling opportunities, produce a change in the feeling and belief components by causing a change in behaviour?

The evidence is mixed, and it may be that the direction of change is situation-specific, varying with the type of purchase and the motivation of the client.

1 Under conditions of **high-involvement** where the costs and or risks of purchase are high, and where status and self-esteem may be involved, clients may search for a long time before coming to a decision. This length of pre-purchase evaluation can give the opportunity to build up a positive belief-and-feeling complex which will steer the decision towards one product in favour of others.
2 In **low involvement** or routine decisions, say yoghurt buying, the consumer is unlikely to be motivated towards a long search and evaluation of alternatives. Thus point-of-sale trials may offer a better opportunity to change behaviour. If such a trial results in purchase, it may bring into action the 'I tried it; I bought it; so it must be good' effect, thereby affecting the other components.

■ THE MEASUREMENT OF ATTITUDES

There is a wide range of techniques available for assessing attitudes, most, but not all, deriving from psychology, rather than from the marketing field itself.

It is important to recognise that while several of these methods use numerical scaling, they do not give truly equal-interval measures. The difference between 'strongly agree' and 'disagree' may not be the same as that between 'agree' and 'strongly agree'. Further, the 'strongly agree' of one person may not indicate the same force of agreement as that of another consumer. These scales, then, are not really like rulers, but they do aim to go beyond the simple ordinal, or ordering, level.

Thurstone

This technique, one of the oldest, is extremely lengthy. Construction of a Thurstone-type scale is not something to be undertaken lightly. It involves four main stages:

1 A number of statements towards the object of the attitude are prepared, varying from strongly in favour to strongly against. At least 100 items are recommended for a 20 item test.

2 These are then submitted to a large panel of independent judges. They rate each item on an 11-point scale from the strongly positive extremity to the extreme negative pole. Their job is not to give their own opinions, but to assess the strength and direction of opinion implied by each statement. For instance, in a study conducted by Thurstone himself, the statement 'I feel the church services give me inspiration and help me to live up to my best during the following week' received an average scale value of 1.7 from the judges as a very positive statement about the church.

3 The ratings of the judges are then compared and items which show close agreement in rating between judges are retained. A set of statements to cover the range from positive to negative extremities in roughly equal steps is then selected.

4 The final test is given to the target group who mark their agreement or disagreement with each item. The score for any individual is then the total of the scaled scores for the items with which agreement is shown.

Likert

This method short-circuits step 2 above by going directly from the preparation of statements to a pilot group. They rate their own opinions for each item on a five-point scale, from 'strongly agree' to 'strongly disagree' with a middle, neutral, point, e.g.

The internal combustion engine is amongst the worst of human inventions.

Strongly agree	*agree*	*undecided*	*disagree*	*strongly disagree*
1	2	3	4	5

The score here is the total of the person's ratings, taking account of the direction of the statement. Agreement with the statement 'Automation will be the death of creativity' is unfavourable to automation, whereas agreement with 'Automation will free people's time for pursuit of their own creative activities' is favourable.

The extent to which score on any one item agrees with total score for each person is then calculated to see how far individual items 'hang together' with the scale as a whole, and poorly agreeing items are discarded for the final version to be given to the target group.

Likert scales are relatively easy to construct, and quite simple to administer. They have been used with children, and for surveys by telephone. However, two people could clearly obtain the same score but with a different pattern of responses, so that further analysis would be necessary to go beyond a simple measure of strength.

Osgood

The **semantic differential** was originally used to study the 'universe of meaning' brought into play by different concepts. It can however be looked at as a means of assessing attitudes on predetermined dimensions. The procedure is quite simple. A stimulus (a person, organisation, or thing) is given and the subject rates it on a scale against various descriptions, which are usually adjectives.

In Fig. 6.3 the job of electrician has been rated against a 7-point scale.

Fig. 6.3

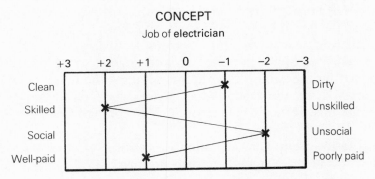

CONCEPT
Job of electrician

The rating points of one person have been joined to give a profile, or graphical representation of his attitude towards the job of electrician. We could then draw a profile for his ratings of the job of policeman, and compare them, or obtain an average profile from many people's ratings. People, companies, products can be compared by this method. Thus, a company wanting to compare its product on relevant attributes with those of a rival could do so by means of the differential, and take action on the results.

The scale offers the possibility of seeing the specific elements involved in an overall attitude towards a particular object or idea. It thus gives more diagnostic information than a score which may summarise an attitude, but blurs the separate aspects. If we add the ratings above, they come to zero – an apparently neutral attitude. But in fact, some aspects of the job are seen as 'good', others as 'bad'.

Osgood himself has suggested that further order can be brought into the 'universe of meaning' by deriving scores for **evaluation** (good-bad), **potency** (strong-weak) and **activity** (active-passive) thereby mapping the concept in a three-dimensional space. What we are getting at by this method is the **connotative** meaning of the concept – the personal response, rather than the publicly agreed, or **denotative** meaning. We all know what margarine is, more or less, but it 'means' different things to each of us. Osgood's method helps to uncover these meanings.

The question of different responses to different words does however raise a problem in the bi-polar words used to define the scales. The word 'social' may have one connotation to one person, but a rather different one to another. Thus the actual scale social-unsocial will not be identical for all the people who complete the scale.

Kelly

Kelly believed that each of us brings our own unique order into the world by the use of **personal constructs**. These are black-and-white, either-or, dimensions, rather than the graded differentials of Osgood's scheme. We can sample them by the **Repertory Grid** or REP test. In this, the subject is given three items, which again can be people, groups, objects or ideas, and asked to group two together as similar in some way, leaving the third element as dissimilar.

The constructs used can be provided, as with Osgood, or they can be elicited, that is, supplied by the subject *after* he has grouped the items. Some workers prefer this method, on the grounds that it does not force dimensions on the subject. Against this, it then becomes difficult to compare one set of responses with another.

In the grid form, group administration is possible. A list of items heads the columns, and sets of three items, or triads are marked off in each row for the subject to compare. (See Fig. 6.4.)

The respondent puts crosses through two which are perceived as similar (the 'similarity' or 'construct' pole), leaving the third (the 'contrast' pole). The poles of the construct are written in the end column. The technique has the benefit of studying the individual's perceptions without forcing 'constructs' upon them.

Fig. 6.4

Sort No.	Chinese	English	French	Indian	Italian	Construct
		A short grid form for different types of restaurant				
1	0	⌀	⌀			European–Asian
2			⌀	0	⌀	Smooth–rough
3	⌀	0		⌀		Exciting–dull
4						
etc.						

Fishbein's attitude model

Martin Fishbein attempted to cope with the problems of the three-component view in several ways.

1 He distinguished the separate elements of belief about an object (or an expectancy) and the evaluation or value of that belief for the individual.
2 He allowed for the specificity of attitudes towards the same object.
3 He allowed for compensation, partly by this specificity, and partly by 'weighting' the belief component and the evaluative.

EXAMPLE 6.2   TWO MEN AND A CAR

Jim and Percy are looking at the same car at an exhibition.
Jim thinks 'Bet that will do more than 100 mph.'
Percy thinks 'Bet that will do more than 100 mph.'
Jim thinks 'Smashing. That would impress the girls.'
Percy thinks 'Horrific. Just a quicker way to die, that's all.'
   Both have the same beliefs, but their evaluations of those beliefs are different. Their expectations of the car's performance are similar, but the value placed on the performance is different.
   Jim sizes up other specific aspects, such as styling, interior comfort, the prestige it might bring him. His overall attitude depends on the number of his beliefs about the car, and the value, or evaluation, of those beliefs.

This incident can be summed up in a general statement: an attitude towards an object is the sum of the number of beliefs about the object, each belief being weighted by the evaluation placed on that belief. In a formula, then:

$$Ao = \sum_{1}^{n} Bi \times ai$$

Ao is attitude towards the object
Bi is the belief about the object
ai is the evaluation of that belief
n is the number of beliefs

Because of the problems in the relation of attitudes to behaviour, however, Fishbein used **attitudes towards behaviour** in relation to the object, rather than attitudes to the object itself. This represents the difference between Jim believing that the car will do over 100 mph (whoever is the driver), and his believing that, *if he buys it*, he will be able to do more than 100 mph. We have moved closer to **behavioural intentions**, which Fishbein believed would be a better predictor of actual behaviour than simply assessing the attitude to the object itself.

The formula is thus somewhat amended:

$$\text{Aact} = \sum_{1}^{n} \text{Bi} \times \text{ei}$$

Aact is the attitude towards a specific act (e.g. Jim's buying the car)
Bi is the perceived belief that that act will produce a given consequence ('If I buy that car, I can do 100 mph')
ei is the individual's evaluation of that consequence
n is the number of consequences involved.

To assess the attitude we therefore have first to assess the belief aspect, and the evaluative aspect.

ASSESSMENT OF BELIEF COMPONENT
A series of statements thought to represent important or salient features of the object is prepared, and rated on a semantic differential scale. Thus if 'power' has been found to be an important feature in choosing squash racquets, a statement might be:

Buying the Panther racquet will increase power

very likely ⌐——⌐ very unlikely
     +3   +2   +1   0   −1   −2   −3

ASSESSMENT OF EVALUATIVE COMPONENT
A statement here might be:

Increased power from a squash racquet is

very desirable ⌐————————————————————————————————————⌐ very undesirable
        +3   +2   +1   0   −1   −2   −3

For this individual, the belief is that the Panther will not increase power, but that power itself is a desirable feature.

COMBINING THE TWO COMPONENTS

A table can now be constructed showing the feature involved, the individual's belief rating, and his evaluative rating of that belief (Table 6.1). We could do this for a sample of the target group, and thus obtain average ratings.

Table 6.1 Comparison of the Panther and Smasher

Feature	Panther			Smasher	
	Belief	B × e	Evaluation	Belief	B × e
1 Will give power	−2	−6	+3	+2	+6
2 Will be cheap	+1	0	0	−1	0
3 Will be durable	0	0	2	−1	−2
4 Brings prestige	−1	−2	2	+2	+4
	Total −8			Total +8	

The belief weightings and the evaluation weightings are multiplied together, and their grand total obtained, following the formula given above.

From this we can get diagnostic information. On the highly desirable feature, power, the Panther fails, but the Smasher does well. On the highest expectation for the Panther, the evaluation is only neutral. Note, however, that different segments even of the squash market might have different evaluations. Power players would welcome power, but many 'touch' players would place much less value on it.

In the extended behavioural intentions model a new element, that of normative compliance is added. This assesses the extent to which a person will 'go along' with the intentions of a particular group.

We now have a measure of the attitude towards a particular behaviour in given circumstances, and this can be added to the strength of the subjective norm or individual motivation to conform to specified group norms. Thus the extended formula is:

$$B \approx BI = w1\,(Ab) + w2(SN)$$

Where B is overt behaviour, BI is behavioural intention, Ab is attitude towards performing the behaviour, and SN is the person's subjective norm, each weighted appropriately by w1 and w2. This could be translated as:

- behaviour is related to behavioural intentions;
- behavioural intentions are a function of attitude towards performing specified actions towards the object, and of subjective motivation to accept specified group norms.

Notice that we have come a very long way from attempting to predict behaviour from global assessments of attitude. Indeed Engel and Blackwell comment:

Beliefs and attitudes, defined in terms of an attitude towards an object *have been expected to carry an impossible weight of prediction.*[6]

Fishbein thus requires specific assessments to be made, so that the results are diagnostic. He does not claim to predict behaviour directly, but behavioural intentions. Where there is close correspondence between the target behaviour and situation, and the measurement procedures, then prediction from behavioural intentions as assessed by the model and overt behaviour may be high.[7]

■ CHANGING ATTITUDES

Foxall underlines the caution needed when assuming that change in attitude can necessarily result in a change of behaviour when he says:

If consumers' verbalised attitudes function independently of their actions, if attitude measurement techniques cannot be reliably employed in any degree to provide a guide to buyer behaviour, and if so-called attitude data possesses little or no predictive validity, the edifice of contemporary marketing practice must begin to crumble.[8]

Nevertheless, much work proceeds on the assumption that a positive change in attitude towards a product will result in increased likelihood of positive behaviour towards the product, so a consideration of research on the issue is well worthwhile.

The classic work on attitude change stems from the Yale University project on communication and attitude change in the 1950s. This and much other work has broken the communication process into four elements:

1 The communicator or source
2 The communication or message
3 The receiver or target
4 The context or situation.

Communicator or source factors

CREDIBILITY
The extent to which we trust and believe in a communicator – his credibility – is an important factor in persuading us towards his point of view.

Thus Hovland and Weiss found students showed greater change towards the communicator's viewpoint on nuclear submarines when the author was said to be the scientist Oppenheimer than when the same message was attributed to

Pravda. No difference was found in the amount of information learned by listeners in the high credibility as compared with low credibility situation.

Similar results have been found in the evaluation of poetry, the high credibility source being T S Eliot and the low credibility source an unknown female student. However, after an interval, the effect of the communicator seemed to lessen, and attitude was determined more by content. This was termed the **sleeper** effect.

ATTRACTIVENESS

A semantic differential was used to determine the attractiveness of communicators. It was then found that positive attitude change towards the communicator's position was linked to his attractiveness. One of the components of attractiveness may be that the communicator is seen as one of us by the target group so that presenters with whom the group can identify may be very effective where credibility from expertise is not vital.

SELF-INTEREST

Whatever influence the communicator may have from prestige or attractiveness will be greatly diluted if he seems to be acting out of self-interest (e.g. because high payments are received to endorse a product). But if a communicator seems to be advocating a position opposed to his own interest, he will gain credibility.

The communication

DISCREPANCY

Early work suggested that the greater the difference between the attitude expressed by the communicator and that of the receiver, the greater the degree of change. However, when account was taken of the degree of involvement of the receiver, and the credibility of the communicator, it was found that on important, or salient issues, greatest change occurred with a credible communicator advocating a position not too far removed from that of the receiver.

Connected with this is the **latitude of acceptance**. This phrase summarises the tendency for people to accept a position within a limited range of their own, but to reject it beyond this range. Thus attempts to move too fast may fail and, with extreme discrepancy, **boomerang** effects may occur, with the receiver holding on to his own position even more strongly because it is under attack.

Besides the size of the change advocated, the direction of intended change is important. **Congruent** changes are those which increase the extremity of a position: positive becomes more positive and vice versa. **Incongruent** change occurs when an attitude lessens in extremity, or moves sufficiently to change from positive to negative. In general it is held that congruent change such as increasing liking for a liked object is easier than incongruent.

ONE-SIDED OR TWO-SIDED COMMUNICATION?

It might be supposed that presenting only the positive side of a position might be the most effective in changing other people's views. After all, why draw attention to weaknesses in one's arguments? But detailed studies have shown that two benefits may result. Firstly, credibility may be increased because the communicator seems 'fair-minded' in disclosing possible objections (some of which may have occurred to the audience anyway). Secondly, the audience may become inoculated against the effects of later counter-argument, since they have heard parts before. Thus, a salesperson might say, 'Now I have heard it said that the price of this appliance is too high. But that is looking only at price, and not at an even more important factor, performance. The performance of this model is, I assure you ....'

It appears that a one-sided presentation is effective with less intelligent and less well-informed groups, and where congruent change is desired. Two-sided arguments may be preferable for more intelligent and informed groups, who could feel insulted by crude, one-sided presentations.

FREQUENCY OF APPEAL

It can be irritating to hear exactly the same message or the same presenter over and over again, and we may very well tune out. In that case, the communication has reached the 'wearout' stage. Sometimes, however, the **mere exposure** effect occurs and a presenter can continue his effectiveness for long periods. In England, the TV personality John Cleese has appeared in commercials over a long period, without 'wearing-out' his welcome, and Robert Morley has had an even longer run.

Even rats are affected by mere exposure! Those exposed to Mozartian music showed a later preference for his music, while those exposed to the music of Arnold Schoenberg preferred his.[9]

Where wearout threatens, change in format and reduction in frequency may produce recovery from the habituation or rejection effects.

APPEALS TO FEAR

Many of our everyday activities carry with them the risk of injury or pain. The kitchen bristles with possibilities of accidents; a car crash is always on the cards; even poor care of the teeth may mean toothache and an unpleasant visit to the dentist. In changing people's attitudes and behaviour in such situations, should we appeal to this fear motive, and if so, how strongly?

Early work on tooth care appealing at different levels to the fear of decay etc. showed that the *less* the fear arousal, the greater was the attitude change and subsequent resistance to counter-argument. Later work suggested that a moderate appeal was most effective. Minimal appeals produce little change, and high-fear appeals may give rise to high anxiety and consequent rejection of the source and communication, particularly where the receiver is highly involved. A summary of recent views suggests that fear arousal can be effective

- with moderate arousal of fear
- when the dangers are real
- when the receiver believes the measures suggested will be effective.

Such considerations are particularly important in, for instance, attempting to modify attitudes towards smoking, or, more recently, towards the dangers of promiscuous and homosexual sex as possibly leading to AIDS. One by-product of the high-intensity British campaign has been to raise fear about quite other kinds of behaviour, such as sharing a toothbrush, and some groundless fears have had to be lessened by further information.

OTHER COMMUNICATION FACTORS
1 Drawing a conclusion: this is suggested as more effective with less intelligent and knowledgeable audiences.
2 Order of presentation: where a two-sided argument is to be presented, should the pros come before cons, or after? The **primacy** effect suggests that hearing good points sets off a good first impression, whereas hearing adverse points first may produce a negative attitude, and rejection of later positive points.

Against this, the **recency** effect suggests that the last heard information leaves greatest impression, so that presenting bad points later may result in negative attitude change.

Receiver factors

People vary in their resistance to attempts to change their attitudes. This is known as **persuasability**. Relevant points here are that:

1 Those low in self-esteem seem more likely to be impressed by others, and thus are more likely to change their views.
2 High intelligence is connected with low persuasability, as is good memory, perhaps because these enable many arguments to be kept in mind, rather than those most recently heard.
3 In early studies, women were found to be more persuasable than men, but even then it was pointed out that this might be more a social than a genetic effect. With greater opportunity for confidence and self-esteem amongst women, this difference may be lessening in many cultures.

Context factors

Group membership may affect attitude change in a number of ways.

COMMITMENT
Many studies have shown that where a person commits themselves publicly to a certain behaviour (say losing weight) there is a greater tendency to convert stated intention to behaviour than when private commitment is made.

CONFORMITY

The effects of group affiliation are often to support individuals against modifiability of attitudes. An early study on Boy Scouts showed that resistance to attack on their values was related to the value they placed upon group membership. Indeed, where membership was highly valued, attack produced even closer adherence to group norms. Once more, beware the boomerang effect!

Some of the various factors involved in attitude change are summarised in Table 6.2.

Table 6.2

Communicator	Communication	Target	Context
Prestige	Discrepancy	Persuasability	Group support
Attractiveness	1 or 2 sided	Self-esteem	Group commitment
Credibility	Fear arousal	Memory	
Intentions	Primacy	Intelligence	
Exposure	Recency		
	Exposure		

■ THEORIES OF ATTITUDES

Balance theory

When a friend expresses opinions close to our own, we feel comfortable with the situation. It's as we would expect. But if someone we dislike expresses opinions similar to our own, or our friend expresses views quite opposite to ours, there may be a slight shock. Things are not as we would expect. In Heider's balance theory it is argued that we aim at balance, and that change may therefore occur to produce balance. The situations are usually represented as triangles.

Let's take A and B as two people, and C as a political party. The diagrams below represent various possibilities of balance and imbalance, with '+' representing a positive attitude, and '−' representing a negative one. The situations are seen from A's point of view.

Fig. 6.5

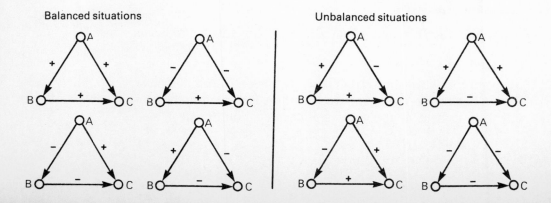

Where the system is balanced, there is no need for change. Things are as they should be. But what will happen where there is imbalance? It might of course be tolerated, but if not there are three main possibilities, as shown in Fig. 6.6.

Fig. 6.6

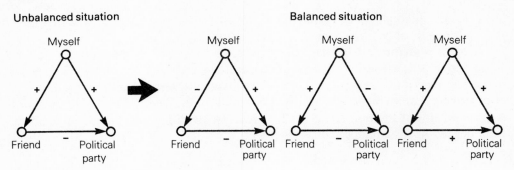

The changes involved are:

1 Attitude towards the friend might change in a negative direction.
2 Attitude towards the party could change in a negative direction.
3 Persuade the friend into greater appreciation of the party.

Criticisms of the theory include the fact that it takes account only of **direction** of attitude, not its **degree** and that it omits many possibilities, such as removing the friend from the system.

Congruity theory

Osgood and Tannenbaum's congruity theory may be considered as a special case of balance theories. However, it goes beyond Heider's approach in taking account of intensity as well as direction of attitude.

Attitude research and learning theory both agree in suggesting that an 'attractive' presenter is a good choice for improving consumer evaluation of products. But supposing we use a very attractive presenter expressing a positive opinion about an object or idea which is negatively evaluated by the consumer? Now, there is incongruity. How can it be resolved?

Osgood and Tannenbaum suggested that there is a movement towards congruity, in that the attitude will change towards the opinion of the presenter, but that the presenter will be less positively rated, because of his putting forward an 'incongruent' view. This is what Tannenbaum found in the 'attractiveness' work mentioned earlier. Attractive people making positive statements which were against listeners' attitudes towards an object moved attitudes in a positive direction, but suffered a loss of attractiveness themselves.

However, it appears that more extreme positions on the attitude scale carry more weight than those nearer a neutral position. In other words, a highly rated presenter will 'pull' attitudes towards his own favourably expressed opinion more strongly than mildly held negative attitudes towards the object will reduce the presenter's attractiveness.

Dissonance theory

This third example again rests on the assumption that discord or dissonance between aspects of an attitude system is a source of tension which can be resolved by moving towards consonance, or agreement, within the system. The particular parts of the system with which Festinger, the proposer of **cognitive dissonance** theory, investigated were cognitions: 'the things a person knows about himself, about his behaviour, and about his surroundings.'

Of particular interest to marketing are situations in which dissonance results from a person's choice. Suppose after careful thought I buy a car. There are some features of other, rejected, cars which were attractive, and some features of the chosen car which are not so attractive. Consequently, post-purchase behaviour might include some doubts, regrets, or dissonance about our choice. The degree of dissonance will vary with:

1 The extent to which rejected alternatives are evaluated as similar to the chosen product. If our choice is clearly ahead of the field, little dissonance occurs, but if others were almost as attractive, dissonance is high. This will involve the number of positive attributes of accepted and rejected choices, and the number of negative attributes of the chosen model.
2 The number of competing alternatives. Dissonance is higher the more alternatives we have discarded.
3 The degree of cognitive overlap or the extent to which the 'field' of rejected alternatives is seen as having similar characteristics to the choice. The greater the overlap, the less the dissonance.
4 The importance of the action. Choosing a cake to go with your tea may produce mild post-choice dissonance, but unlikely to compare with the dissonance produced after buying an expensive car.

The factors are briefly summarised by the equation:

Amount of dissonance associated with choice k =

$$\frac{\text{Sum of beliefs dissonant with k}}{\text{Sum of beliefs consonant with k}}$$

How are we to reconcile the dissonance?

1 Increase the attractiveness of the chosen alternative, and decrease that of the rejected alternative. This will particularly occur where there is close agreement in evaluation of the alternatives. Look for the good points of the car you chose, and emphasise the poor points of those you rejected.
2 Change or revoke the behaviour: do not purchase again; send back 'approval' goods. But in many cases, the action is difficult to revoke (marriage?).
3 Admit we chose wrongly!

The second type of situation to which dissonance theory applies is that where the public behaviour of an individual is at odds with his internal evaluation. Someone, for instance, expresses a point of view which is at variance with his true feelings. Where this is done under compulsion, it is known as **forced compliance**.

Dissonance theory predicts here that the *greater* the inducement or compulsion, the *less* will be the dissonance, and vice versa.

EXAMPLE 6.3   BORING? OF COURSE NOT!

1 Students did a rather boring task.

2 Their attitudes towards it were measured.

3 They were then offered either $1 or $20 to tell later students that the task was quite interesting.

4 Attitudes towards the task were again measured after this public commitment.

5 Which group should become more positive in their attitude to the task? Those given $1 or those given $20?

6 The answer, perhaps surprisingly, is the $1 group. Why?

7 Because, offered a biggish incentive, we say, 'OK I lied to get the money. But I didn't really like it.' We hold on to the attitude.

But are we the sort of person to lie for $1? Of course not. So we resolve the behaviour-attitude dissonance by changing the attitude: 'I really did like it!'

In the first case, the reward is considered sufficient justification for the behaviour, so there is little dissonance. In the second, the reward is too slight to justify the behaviour, so there is dissonance.[10]

Dissonant messages for marketing

1 The post-purchase situation suggests the following:

(a) doubts and dissonance will be highest with irrevocable and voluntarily undertaken actions; with several alternatives; with many 'plus' points for the alternatives and with high involvement with the decision;

(b) post-purchase behaviour may include: upgrading the chosen alternative and down-grading the remainder; brand loyalty shown by repeat purchase after temporary dissonance (thus confirming the 'rightness' of the original choice).

2 The counter-attitudinal situation occurs when a customer is persuaded to try a product to which he is not currently favourable. Where the incentive is not high, dissonance may be resolved by a more positive attitude towards the product, as in the 'boring task' experiment. But if too great an incentive is given, then there is the danger, certainly with a low involvement item, that although purchase is made, attitude remains unchanged, and buying ceases when reinforcement ceases.

■ SELF ASSESSMENT QUESTIONS

Marks

1 Write 'balanced' or 'unbalanced' against these 'triangles'.
  (a) John likes Mary. They both like Milk Tray. _ _ _ _ _ _ _ _ _ _ _
  (b) Bill hates John. They both like Guinness. _ _ _ _ _ _ _ _ _ _ _
  (c) Jane dislikes Anna. They both hate red wine. _ _ _ _ _ _ _ _ _   (3)

2 The following belief and evaluation ratings for two brands of shoe were obtained on scales from −3 to +3. Using the Fishbein Aact formula, find the total belief-evaluation score for each.

Attribute	Evaluation	Brand A	$b \times e$	Brand B	$b \times e$
		Belief (b)			
Hard-wearing	+2	+3	—	+1	—
Price below £10	−1	−2	—	+1	—
Comfortable	+3	+2	—	−1	—
Good styling	+1	+1	—	+1	—
		Total: _ _ _ _		Total: _ _ _ _	

(2)

3 Write 'true' or 'false' against the following:
  (a) According to congruity theory, if a person is rated +3 and endorses a product rated by the consumer at −1 the product is likely to gain more in attractiveness than the person loses. _ _ _ _ _ _ _ _
  (b) Attitude change depends greatly on whether the person believes the information given. _ _ _ _ _ _ _ _ _ _ _ _ _ _ _ _ _ _ _
  (c) A convicted criminal arguing for harsher punishment for his type of crime could produce positive attitude change towards his position. _   (3)

4 Mr Jackson chooses a new car which does not perform at all well. Which of the following is his most likely post-purchase reaction:
  (a) Emphasising the good points of rejected alternatives.
  (b) Emphasising the bad points of rejected alternatives.
  (c) Emphasising the bad points of the chosen car.
(a), (b) or (c)? _   (1)

5 Put the right names against these descriptions:
  (a) The consumer indicates agreement with statements on a 5-point scale. _
  (b) Includes a measure of subjective norm. _ _ _ _ _ _ _ _ _ _ _ _ _
  (c) Uses 'similarity' and 'contrast' poles. _ _ _ _ _ _ _ _ _ _ _ _ _
  (d) Potency, activity and evaluation are major dimensions of his approach. _

(e) Deals with dissonance between different cognitions. _ _ _ _ _ _ (5)

> Kelly Osgood Likert Festinger Fisbein

6 Arrange the following into **communicator**, **message** and **receiver** factors.

> persuasability   credibility   one/two sided
> attractiveness   fear appeals   intelligence

COMMUNICATOR   MESSAGE   RECEIVER
(a) _ _ _ _ _ _ _ _   (c) _ _ _ _ _ _ _ _   (e) _ _ _ _ _ _ _ _ _ _
(b) _ _ _ _ _ _ _   (d) _ _ _ _ _ _ _ _   (f) _ _ _ _ _ _ _ _ _ _

(6)

(Total: 20)

(Answers are on page 220)

■ STUDY AND EXAMINATION TIPS

Syndicate study

1 If you are part of a tutorial group, or have friends working for the same examination, you would probably find the 'syndicate' approach quite helpful. Form yourselves into small groups of up to six people.

2 It can work in two ways:
   (a) Preparing the information. Everyone reads a chapter. But different people make themselves responsible for a given part, producing:

● resumés/check lists of important points (e.g. on attitude change)
● additional material from other sources
● practical illustrations (e.g. of attitude change, approaches in different media, and for different products/services)
● quizzes on specific points

   (b) Using the information. When examination time approaches, the members of a syndicate take a question, and use their material to prepare a (fairly detailed) plan for it individually. Approaches are then compared and evaluated, perhaps with tutor assistance.

3 See if your syndicate comes up with a more effective outline for Question 2.
   (a) *Early views on attitudes*

● the three-component or 'latent process' view
● the assumption of consonance between the components
● the assumption that attitude and behaviour were necessarily related: positive attitude → positive behaviour

   (b) *Fishbein's work*

● the move towards attitude-to-action, rather than attitude-to-object
● the move towards behavioural intention as the closest predictor for behaviour

- the move towards specific features of an attitude (e.g. to different attributes of a product)
- the compensatory nature of the approach: expectancy times value, or belief times evaluation
- the inclusion of social forces in the extended model (the subjective norm)

(c) *Implications for marketing*

- Earlier work suggested that change in attitude would result in change of behaviour.
- Therefore much effort was concentrated on presentations aimed at changing attitudes.
- In order to see if attitudes had changed, it was necessary to measure them. Therefore much work focussed on attitude measurement in a global sense.
- Fishbein's approach suggests that the concentration in measurement should be on behavioural intention, specifically sub-divided according to the *situation* and *attribute* involved.
- This gives more diagnostic information – e.g. on the value placed on different attributes of a product, and on the specific beliefs of consumers about product attributes.
- This in turn can give specific guidance on product strategy. Note: If you can make use of the various formulae, do so. They will help to focus your mind on the important points. But don't just put the formulae down parrot-fashion: explain them.

■ EXAMINATION QUESTIONS

1 A principal goal of marketing communication is to change attitudes or create favourable attitudes towards a brand or product. What are the main methods used to achieve this?

2 Does Fishbein's work represent a major advance to an understanding of attitudes when compared with earlier work?

3 'It is dangerous to assume that a knowledge of attitudes is in itself predictive of behavioural consequences in given situations.' Discuss this statement and its implications for marketing strategy.

4 Briefly outline the theory of cognitive dissonance. Discuss its implications for marketing and evaluate its usefulness in marketing practice.

5 Guinness once won an award for a poster whose headline ran: 'I've never tried it because I don't like it.' What light, if any, does this poster shed on the attitude-behaviour controversy?

6 Briefly outline any *two* attitude quantification techniques, and discuss the extent to which they provide a satisfactory measurement of attitudes.

7 | **Personality**

All that a man is. Gordon Allport.

■ INTRODUCTION

Mr D goes along to the supermarket very early on Wednesdays, arriving at 8.00 am precisely, just as the doors open. He doesn't like meeting people very much, and anyway the quietness of the store allows him to work his way methodically through his checklist. When he gets to the checkout, he manages a slight smile at the cashier, but is relieved to be home again on his own. He is never very sure of himself with other people, but quite self-confident handling complicated computer software. In fact, other computer experts respect his judgement, and turn to him readily for advice, and read his columns in the computer magazines. As he leaves, the cashier shakes her head, and wonders if Mr D is very unhappy, or if she has offended him somehow.

When Ms E goes to the supermarket, practically everyone there knows it. She might arrive any time, in-between the hectic episodes of her life. There is bound to be someone she knows, who gets an enthusiastic greeting and the benefit of her advice on what is the best shampoo to use for greasy hair. The trolley is filled rather erratically as she goes from one acquaintance to another. When she gets to the checkout, the other customers sometimes get cross because she is bound to dash off just as her goods are checked. Some impulse has crossed her mind, and she simply *has* to make sure she gets that last vital purchase. In spite of this, she is well-liked, and has quite an influence amongst her wide circle of friends, who think she is very self-confident, though some do wonder if she is as confident inside as she appears.

Mr D and Ms E obviously have different personalities. In their different ways, they have influence on the opinions of others. They have their own estimates of themselves, and other people form their own judgements of them. There seems to be both an inner and an outer aspect to their personalities – their outward behaviour and their inner feelings; their estimates of themselves, and those made by other people.

In this section we will look more systematically at

1 Two approaches to personality: Freud and Cattell
2 Life-styles
3 Personality and new products
4 How we see ourselves: the self-concept
5 How we see others: person perception.

■ FREUD'S THEORY

Although Freud began his psychological investigations in the 19th century, and died in 1939, the general influence of his work has been long-lasting not only in psychology, but in cultural activities such as novels, drama and art. Some attempts at applying the theory to marketing have been made, but so far no systematic, full-scale application has developed.

The theory is largely **explanatory**. It seeks to unravel the factors behind behaviour, rather than to predict it. For Freud, little, if anything, in human life occurs by chance. Rather, it is the result of previous forces, often from childhood, upon the individual. His is a **deterministic** viewpoint, with scant room for individual freedom of choice.

The major points emerging from his writings can be divided into **dynamic**, **structural** and **developmental** aspects.

Dynamic aspects

Freud thought of a psychic energy, parallel with physical energy, which could flow between the different structures and layers of personality. In later work, he divided this into two sets. The libidinal, or life-enhancing forces, such as seeking food, drink, and sexual activity, formed one group, the sexual instinct itself being called libido. The second group consisted of destructive forces, aimed at harming others and even oneself.

The two groups need not operate independently. In eating, for instance, the life forces are satisfied, but by the same act, something is destroyed. Our chicken dinner satisfies our appetite, but costs the life of another living organism.

Most people are well aware that Freud concentrated on the sexual instincts as a central part of his theory. It is important, however, not to identify this with purely physical aspects of sex. Freud also emphasised the need for the loving side of personal relations.

Structural aspects

THE UNCONSCIOUS
Although he was not the first to write about it, Freud is famous for his emphasis on the unconscious aspect of our lives. He argued that our much prized

rational, conscious, self is but one small part of our personality, the remainder being unknown to us, yet operating to affect our thoughts, behaviour and feelings. It is as if we thought that a small island was floating on the sea, and ignored the much greater part lying below, and supporting what we can actually see.

THE ID

The id lies completely within this hidden part. It is the first structure, born within us as the instinctual source of our psychic energy. It is blind to outside reality, and follows the pleasure principle in that it seeks immediate gratification of the tensions generated within it. A small child howling with rage at the frustrations of hunger is perhaps a good example of pure id activity. Various picturesque descriptions have been given to it, such as 'the dynamo of the desires', 'a whirlpool of wild wishes'. *The id represents the biological aspect of personality.*

THE EGO

The ego develops because the blind desires of the id are not adjusted to the demands of reality. Hence energy is released which can be used to channel the unconscious wishes in ways adaptable to reality. The young child has to learn that not everything is good to grab and suck, that some things are unpleasant or harmful.

   The ego can also delay satisfaction, in deferred gratification. Students, for instance, delay financial independence to secure more beneficial qualifications. The ego is conscious, performs the functions we have considered in earlier sections, and has been called the 'executive of the personality'. *The ego represents the cognitive, reasoning, aspects of personality.*

THE SUPEREGO

The superego, largely unconscious, serves to prevent the id from offending against a moral code derived, via the parents, from the cultural norms and values of the surrounding society. Because of this early formation, particularly where strong religious values are involved, it will continue its guidance function even when the person finds himself in a society with different values. By means of the ego-ideal it strives for perfection rather than pleasure, and by means of the conscience it can arrest id impulses: 'Thou shalt not ...'. *The superego represents the moral aspect of personality.*

Developmental aspects

The psychic energy can also flow between different areas of the body, known as the erogenous zones. At each of the **psychosexual stages** a particular zone is the focus of energy, interest and pleasure.

   At the first, **oral** stage, the mouth is the focus, initially for satisfaction of life impulses by sucking and eating, and later for the aggressive forces by biting and spitting. Next, with toilet training, the **anal** stage is reached, followed by the **phallic** stage, where interest is on the genital areas, though true adult sexuality is not present. Finally, after the **latency period** the **genital** stage is reached, and with it the possibility of full adult sexuality. Normally, there will be a progression, in order, through these stages. But where the crisis of a particular stage is not fully resolved, the after effects may last through into the formation of adult personality characteristics.

   Fixation occurs when progression stops at a stage. **Regression** is when we drop back to earlier stages – perhaps overeating when we are lonely and depressed. The form of the behaviour may however be quite different from that in the original stage. A dependency on physical feeding in the oral stage may have as its consequence a need for approval, or for possession of things.

Mechanisms of defence

The id, ego and superego do not, of course, exist in the way heart, kidneys and lungs do. They are 'as if' creations to explain the forces at work within us: instinctual drives, cognitive processes, and moral values and expectations. Inevitably, conflict between them can arise, and to cope with the anxiety resulting from this, we may make use of the **mechanisms of defence**. Amongst these are:

1 **Repression**. Painful feelings and memories are unconsciously forced out of consciousness, yet remain active there, unknown to us, affecting our reactions. Sometimes they will re-emerge, in dreams or the famous 'Freudian slips' where we say something quite different from what we intended. These Freud called the 'return of the repressed'.
2 **Projection**. One way of avoiding anxiety from unacceptable feelings and thoughts is to attribute them to others. So in projection, we see these impulses in others, and fail to recognise them in ourselves.
3 **Displacement**. Sometimes it may not be possible to release an impulse, say of aggression, directly onto the object causing it. We may then displace it onto some other target – for instance by shouting at a subordinate after a rough time with the boss. Or we may change its character, as when we get back on someone, not by physical attack, but by spreading rumour and gossip about them. Where the displacement is towards a more socially acceptable outlet, it is often known as **sublimation**. Freud himself analysed the Madonna paintings of Leonardo da Vinci as a sublimated expression of longing to regain his mother, from whom Leonardo was separated early in life.

Marketing messages from Freud

UNCONSCIOUS MOTIVES
If consumers' motives are sometimes unconscious, unknown even to them, how can we find out about them? Motivation research was one method, but some of

its findings caused consternation. Do women bake cakes as a symbolic desire to give birth? Do men wear braces on their trousers because of a fear of castration? It is easy to mock, but the notion that consumers may have many motives, 'layered' in terms of their conscious awareness of them is a good corrective to the over-simplified idea that consumers always know why they are buying. Even if we do not accept subliminal perception, we should remember that quite small or short elements of a presentation can trigger off associations in an individual consumer's mind, beyond the fringe of the main theme.

But unless we accept the idea of a similar, collective, unconscious amongst consumers, we have to interview each one to find his precise motives!

SEX
As pointed out, Freud did not equate sex with physical lust. Appeals to 'naked sex' might offend against the superego in some people. They might produce perceptual defence in others. For the more sexually permissive, they might prove merely laughable. Research has indeed suggested that sexual-romantic themes were more effective in gaining attention to advertisements than those involving nudity, and that brand names associated with sexual illustrations were recalled *less* often than those without.

THE ID, EGO AND SUPEREGO
It is easy to fit Freudian theory onto situations. But whether the theory can be used as a design strategy, and whether it is the only explanation, are different questions.

EXAMPLE 7.1 WHAT'S COOKING, GOOD LOOKING?

An athletic young man comes into a room, throws down his squash racquet (virility symbol?). He takes off his shirt and dances a few quick steps (appeal to sexual instincts?). Takes a convenience food packet out and puts it in the microwave (ego decision, solving problem of pressure of time?).

Meanwhile an attractive girl (sexual instincts?) steps into her car, carrying a bunch of roses.

Food is ready. Man takes a quick taste (oral gratification?), puts on shirt and has supper ready as girl enters. Superego is appeased by good deed of preparing food.

We could of course also see this as appealing to the dual role view of Chapter 5: the man is physically active, but also caring. The woman is attractive, but portrayed as independent rather than dependent, and quite willing to take the initiative by bringing the roses. Alternatively, the whole thing could be a sophisticated send-up!

■ TRAIT THEORY

Try this simple test. Write down the fewest number of adjectives you could use to give someone who didn't know you a reasonable idea of your personality.

It's probable you wrote down between three and ten. These words describe important features of your personality. If you wrote 'polite', then this suggests that in a lecture, at the supermarket checkout, at a party, your behaviour will have certain similar characteristics, quite different from that of someone who might be called 'rude'. If your friends describe you as 'polite', then this enables them to predict, to some extent, how you will behave in a range of situations.

Allport and the beginning of trait theory

Such 'chunks' of behaviour were first systematically studied by Allport. He called them traits, or predispositions to respond in a similar manner to different kinds of stimuli. He felt they were 'real', located inside the individual, but agreed that they could be observed empirically, in consistencies within behaviour.

With Vernon he produced the 'Study of Values', which aimed at deep-seated traits, such as the **economic**, where value is placed on what is useful, or the **social**, where love of people is important. Sample items similar to those in Part II of the test are given in Example 7.2.

EXAMPLE 7.2   THE ALLPORT-VERNON STUDY OF VALUES

In your opinion, can people whose full time work is in business spend Sunday best in:

(a) working towards a higher educational qualification
(b) playing a sport competitively
(c) attending a play
(d) going to church and reflecting on the sermon?

The subject gives 4 points to his first choice, 3 to the second and so on.

You might like to try to identify the values aimed at by these questions. The full six are theoretical, economic, social, aesthetic, political and religious.

This approach, which assesses observable, if verbal, behaviour in standard situations, seems to promise more for marketing than those which necessitate an exploration of the darker recesses of consumers' minds. However, it does rest on the belief that there is a 'something' within the person which 'causes' his behaviour to be consistent in certain ways. This 'inner' assumption draws heavy criticism from the more behaviourist and objective psychologists such as Eysenck and Cattell.

Cattell and the 16PF

Cattell made the ambitious claim that personality is:

that which tells what a man will do when placed in a given situation.[1]

If that were true, and the situation was a marketing one, how fortunate we would be! Assessments of personality and knowledge of situations would enable us to predict consumer behaviour perfectly! In mathematical form, Cattell states

$$B = f(S.P)$$

meaning that *B*ehaviour is a function of the *S*ituation and the *P*ersonality of the individual involved.

This personality can be assessed in terms of **traits**. Several of them may be involved in any one situation, and the situation can sometimes very strongly determine which actual behaviour occurs. Calmness and politeness on the telephone may be replaced by frantic pressure should a fire break out! Indeed, Cattell said that

lack of allowance for the situation is one of the main causes of misjudging personality.[2]

Cattell also pointed out the two-way nature of traits. We infer the trait from observable behaviour, but then can use it to predict behaviour. His own '16 Personality Factor Questionnaire' (16PF as it is often called) derived traits from responses to written questionnaires. These factors he called **source traits**, meaning that they give rise to a particular range of observed behaviours. Their names are sometimes rather fearsome, but they can be connected to everyday descriptions. The dimension of **Parmia** is associated with boldness and spontaneity, whilst its opposite, **Threctia** expresses itself in shyness. (Mr D and Ms E?)

From a person's standing on each of these traits in relation to average scores, a profile can be drawn, which shows a kind of 'map' of personality, as shown in Fig. 7.1.

Fig. 7.1

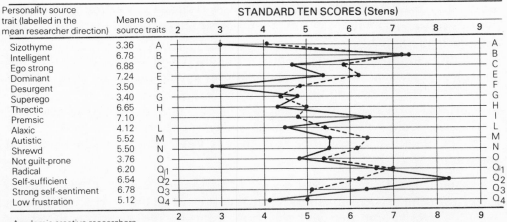

Academic creative researchers
Industrial, applied creative researchers

Here the average scores of a group of academic, creative scientists have been 'profiled' against the profiles of creative, but industrial, scientists. On some factors, clear differences emerge: the academics are more withdrawn, more self-sufficient, but less dominant.[3] If we could segment different groups of consumers in such a way by personality profiles, we might be able to use the predictive aspect of trait theory to forecast their behaviour.

However, Cattell himself gives warnings about assuming a straight trait-behaviour relation:

1 Situational factors. The consumer who is normally decisive in making purchases may suddenly show indecisive behaviour when selecting a ring for his girlfriend.

2 Role factors. A father might reprimand his child for burping at the table (role of father) but make no comment should a guest do so (role of host).

3 Faking and social desirability. Where someone realises what the purpose of a questionnaire is, they may respond to the questions not as they really feel, but in order to produce a particular, usually desirable, impression.

An early attempt to use personality measures to predict consumer behaviour was made by Evans.[4] He used the Edwards Personal Preference schedule in an effort to predict ownership of either a Ford or Chevrolet car. Using the test alone, he was correct in 63% of cases – only slightly better than chance. But using more objective and demographic variables, he was able to predict correctly in 70% of cases.

Even if personality tests were useful in predicting behaviour, there would still be problems in turning this to account:

1 From a promotional viewpoint, it would be necessary for people with common trait patterns to show other common features, such as income, age, or location. Otherwise, correct choice of media exposure would be very difficult.

2 The majority of trait approaches have been developed outside the marketing field. Thus, even if measures have good reliability and validity in their original usage, they may not transfer adequately to specialised marketing application. For this reason, adaptations of trait approaches to fit particular marketing needs have been attempted.

3 If a tidy pattern of personality-product choice could be found, all well and good. But supposing that several trait patterns could lead to the same choice? The picture is no longer so tidy (see Fig. 7.2).

4 Individual personality is unique. Marketing aims at large aggregates of individuals. Unless personality testing can reveal clear patterns within these which are of sufficient size to be economically viable, it will not have practical application.

The idea that a single measure such as personality can be a magic key to predicting complex consumer behaviour is at present an unproved one. Hence a more all-inclusive approach has been developed, using the concepts of **life-styles** and **psychographics**.

Fig. 7.2

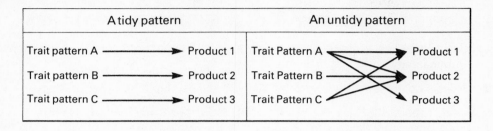

■ LIFE-STYLES AND PSYCHOGRAPHICS

Life-styles can be explained as summarising the way people live, the way they spend their time and money, and reflect the underlying values they may have.

Psychographics exists to give an operational measure of life-style. It offers the possibility of quantified data, in contrast to the more qualitative, in-depth information obtained from personal interviews.

The term 'AIO' measure is also used where attention is focussed on the activities, interests and opinions of consumers. Table 7.1 gives an example of some of the areas which might be covered (together with some demographic variables) in this approach.

Table 7.1

Activities	Interests	Opinions	Demographics
Entertainment	Family	Politics	Age
Shopping	Food	Education	Life-cycle stage
Work	Achievements etc.	Future	City size

The information is often obtained by a Likert-style scale (Chapter 6) e.g. for holidays:

A cabin by a quiet lake is a great place to spend the summer.
Strongly agree/agree/no opinion/disagree/strongly disagree

The purpose of such studies is to enable effective communication with particular groups of consumers, and to represent products to them in a way compatible with their life-style, including their values. A non profit-making application to a social issue is shown in Example 7.3.

EXAMPLE 7.3   LIFE-STYLES OF GOOD TIMERS AND NERDS

1 Four-point scales were given by telephone on 15 separate points to young men in an American city.

2 Analysis of these Attitude/Interest/Activity scales suggested four groups:

- Good Timers (23%) who often went to parties, and had a macho, 'kicks' orientation. They drove fast, listened to 'rock' stations, had the highest admitted incidence of drink-driving, but showed little other problem behaviour.
- Well-adjusted (27%) claimed to be happiest, average partiers, next to lowest in driving after drinking, and showed little problem behaviour.
- Nerds (24%) most dissatisfied with themselves, lowest in partying, macho behaviour, problem behaviour and reported the lowest level of drink-driving.
- Problem-kids (24%) above average in tendency to have problems, average in other measures, with the second highest reported drink-driving.

1 It looks, because of the size of the segment and their high drink-driving, that the 'good-timers' could be a profitable target for anti-drink campaigns. But how should the material be presented?

2 They are concerned with pleasure for themselves, not risk to others. Not showing fear and taking risks are part of the macho image, so safety appeals will fail.

3 As part of their belief system, they think being drunk is fun, believe the chances of an accident or losing their licence are low, think drink helps them with girls, and anyway, who's affected by a few drinks? Not much hope there!

4 The authors suggest an approach based on the belief that a *real* man's control *is* threatened by drink, and that a *real* man doesn't need alcohol to have fun.[5]

5 How would you approach the 'good-timers'? What medium? What method? What message?

■ JUDGING OURSELVES: THE SELF-CONCEPT

The self-concept and the ideal self

Although not an actual theory of personality, the self-concept is an important feature of personality. It may be described as one's image of oneself, including 'What I am', and 'What I can do', rather like the short description you gave of yourself earlier. This image is however not only produced from our own judgement on ourselves, but from the 'looking-glass' self, that is, the way other people seem to regard us. Eyes that wander about may suggest that we are being boring. Student eyes riveted on a lecturer *may* (but by no means always) indicate that she is worthy of interest and attention.

We tend to select out experiences to confirm our self-concept. But also we can, it seems, be influenced towards the view of us expressed by other people, and by important experiences.

EXAMPLE 7.4   CHANGING THE SELF-CONCEPT

A   Ugly duckling becomes swan

1 A group of male students played what they thought was a joke on a rather dull, unattractive girl: they treated her as if she were very attractive and popular.

2 Before that year ended, her manner had become more easy in interpersonal relations, and she felt that she was indeed popular.[6]

B   Challenge brings change

1 Two studies have measured the self-concepts and ideal-self of groups of young men exposed to considerable physical stress before and after the experience. One group attended an American Outward Bound school. The other went on an Arctic expedition.

2 While slightly conflicting in some ways, both indicated a reduction in the gap between ideal self and self-concept.[7,8]

Two messages for marketing are indicated here.

1 Consumers might be encouraged to see themselves in a new light (i.e. modify their self-concept) by appropriate messages.
2 'Challenge' type holidays and experiences could be presented as fostering self-confidence, initiative and leadership qualities, as well as being enjoyable.

Besides assessing ourselves as we are, we also can think of 'How I would like to be.' This is the ideal self of aspirations and ideals. Here marketing needs to know not only what people are and what they do, but what they would like to become. 'The good mother ...' can be portrayed using a product. Those who use the product are confirmed as 'good'. In those not using, we might set up a tension between self and ideal self (but the opposition are likely to be doing the same anyway!).

Conflict and the self

We do not always see ourselves objectively, so there may be a gap between our self-concept and our experiences (we think we are academic, but fail the exam). There may also be a gap between ourselves as we are, and ourselves as we would like to be. Such factors may affect our self-esteem, or the way in which we evaluate our self-concept. High self-esteem, and we feel confident, ready to face things. Low self-esteem, and we lack confidence in tackling things. If we are not careful, this reduces our performance still further, and the slippery slope of failure may be beneath us.

Consumers and the self-concept

Classical studies of the relation between consumer product choice and their self-concept showed some tendency for consumers to see themselves in a similar way to owners of the same product, but different from owners of different brands. Thus Grubb[9] found these differences (amongst others) in the self-images of Volkswagen and Pontiac owners:

Volkswagen owners
- Thrifty
- Practical
- Conservative
- Economical

Pontiac owners
- Flashy
- Adventurous
- Pleasure-seeking
- Status-conscious

Children appear to learn early that material products carry social significance. They can thus enhance their status, and hence their self-concept by purchasing or possessing products. This occurs in two ways:

1 The child transfers to himself the social meaning of the product: 'I own a Dogo' (supposing Dogos to be highly desirable).
2 This ownership and its associated status is communicated by the child showing or sharing the product with others ('Hey, he's got a Dogo!').

This enhanced 'looking glass self' is then reflected back to the child, again improving his self-esteem. It has been estimated that a quarter of television advertising to children contains self-concept appeals.

■ JUDGING OTHERS: PERSON PERCEPTION

Physical objects give signals to us, which we then organise and interpret. So, of course, do people. But there is one major difference between the perception of people and of objects: other people are aware that we are observing and forming impressions of them, and in turn, we are aware of the observations of others. The signals of people are not just passive, like the reflection of light from a polished table. They are often intentional, and convey meaning, in a language without words.

Forming impressions of others

The signals given by other people will include their manner of dress, their appearance, the movements of the body, especially face and hands, their speech. From these we will form an impression of their apparent status, and begin informally to build up a picture of the traits of the other person.

These first signals and our interpretation of them are likely to be quite important, whether in the formal context of an interview, or in less formal encounters such as meeting a professional colleague over lunch. The **primacy** effect suggests that early impressions last long.

Besides these direct signals, there will be other secondary information. Other people may have passed on their views, either on references, or by word-of-mouth. These will interact with our own experience, perhaps colouring it before we have even met the new person. Part of this information may be negative, which has been shown to have a very strong influence on impressions.

The purpose of our appraisal will affect what factors we weight most heavily. For the job of an office cleaner, accent and grammar might count for little. But for the job of receptionist, they are very important.

As we get to know a person, we will distinguish between merely temporary behaviour – being out of sorts, for instance – from longer-lasting traits. These we will not build up piece by piece like a jigsaw, but rather as an impression of the whole person. A sort of 'person gestalt' will emerge, like the gestalt we form of a physical display. However, such a gestalt can be changed just as a physical gestalt can, by a slight change of its parts. A sudden outburst of completely unjustified temper may completely shatter the impression of a quiet, well-controlled manager.

Errors in person perception

THE HALO EFFECT
There is a danger that when we assess a person highly in one area, we may do so in others, whether or not such high ratings are really justified. Athletes may be listened to on topics about which they are not really knowledgeable. Whiz-kidd executives who are doing well may be thought incapable of doing wrong. The other side of the halo has, not surprisingly, been called the 'horns' effect. Give a dog a bad name – and it sticks. A bad impression of a person in one area may spread to darken our impressions of other aspects of personality.

THE CONTRAST EFFECT
If an interviewer sees someone of rather dull personality, followed by a slightly more lively candidate, the second may gain from the contrast with the first. In meetings, some people will avoid following the contributions of lively speakers, because this makes them – by contrast – look dull and ineffective.

THE FUNDAMENTAL ATTRIBUTION ERROR
As Cattell pointed out, most of us tend to place the causes for a person's behaviour within them, rather than in external circumstances. Further, we tend to assume that certain traits will occur together. We also tend to put the causes of success within ourselves, e.g. because we tried hard, but put the causes of failure outside (such as bad luck). But when other people succeed, we may reverse the argument. 'You slipped, but I was pushed' is a summary of this effect.

STEREOTYPES
In the extreme, we may assume that a whole cluster of traits is typical of all

members of a particular group. All Scots are mean, all bankers are hard-hearted. Thus an individual is not judged on their own merits, but against the supposed qualities of their race, or sex, occupation or age. Research involving an analysis of over 100 studies showed that white raters rated whites higher than blacks, with the opposite occurring for black raters.

Stereotypes can be held towards countries. Studies of attitudes towards 'country of origin' have shown quite distinct patterns towards products of different countries.

EXAMPLE 7.5   WHAT'S IN A COUNTRY'S NAME?

1 A longitudinal study has been carried out in Finland towards products from several countries, including West Germany, England and Japan.

2 Amongst the points considered were workmanship, technological advancement, reliability and length of life.

3 Over the period 1975–85, the position of Japan improved on almost all indicators. That of England declined slightly.

4 The authors repeat their earlier advice:
'The exporter…should pinpoint the attitudinal dimensions providing barriers to successful marketing, and determine the need for, and feasibility of, corrective action.' [10]

The field of person perception is a very wide one, but central to many business and marketing situations. It has two main functions:

1 Interpreting accurately the non-verbal as well as verbal messages of others. In board rooms, in presentations, in selling situations, in interaction between colleagues, the ability to 'know what is going on' is very important – and non-verbal cues can be very informational. This might be called the decoding function.
2 Using non-verbal cues to advantage. This is the encoding aspect. But there are two features here as well:
  (a) non-verbal cues can 'leak' our true feelings, and belie our spoken words. (The friend says, 'How interesting!' but the eyes glaze and the head droops.)
  (b) but they can enhance and supplement our words, drawing attention, giving emphasis.

Non-verbal cues open up a second channel. Make use of it.

■ PERSONALITY AND COMMUNICATION: OPINION LEADERS

There has always been a tendency to regard the mass media as able to impose opinions on a more or less passive public. But early work in the 1940s and 1950s had already cast doubts on the relative effectiveness of media as compared with personal communication. In one study of marketing shifts from brand to brand, personal contact was the most influential source in relation to total exposure, exceeding radio in its effect. Nevertheless the one-step view of media communication was originally widely held.

One step or two?

This early view has also been called the 'hypodermic' view. The media were thought to inject ideas directly into a passive public. One direct step, and the message came across. Katz and Lazarsfeld,[11] however, found that in communities, certain people were turned to for advice, and thus might be termed **opinion leaders**. This in turn led to the development of the **two-step** view of communication. This view argues that as well as any direct exposure to media influence, people will also be exposed to opinion leaders, who will interpret and filter the information from the media to the 'rank and file'. Thus there could be several types of influence operating:

1 Direct influence of media on individuals: no contact with opinion leader.
2 Direct influence of media on individuals, mediated by contact with opinion leader.
3 Direct influence of opinion leader, no influence from media.

Fig. 7.3

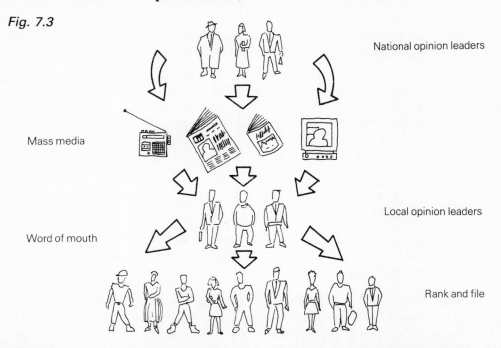

National opinion leaders

Mass media

Local opinion leaders

Word of mouth

Rank and file

Note that, as pointed out in Chapter 5 on socialisation, the media have their own opinion leaders, so that in a sense we have three steps in the layers of communication.

Who are the opinion leaders? How can we find them? How can they help marketing?

Numerous researches have studied opinion leaders. Not all agree, but certain fairly consistent trends have emerged.

1 They have a wide range of social contact.
2 They tend towards independence.
3 They have more contact with and interest in the media.
4 They often come from similar backgrounds to those they lead. (Social proximity.)
5 In mixed social systems, however, they may be of higher status.
6 They are more innovative, and are receptive to new products.
7 They are likely to have more interest in the area in which they lead.

This last point raises the question, how wide is the influence of such leaders? Do they lead for a wide range of products and ideas (**polymorphic**) or is their leadership product-specific (**monomorphic**). The general answer seems to be that they advise and lead for a range of related products, but not for products in general. (Presumably Mr D would be a leader within the computer field, but hardly for hair shampoo.)

Amongst the methods which can be used to identify opinion leaders are:

1 **Sociometry**: asking people within a given social system who they would turn to for advice or information on a given topic, and who offers information and advice to them. This can then produce a network or map of the information system to which the person belongs.
2 **Key informant method**: informed members of a social system are asked to name those who have influence on the behaviour of others.
3 **Self-designating method**: people are asked to assess their *own* influence on others in a particular situation.

Information is thus gained about what people offer advice, and to whom, and what people seek advice, and from whom.

In today's sophisticated climate towards technology and persuasion, it is unlikely that the two-step flow is simply one of exposing information via the media to opinion leaders who then, like disciples, pass on the gospel to the others. Nevertheless, it may well be worth making an effort to reach them, since clearly they do exert influence.

1 Specialist influencers can be reached through specialist media (Mr D and computer journals), or by the use of specialised mailing lists. These could be used both for direct mail approaches, and for comparison of lists, to identify those who receive from several sources, and thus may have expertise and influence.
2 Observational learning suggests that seeing an influential person use a product

may persuade people to imitate their behaviour. Hence, loan of a new product to people known to be influential to the target group may prove profitable in two ways: by others seeing the product used, and by the opinion leader, after successful trial, passing on their opinion to others.

■ SOCIAL INFLUENCES ON THE ADOPTION OF NEW PRODUCTS

A large proportion of new products fail to get a grip on the market, whereas others are taken up and maintain a good position. Two sets of factors are probably involved.[12]

1 Are all new products really new? The answer is that some are newer than others:

(a) a continuous innovation is one which simply modifies an existing product (e.g. fluoride added to toothpaste).

(b) a dynamically continuous innovation involves a more considerable change, such as compact discs coming into the hi-fi area.

(c) a discontinuous innovation adds a new set of possibilities for consumer behaviour (e.g. the advent of television).

2 What product and promotional factors favour adoption? These include:

(a) relative advantage: does the product offer a sufficiently significant advantage in the consumer's mind over the one currently used to merit at least a trial? (Note that the consumer must be convinced of this, rather than the producer or marketer.)

(b) compatibility: to what extent is the product compatible with existing values and experiences of potential adopters?

(c) complexity: how complex does the operation of the product seem to be to the consumer? Perceived complexity can be reduced by the design of the product, or by good explanation, or by demonstrations of its simplicity.

(d) trialability: how easy is it for the consumer to try the new product without being committed to purchase? This is easy enough for a low involvement routine purchase such as yoghurt – a stall near the supermarket entrance will encourage trial. But what about high risk, high involvement items such as a car with novel features?

(e) observability: how visible is the use of the product by others? Bandura's view of the importance of observational learning suggests that the more an individual sees use of the product, the greater the thrust towards trying it himself. Sports goods are frequently given to sponsored sportsmen, giving wide and high prestige exposure. Just seeing someone else have new double-glazing may tilt the balance in favour of a new firm, who may offer free or heavily reduced installation in return for photographs or even visits by potential customers.

Stages of adoption

The stages by which an individual consumer comes to adopt (or reject) a new product are:

1 Knowledge. The consumer has been exposed to the product and is aware of it, without coming to a decision as to whether he needs it. Initial knowledge is likely to come from the mass media.

2 Persuasion. At this stage, the consumer forms a favourable or unfavourable attitude towards the product, based on going over the advantages and disadvantages, and the perceived risks of adopting it. To help reduce any risks, the consumer may seek further information.

3 Decision. The consumer may adopt, to make use of the product on more than trial basis, or to reject. In that case he may reject actively, after consideration or trials, or passively, by never really considering adoption.

4 Implementation or use. Here it is important for intention to be translated into purchase, to facilitate the transfer from mental trial to actual use.

5 Confirmation. Again there may be two outcomes. With reinforcement and lack of dissonance (the product satisfies the consumer) then continued adoption will occur. But if dissatisfaction or dissonance occurs, then discontinuance will result.

The stages by which numbers of consumers come to adopt the innovation are regarded as a kind of wave, spreading through the population in steps, as different classes of consumer take on the product (see Fig. 7.4).

Fig. 7.4

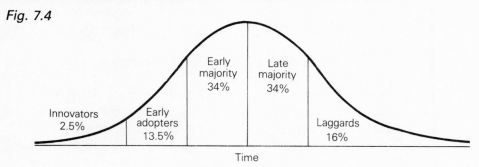

It can be seen that in terms of time, five segments are identified: innovators, early adopters, early majority, late majority, laggards. The proportions of these are said to follow those of the normal curve, though Rogers admits not all diffusion processes show a true normal distribution.

Of these, the innovators are very relevant to marketers, since once a product begins to be adopted, its continued adoption may depend on the acceptance-rejection process of first users. In fact, innovators seem to have much in common with opinion leaders. Summaries of researches suggest they are often:

1 Of high social status, well-educated, upwardly-mobile. Income is of course relevant as high risks may be involved in trying an expensive product.

2 More cosmopolitan, or wide reaching, in their communication patterns, have more media exposure, are more aware of innovations, and seek information about them. They are more venturesome and open-minded, with a wide range of social contacts.

3 More intelligent, rational and creative, but not rigid or dogmatic.

Rogers originally used the following descriptions of the classes:

Innovators: venturesome

Early adopters: respectable, the man to check with

Early majority: deliberate. 'Be not the last to lay the old aside, nor the first by which the new is tried'

Late majority: sceptical

Laggards: traditional. 'Whilst most individuals in a social system are likely to look to the road ahead, the laggard has his attention fixed on the rear view mirror.'

Clearly there are possibilities here for segmentation. But a number of questions remain.

1 Are the same people involved in the same segment for all products? As with the opinion leaders, probably not. Therefore innovators and early adopters particularly need to be identified for the product.

2 Rogers' early work was based on less developed societies. Does the wave concept apply to all products? The comedian Lenny Henry helped to raise thirteen million pounds by his 'Red Noses' campaign, when everyone interested wore a red nose on a particular day. Was the adoption curve a normal one here?

3 How is the stage of the curve to be determined? If the 'phase' of the curve cannot be determined, how can market strategy be changed to suit the characteristics of a particular segment?

In spite of these criticisms and the presence of other models, the Rogers approach has remained influential for over a quarter of a century already.

■ SELF ASSESSMENT QUESTIONS

Marks

1 Write the correct Freudian structure against these statements:
(a) the source of instinctual energy _ _ _ _ _ _ _ _ _ _ _ _ _ _ _ _ _ _
(b) the moral aspect of personality _ _ _ _ _ _ _ _ _ _ _ _ _ _ _ _ _ (2)

2 Give the correct defence mechanism for these statements:
(a) 'He hit me back first'. _
(b) 'I certainly do not remember being insulting to you'. _ _ _ _ _ (2)

| regression repression projection identification |

3 Cattell uses _ _ _ dimensions in his assessment of personality. (1)

4 Fill in the complete words of the 'AIO' measures in psychographics

   (a) A _____

   (b) I _____

   (c) O _____ (3)

5 (a) 'All football players are rough and stupid.' This is an example of a s _____

   (b) A person who rates one product of a company highly might over-rate other products of the same company. This is a form of the h _____ effect. (2)

6 What type of person might influence the impact of a television communication on viewers, according to the '2-step' theory?

O _____   L _____ (1)

7 Write 'True' or 'False' against these statements about opinion leaders:

   (a) more interest in and contact with the media _____

   (b) are conservative, and unwilling to consider new products

_____ (2)

8 Choose the right term to go with the following:

   (a) what we think of ourselves _____

   (b) what kind of person we would like to be _____

   (c) the way we see ourselves reflected in the mirror of other people's reactions towards us _____ (3)

> ideal self   looking-glass self   self-concept

9 Write 'true' or 'false' against these statements.

   (a) innovators are more 'cosmopolitan' than others _____

   (b) the 'early majority' form about ⅓ of the diffusion wave ____ (2)

10 Put the right product characteristic against these:

   (a) ability for the consumer to 'have a go' with the product ____

   (b) 'I never thought word-processing could be so easy.' _____ (2)

> observability   compatibility   trialability   complexity

(Total: 20)

(Answers are on page 220)

■ STUDY AND EXAMINATION TIPS

Help! I don't understand the question!

1 Except for the masochistic and case-hardened, examinations can be somewhat stressful. It's a common experience to be bewildered by a question in the examination, only to find from the discussion afterwards that you knew all the material – but didn't recognise the question. Or sometimes, the question may be very long, and you find it difficult to sort out what's needed. By all means look for the straightforward ones where you can see the required answer from the question. But don't ignore questions just because they seem long.

2 Let's 'unpack' Question 1, which looks rather fiendish at first sight.
(a) It has three main parts: a theoretical beginning.
(b) An application of the theory to a specific product.
(c) An examination of the problems of using a particular element of the theory (the 'opinion leader'). Note that you're given a useful 'prompt' by the provision of the technical term in the last part.

3 So a possible plan might be:
(a) A comparison of the 'traditional' one-step, and the amended two-step, processes, highlighting the position of the opinion leaders. A brief general outline of their function and characteristics would be appropriate here.
(b) Comparison of the advantages and disadvantages:
(i) One-step: apparently direct contact with the consumer, e.g. through magazines, television, point-of-sale demonstrations, but does not have the benefit of the influential social forces of the mediating opinion leaders.
(ii) Two-step: provided opinion leaders can be found, or inserted into the campaign, the benefits of direct contact can be combined with the influence of people who hold a significant position (for the product) in the consumer's social system. But how easy is it to find and use such people?
(iii) Application: remember hair-care products are mentioned. What sort(s) of people would lead in this field? What advantages would come from using them?
(c) Problems of finding opinion leaders and using them.
(i) Opinion leaders do not generally lead over a wide range of products: they have influence in fields of related products. Thus marketers need opinion leaders who are influential in the chosen product area.
(ii) While there are some general characteristics of opinion leaders, marketers cannot survey vast numbers of consumers to find the leaders. Nevertheless there are methods for finding the *type* of person (sociometry, key informant, and self-designating techniques). Other methods include identification from mail-shot lists, and the *insertion* of opinion leaders (e.g. well-groomed and knowledgeable demonstrators at points of sale; attractive and well-known presenters in commercials).

■ EXAMINATION QUESTIONS

1 Examine the relative advantages and disadvantages of the one-step and two-step models of the communication process, especially when applied to the marketing of mass consumer (e.g. hair care) products. Why is the concept of the 'opinion leader', crucial to the two-step model, so difficult to utilise in marketing terms?

2 To what extent should marketers take any notice of Freud's work?

3 Why have researchers been unable to find a consistent relationship between personality and consumer behaviour? Does this invalidate the use of personality factors as a marketing variable?

4 It is often said that new products are the life blood of any company. But how do new products become regularly and widely adopted? Give relevant examples to illustrate your argument.

5 Assess the usefulness of life-style research (psychographics) for the market segmentation strategy of either:
    (a) a large furniture manufacturer, or
    (b) a sports-wear manufacturer.

8 | Models and marketing

Men may come and men may go, but models go on for ever.
Adapted without permission from Lord Tennyson's 'The Brook'.

■ INTRODUCTION

Suppose you are in a large, unfamiliar city. It's quite likely you'll buy a map of the city to help you find your way round. This is a sort of **model** of the city. It isn't a model which tries to reproduce everything on a small scale; it isn't like the model villages which show the smallest detail of the real thing. It would be very inconvenient to have to carry that type of model around. So we use a map which doesn't look like the city at all, but represents the important features in a way we can understand. We might use different kinds of map for different purposes – a theatre map for entertainment, a transport map for the transport system. We might want a very detailed map of the city, or a map of the country showing that city in relation to the rest of the country. These maps would concentrate on some features, and ignore others.

Similarly, many workers have tried to reduce the complicated elements of marketing to simplified pictures which represent what is going on. Thus there are models which represent the ways by which consumers come to make choices about products; about the forces at work within an organisation about to make an expensive purchase; about the ways by which new products come to be accepted and taken up by consumers. *A model represents some aspect of a real situation.* The situation we shall be examining in this chapter is consumer buying, and we will look at various models of consumer behaviour.

Don't be surprised if alternative models of the same process seem very different indeed. An illustrated map of London with drawings of Tower Bridge and the other sights looks very different from the bare black and white of a street map, but it represents the same situation. Remember also that small models can be put together to form large, comprehensive, models, just as the pages of an A–Z guide join together to make a complete map of a town.

■ TYPES AND PURPOSES OF MODELS

We can divide marketing models into a number of categories:

1 By their function as descriptive or predictive models.
2 By their range, as specific or general models.
3 By whether they concentrate on external factors (black box) or on internal factors (personal variables) or on a full combination of the two (grand or comprehensive).

Descriptive or predictive

Some models simply summarise what is going on. Thus a flow diagram on the wall of a publishing company might show the processes necessary before a book actually reaches the bookshops. Here there is no attempt to go beyond representing in a clear form the many complicated processes involved. This is a descriptive model.

But as we saw in the first chapter, being able to predict rather than merely describe is a powerful tool. Hence some models help the marketer to predict what will happen 'if' – that is, how some change in a part of the marketing process will affect its outcome. A good descriptive model, by providing an accurate base, may enable academic students of marketing to test out hypotheses and generally serve as a focus for discussion and clear thinking. *Prediction tests out the accuracy of description.*

Specific or general?

To have an elaborate model of how a consumer comes to choose a particular bar of chocolate might be helpful to a chocolate manufacturer, but far less helpful to someone who sells high performance cars. But if a general model can be provided which indicates some common features of consumer behaviour, it can then be refined and made more specifically suited to a particular buying situation.

Consider the very simple model of Fig. 8.1.

Fig. 8.1

input → processing → output

This has a very wide and general application. Aeroplanes, ships and cars take in fuel, and convert it to power. Televisions take in electromagnetic waves, and convert them into visual and auditory signals. Consumers take in stimuli and information about products, re-organise it, and respond by buying, not buying, recommending and so on. The basic general model can then be made more specific, as shown in Fig. 8.2.

Fig. 8.2

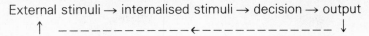

External stimuli → internalised stimuli → decision → output

(Zaltman and Wallendorf[1])

In consumer terms, various external (e.g. product) stimuli are processed into internalised stimuli, then fed into the decision processor, which produces the final response or output.

This model can in turn be developed by focussing on each of the four stages to provide a fuller picture of what happens in each. Notice that one simple addition – that of the feedback loop from post-decision stage to reception of stimuli – raises questions about the effects of post-purchase consequences on consumers' later reaction to products.

External variables, internal variables, or both?

You are thinking of buying a new television. You've had experience of your own model, of friends' models, and have casually noticed advertising about other makes. This is external information from the past.

Now you go into shops, read catalogues, and are exposed to stimuli from the present. The selection and interpretation process we studied in Chapter 2 gets to work, and combines with your memories of past experience (Chapter 3) to move you towards a decision. Other social and psychological factors will interact with the more cognitive elements. But you will also have purposes and expectations, of what exactly you want the set to do, and how it will perform. Anticipation of the future plays its part.

We can make a general model of this specific incident by abstracting certain elements which will be common to many such buying situations.

1 There are influences from the **past**.
2 There are influences from the **present**.
3 There are expectations for the **future**.
4 Some of these influences come from outside, from the environment. They are **external**.
5 Some will come from inside, as **internal** factors, either:
   (a) long-standing, such as personality traits;
   (b) shorter term, such as a sudden interest in teletext models inspired by playing with a friend's machine.

From these elements we can construct a simple model (see Fig. 8.3).

■ BLACK BOX MODELS

These focus on the external aspects of a situation, rather than the internal state of the consumer. Thus, Kotler's early model of the flow from input to response via the consumer is shown in Fig. 8.4.

Notice that only observable variables are included. The consumer serves as processor, but we are given no indication of what goes on in this processor. This is not necessarily a fault. If we find that advertising which highlights the quality

Fig. 8.3

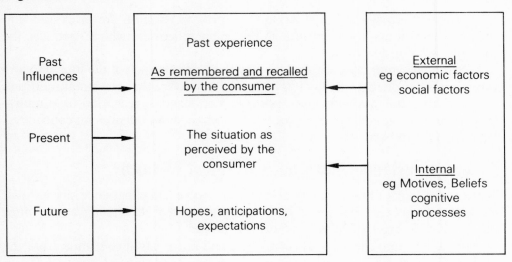

Fig. 8.4

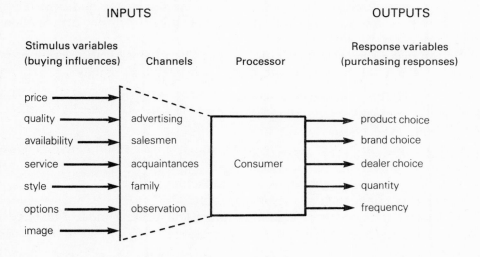

of a product brings increase in consumer choice of our product, we need not necessarily look any further. If we find that a more positive brand image leads to increase choice of our brand, the model has done its work, at least for this purpose.

An illustration of how a study of relations between input and output may give rise to general findings about consumer behaviour is given in Example 8.1.

EXAMPLE 8.1 LOW RATINGS, HIGH LOYALTY?

1 By metering the viewing of a panel of viewers, information was objectively obtained on what programmes were most popular *and* how often families/individuals repeat viewed programmes.

2 'Viewing' was defined as having the programme on during its middle minute.

3 Comparison of rating with repeat-viewing showed a 'double jeopardy' effect: *'the few viewers of low-rating programmes watch them even less regularly than average'*.

4 Thus, by an objective investigation of inputs (the available programmes) and outputs (choice of a particular programme) a pattern emerges which is perhaps against the common-sense idea that minority programmes attract a hard core of dedicated viewers.

(Ehrenberg and Wakshlag[3])

■ PERSONAL VARIABLE MODELS

Personal variable models tend to focus on internal factors, the **intervening variables** of the S-O-R type of model. The evidence for these may be from actual behaviour (e.g. the inference of attitudes from responses to attitude scales) or the variable may be put in the model because it then gives better explanatory and predictive power. We build the model 'as if' the construct were there.

Linear additive models

We have already met one model of this type in Chapter 6, when considering the work of Fishbein. He argues that a consumer's intention of using a specified product in a specified way in a specified situation results from the addition of two factors:

1 Attitude towards the particular behaviour. This results from several expectancy-value components, each formed from the product of

- a belief that a certain outcome will result from the behaviour
- evaluation of that outcome.

2 Subjective norm. This represents the influence of 'important others' – what we think other people who are important to us think we should do. It is the additive sum of separate elements relating to our tendency to fall in the way we think particular people would expect us to behave. Again, each element is formed of two components:

- normative belief (the extent to which we feel the other person thinks we should or should not behave)
- our motivation to comply with that expectation.

Again, each element is the product of the two components, so it might be better to describe the model as additive-multiplicative.

A number of predictions can be made from this extended model.

1 Different products may call for different weightings of the belief and norm elements to predict consumer behaviour accurately.

2 Knowledge of behavioural intentions is the best predictor of behaviour.

3 Changes in attitude towards a behaviour will result from changes in the belief and evaluation components.

4 Changes in the subjective norm will result from changes in the normative and motivation components.

These predictions can then be **operationalised**, or turned into specific situations through which the predictive power of the model can be assessed.

EXAMPLE 8.2   SOCIAL AND SOLITARY DRINKING

1 Students were asked to indicate their feelings about purchasing two different brands of beer, either for themselves, or to serve to friends at a party.

2 It was argued that the attitudinal (expectancy-value) element would dominate in the solitary situation, but that the normative element would be more important in the social situation. The scale used reflected Fishbein's measures.

3 The predictions were confirmed for one beer, but not for the other.

4 However, evidence from other products has tended to support the predictive power of the model.

(Experiment by Miniard and Cohen[4])

Other 'internal' models

The decision-process used by the consumer can often be regarded as **non-compensatory** or **compensatory**.

NON-COMPENSATORY

In this process, as suggested by the name, poor attributes of a product *cannot* be compensated for by good attributes. There are several varieties:

1 Lexicographic The most important attribute to the consumer is chosen, and the brand which excels on that is chosen. If there is a tie on this attribute the second most important is examined, and so on. Notice that different consumers could have different rankings of attributes. The processing sequence in this case is by attribute, rather than by brand, since the consumer compares separate attributes rather than the whole of the attributes of one brand against those of another.

2 Threshold or elimination Again the most important attribute is taken, and a cut-off, or threshold is set. Brands which satisfy this requirement (e.g. 'It must contain fluoride') are accepted, others rejected. If more than one brand is left, elimination continues for successive attributes till there is only one survivor.

3 Conjunctive In this process, a set of cut-offs is set for *all* the attributes important to the consumer. Each brand is then examined on all the criteria. If a brand satisfies all, it is accepted.

COMPENSATORY
Here, perceived weakness in one attribute may be offset by perceived strength in another. The general strategy is thus to process by brand, weighting each attribute in turn to produce an overall brand estimate. In its simplest form, this is a **trade-off** model, since the less desired outcomes are traded-off against the more desirable ones. Excellent quality may be regarded as a good trade-off against higher price, good after-service facilities may compensate for a longish delivery period.

In more complex forms, there are **multi-attribute** models. Fishbein's is an example of such a model. Belief and evaluation are mutually compensatory, as are normative compliance and motivation to conform.

■ COMPREHENSIVE MODELS

These are also referred to as **Grand** or **Theoretical** models. Rather than deal with actual purchases or situations, they present an abstract view of the buying process. Often, they concentrate on the buyer's decision-making, and hence are referred to by that title.

The Nicosia model[5]

This model may be thought of as a computer-type program, divided into four main sub-routines, output from one routine serving as input for the next. Though originally applied mainly to new product situations (and therefore starting at the beginning), the process, once begun, can be seen as entered at any point. Fig. 8.5 shows the model, and should be followed along with the description below.

The four fields involved are:

1 From message to attitude. This field has two sub-fields:

(a) The firm's attributes. These include the products, types of media exposure, intended audience.

(b) The consumer's attributes. These include situational factors applying to the consumer, cognitive and personality factors, such as the processes of selective attention, perceptual bias and the other features of information processing discussed in Chapters 2 and 3. A message will be encoded by the firm, and the consumer will decode it from his own particular standpoint. Where a positive attitude results, Field Two will be entered.

Fig. 8.5

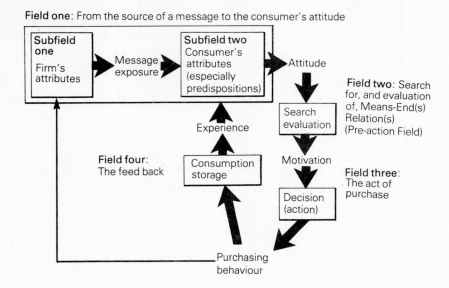

Field one: From the source of a message to the consumer's attitude

2 Search and evaluation. This is a problem centred field, with the consumer gathering further information, and making comparative evaluations of the resulting 'data banks' on the product and its rivals. The search will be partly internal, producing both conscious and unconscious associations with the brand, and external, with information perhaps from family, friends, colleagues as well as commercial inputs.

Some of these sources may produce dissonant information – that is an opinion from one source may contradict that from another – but the consumer will aim to resolve these dissonances. If the resulting evaluation is negative, then the process will be quitted. If a positive evaluation results, it will carry forward to Field Three motivationally, as an intention to consider purchase of the product.

3 From motivation to action. Although the consumer may have formed an intention to buy, there may be circumstances which could prevent his buying, such as unavailability. If purchase is possible, then Field Four is entered.

4 Feedback. In this field, consumption or storage of the product will occur, and the consumer will evaluate the consequences of his purchase. A particular feature of the Nicosia model is that it includes feedback both to the consumer *and* to the firm. By the act of purchase, the consumer feedbacks information to the firm, and may supplement this in other ways. In response to this feedback, the firm may alter its message, beginning a new cycle with changed input.

Meanwhile, the consumer has been receiving feedback from the post-purchase consequences of his decision. These may cause him to re-enter Field One with a changed view of the product and the firm. Thus the relations between firm and consumer can be seen as **reciprocal**, each entwined with the other.

Assessment of the Nicosia model

1 The model portrays the stages suggested by Kotler as a general purchase model (see Fig. 8.6).

Fig. 8.6

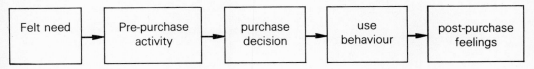

2 However, the activities of the firm are systematically related to those of the consumer.

3 Although originally applied to advertising, it is general enough to be tried out in other fields.

4 Again, as a general model, it can be refined (as done by Nicosia) to provide further explanation of each of the fields.

5 As outlined above, it may appear a mechanistic process. In practice, complex consumer activity may be much less tidy than the neat flow diagram suggests.

6 It avoids the trap of assuming we can stop at the 'message-attitude formation' stage: other processes and situations may occur.

The Howard-Sheth model

This model can be looked at as an elaboration upon an input-processor-output model, with the processor divided into two sections, involving perceptual constructs and learning constructs respectively. This results in four blocks which will be examined in turn. The blocks have been labelled on Fig. 8.7 so that you can follow the chart more easily.

1 Inputs (Block A). These 'signals' are divided into three types:
    (a) significative: the actual 'messages' arriving from the products themselves;
    (b) symbolic: messages *about* the products, e.g. by advertising;
    (c) social: information and influence arising from family, reference groups, and membership of a particular social class.

2 Processing variables (Blocks B and C). These fall into two classes: perceptual and learning. Howard and Sheth refer to them as **hypothetical constructs** since they must be inferred from behaviour, rather than observed directly. They are affected by the **exogenous** variables which lie outside the processing system (e.g. culture, social class, pressure of time and financial status).

The process from exposure to the stimuli to changes in the internal variables might run as follows:

    (a) I need to update my computer system. I have loosely attended to magazine and television adverts, and wandered into High Street stores. But I'm not at all clear yet what specific computer might suit me (**stimulus ambiguity**);

Fig. 8.7

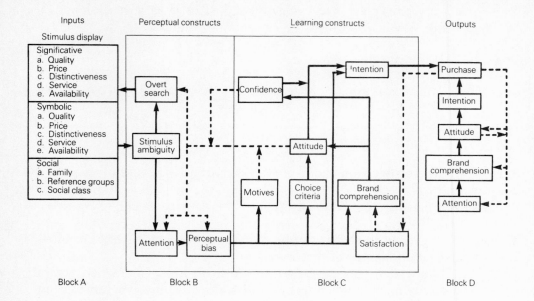

(b) therefore I change my rather loose inspection for a more concentrated search for clear information (**overt search**). This might come from specialist journals, *informed* salesman, other users;

(c) however, I may misunderstand some of this information, or select it out, because it seems irrelevant to my needs (**perceptual distortion** and **selective attention**);

(d) now my **choice criteria** will begin to operate. Exactly what do I need a new system for? To keep up with other users? For word-processing mainly, or general use in connection with marketing? Here three important situations may arise:

• if I'm not really clear about my criteria, or the specific offerings of different systems, then I must engage in much searching: **extended problem solving**;

• if I know my criteria, and simply have to search to find the product which fits them, then the search is smaller, and I use **limited problem solving**;

• if I know both the criteria, and the products which satisfy them, I can quickly solve the 'problem'. This is a **routinised** response, which of course does not apply to the rather expensive and novel decision involved in buying a new computer.

(e) as a result of my searches, I will have formed an attitude towards products in my intended range. Further, according to the strength of my beliefs about the product, I will have a certain level of confidence;

(f) the greater the degree of confidence, the greater the intention to purchase a particular system;

(g) finally when the level of confidence is sufficiently high, I will move towards purchase.

In following through these steps, we are really plotting the route through the hypothetical constructs. These however also issue in outward, observable, behaviours, the output variables.

3 The output variables (Block D). These are quite clear cut, and form a hierarchy of effects in which establishment or change of one variable leads on to change in another, but with feedback loops between them.

(a) in our example, my attention may be caught by a shop display for a personal computer;

(b) because I am interested, I find out more, improving (hopefully) brand comprehension. I shall of course be doing this for several brands and models;

(c) this will lead to the formation of attitudes towards the range of which I am aware (remember the 'sets' of Chapter 2?);

(d) in turn, for the evoked set, an 'intention to consider purchase' will be formed;

(e) finally, the chosen purchase will (may?) be made.

The following points can be made about the model:

1 The model has developed steadily since its early version in the 1960s[8] indicating that it is alive and well.

2 Heuristically, that is, in terms of generating ideas and discussion, the model has been very successful.

3 The variables, though clear cut in the model, are less easy to translate into operational terms. In particular, the distinction between **endogenous** (within the main processing system) and **exogenous** (outside the system) does not always seem clear cut.

Engel, Kollat and Blackwell[9]

This model is often known, more or less affectionately, as the EKB model. With the arrival of a different co-author, Miniard, the originators suggest it might be re-initialled as 'EBM'. The advantages of models are summarised by them as:

- explanations are provided for behaviour
- a frame of reference is provided for research
- a basis is provided for management information systems.

They quote Ajzen and Fishbein's theory of reasoned action, including the statement that:

human beings are usually quite rational and make systematic use of the information available to them ... people consider the implications of their actions before they decided to engage or not engage in a given behaviour.

Fig. 8.8

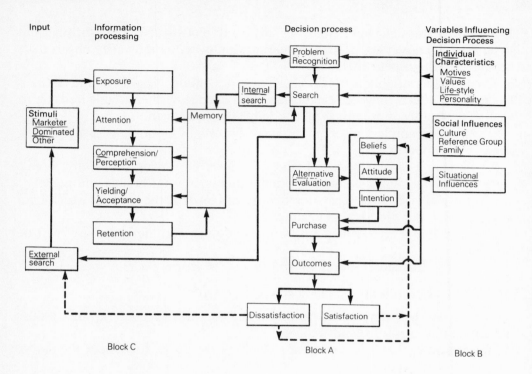

While it is recognised that the level of active reasoning used will depend on the purchase and the situation, the model is very much a decision-making one, with five major stages, again labelled as blocks for easier reference (see Fig. 8.8).

1 DECISION PROCESS STAGES (BLOCK A)

This is the central, executive block, the main program if you like, which is linked with other sub-systems. Its components are:

- problem recognition
- search
- alternative evaluation
- purchase
- outcomes

2 PROBLEM-RECOGNITION

From realisation of a non-ideal state ('My computer system isn't adequate'), the consumer is motivated towards a search process aimed at solution. (But circumstances, such as lack of cash, might cause the system to be put on 'hold'.)

The realisation might come from within, or be stimulated, e.g., by commercial information. The full set of influences at this stage are (Block B)

- individual characteristics: motives, values, life-style and personality
- social influences: culture, the reference group, the family
- situational influences

3 SEARCH

This may be carried out both internally and externally. An internal search may reveal, through memory, that there is a solution readily available. While this is likely with routinised behaviour it is not likely with a fairly expensive and complex item like a computer.

If a solution is not reached, then external search will be necessary. This will expose the consumer to information which he will then process (Block C).

(a) inputs to this system will come from either market-dominated or commercial sources or, for example, knowledgeable friends.

(b) information processing phases are similar to those outlined in Chapter 2:

- exposure
- attention
- perception and comprehension
- yielding and acceptance
- retention

Successful exposure will lead to attention, the allocation of information-processing capacity to the stimuli. (Remember selective attention?) Short-term memory will store the information, to be compared with other information from long-term memory.

If the message exposure has been successful in relation to the consumer's information-processing system, then perception and comprehension of meaning will occur – hopefully, as the marketer intended.

This interpreted message can now be compared with existing beliefs and attitudes. If the message is sufficiently persuasive, then there will be a re-structuring and modification of these. (Our study of attitude change is very relevant here.) This penetration of the intended message results in yielding or acceptance, and its meaning (the semantic aspect) will be stored (retention). In fact, there will be several data banks available, relating in our case to different computer systems. How are we to choose? We enter the alternative evaluation system.

4 ALTERNATIVE EVALUATION

This includes a chain of effects

- beliefs
- attitude
- intention

Central to beliefs are the product attributes which are thought to be relevant to the desired outcomes. Where these attributes are evaluated favourably, a favourable attitude will be formed, which may result in an intention to purchase.

This then moves us on to the purchase and outcomes phase.

5 PURCHASE AND ITS OUTCOMES
The main outcomes will be satisfaction or dissatisfaction:
(a) satisfaction will have a favourable feedback effect on the belief-intention chain;
(b) dissatisfaction will have an unfavourable effect in relation to the beliefs and attitudes about the product, and will also, as a non-ideal state, be likely to begin the external search again.

We could also refer to these outcomes as consonance or dissonance in the language of Chapter 6.

The analysis so far has been of extended problem solving. Like the Howard-Sheth model, the EBM approach considers several levels of decision-making.
1 **Extended problem solving** occurs when:
(a) there is time for adequate evaluation;
(b) relevant product attributes can be distinguished;
(c) the purchase is important to the individual (high involvement).
2 **Limited problem solving** occurs when:
(a) differentiation of product attributes is less;
(b) involvement is lower.
3 **Routinised problem solving**. It's satisfying to repeat a successful purchase, expecting and receiving satisfaction. Thus the extended decision model may be condensed to a quickly executed loop:

• problem recognition
• internal search
• intention
• purchase
• satisfaction

It might be argued, therefore, that under RPS brand loyalty and repeat-purchase would be high. But studies show that multi-brand purchases are made, indicating that loyalty is not high. Incentives rather than persuasive campaigns may therefore be the strategy needed.

It is suggested by the authors that brand-switching under low involvement may be due to **variety seeking**. We saw in Chapter 4 that humans do *not* always seek to maintain an ideal state. Hence 'a change' may be wanted. So statements like 'Fancy a new taste?' may be effective for over-routinised situations. This effect was also referred to by Howard and Sheth as the **psychology of complication**, in which the consumer breaks out of a routinised situation, resolves the new, small problem, settles back into the new routine and so on in a cycle of routine–non-routine behaviour.

The EKB or EBM model brings into play much of the material studied throughout this book, and attempts to co-ordinate it into an effective model of the decision process. But it and the Howard-Sheth model are open to several possible criticisms.

1 *Do* consumers go through the elaborate stages suggested, especially under low involvement? This point is dealt with to some extent by the routinised process. But is there any actual division of processes in repeat-buying, or is it just habit, for maintenance of brand, or impulse for varying the brand?

2 Are the models too rational? Katona[10] argued in his paper 'Rational behaviour and economic behaviour' that economics can benefit from the social sciences, and vice versa. The inclusion of the exogenous variables in the Howard-Sheth models and of the general motivating influences block in the EBM model prevent them being purely rational product utility-cost designs, and both include psycho-social variables.

3 Both contain a chain of effects. We saw in Chapter 6 that care is needed in assuming one-way traffic in any chain involving attitude and behaviour. The Howard-Sheth model does however allow for feedback effects between the elements of the chain, as does the EBM from the satisfaction-dissatisfaction outcomes.

■ SELF ASSESSMENT QUESTIONS

Marks

1 Put the right type of model against the following descriptions:

(a) Products are rejected if they are below a certain minimum level on important attributes. _____

(b) Consumers weigh the good and bad points of a product against each other when considering purchase. _____   (2)

lexicographic   threshold   trade-off

Howard-Sheth Model

2 List the four main stages of the Howard-Sheth model

(a) _____ (b) _____ (c) _____ (d) _____   (4)

3 Complete the output stages of the Howard-Sheth model by using the words provided.

attitude intention brand comprehension	attention
	(a) _____↓
	(b) _____↓
	(c) _____↓
	purchase

(3)

4 Put the right term against the following descriptions:

(a) Distortion and forgetting of sales and product information.

_____

(b) Inability to reach a clear decision through insufficient information. _____ (2)

> extended problem solving   perceptual bias
> stimulus ambiguity   overt search

Engel, Kollat and Blackwell Model

5 Complete the stages of the decision process by using the words on the left.

problem recognition

outcomes

(a) _____

search

(b) _____

alternative evaluation

purchase

(c) _____

(3)

6 (a) Helen is considering switching from one brand of toothpaste to another. She will probably do some _____ problem solving.

(b) Mr and Mrs Newed are thinking of getting a new compact disc player, never having had one before. They will need to do some _____ problem solving.

> routine   extended   limited   (2)

Nicosia Model

7 Put the most suitable description against each of the 'fields' of the Nicosia model.

Field One: (a) _____
Field Two: (b) _____
Field Three: (c) _____
Field Four: (d) _____   (4)

> Search and Evaluation   Firm and Consumer attributes
> Feedback   The act of purchase

(Total: 20)

(Answers are on page 220)

■ STUDY AND EXAMINATION TIPS

The use of diagrams

1 This book, and indeed any other text on a similar topic, contains many figures and diagrams. How far should you try to remember them?

2 Often, a diagram will be there to supplement verbal explanations – to give you two ways of 'encoding' the material (remember Chapter 3?). Sometimes, as in the 'flow' type of model, it is very difficult to follow the verbal argument without seeing how the pieces lock together.

3 Should you try to reproduce a model such as the Howard-Sheth in your examination paper?

(a) A beautifully drawn diagram may look very impressive, but if it is the main contribution you offer, the examiner has no means of knowing whether you have really understood anything about the model.

(b) Therefore you must be sure that you can answer the question *and* have the bonus of the diagram – but make sure you can do it. Mistakes would be rather obvious.

(c) On balance, then, the advice would be:

(i) For complex diagrams, use them to aid your study in association with the text: don't ignore them. But think carefully whether the trade-off between time and presentation in an answer is worth-while.

(ii) Simpler diagrams may however be used to punch home a point. In an answer on the attitude-behaviour relation, for instance, a simple two-way diagram (Attitude ⟺ Behaviour) will show you know the traffic is not just down a one-way street.

4 Whether you use a diagram or not, remember that the examiner asking about a particular model is likely to expect:

(a) A general description of the model, expressed logically in terms of its major elements (e.g. the stimulus-constructs-responses blocks of the Howard-Sheth model).

(b) Some awareness of the components of each element (e.g. the significative, symbolic and social components of the stimulus block).

(c) As demanded by the question,

(i) examples of how the model would apply practically (e.g. how well-informed sales people, and good informational material could resolve 'stimulus ambiguity' in favour of a given product (Question 2)).

(ii) an evaluation as a model: whether it is only descriptive, or whether it is explanatory and predictive; how far it has been heuristic in generating new ideas; what criticisms have been made; what empirical work has been done.

■ EXAMINATION QUESTIONS

1 Evaluate the success of behavioural modelling as a technique for explaining and predicting consumer activity in the market place, with particular reference to *one* of the following three: Howard/Sheth, Engel/Kollat/Blackwell, or Nicosia.

2 Show how the Howard-Sheth model of buyer behaviour could be usefully applied by a company in the motor industry to the sequence of processes culminating in the purchase of a new car.

3 What role can the modelling approach play in developing a better foundation for marketing?

4 Discuss the view that behavioural modelling saves marketing from becoming an unwieldy mass of scattered facts.

5 Compare and contrast the Howard-Sheth model of buyer behaviour with that of Engel, Kollat and Blackwell.

9 | Organisations I

The managerial function finds its only outlet through the members of the organisation.
H Fayol.

■ INTRODUCTION

We have looked so far at the individual consumer and factors affecting buying behaviour. You may well feel that this is the heart of the marketing process. But before any product reaches the consumer, a great deal of effort will have been put in by people working together in an organised rather than individual way.

When a new computer comes onto the market, the research department will have developed it; the marketing department will have investigated consumer needs; the advertising department will have implemented a plan for bringing the new product favourably to the attention of consumers; and all of these groups will have worked together, more or less harmoniously, under the umbrella of one organisation.

Very possibly you will become a member of a large organisation, and a knowledge of what is good practice within organisations will therefore be of value to you. A second reason for studying organisations is that they, as well as individuals, are consumers. The salesperson who can persuade a large organisation to adopt a particular word-processor has achieved an important and valuable sale. So a knowledge of what is termed organisational buyer behaviour or industrial buying is vital to those involved with this type of market.

In this section, we will examine:

1 The nature and structure of organisations
2 The development of organisational theory
3 Communication in organisations
4 Organisational buyer behaviour

■ WHAT IS AN ORGANISATION

Schein gives this definition:

An organisation is the planned co-ordination of the activities of a number of people for the achievement of some common, explicit purpose or goal, through division of labour and function, and through a hierarchy of authority and responsibility.[1]

This is similar to the description of a group, but two additional points should be noted.

Division of labour

Organisations are formed of individuals. In any but the smallest, no one individual could perform all the tasks necessary. Thus a structure which selects or trains those people best suited to the varied tasks needed, and makes their functions quite clear, is likely to be effective.

Hierarchy of authority and responsibility

A keyword in the definition is co-ordination. Without co-ordination, the organisation would be no more than a collection of individuals, each pursuing separate ends. With a clear structure, individuals know to whom they report, from whom they receive instructions, and are kept in touch with those working on similar projects.

These points were particularly stressed by the writers Max Weber (1864–1920) and Henri Fayol (1841–1925). A football example might illustrate their importance. Eleven young children are likely, left to themselves, to converge on the ball, each intent on driving it towards the far goal. Chaos! Contrast that with the smooth working of a top-class team. Each player knows his territory and his tasks, and together they work under a captain and manager, who aim to bring out the best in each player for the mutual benefit of the team. Notice also that the team will continue even if individual players leave.

- the organisation depends on individuals
- the individuals depend on the organisation
- the organisation is more than the sum of the individuals.

■ DEVELOPMENT OF ORGANISATIONAL THEORY

Schein has suggested that three major ways of looking at the motivation and management of workers can be seen during this century. These are

- rational-economic assumptions

- social assumptions
- self-actualisation assumptions.

These in turn produced changes in management strategy and the organisational structures employed.

Rational economic man

The model here is that of workers who seek to maximise their profits for any given level of effort, who are not able to contribute anything to the initiation of new methods, but who will carry out instructions if motivated by an adequate reward system. The tasks of management and workers are thus different.

1 Management is required to produce effective means of production, to see these are carried out, and to ensure that the financially motivating scheme is an adequately motivating one. *Management takes the lead, is active, and controls workers.*

2 Workers should be motivated towards effective carrying out of the tasks set by management. *Workers are passive, working under incentives for their own benefit, rather than that of the organisation.*

In spite of this split, however, it was argued that the separate pursuits of self-interest would result in a balanced system. This view, elaborated later into 'Theory X', was typical of early thinking on management-worker relations.

F W Taylor, who wrote *The Principles of Scientific Management* in 1911, refined the rather crude outline above. He suggested that:

1 Effective production could be aided by the development of scientific work-study methods and by the selection and training of workers so that they were well-fitted for the highest level of task of which they are capable.

2 Workers would co-operate in schemes involving these principles since they would see that it was in their interest to maximise their personal outcomes.

Taylor did not see managers and workers as necessary enemies. He wrote of

the intimate cooperation between all members of the team which is characteristic of scientific management,

and that

The new way is to teach and help your men as you would a brother; to try to teach him the best way and show him the easiest way to do his work.[2]

His explanation for the disagreements between the two sides involved:

1 The very natural fear on the part of workers that if equal or higher productivity could be obtained with fewer staff, layoffs would occur.

2 The consequence of this fear in restriction of output by workers.
3 Inefficient methods of work.

Taylor himself was able to show that improved methods could indeed lead to increased productivity.

EXAMPLE 9.1   TAYLOR AT WORK

1 Taylor increased the wages of efficient loaders at the Bethlehem Steel works by 60%, after designing and organising more effective methods of loading.

2 The works was able, over a three-year period, to reduce the loading force from 500 to 140: a drop of 72%.

3 This in turn halved the overall handling cost per ton of material, and in the last six months of the period, gave a saving of 39 000 dollars.

4 Taylor wrote *'scientific management has nothing in it that is philanthropic'*. Management is there to make a profit. But his writing is full of respect for workers, and he does *not* seem to have been a cold, hard, slave-driver.

Although Taylor believed that management and workers could co-operate in a rational economic enterprise, to their mutual advantage, 'scientific management' has been criticised as an unethical way of regarding workers, and on factual grounds because, as we shall see, the expected gains in productivity are not always obtained.

Social man: the human relations approach

In the 1920s and 30s a long series of investigations was carried out at the large Western Electric plant at Hawthorne. One of these was described in Chapter 1 – changes in the 'non-human' environment, lighting, failed to produce the expected changes in output, since even when the level of lighting was severely *reduced* in the experimental group, production continued to *rise*. As a result, further investigations were carried out under the leadership of Elton Mayo.

THE RELAY ASSEMBLY GROUP
A small group of women whose normal output had been unobtrusively measured were placed with an observer. Thirteen different work conditions (such as varied wage schemes, rest pauses, free snacks etc.) were changed over a two-year period, each change being discussed with the women. Output rose with all but one of the changes, to a level 30% over the original baseline. And on one occasion when privileges were reduced, output still rose.

Again it seemed that the independent variables were not consistent in their effect upon output. It was therefore concluded that some other, hidden factors were at work. These included what might be called 'social recognition' – an awareness that special interest was being taken, that they were not being treated simply as work units. Other factors were relative freedom from rigid supervision, so that women were able to develop their own group spirit and cohesiveness.

This tendency for novel and social factors to cause changes on their own, over and above those due to the supposed independent variable, has since been called the 'Hawthorne effect'. It occurs in all fields of social study, and requires care to prevent misleading conclusions being drawn about the effects of new methods and schemes.

It also draws attention to the non-mechanical aspects of groups. As Mayo said:

Six individuals became a team, and the team gave itself wholeheartedly and spontaneously to co-operation in the experiment. They felt themselves to be participating freely, and without afterthought, and were happy in the knowledge that they were working without coercion from above or limitation from below.[3]

THE BANK WIRING OBSERVATION ROOM

Fourteen men in a separate room were observed as they wired up electrical equipment ready for soldering by other members. The final product would then be checked by two inspectors. In this case, there was *no* rise in output, no Hawthorne effect. Instead, there was a restriction of output to a self-chosen norm, less than could have been achieved at maximum efficiency. Those who produced too much were labelled 'rate-busters' or 'speed-kings'. Those who produced too little were called 'chisellers'. Sanctions including 'binging' – a sharp blow to the biceps – were imposed on those breaking the norms.

Various actions against company norms, such as trading jobs, and reporting falsely low figures one day to get an easy day the next were frequent. Group pressure was put on the inspectors to condone these practices, and one eventually asked for a transfer. Although there was an overall group identity, sub-groups formed between those who considered their work of a superior nature, and the remainder, each tending to keep together and have their own norms and ways of spending break time.

Here there is a different picture. Instead of group cohesiveness leading to satisfaction and increased output, the forced cohesiveness led to a reduction in output. Both situations, however, serve to emphasise the need to consider *social* and not merely economic factors in management. Besides the formal organisation of a company, there will exist informal groups, themselves capable of setting and enforcing their own norms and values.

The systems approach

OPEN AND CLOSED SYSTEMS

The scientific management approach viewed production mainly as a technical system concerned with the conversion of materials (input) to products (output), while the Hawthorne experiments showed the importance of social systems as well. The systems view suggests that neither of these systems can be considered in isolation. Rather, management should concentrate on the relations between the systems, and the best means of co-ordinating them for any given situation. But in doing so, managers should not simply look inwards, which would produce a closed system, out of touch with the environment and consequently likely to be inflexible in the face of demands for change. An open system on the other hand would allow the organisation to be balanced in its relations with external forces, and thus more adaptive to requirements for change and development.

THE CONTINGENCY APPROACH

Scientific management was associated particularly with hierarchical or top-down forms of structure, and it was hoped that it might be possible to specify ideal forms of organisational structure which would of themselves produce efficient running. These would then form universal principles of management. The systems approach makes no such claim. The systems and their inter-relationships must be adapted to the situations in which they operate. It is, then, a contingency viewpoint, emphasising the need to look at each organisation uniquely, to gain the best match between its form and the internal and external demands upon it. The idea of a 'recipe' which can produce efficiency independently of circumstances is not part of systems theory.

SOCIO-TECHNICAL SYSTEMS

The way in which systems theory can pull together other views was shown quite early by the Tavistock group of industrial researchers. They found that a change in coal mining techniques from traditional small-group to large unit production disrupted the tight, almost family-like cohesiveness, of the earlier method. The benefits of new technical facilities were reduced by the negative social results.[4]

The socio-technical view thus emerged, as illustrated in Fig. 9.1.

Fig. 9.1

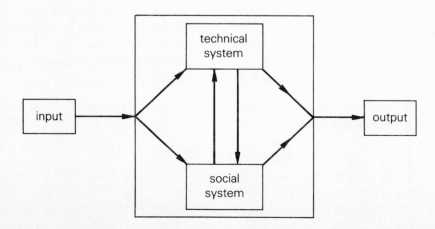

An organisation will have technical means of transforming input materials into products. These will include machines, methods of working, and structuring of work-groups. But there will be an interaction between the technical aspects and the people operating the technical system, as shown in the Hawthorne and Tavistock studies. Management cannot simply impose a technical operating system without regard to its impact on those putting it into action. As Schein says,

the initial design of the organisation must take into account both the nature of the job (the technical system) and the nature of the people (the social system).[5]

Self-actualising man

As a result of 'humanist' psychologists, such as Maslow (Chapter 4) a view of humans developed which held that, in the right circumstances, we have a strong tendency to release whatever potential we have within us. We will be looking at the particular applications of this view to work situations in Chapter 10. The essence of the approach can however quickly be seen by contrasting Theory X, a summary of traditional views, with Theory Y, which represents more modern ideas.

EXAMPLE 9.2   McGREGOR'S THEORY X AND THEORY Y

Theory X: Traditional

1 The average human being has an inherent dislike of work, and will avoid it if he can.

2 Thus most people must be controlled or coerced to get them to put forward adequate effort towards achieving organisational goals.

3 The average human prefers to be directed, wishes to avoid responsibility, has relatively little ambition, above all wants security.

Theory Y

1 The general principles of Maslow's hierarchy are accepted.

2 The expenditure of physical and mental effort in work is as natural as play or rest.

3 Man will exercise self-direction and self-control in the service of objectives to which he is committed.

4 The average human being learns under proper conditions not only to accept but to seek responsibility.

5 The capacity to exercise imagination, ingenuity and creativity in the solution of organisational problems is widely, not narrowly, distributed.

McGregor summarises by saying:

So long as the assumptions of Theory X continue to influence managerial strategy, we will fail to discover, let alone utilise, the potentialities of the average human being.[6]

◼ THE STRUCTURE OF ORGANISATIONS

Schein has argued that the view of man taken by management affects not only organisational practices, but organisational structure. Here we will begin with the classical view of organisations, and show some amplifications and modifications.

Classical hierarchical theory

This theory, associated with the scientific management view, involves the familiar organisation chart as in Fig. 9.2.

Fig. 9.2

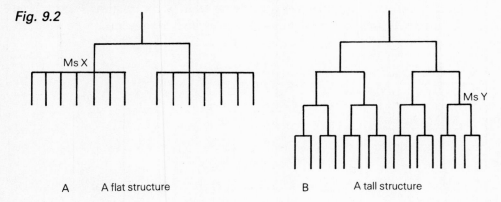

A   A flat structure   B   A tall structure

DEPTH AND SPAN
The characteristics of any organisational structure can be looked at in terms of depth or span. A structure with many levels is described as a tall structure, while that with few levels is flat. The number of levels from highest to lowest is known as the depth of control (or chain of command) while the number of people directly responsible to any one individual is the span of control.

Structure B in Fig. 9.2 is a tall structure, with considerable depth of control. A is a flat structure with a short chain of command. Ms X in Structure A has a wide span of control, while Ms Y in B has only a narrow span of control.

IS THERE A PERFECT STRUCTURE?
In the early days of organisational theory, it was thought that it would be possible to describe the 'perfect' organisational structure, which would function effectively in any circumstances. Later, situational demands were included, and the 'correct' number of individuals in the span of control at different depths was

searched for. But we have seen that both social and technical influences may play their part, and the idea of universal principles of structure has given way to structures fitting circumstances – the contingency approach.

Mechanistic and organismic structures

The hierarchical structure is very effective for defining responsibilities, flow of communication and implementing higher level decisions. Burns and Stalker have referred to this pattern as **mechanistic**. Typically, it will operate very well in situations where routine, long-term, production takes place in a relatively unchanging environment. Its channels function like a well-oiled machine, its 'cogs' operate in the way expected of them.

But where change is vital to survival, this well-established machine may prove ill-adapted. Its communication patterns tend to be downward, reducing the possibility of worker-contribution to change. Horizontal communication (e.g. between departments) is weak, so that cross-fertilisation of ideas is lessened. In contrast, the **organismic** model is more flexible, with greater horizontal communication, and a less formal and centralised structure. The structural factors of each are shown in Table 9.1.

Table 9.1

Organismic	Mechanistic
• Low task specialisation	• High task specialisation
• Horizontal communication	• Vertical communication
• Authority structure flexible	• Strict hierarchy of authority
• Low formalisation	• High formalisation
• Knowledge and control spread through organisation	• Knowledge and control at the top
• Conflict resolved by discussion	• Conflicts resolved by people in authority

Adapted from Burns[7]

It is of course too simple to assume that a large organisation will run completely on either mechanistic or organismic lines. Thus, Lawrence and Lorsch examined production, sales and research departments in ten organisations. The results are summarised in Table 9.2.

Table 9.2 Differentiation of departments

Department	Structure	Time-span	Focus
Research	informal	long	quality
Production	formal	short	efficiency
Sales	formal	short	relations

Thus the 'organisational mix' of formal and informal structure may depend on

- the nature of the department
- its relation with organisations outside
- the external climate: rapid change may require flexible organisation. A mechanistic structure suits a static situation.

The horizontal linkage model

Organisations exist in an environment. To survive, they must respond to that environment, and any changes in it. Between them and the environment there are **boundaries**, where the internal system of the organisation is in touch with the various systems of the outside world.

Thus the research department of an organisation will be scanning the professional environment for the latest developments and activities of competitors. Such imported information will help to tune the inner research system to the outer climate. At the same time, the marketing department will be importing information about consumer needs, success of previous products, and performance of competitors' products.

These two importing processes would be useless if the two departments did not freely communicate and plan together so that the research development took notice of marketing applications and vice versa. We thus get what is called the **horizontal linkage model**.

Fig. 9.3 Horizontal linkage model

Figure 9.3 emphasises three important factors:

1 Research and marketing departments must be highly competent.
2 They must both be closely linked to the outside world.
3 They must communicate and co-ordinate closely together.

The idea of boundary activities *within* the organisation has been put forward by Likert, who conceives of the system as a series of overlapping group structures.

Fig. 9.4

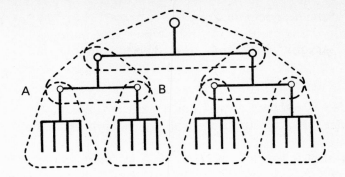

Those who belong to two or more overlapping structures are called link pins (see Fig. 9.4).

A, the Head of Marketing, is able to make horizontal links with his opposite number in Research, and with his subordinates in his own department. Both horizontal links (between departments) and vertical links (within departments) are available to him. After discussion with Research, he can pass on ideas to his staff, and receive feedback from them. Such people are thus important focal points in organisations, as are the link pins between the organisation and the environment.

Because of the multiple roles of these focal individuals, and their associated role expectations, they may be exposed to **role conflict** and **role ambiguity**. Where a salesman is expected to push a given line, against resistance from retailers, he may experience conflict. Where expectations are not made clear, there may be role ambiguity. And where his overlapping roles are simply too many – he is in contact with too many groups and their varied expectations – there will be **role overload**.

The impact of technology

Woodward studied 100 firms in Essex, England, and categorised them into three groups, according to the complexity of their technology.[10]

1 Unit and small batch production. Typically, customised products are made for individual customers or small runs of specialised orders are carried out.
2 Large batch, mass production technology as in assembly line processes.
3 Continuous processes, where raw materials are continuously processed as in oil refining, cement manufacture, beer making.

She found that the typical organisational pattern of the three groups differed, and that the successful firms were those which kept close to the typical pattern for their group. As the complexity of technology increased (that is, from small batch to continuous processes) a number of structural factors changed.

● the span of control of the chief executive increased considerably with technological advance

- the depth of the hierarchy increased
- the proportion of administrative and support staff increased
- organismic, flexible structures seemed best suited to small batch and continuous processes. Mechanistic structures seemed better suited to the middle, large-batch group.

Such results led Woodward away from her earlier expectation that structures would be similar for successful firms in all types of process to the statement that

Different technologies imposed different kinds of demands on individuals and organisations, and those demands had to be met through an appropriate structure.[11]

Technology is thus seen as a mediating factor which interacts with an appropriate structure to produce effectiveness.

However a later study at Aston University suggested that this 'technological imperative' applied only to those parts of the organisation directly affected by technology – the production side – rather than administrative parts such as marketing and accounting. In addition, they found that size was more directly related to structure than technology. This then led to the more cautious suggestion that technology can be seen to have an effect on structure *provided* size of company and nature of department are taken into account.

Again, therefore, we have moved away from any universal principles towards the contingency view, that effective structures must take into consideration a wide range of factors.

■ ORGANISATIONAL CHANGE

We have seen that organisations exist in an environmental climate, and to prosper, they may need to adapt to changes in that climate. Alternatively, they may be so powerful as to resist change, or even themselves to produce environmental change. A typical example in Southern England has been the transformation of unsightly gravel pits to parks with lakes for boating, wind-surfing and a variety of recreational activities. Here, the firms have taken account of the swing towards leisure, the greater availability of personal transport, and the ecological and conservationist movements. Both the organisations and the environment have received benefits.

Factors leading to change

THE DEVELOPMENT OF NEW TECHNOLOGY
Woodward's study showed that technology might have an effect on overall structure. Internal changes in practice may also occur, as when the introduction of word-processors moves filing and retrieval operations from cabinet to cassette and disc.

CHANGES IN THE ECONOMIC CLIMATE
These may bring moves towards expansion or restriction as growth or depressed conditions arise. The expansion of the London Stock Market following the 'Big Bang' and its hi-tech equipment was fairly quickly reversed by the crash of 1987, with back-room staff dismissed, and the volume of small investor business dropping rapidly.

CULTURAL VALUES AND NORMS
A startling change resulted from the worries over AIDS in the late 80s. Linked with 'safe sex', the contraceptive sheath increased sales, but, perhaps more significantly, could be advertised both on television and on public hoardings. Points-of-sale could be established beyond the High Street chemists. And the image portrayed could be that of a caring couple, rather than that of a selfish male out for self-gratification. From being a furtive article, the condoms acquired sufficient respectability to be handed out as examples to solemn gatherings of head teachers and, on one occasion, to a startled Princess!

Factors to assist change

ORGANIC STRUCTURES
These have been shown to facilitate new ideas but their very flexibility and less well-defined work-roles makes them less able to implement change. Research has shown that, in general, mechanistic forms are more effective in the implementation of change.

This has led to the idea of an **ambidextrous** approach. Different types of organisation might exist at the same time in different sections – the Research Department being organic, the Accounts more mechanistic. Or an organisation might switch from one to another according to the impact of environmental forces towards change.

COSMOPOLITAN ORIENTATION
This occurs when key managers have a professional interest beyond a single organisation. It may be shown by holding office in professional organisations, publication of papers in professional journals etc. In such cases, there is likely to be a greater receptivity to innovation than where it is absent.

EXAMPLE 9.3   TO BUY OR NOT TO BUY?

1 In a hospital, the cosmopolitan orientation of radiologists and administrators was assessed.

2 The extent to which the hospital purchased novel radiological equipment was also assessed.

3 It was found that most innovations were made where radiologists were cosmopolitan, but administrators were more local in outlook.

4 It was argued that by their boundary contacts, radiologists were aware of, and pushed for, innovations, while administrators had the local power to implement them.[12]

Schein argues that organisational effectiveness for coping with change hinges on good communication, flexibility, creativity, and genuine commitment. This in turn argues for:

1 Recruitment, selection and socialisation practices which are a stimulus rather than an insult to people.
2 The recognition of developmental changes in people.
3 Provision for effective group action.
4 Ever-ready willingness to redesign organisational structure.
5 Leadership in goal setting and definition of values.[12]

Several of these points will be covered in Chapter 10.

■ COMMUNICATION IN ORGANISATIONS

In order for things to change, there must be communication. In order for people to relate to each other, they must communicate. Here we will look at different 'flows' of communication and at some of the problems of communication in organisations.

Direction of communication

Communication in organisations may be thought of as flowing in two main directions: vertically and horizontally.

VERTICAL
Downwards communication will often consist of instructions, orders, the translation of company policy into operational terms. Upwards communication will give feedback. This may involve facts as in output or sales figures, or a report on the success of a project. It may also consist of opinions or reactions to suggested changes. And, very importantly, it may contain suggestions for new action to be considered for possible adoption.

With a too top-heavy structure, and little feedback from below, the contribution and perhaps good faith of those actually doing the job may be lost.

HORIZONTAL
Here there is communication within and between departments – a form of cross-fertilisation. In its absence, there could be 'islands' of non-communication, one sector of the organisation being unaware of the ideas and feelings of another.

Tall structures tend towards vertical communication, while flat structures tend towards horizontal.

Fig. 9.5

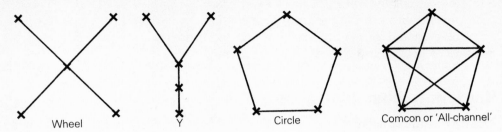

Wheel   Y   Circle   Comcon or 'All-channel'

Communication networks

Leavitt[14] worked with a number of 'networks' of communication, with different patterns within them. Some are shown in Fig. 9.5.

The circle and the comcon are de-centralised, since there is no central member through whom all information passes. The wheel and the Y are centralised, since one person at the focus can have an overview of all information.

It has generally been argued that centralised networks are effective for routine situations, where one person can handle the various inputs successfully, but in more complex situations, where the demands on expertise or decision-making are too great, a decentralised form may be necessary.

Leavitt's findings came from laboratory studies, and thus should not be translated without thought into operational situations.

Organisations and non-verbal communication

Market the marketing agency! Just as we saw that product image can be improved by packaging, so corporate image can be communicated by signals around the environment.

1 Carpets, painting, furniture, can convey an 'organisational style' just as they can convey an individual life-style. Young artists are now commissioned to provide paintings for office walls.
2 The arrangement of furniture and rooms can convey an open or a closed attitude. The open door conveys 'I am available. Want to discuss anything?' The closed management door in a separate management suite may convey 'I'm busy. Go through channels to get to me.' Open plan offices enable horizontal communication to occur, but may not of course suit the introvert, who needs time and quiet to develop his own ideas.

Informal communication

Besides the formal patterns of communication, there will be informal channels. The 'grapevine' is a typical example of how ideas can suddenly spread through an organisation without any formal communication having been issued.

Sometimes this may be harmful, where rumour and gossip about management intentions circulate. But informal communication can also be helpful. A shared coffee-break with a colleague from another department can produce a new idea, or resolve an old problem. Space and time, properly used, can facilitate the meeting of people and the exchange of ideas.

Barriers to communication

Effective communication cannot really be said to occur if the intended meaning does not come over. Amongst the problems which may occur, say in transmitting an important message about change, are:

1 Lack of clarity in the idea itself: if you haven't a clear idea, how can you communicate clearly?

2 Lack of clarity in the encoding of the idea: choose your words and style to fit the receiver. Not all receivers can decode what you can – and it's *your* fault, not theirs, if they can't. Government departments have been notorious in the past for 'gobbledegook' messages which readers cannot interpret.

3 Misinterpretation (or later misrepresentation to others) may occur where attitudes are hostile to the message. Listen to any management–union confrontation on the media, and you will see each side carefully using the other's messages to its own advantage.

4 Overload: Keep it short and simple!

■ ORGANISATIONAL BUYING BEHAVIOUR

Earlier sections have focussed on the individual consumer and his behaviour. Here we consider situations where buying and selling occur between organisations. Firstly, we should look at some important differences between individual and organisation buying situations.

Individual and organisational buying

1 Many consumer decisions are taken by one person, although we have seen some exceptions in family decision-making. In contrast, many organisational decisions will involve many people. It is common to call the group involved the **decision making unit (DMU)** or the **buying centre**.

The roles of those concerned will include:

(a) the **initiator**, who starts things moving by recognising a need;

(b) the **influencer**, anyone whose suggestions and advice are considered by other members;

(c) **deciders**, who have the power, either formal or informal, to make the final decision;

(d) **buyers**, who implement the chosen purchase. They may or may not be the same people as the deciders. For technical or high risk purchasers, a purchasing agent may simply carry out the requirements of an engineer or senior executive;

(e) **users**, those working with the purchase. Clearly their needs and opinions on previous purchases must be available to those closer to actual purchasing;

(f) **gatekeepers** can be any of the above. They bring information into the organisation or distribute it within. A simple example is that of a receptionist who directs people to appropriate individuals or sections. At higher levels, an engineer might decide which outside representatives should attend a meeting to discuss possible purchases.

2 Because so many people are involved, there is a much more complicated pattern of needs to be satisfied. The engineer needs to consider the efficiency of his processes. The accountant has to consider the cash flow. The personnel department have to anticipate likely staff reaction to change. Thus a decision which satisfies all those involved may be difficult to reach, and some form of conflict of interest may be inevitable.

3 Although many organisational purchases, such as office supplies, are routine, others involve one-off, highly complex decisions. For a publishing firm to move towards a new form of printing is far removed from an individual consumer purchasing a pen for his own use.

4 Thus the risks involved should a wrong decision be taken are much more severe. They may be divided into two main groups:

(a) organisational risks to the efficiency and therefore financial status of the company;

(b) personal risks involving the status and credibility of individuals close to the decision-making process. They stand to take the blame should problems follow the decision. This in turn may lead to interpersonal problems where one group resents the imposition of a decision upon it, with unfortunate consequences.

5 Post-purchase consequences are likely to be given greater emphasis in organisational buying. The need for extra training of staff, for certainty of service, for modifications to premises to accommodate new machinery, will all be weighed in with the actual performance specification.

6 We can thus say that organisational buying will often involve high risk and high involvement.

■ MODELS OF ORGANISATIONAL BUYING

The actual purchase situations likely to be faced by an organisation have been divided into:

1 **Straight re-buy**. Goods have been purchased before and there is little need for information search either about product or sellers.

2 **Modified re-buy**. Similar purchases have been made before, but the situation

is now sufficiently different for new information to be needed about product or seller.

3 New task. This is the most complex type of decision faced. A new purchase will involve a higher level of search against a background of the needs and problems of those who will be affected by the purchase decision.

These basic divisions have been amplified to take account of:

1 Novelty of the purchase: the experience of the organisation in purchases of this sort.

2 Complexity: the level of information search needed; the number of individuals and groups involved in and affected by the decision; the post-purchase consequences as described above.

3 Importance: the assessed effect on productivity and financial performance. (Note the similarity here to the levels of the consumer/buyer models.)

Finally, models themselves have been divided into:

1 Task models which focus on the economic factors involved in specific purchase situations.

2 Non-task models, focussing more on the psychological and social forces at work.

3 Decision models, which look at the decision process from start to finish.

4 Complex models which, like those for individual consumer behaviour, try to cover all aspects of purchase situations.

It is important to remember that, as with consumer buying models, there is no one universal buying process. Styles and personnel will vary from situation, and even within one organisation, those involved and the type of information-seeking and decision-making they use, will depend on the stage the purchase process has reached. As one example, we will look at the Sheth model.

The Sheth model[15]

The Sheth model (see Fig. 9.6), while complex, is particularly concerned with the decision-making process and the psychological factors involved.

EXPECTATIONS
The core of the model lies in the expectations of those involved in the decision process (Block 1 in Fig. 9.6). These bring with them different backgrounds contributed to by their professional education, their role interpretation, and their personal life-style.

ACTIVE SEARCH
Depending on the degree of their involvement, they will conduct an active search through their sources of information (Block 1b). As with the Howard-Sheth model, this information will be filtered and interpreted according

Fig. 9.6

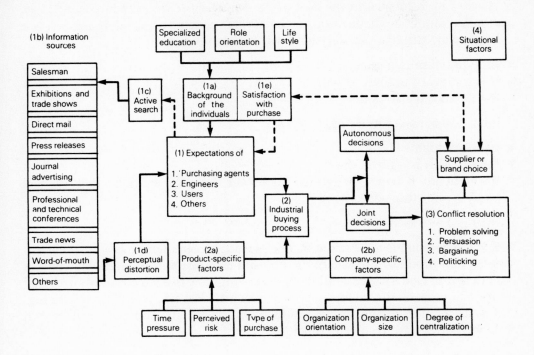

to the orientation of the individual. A hard-pressed accountant may see the 'same' information differently from an engineer anxious to move towards more advanced equipment.

COMPANY- AND PRODUCT-SPECIFIC FACTORS
Joining with these individual influences to affect the buying process (Block 2) will be factors associated with the product itself, and factors deriving from the company (Blocks 2a and 2b).

1 Product-specific factors will include how quickly the product is needed (time-pressure), the perceived consequences of making a wrong decision (perceived risk) and the type of product to be purchased. A 'straight rebuy' purchase of routine material will obviously involve less activity than an expensive 'new-task' decision.
2 Company-specific factors are the orientation of the company – whether towards production or engineering, which clearly will affect the power of individuals or groups to influence the decision, the size of the company, and, related to this, the complexity of the company.

AUTONOMOUS AND JOINT DECISIONS

These product and company factors will then interact with the individual factors of Block 1 to influence, in the first place, whether the decision is taken by one person (an autonomous decision) or by several people (a joint decision).

In general, autonomous decisions will be taken when:

- time pressure is high
- it is a repeat-purchase situation
- the perceived risk is low.

Joint decisions are more likely when:

- risks are high
- the decision is a novel one
- the company is large (though the higher the degree of centralisation, the less likely a joint decision).

CONFLICT

Where the decision is to be taken by one person, he can then proceed to choice of supplier and product. But where the decision is to be joint, progress may be less smooth and indeed involve conflict. It is very unlikely in such circumstances that an optimal or perfect conclusion will be reached. Rather, it will be **satisficing**, that is, it will meet certain criteria. Which criteria become dominant will depend on how conflicts are resolved (Block 3).

1 Problem-solving is likely when conflict centres around consequences of choosing particular suppliers or brands, and may be beneficial in that further active search may produce alternatives or a clearer picture.

2 Persuasion may occur without further problem-solving when those against a decision move towards accepting the majority view.

3 Bargaining. Where conflict cannot be resolved by problem-solving or persuasion, and deep-rooted differences remain, two **non-rational** techniques may be used. In the first, the dissenting person or groups goes along with the decision against a promise of a return concession in the future.

4 Politicking. In this second non-rational technique, power influences between groups will be brought into play. Once a decision has been reached, the choice of supplier or brand can be made. But even though internal problems may have been settled, there may be external factors which can effect this part of the process (Block 4).

■ MESSAGES FOR MARKETING

Organisational buying

Because of the greater complexity of organisational buying, sellers need to take account of:

1 The type of purchase (as seen by the buying company). New task purchases will need greater informational input than rebuys. Different people will be involved at different levels of purchase.

2 The strength of the various personal influences, so that approaches are made in the right quarter. Notice that for some products, users may be very important, though not directly concerned with decisions. Drawing the attention of software users to a new, effective business series by television advertising may help to create a ground-swell towards adoption in the 'silent majority' supplementing more personal contact. Such personal contact is of course vital in identifying the influences within a particular organisation.

3 Changes in the balance of influence as the decision process develops. The initiator may be important at early stages, then the influencers, with the deciders having power at the later stages. Timing of contact and presentation is therefore important.

No organisation is an island

The danger with large organisations is that sub-structures become isolated from each other. Hence communication is vital:

1 Throughout the organisation: e.g. a house journal, well-presented notice boards.

2 Between departments – marketing heads meet development heads. (Horizontal communication.)

3 In departments: e.g. the sales department whose members typically are frequently separated from the home base. This can provide information benefits both for the salesforce (e.g. new plans, products and presentations – downwards communication) and for management (e.g. by suggestions from the salesforce – upwards communication). There will also be social benefits by increasing the feeling of belonging and reducing the pressure of isolation, known to be a factor in producing stress.

4 With the environment: boundary workers should be encouraged to feedback information (e.g. salespeople on reactions to products, other products in the field) to prevent the organisation being isolated from the environment.

■ SELF ASSESSMENT QUESTIONS

Marks

1 Put the right name against the following:
(a) scientific management _____
(b) social man _____
(c) self-actualising man _____   (3)

> Hawthorne   Maslow   Taylor

2 Write 'true' or 'false' against these statements:
(a) Flat structures have narrow spans of control. _____
(b) Mechanistic structures are good for creative situations. ___
(c) Oil-refining is an example of a large-batch process. _____
(d) The 'wheel' is a centralised structure. _____
(e) Centralised structures are best for complex decisions. ____   (5)

3 Which role in the decision making unit involves the following functions:
(a) Controls the flow of relevant information. _____
(b) Their advice and suggestions are considered by others. ___
(c) Recognises a purchasing need within the organisation. ____   (3)

> initiator   influencer   decider   buyer   user   gatekeeper

4 Which types of purchase does each of these represent?
(a) Re-ordering stationery supplies from a known and trusted supplier. _____
(b) Changing stationery supplies because the usual source is no longer trading. _____
(c) Purchasing a new type of machine. _____   (3)

> new task   modified re-buy   straight re-buy

5 Put the following under the headings of 'product-specific' or 'company-specific' according to the Sheth model.

> time pressure   orientation   size   perceived risk

Company-specific   product-specific
(a) _____   (c) _____
(b) _____   (d) _____   (4)

(Answers are on pages 220–1)

6 Give two ways which the Sheth model suggests are used to resolve conflicts.

(a) _____

(b) _____ (2)

(Total: 20)

(Answers are on pages 220–1)

■ STUDY AND EXAMINATION TIPS

1 We're almost at the last chapter, and no doubt your examination is not too far away. Here are some suggestions for using time in the examination.

2 Check from past papers and present regulations how many questions are to be answered, and how long you have to answer them. This will give you the average time available for each. Take off about 5 minutes per question to allow for reading the paper and making your plans. This will give you your writing time per question.

3 Check from your previous work approximately what you can expect to write in that time. There is no doubt that people vary greatly in their writing speed.

4 Whatever else you do, **answer the right number of questions**. There is no point in doing three questions, however brilliantly, when four are definitely required. The examiner can only give you zero for an unanswered question.

5 *Sometimes* examiners will recognise pressure of time on a student, and accept answers in note form for the last question attempted. But don't rely on it! Write in connected English whenever possible.

6 A possible set of notes for Question 2 (to be expanded into a full answer) could be:

(a) Mechanistic and organic structures are two rather contrasting patterns of organisations.

(b) Mechanistic structures have: (list the main characteristics).

(c) Organic structures have: (list the main characteristics).

(d) Organic structures are flexible, well suited to innovation, and responsive to changes in the external environment.

(e) Mechanistic structures are effective in routine and settled conditions, and have been found good for implementation of change.

(f) Since there is unlikely to be a set pattern in a *new* marketing department, at least some part of the organisation should be organically structured, allowing for the generation of new ideas.

(g) But a settled framework should also be developed, to give security, clear division of authority and responsibility, and to be available to convert innovative ideas into effective practice. A mechanistic structure is helpful for this.

(h) Thus the initial organisational pattern should include elements of both forms of structure.

■ EXAMINATION QUESTIONS

1 Why do sales staff sometimes resist changes introduced by management? What techniques may be employed (by managers) in order to reduce the level of resistance associated with the implementation of change?

2 What do you understand by the terms 'mechanistic' and 'organic' (or 'organismic') when applied to organisation structure?

  If invited to set up a Marketing Department from scratch, would you recommend that it be established on 'mechanistic' or 'organic' lines? Give reasons for your recommendations.

3 Discuss the main behavioural influences affecting organisational buying decisions.

4 What part do social factors play in organisational buyer behaviour? Illustrate your answer with relevant examples.

5 Select any model of organisational buyer behaviour, and explain how you would use it to develop a marketing strategy for either a computer software company (e.g. Ashton-Tate) or an independent management college offering courses to managers in industry (e.g. Ashridge).

6 It is now quite normal to see micro-computers for business use being advertised on British commercial television, a medium more normally regarded as best suited to fast-moving consumer goods. How do you account for this trend towards the use of television as a business-to-business advertising medium?

10 Organisations II

Scientific management requires the scientific selection and then the progressive development of the workmen. Taylor.

■ INTRODUCTION

Organisations are composed of individuals, and however well designed the organisational structure may be, it will depend on the efficiency and motivation of its members for success. If people are working at jobs for which they are not suited, or in conditions which do not motivate them, the organisation will suffer.

It is therefore important for managers to appreciate the importance of:

1 Selecting the right people for the right positions;
2 Providing training where new techniques are needed, or where there is a shortfall of trained workers;
3 Ensuring that motivation is maintained at all levels.

It is these three aspects which we will consider in this chapter.

■ SELECTION

Selection has been called fitting the man to the job. If there is a position to be filled then, as Taylor pointed out in *Scientific Management*, it makes sense to be sure that man and job can work harmoniously together. Hence we want to establish, before any work has been done, who is likely to succeed in the post, and who is not. In other words, we want to predict success in a given field. To do this, we need to know very clearly what the job requirements are, by means of a **job analysis**, and what sort of person would best fit the job, which involves a **personnel specification**.

Job analysis

By observation of existing workers, interviews, questionnaires such as the Job Description Index, the aspects of the job leading to success or failure, to satisfaction or dissatisfaction are established. It will be easier, of course, to provide such a 'job blueprint' for a relatively routine activity than it will be for a manager who is expected to innovate and reorganise within a company.

Personnel specification

The requirements of the job are now translated into the skills required of the person doing the job. A model which has a long history in the formation of personnel specifications and in selection generally is Rodger's Seven-Point Plan.

1 **Physical characteristics**, e.g. strength, height, attractiveness.
2 **Attainment**. Relevant qualifications, previous experience and training.
3 **General intelligence**. While general ability cannot be the sole guide to success, there is a broad banding of levels of intelligence associated with success in different jobs.
4 **Special aptitudes**. In addition to general ability, what special skills – manual, verbal, inter-personal – are needed?
5 **Interests**. Would any special interests be of value to the post, e.g. in fostering internal and external relations?
6 **Disposition**. Are any special qualities of temperament, such as tolerance or sympathy, likely to be involved?
7 **Circumstances**. In selling particularly, there may be situations involving travelling, going overseas, which might be difficult for some candidates.

Having found what is required for the job, and from that what kind of person we are looking for, we need next to find them – the selection stage.

Selection methods

THE INTERVIEW
Interviews are one of the oldest methods of selection, and are still widely used, in spite of considerable evidence suggesting they are not very effective. Amongst the disadvantages are:

1 Inconsistent standards between interviewers, so that a candidate's chances vary with who does the interviewing. This may result from different emphasis being given to different abilities, or from exploration of different topics.
2 Inconsistent standards by the same interviewer. Particular attitudes towards certain groups may prejudice selection of members of those groups. On the other hand, the interviewer may get along well with certain types of candidate.
3 There is evidence that first impressions count heavily: interviewers may make their minds up very early on.

4 Previous information (e.g. the application form) may 'set' the interviewer towards a particular view of the candidate before even seeing him/her.

Amongst the advantages are:

1 Face validity: Many people feel dissatisfied if they do not get a personal, face-to-face interview. It feels right to them to meet someone from the organisation personally, rather than via impersonal correspondence or simply pencil and paper tests. Interviews give the applicant a chance to interview the organisation – and maybe reject it!
2 In small firms, social relations may be very important. The interview gives a better chance of assessing this than more impersonal methods. This may be very important for later harmony in the firm!
3 Where, as with sales representatives, social skills are required, the interview offers at least a sample of such skills, and thus helps to suggest what external social relations will be like.

Interviews are much more effective when they are structured. A checklist based on the job analysis and the Seven-Point Plan ensures that vital areas are adequately covered. Board interviews, with several people exploring different areas, and pooling their judgements, can remove some of the problems of individual reactions to candidates. They may however be somewhat off-putting to nervous applicants!

TEST METHODS
Because of the subjective nature of the interview, many experts recommend the use of objective tests as a supplement to personal contact. Often, these assess the candidates under precisely similar conditions, so that each has a reasonably equal chance.

In using such tests, it is vital to consider reliability and validity. Very briefly, reliability indicates consistency. A test would be little use if it gave widely different results if given to the same person after an interval of only a week. Validity indicates whether the test measures what it claims to measure. Of particular importance in selection is predictive validity which assesses how far the test can forecast. For selection of a VDU operator, for instance, we would want a test which 'selects in' those likely to be efficient operators, and 'selects out' those who will not prove to be efficient.

Test batteries formed of several objective measures may be used where a large number of candidates have to be allocated to a wide range of jobs (as in Armed Forces Selection procedures) but smaller operations may find individual tests effective. But it is of course essential that whatever procedure is used, it does pick out those with adequate capabilities for the job.

Amongst the type of objective test which may be used are:

1 Achievement tests. These assess what has already been learnt, as in the case of a test of office procedure, or computational skill.
2 Aptitude tests. These try to assess the potential of a person for a given field,

rather than what he can now do in it. They can be useful in deciding who will best profit from training.

3 General ability. While the concept of intelligence is less powerful than it was, it is still felt that there is a set of high-level reasoning skills which have relevance to a wide range of occupations. In general measured ability declines with lower occupational group.

4 Personality. It might be thought that tests of personality would be particularly useful in the selection of salespeople. The evidence is however not very strong. One problem which particularly applies to personality tests is that of faking. This occurs when a person realises the general drift of questions in a questionnaire, and deliberately, or unconsciously, 'fakes' his answers to produce a given impression. Thus, if a job seems to call for extroverted characteristics, an applicant might obligingly produce a high extrovert score – which might not reflect his 'true' personality.

'WHOLE PERSON' METHODS
Many psychologists such as Eysenck strongly argue the advantages of objective tests over interviews and other more subjective procedures.[1] Against this is the argument that tests are **atomistic** – they break the person down into small bits. Therefore **holistic** methods which try to assess the person 'in the round' have been developed. In these, besides having interviews and tests, the candidate is put in real-life situations resembling those they will face in the post.

Armed Forces typically use group projects to assess leadership and interpersonal skills. The English Civil Service has used weekend programmes in a similar way. In marketing, such an approach might involve candidates presenting a prepared project for discussion and criticism by other candidates. On a lesser scale, the in-basket techniques can be used. Here, the candidate picks a problem from his in-tray, and presents a solution to it.

The intention is to get the feel of the 'whole' candidate, rather than assemble them like a jigsaw from various bits of information.

Messages for marketing

The messages will in principle be similar across a broad spread of organisations, and include:

1 Find out what is required for the job. What, exactly, is required from your salesman, receptionist, accountant? (job analysis).
2 Find what kind of person would most effectively fit those requirements (Personnel specification).
3 Find the person!
4 In finding them, particularly consider:
   (a) the cost-effectiveness of the selection procedures. There is no point in an elaborate procedure when a simple track record, on-the-spot test, and interview would suffice;

(b) the type of skills which are most relevant. If social skills are likely to be important, then the selection procedure should give opportunity for these to be displayed (e.g. in interview);

(c) do your utmost to ensure the procedures and tests are reliable and valid.

Fitting the job to the man: classification

Complementary to selecting the right person for a job is that of arranging the job so that the person can work most effectively at it. This can involve three aspects.

1 **Environmental conditions**, for example:

(a) times of working, rest pauses, shift systems, flexi-time can all affect the performance and satisfaction of workers. Early studies suggested that above a certain length of day, no benefit in production was gained from longer hours;

(b) heat and noise have been shown to be detrimental to good performance, while music, though not necessarily increasing performance, has increased satisfaction.

2 **Display and control**. Where displays have to be read and controls operated, ergonomics can be important. You quickly appreciate the difference between a car whose controls are easy to reach and whose displays are easy to read and one where controls seem cramped and displays are far from clear. Ergonomics concentrates on equipment design, to fit the task to the person, but can include the environmental factors listed above.

3 **Social aspects**. This is perhaps the most important issue for marketing. The whole of Chapter 9 stressed the need to take account not merely of the economic functions of individual and groups, but also their social interactions. Thus over and above any 'job engineering', which eases the material aspects of a post, there will be a need to ensure that the social setting contributes to job efficiency and satisfaction. This will include attention to the social and recreational needs of the employee, but will also include the need for support from superiors, for feeling part of the total organisation, for loyalty towards a working group without antagonism towards others within the organisation. The Tavistock 'longwall' studies showed that mechanical efficiency without supportive social relations is an inadequate solution.

■ TRAINING

Training has a wide range of applications in any reasonably-sized organisation.

Orientation

Large organisations can be very forbidding to the newcomer, and a programme which welcomes new entrants, shows them how things run in general, and what opportunities there are may be very helpful in developing satisfaction, or **organisational commitment**.

Specific training

Where a person needs to develop new skills to perform a task efficiently, a training programme can assist, particularly where the skills are capable of being broken down into clear-cut steps. This may well apply to sales personnel, or to interviewers.

Development training

It will benefit both staff and company if training is not only given for the present position, but also for future positions. Such 'programmes' will be less precise than those for specific posts, and may concentrate on management skills and interpersonal relationships.

Some general principles can be used to guide the training process:

1 The training programme should take account of the 'training gap' between trainee capability and course requirements. Too great may result in frustration, too little in boredom.

2 Feedback on performance and positive reinforcement should be given at each stage. Self-assessment can be offered by video recording of, for instance, a sales discussion.

3 A typical programme would involve showing trainees new techniques, allowing them to practise them, and finally feeding back information on their success.

4 It is often found that training seems effective within a training programme, but trainees revert back to older habits when back in the 'real-life' situation. It is important therefore for trainees to be able to generalise their learning beyond the confines of the course itself. It is also important that trainees should feel committed to the use of their new skills *after* the programme has ended.

5 Attitudes towards training are important. If a programme is seen as helpful both to the individual and to the organisation, then transfer to the working situation will be smoother than if it is seen as just another management gimmick.

6 Training which is too specific, and fails to offer general principles, may be ineffective because:

(a) it is too geared to a particular activity;

(b) it becomes a routine which, in the case of sales representatives, for example, may lead to irritation.

◼ WORK MOTIVATION

In this section we will look at theories of motivation which have particular relevance to work situations. We have already looked at McGregor's Theory X and Theory Y in Chapter 9. This theory summarises the difference between motivation as external, depending on incentives (Theory X) and motivation as arising from internal drives towards the use of initiative, responsibility and self-realisation (Theory Y).

On the one hand, workers are seen as relatively passive, responding to motivational packages of pay and perks; on the other, they are looking for the satisfaction of reaching self-chosen goals. This distinction between material and psychological satisfactions, between the growth and deficit levels of Maslow's hierarchy, is implicit in Herzberg's **two-factor** theory.

The two-factor theory

Herzberg asked 200 engineers and accountants to list quite specific events which had caused them particular satisfaction or dissatisfaction in their job. This is the **critical incident technique**. From an analysis of their responses, he concluded that two different sets of factors were at work in producing satisfaction or dissatisfaction.

The 'satisfiers' he called **motivators** and the 'dissatisfiers' he called **hygiene** or **maintenance** factors. They are summarised diagrammatically in Table 10.1.

Table 10.1

Motivators	*Maintenance factors*
Presence leads to satisfaction	*Poor quality of factors leads to dissatisfaction*
• Promotion opportunity	Company policy
• Opportunity for personal growth	Physical conditions
• Recognition from management	Relations with others
• Responsibility	Quality of supervision
• The nature of skills involved	Job security
• Achievement	Pay

It is important to note two points about the effect of the different factors:

1 Even when the hygiene factors are well controlled, positive satisfaction does not necessarily result. Good pay, good social facilities, a pleasant environment may not of themselves produce a positive feeling towards the job. An employee might tolerate the job because of what it brings, but without really relishing it. The work is done for what it brings, not what it gives. Herzberg comments:

At the psychological level, the two dimensions of job attitudes reflected a two-dimensional need structure: one need system for the avoidance of unpleasantness and a parallel need system for personal growth.[2]

2 It may be that the factors operate differently for different types of people. There may be some for whom the hygiene factors are sufficient. Their *positive*

motivation may lie elsewhere, and they may reject the demands of responsibility and initiative. Others, however, may feel dissatisfied with the lack of opportunity offered to exercise their potentials. They suffer from **qualitative underload** – that is, the demands of the job do not match their capabilities – and this is known to be a cause of stress.

Herzberg's work has been criticised on a number of grounds:

1 The critical incident technique may have led to bias in reporting of satisfying and dissatisfying experiences.
2 Later work has not consistently supported the two-part division.
3 Motivators have been reported as causes of dissatisfaction; hygiene factors as causes of satisfaction, particularly for 'blue-collar' workers.

Nevertheless, Herzberg drew attention to the importance of both lower and higher levels of Maslow's hierarchy. Thus managers need to do more than simply attend to basic safety and social needs. This view has resulted in exploration of more specific ways of enhancing job satisfaction.

1 JOB ENRICHMENT OR VERTICAL LOADING

Here workers are given responsibilities over and above those normally attached to their job. The evidence for success with this technique is mixed, and clearly there are problems if more responsibility for one worker is seen as encroaching on that of others.

2 JOB CHARACTERISTICS MODEL[3]

This more sophisticated approach considers three critical psychological states:

1 Experienced meaningfulness of the work itself. This is contributed to by **skill variety**, calling upon the varied abilities of the worker; by **task identity** which involves the worker in a whole rather than partial task, and by **task significance** which is the extent to which the job is seen as significant for *others*.
2 Experienced responsibility for the outcomes of work. This is enhanced by **autonomy** where the worker is given discretion to carry out a job as he sees best, rather than under direction from above.
3 Knowledge of results of the work. This is achieved by **feedback**. A very simple instance would be the use of a sales chart.

The model is shown in Fig. 10.1.
One study of the model is summarised in Example 10.1.

EXAMPLE 10.1   JCM IN PRACTICE

1 Clerical workers were allowed to choose what jobs they would perform (skill variety).

2 They were responsible for complete tasks (task identity).

3 A clear indication was given of how their work fitted into the organisation as a whole (task significance).

Fig. 10.1 The job characteristics model

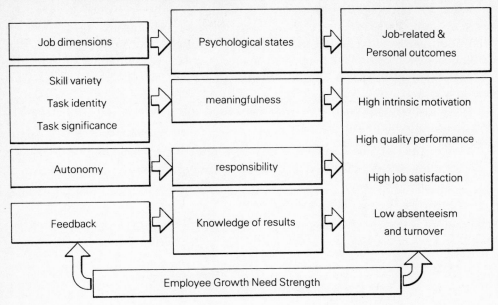

4 They set their own schedules and were responsible for assessment of their work (autonomy).

5 They kept their own records of productivity (feedback).

6 Compared with a control group, the experimental group showed *higher* internal motivation and satisfaction with jobs, and *lower* absenteeism and turnover.

7 But the quality of work performance was not greatly higher for those performing the enriched jobs.

8 Thus three of the four predicted outcomes of the model were supported.[4]

Expectancy theories

An **expectancy-value** theory suggests that in the work situation, a worker expects that the results of his efforts will be rewarded by something of value to him.

One of the earliest expectancy approaches was that of **Vroom**. He proposed that motivation was the joint result of the person's expectation of an outcome and the **valence** of that outcome – that is, its perceived attractiveness. This outcome might then be instrumental in obtaining a more remote but attractive reward. His view can be expressed in a simple equation:

$$\text{force of motivation (F)} = \text{expectancy of desired outcome (E)} \times \text{valence of desired outcome (V)}$$

An important initial point here is that the attractiveness of a 'reward' may not be the same for all people. For some, a straightforward pay rise may have high valence, and increase motivation. For others, recognition of ability by promotion, without so high a pay rise, may be a highly desirable outcome. This emphasises the need to take account, where possible, of individual preferences, and again suggests that a simple reliance on monetary incentives may be too simple a view.

Vroom's early approach has been expanded into several 'VIE' models. The essential components of these are:

1 Valence: the perceived attractiveness of a reward for performance.
2 Expectancy: the belief that effort will result in performance, which in turn will be
3 Instrumental in achieving a desired goal.

A version of this type of theory is that of Lawler and Porter[5] shown in Fig. 10.2.

Fig. 10.2

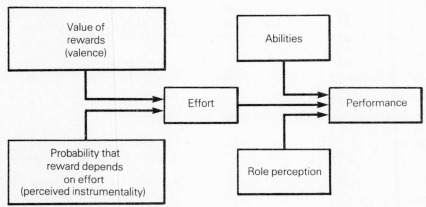

Here the translation of effort into performance is moderated by the person's abilities in relation to the post, and his perceptions of the activities and behaviours he feels are properly associated with it.

Motivation can thus be affected at three levels:

1 If the offered reinforcement has little valence, motivation and performance will drop.
2 If effort is not translated into the performance required to achieve the reinforcement, expectancy will drop, and with it performance. A salesperson may embark on a programme for a new product with enthusiasm, in hopes of good sales and commission, only to find heavy post-purchase problems from retailers. His expectancy and therefore his motivation to press this product will inevitably lessen.
3 Programmes which make clear the relation between effort and reinforcement should be more effective than those which do not. If salespeople know clearly the relations between their efforts with specific products and the resulting

reinforcements they will be able to plan their work to maximise their outcomes, and management will have a powerful tool for controlling the activities of its sales force.

Equity theory

This theory, proposed by Adams in 1965, suggests that in comparing their work situations, people take account of the following:

1 Inputs, including hours worked, qualifications, responsibilities.
2 Outcomes, including pay, privileges, status, holidays. They then compare their outcomes (roughly, what they get from their job), with their inputs (what they put into it). This is the outcome/input ratio.
3 This outcome/input ratio is estimated for themselves and for the worker with whom they are making the comparison.

Three main consequences may result.

1 Equity. The ratios are equal: 'taking account of the different inputs and outcomes, I feel that I get a fair deal compared with my comparison worker'.
2 Overpayment inequity: 'my ratio is higher: I get more out per unit input than my comparison person'.
3 Underpayment inequity: 'I get less out per unit input than the other'.

The two unequal situations will produce psychological consequences of guilt and anger respectively, as shown in Fig. 10.3.

Fig. 10.3

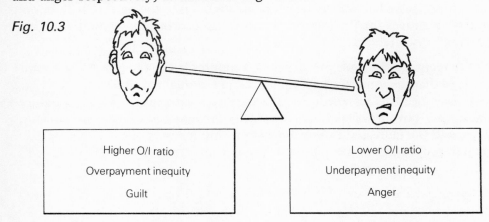

Higher O/I ratio	Lower O/I ratio
Overpayment inequity	Underpayment inequity
Guilt	Anger

Some methods which may be used to reduce the inequity are shown in Table 10.2.

It is clear that workers are likely to be dissatisfied if they find other workers with better rewards for equal effort than they feel they have. In the end, this might lead to loss of staff to companies with better incentives. On an international scale, it may lead to a 'brain drain' where, say, English doctors are attracted to other countries because the outcome/input ratio is perceived as significantly higher.

Table 10.2   Reaction to inequity

Type of reaction	Underpayment	Overpayment
Behavioural	Lower own efforts (reduce input)	Raise own inputs (e.g. work harder)
	Try to raise outcomes (ask for rise)	Try to lower outcomes (don't press for rise)
Psychological	Convince self that other is really more qualified	Convince self that own high inputs (e.g. qualifications) are high and justify outcomes

A second, more difficult, form of comparison, is that of comparable worth. Here, an attempt is made to compare the situations of people in somewhat different occupations, such as a nurse and a policeman. Equity is important here, to avoid the drift from occupations which are seen as having low outcome/input ratios to those which appear to have high ratios.

■ MONEY AND MOTIVATION

Taylor's view of money as a prime motivator has persisted for a long term. More recent views, described above, have drawn attention to the need to look beyond financial incentives for the most efficient means of work motivation. This may be related to two factors.

1 The percentage of people in a developed country below the poverty line is now far less, so that the importance of money as an essential instrument for satisfying purely basic needs is lessened. Social security systems may also have produced the so-called 'poverty trap' where it actually proves disadvantageous to work.
2 This, and the increased professionalism within many organisations, has led to a greater proportion of people with 'growth' as opposed to 'deficit' needs to satisfy.

We can consider the place of money in relation to several motivational theories.

Maslow, Theory X and Theory Y

Money will certainly supply the basic needs, provide for shelter and security, and, for some people, provide a source of self-esteem: the bigger the salary, the greater the self-esteem. It might buy friends – but is that what is really meant by belonging?

Where it is likely to fail is in the growth needs, and in satisfying needs for initiative and responsibility, as indicated in Theory Y. *Money fits in well with*

Theory X approaches, but cannot fulfil of itself all the functions demanded by Theory Y.

The two-factor theory

Money is clearly indicated as a **maintenance** factor. Poor wages and salary schemes will invite dissatisfaction and work-force problems. But Herzberg reminds us that even when the financial incentives are well-designed and presented, they may not of themselves be sufficient to produce satisfaction. We have built the foundations without erecting the superstructure. *Money may prevent dissatisfaction, but might not produce satisfaction.*

VIE theories

Money is undoubtedly instrumental in achieving desired goals. But the valence of money as a goal in itself will vary from person to person. This is good in one way, since management can offer money which is exchanged for personally desired rewards at the choice of each individual worker. It would be very tiresome for the wages department to ask each worker what goods he wanted each week, and supply them from a general warehouse!

On the other hand, for some people there are more valued outcomes than just money as a reward for work, as suggested by the two-factor theory. *The valence of money is not the same for all workers.*

Equity theory

Here we must remember that we are dealing with comparisons. Firstly, workers can compare what they get with what they give. But perhaps more importantly, in the pub, over coffee, through the media, they can compare their 'deal' with that of workers in similar positions. If the 'money scales' are weighed against a worker, management can expect problems, varying from lessened motivation and productivity to strike action. But money is not the only balancing factor available.

EXAMPLE 10.2   DOES STATUS BALANCE EFFORT?

1 Students were hired to proof-read, at what they regarded as a fair rate.

2 After an initial period, some students were given the title 'senior proof-reader'. This required them to stay an extra hour to check other students' work. They did not receive any extra payment for this.

3 Their performance was compared to that of students who were asked to stay, without being accorded any extra status.

4 The 'titled' students thus had an increase in both input and outcome. They maintained their high performance.

5 The 'untitled' students had an increase in input without any corresponding increase in outcome. What does equity theory predict would happen?

Greenberg and Ornstein[6]

Money can be used to adjust the scales of inequity – but is not the only weight available.

All this may seem very critical of money as a motivator. But of course, it is a very effective one for most people. But there are things in life that money can't buy, such as self-respect and the respect of others. Unless management recognises these 'warm' factors, there is a danger of a cold, clinical approach which is ill-suited to modern conditions. *Money may motivate some workers all of the time, other workers most of the time, but it cannot motivate all workers all of the time.*

■ THE PSYCHOLOGICAL CONTRACT

Most employees are able to refer to a formal agreement, often in writing, laying down conditions relating to their work. However, there is a further, more subtle 'bond' between employees and organisation, which Schein refers to as the **psychological contract**.[7] This may be looked at both from the individual and organisational viewpoint, and can be applied both to commercial and non-commercial organisations, such as clubs.

1 The individual. For his part, the individual accepts his role and its expectations within the organisation. This may involve acceptance of the authority structure, and of commitment to the organisation's goals.

But he will also have expectations of what the organisation will do for him. This will include basic issues like pay, security of post, encouraging rather than depressing work conditions. But it will also include for many the opportunity to develop, fulfilling higher, growth, needs. And all members are likely to expect treatment which respects, rather than demeans, them.

2 The organisation. In return, the organisation will expect the employee to further its goals at an appropriate level, to enhance rather than detract from the corporate image, and perhaps to make sacrifices under times of strain.

Where these two sides work harmoniously together, there will be **organisational commitment** by the individual, so that he feels in tune with the organisational climate and its associated goals. Where there is lack of harmony in expectation and performance, on either side, there is the risk of unrest from workers, or disappointment on the part of management. The important point is that much unrest and dissatisfaction may come, not from formal obligations, but from these unwritten but powerful expectations.

The contract can also be looked at **developmentally**, again from the individual or organisational viewpoint. It does not remain static, but changes as the individual and organisation change.

1 The individual:

(a) early in their career, many people may expect to be challenged to see what they can achieve and contribute. Lack of challenge may bring disappointment and a loss of motivation;

(b) once an area of contribution has been found, the individual may hope for development and an opportunity to specialise, to become productive, perhaps to gain respect from expertise, which may be used to bring along aspiring younger members;

(c) for some, productivity may lessen at later stages. They may hope not to be summarily dismissed, but encouraged to continue to contribute, perhaps in a more advisory than active capacity.

2 The organisation. When the organisation is young, or in difficulty, it may expect extra drive and commitment to help in survival. When things are going well, expectations of steadiness and consolidation may be prominent.

This relation between the two parts is thus a **dynamic** one, capable in good circumstances of constant amicable renegotiation, but in bad, producing tension and even action. This will be so, as in equity theory, when workers in industry see practices such as frequent management–employee consultation in other similar organisations, but absent from their own. Outcomes are not merely material.

We thus reach the final 'view' of man suggested by Schein: **complex man**. With it comes the idea that management must be flexible not only to the structure and style appropriate to a situation, the organisational level, but also to the intricate interplay between individual and organisation. As Schein said:

Perhaps the most important implication is that the successful manager must be a good diagnostician and must value a spirit of enquiry.

Complex man, diagnostic management.

■ SELF ASSESSMENT QUESTIONS

Marks

1 Put the right term against the following:
(a) The perceived value of a reward to a worker. _ _ _ _ _ _ _ _ _
(b) The belief that effort will result in performance. _ _ _ _ _ _ _ _
(c) The belief that performance will bring some reward. _ _ _ _ _

(3)

> instrumentality   valence   expectancy

2 Put the following factors under the headings of 'motivators' or 'maintenance'

> supervision   achievement   pay   responsibility

	Motivators		Maintenance
(a)	_ _ _ _ _ _	(c)	_ _ _ _ _ _
(b)	_ _ _ _ _ _	(d)	_ _ _ _ _ _

(4)

3 Whose theory involves the factors given in Question 2? _ _ _ _ _   (1)

4 Ms Janes talks to Ms Handley. They are in similar jobs, but on balance, Ms Janes feels she has a better outcome/input ratio than Ms Handley.
(a) According to equity theory, what emotion might Ms Janes feel? _
(b) What emotion might Ms Handley feel? _ _ _ _ _ _ _ _ _ _ _ _ _
(c) From *Ms Janes'* viewpoint, there is an _ _ _ _ _ _ _ inequity.
(d) Who might tend to work harder after their talk (Ms J or Ms H)?   (4)

> overpayment   underpayment   satisfaction   guilt   anger

5 Put the most suitable term against the following:
(a) Giving a false impression by answers to a personality test. _ _
(b) Assessment methods which try to build a picture of the 'whole person'. _
(c) 'Fitting the man to the job'. _ _ _ _ _ _ _ _ _ _ _ _ _ _ _ _ _ _ _
(d) 'Fitting the job to the man'. _ _ _ _ _ _ _ _ _ _ _ _ _ _ _ _ _ _ _   (4)

> ergonomics   faking   holistic   selection

6 Write 'true' or 'false' against the following:
(a) Money is the most effective motivator for all people in all circumstances. _
(b) 'Contracts which are written on paper are the only ones worth bothering about.' _
(c) Theory X regards workers as incapable of exercising initiative on behalf of the organisation. _
(d) I now know enough to pass *any* examination.
_   (4)

(Answers are on page 221)   (Total: 20)

■ STUDY AND EXAMINATION TIPS

The examiner gives an example – use it!

1 Sometimes the examiner will leave it to you to supply the practical examples. But more and more, examiners give a theme around which the answer should be organised.

2 In such cases, as in Question 1, you *must* use the example:

(a) if you don't, you will definitely lose marks;

(b) if you use the suggested example well, you have ample chance to show your ability to develop 'working theory' – that is, to see theory and practice **not** as two distinct elements which you desperately try to join, but as an automatic part of your marketing decision-making. That should be the main aim of your studies in an area such as this.

3 How does this work in practice? Question 1 offers an opportunity.

(a) Obviously, you have to state what the psychological contract is. Distinguish it from formal contracts, and answer the question posed by the second sentence by referring to the problems which can occur when this 'hidden' contract is unsatisfactory.

(b) Point out that the contract has two sides:

(i) expectations of the employee;

(ii) expectations of the organisation.

(c) Note also that these expectations may vary with the stage of the employee's career and the state of the organisation (e.g. flourishing/declining).

(d) Now show how this applies to a graduate. Check before you write that you are aware of the exact situation: the marketing department of a large multinational. You must try to bring each point into your answer. How could this be done?

(e) The graduate, perhaps more than an office worker, will expect development in their career. This will involve not only promotion possibilities, but also opportunities to acquire new skills. Thus overseas visits may be welcomed, though probably with only limited responsibility to begin with. This will give first-hand experience of the cultures dealt with, and fruitful understanding of key people and practices in the relevant sections of the business world.

Having shown by this, and by involvement in practical activities such as sales promotions, that she is not just a back-room girl straight from college, she may well expect promotion. As she develops into the middle period of her career, she will hope for opportunities to use her initiative (e.g. by being encouraged to develop a programme for a previously unpenetrated area (autonomy)), to look towards higher responsibility (job enrichment) and, most importantly, to receive feedback on her performance from people whose opinion she respects, such as the Marketing Manager. During this period, she will expect to give her utmost to the organisation, even when occasionally this conflicts with outside commitments.

As she moves towards retirement, she may expect to be employed usefully, rather than simply discarded. For instance, although involvement in new projects and areas might lessen, she could be of tremendous value as a mentor, showing new graduates the way to shape their careers and contribute to the organisation. In this way, her career would come to a satisfactory full-circle, and a new professional life would begin.

(f) Now develop for yourself the second part, dealing with the expectations of the organisation. Emphasise organisational commitment and willingness to accept the authority structure of the organisation.

(g) Finally, you could point out that there is no 'universal' psychological contract. The theory of rational-economic man highlighted monetary features; social man emphasised relationships; complex man implies a diagnostic approach, and the need for each employee to be considered as an individual. A psychological contract which is suitable for a graduate in a marketing department may not be at all suitable for other situations and other workers.

■ EXAMINATION QUESTIONS

1 It has been argued that there is an implied 'psychological contract' between an organisation and its individual employees. What is the basis for this view? How might the 'contract' be formulated for, say, a graduate recruit to the marketing department of a large multinational?

2 Critically review some major theories of motivation at work, such as Herzberg's Motivation-Hygiene model, Expectancy Theory, and Equity Theory. To what extent can these three theories be reconciled with each other?

3 What aspects of organisational structure can affect the individual's level of job satisfaction?

4 The personal interview as a method of selecting employees has often been criticised because of its inherent subjectivity. What factors can produce bias in the recruitment interview, and how can they be overcome?

5 Have theories of motivation created rather than solved employee behavioural problems and demands?

6 With reference to studies of employee motivation, discuss the importance of financial reward as a motivating factor.

Answers to self assessment questions

Chapter 1

1.1 (a), (b), (c): Any three from: Description, Explanation, Prediction and Control
1.2 (a) Subjective
    (b) Objective
1.3 (a), (b), (c): Any three from: Survey, Experiment, Interview, Observation
1.4 (a) Ordinal
    (b) Ratio
1.5 (a) Independent
    (b) Dependent
    (c) No (Why?)
1.6 (a) Population
    (b) Sample
    (c) Primary
    (d) No (Why?)
1.7 (a) Experimental
    (b) Control
    (c) Post-test

Chapter 2

2.1 102 gm
2.2 (a) Habituation
    (b) Absolute
    (c) Difference
2.3 (a) Unawareness
    (b) Inept
    (c) Evoked
    (d) Inert
2.4 (a), (b) Motives, Interest
    (c), (d) Repetition, Novelty
2.5 (a), (b) Figure/Ground, Similarity
2.6 (a) Selective attention
    (b) Perceptual defence
    (c) Selective exposure
    (d) Subliminal perception
2.7 (a) False
    (b) False

Chapter 3

3.1 (a) Skinner
    (b) Bandura
    (c) Tolman
    (d) Kohler
3.2 (a) Continuous
    (b) Intermittent
    (c) Fixed ratio
    (d) Variable interval
3.3 (a) Generalisation
    (b) Extinction
    (c) Discrimination
3.4 (a) Observational learning
    (b) Vicarious reinforcement
    (c) Trial and error
    (d) Insight
3.5 (a) Short-term memory
    (b) Long-term memory
3.6 (a) Acquisition or encoding
    (b) Retention or storage
    (c) Retrieval or recall

Chapter 4

4.1 (a) Homeostatis
    (b) Curiosity
    (c) Approval
4.2 (a) Esteem
    (b) Safety

(c) Growth
(d) Deficit
4.3 (a) True
(b) False
(c) False
4.4 (a) Frustration
(b) Aggression
(c) Constructive
(d) Displace-
ment
(e) Regression
4.5 (a) False
(b) False
(c) False
4.6 (a) Extrinsic
(b) Intrinsic

Chapter 5
5.1 (a) Norm
(b) Role
(c) Inter-role
conflict
(d) Intra-role
conflict
5.2 (a) Laws
(b) Folkways
(c) Artefacts
5.3 (a) Dissociative
group
(b) Aspirational
group
(c) Formal group
5.4 (a) False
(b) False
(c) True
5.5 Any three from:
Family, School,
Peer Group,
Mass Media
5.6 (a) Role-playing
(b) Selective
reinforcement
5.7 (a) Full Nest II
(b) Empty Nest I

Chapter 6
6.1 (a) Balanced
(b) Unbalanced
(c) Unbalanced
6.2 (a) 15
(b) −1
6.3 (a) True
(b) True
(c) True
6.4 (b)
6.5 (a) Likert
(b) Guttman
(c) Kelly
(d) Osgood
(e) Festinger
6.6 (a), (b) Credibil-
ity, Attractive-
ness
(c), (d) Fear
appeals, One/
Two sided
(e), (f) Intelli-
gence, persuasa-
bility

Chapter 7
7.1 (a) Id
(b) Superego
7.2 (a) Projection
(b) Repression
7.3 16
7.4 (a) Activity
(b) Interest
(c) Opinions
7.5 (a) Stereotype
(b) Halo
7.6 Opinion leader
7.7 (a) True
(b) False
7.8 (a) Self concept
(b) Ideal self
(c) Looking-
glass self
7.9 (a) True
(b) True

7.10 (a) Trialability
(b) Complexity

Chapter 8
8.1 (a) Threshold
(b) Trade-off
8.2 (a) Stimuli
(b) Perceptual
constructs
(c) Learning
constructs
(d) Responses
8.3 (a) Brand com-
prehension
(b) Attitude
(c) Intention
8.4 (a) Perceptual
bias
(b) Stimulus
ambiguity
8.5 (a) Search
(b) Alternative
evaluation
(c) Outcomes
8.6 (a) Limited
(b) Extended
8.7 (a) Firm and
consumer attri-
butes
(b) Search and
evaluation
(c) The act of
purchase
(d) Feedback

Chapter 9
9.1 (a) Taylor
(b) Hawthorne
(remember it's
not a person)
(c) Maslow
9.2 (a) False
(b) False
(c) False

(d) True

(e) False

9.3 (a) Gatekeeper

(b) Influencer

(c) Initiator

9.4 (a) Straight re-buy

(b) Modified re-buy

(c) New task

9.5 (a) Orientation, size

(b) Time pressure, perceived risk

9.6 (a), (b) Any two from: problem-solving; persuasion; bargaining; politicking

Chapter 10

10.1 (a) Valence

(b) Expectancy

(c) Instrumentality

10.2 (a) Achievement, responsibility

(b) Pay, supervision

10.3 Herzberg

10.4 (a) Guilt

(b) Anger

(c) Overpayment

(d) Ms J

10.5 (a) Faking

(b) Holistic

(c) Selection

(d) Ergonomics

10.6 (a) False

(b) False

(c) True

(d) Well, give yourself a mark anyway. Good luck!

References

CHAPTER 1

1 Williams, K.C. 1981. *Behavioural Aspects of Marketing*. London: Heinemann.
2 Atkinson, R.L. Atkinson, R.C., Smith, E.F., and Hilgard, E.R. 1987. *Introduction to Psychology*. Orlando: Harcourt, Brace, Jovanovich.
3 Houston, F.S. and Gassenheimer, J.B. 1987. Marketing and Exchange. *Journal of Marketing*. 51, No. 4, pp. 3–18.
4 Ballbué, F. 1963. *Essentials of Economics*. Foundation for Economic Education.
5 Rothschild, M.L. and Gaidis, W.C. 1981. Behavioural Learning Theory: its relevance to marketing and promotions. *Journal of Marketing*. 45, No. 2, pp. 70–78.
6 Allport, G.H. 1947. The use of personal documents in psychological science. New York: S.S.R.C.
7 Tull, D.S. and Hawkins, D.I. Third edition, 1984. *Marketing Research: Measurement and Method*. London: Collier MacMillan.
8 Oppenheim, A.N. 1966. *Questionnaire Design and Attitude Measurement*. Heinemann Educational.

CHAPTER 2

1 Howard, J.A. and Sheth, J.N. 1969. *The Theory of Buyer Behaviour*. New York: Wiley and Sons.
2 Narayana, C.L. and Markin, R.J. 1975. Consumer behaviour and product performance. *Journal of Marketing*. 39, No. 4, pp. 1–6.
3 Williams, T.G. 1982. *Consumer Behaviour*. St. Paul: West Publishing Co.
4 Ulin, L.J. 1962. Does page size influence advertising effectiveness? *Media/Scope*. 14.
5 Allison, R.L. and Uhl, K.P. 1964. Influence of beer brand identification on taste perception. *Journal of Marketing Research*. 1.
6 Quoted in: Engel, J.F., Blackwell, R.D. and Miniard, P.W. Fifth edition, 1986. *Consumer Behaviour*. New York: Holt, Rinehart and Winston. p. 221.
7 Brown, R.L. 1958. Wrapper influence on the perception of freshness in bread. *Journ. App. Psychol.* 42.
8 McGinnies, E. 1949. Emotionality and perceptual defence. *Psychological Review*. 56.
9 Packard, V. 1981. *The Hidden Persuaders*. Scottsdale: W.S.P.
10 Moore, T.E. 1982. Subliminal advertising: what you see is what you get. *Journal of Marketing*. 46, No. 2, pp. 38–47.
11 Moore, T.E. 1982, see above.

12 Tull, D.S. and Hawkins, D.I. Third edition, 1984. Marketing Research: Measurement and Method. London: Collier MacMillan.

CHAPTER 3

1 Williams, T.G. 1982. *Consumer Behaviour*. St. Paul: West Publishing Company.
2 Thorndike, E.L. 1911. *Animal Intelligence*. New York: MacMillan.
3 Quoted in: Miller, G.E. 1962. *Psychology: The science of mental life*. Harmondsworth: Penguin.
4 Gorn, G.J. 1982. The effects of music in advertising on choice behaviour: a classical conditioning approach. *Journal of Marketing*. **46**, No. 1, pp. 94–101.
5 Nord, W.R. and Peter, J.P. 1980. A behaviour modification perspective on marketing. *Journal of Marketing*. **44**, No. 2, pp. 36–47.
6 Skinner, B.F. 1971. *Beyond Freedom and Dignity*. New York: Knopf.
7 Skinner, B.F. 1971, see above.
8 Bandura, A. 1977. *Social Learning Theory*. New York: Prentice Hall.
9 Nord, W.R. and Peter, J.P. 1980, see above.
10 Tolman, E.C. 1932. *Purposive Behaviour in Animals and Men*. New York: Appleton Century.
11 Droge, C. and Darman, R.Y. 1987. Associative positioning strategies through comparative advertising. *Journal of Marketing Research*. **24**, pp. 377–388.

CHAPTER 4

1 Baron, R.A. Second edition, 1983. *Behaviour in Organisations*. Newton, MA: Allyn and Bacon.
2 Harlow, H.F. and Suomi, S.J. 1970. Nature of Love – simplified. *American Psychologist*. **25**, pp. 161–8.
3 Heron, W. et al. 1956. Visual disturbances after prolonged perceptual isolation. *Canadian Journal of Psychology*. **10**, pp. 13–16.
4 Zuckerman, M. 1979. *Sensation seeking beyond the optimal level of arousal*. Hillsdale, N.J.: Erlbaum.
5 Maslow, A. Second edition, 1970. *Motivation and Personality*. New York: Harper and Row.
6 Murray, H.A. 1938. *Explorations in Personality*. New York: Oxford University Press.
7 McLelland, D.C. 1961. *The Achieving Society*. Princeton: Van Nostrand.
8 McLelland, D.C. and Boyatizis, R.E. 1982. Leadership Motive Pattern and long-term success in Management. *Journal of Applied Psychology*, **67**, 737–743.
9 Atkinson, J.W. and Litwin, G.H. 1960. Achievement motive and text anxiety, conceived as a motive to approach success and avoid failure. *Journal of Abnormal and Social Psychology*. **60**, pp. 52–63.
10 Tull, D.S. and Hawkins, D.I. Third edition, 1984. London: Collier MacMillan.
11 Tull, D.S. and Hawkins, D.I. 1984, see above.

CHAPTER 5

1 Baron, R.A. Second edition, 1986. *Behaviour in Organisations*. Allyn and Bacon, Inc.
2 Sherif, M. 1935. A study of some social factors in perception. *Archives of Psychology*. **27**, No. 187, 1–60.
3 Venkatesan, M. 1966. Experimental study of consumer behaviour conformity and independence. *Journal of Marketing Research*. **3**, pp. 384–387.
4 Engel, J.F., Blackwell, R.D. and Miniard, P.W. Fifth edition, 1986. *Consumer Behaviour*. New York: Holt, Rinehart and Winston.

5   Sherry, J.F. Jr. and Camargo, E.G. 1987. May your life be marvellous. *Journal of Consumer Research*. **14**, pp. 174–188.
6   Mueller, B. 1987. Reflections of Culture. *Journal of Advertising Research*. **27**, No. 3, pp. 51–59.
7   Berger, P.L. 1966. *Invitation to Sociology*. Harmondsworth: Pelican.
8   Berger, P.L. 1966, see above.
9   Engel, J.F., Blackwell, R.D. and Miniard, P.W. 1986, see above.
10   Qualls, W.J. 1987. Household decision behaviour: the impact of husband's and wife's sex role orientation. *Journal of Consumer Research*, **14**, No. 2, pp. 267–270.
11   Qualls, W.J. 1982 . Changing sex roles: its impact upon family decision making. *Advances in Consumer Research*. **9**, pp. 268–270.

CHAPTER 6

1   Ribeaux, P. and Poppleton, S.E. 1978. *Psychology and work*. London: Macmillan.

2   Rosenberg, M.J. and Hovland, C.I. 1960. Cognitive, affective and behavioural components of attitudes. In: attitude organisation and change. New Haven: Yale University Press.

3   Krech, D., Crutchfield, R.S. and Ballachey, E.L. 1962. *Individual in Society*. New York: McGraw-Hill Book Company.

4   Engel, J.F., Blackwell, R.D. and Miniard, P.W. Fifth edition, 1986. *Consumer behaviour*. New York: Holt, Rinehart and Winston.

5   De Fleur, M.L. and Westie, F.R. 1963. Attitude as a scientific concept. *Social Forces*. **42**, pp. 17–31.

6   Engel, J.F., Blackwell, R.D. and Miniard, P.W. 1986, see above.
7   Tuck, M. 1976. *How do we choose?* London: Methuen Essential Psychology.
8   Foxall, G.R. 1981. *Marketing Behaviour: Issues in Managerial and Buyer Decision-making*. Aldershot: Gower.
9   Zajonc, R.B. 1968. Attitudinal effects of mere exposure. *Journal of Personality and Social Psychology*. Monograph Supplement **9**, No. 2, pp. 1–29.
10   Festinger, L. and Carlsmith, J.M. 1959. Cognitive consequences of forced compliance. *Journal of Abnormal and Social Psychology*. **58**, pp. 203–211.

CHAPTER 7

1   Cattell, R.B. 1965. *Scientific Analysis of Personality*. Harmondsworth: Penguin.
2   Cattell, R.B. 1965, see above.
3   Cattell, R.B. and Butcher, H.J. 1968. The prediction of achievement and creativity. New York: Bobbs-Merrill. pp. 281–306.
4   Evans, F.B. 1959. Psychological objective factors in the prediction of brand choice: Ford versus Chevrolet. *Journal of Business*. **32**, pp. 340–369.
5   Lastovicka, J.L. et al. 1987. A life-style topology to model young male drinking and driving. *Journal of Consumer Research*. **14**, No. 2, pp. 257–263.
6   Guthrie, E.R. 1938. *The psychology of human conflict*. New York: Harper.
7   Clifford, E. and Clifford, M. 1967. Self-concepts before and after survival training. *British Journal of Social and Clinical Psychology*. **6**, pp. 241–8.
8   Payne, J., Drummond, A.W. and Lunghi, M. 1970. Changes in the self-concepts of leavers who participated in an Arctic expedition. *British Journal of Educational Psychology*. **40**, pp. 211–6.
9   Grubb, E.L. and Hupp, G. 1968. Perception of self, generalised stereotypes and brand selection. *Journal of Marketing Research*. **5**, pp. 58–63.
10   Darling, J.R. 1987. A longitudinal analysis of the competitive profile of products and associated marketing practices of selected European and non-European countries. *European Journal of Marketing*. **21**, No. 3, pp.

11 Katz, E. and Lazarsfeld, P.F. 1955. *Personal influence: the part played by people in the flow of mass communication*. Glencoe, Ill.: Free Press.
12 Rogers, E.M. Third edition, 1983. *Diffusion of Innovations*. New York: The Free Press.

CHAPTER 8

1 Zaltman, G. and Wallendorf, M. 1979. *Consumer behaviour: basic findings and managerial implications*. New York: Wiley.
2 Kotler, P. 1965. Behavioural models for analysing buyers. *Journal of Marketing*. **29**, No. 4, pp. 37–45.
3 Ehrenberg, A.S.C. and Wakshlag, J. 1987. Repeat viewing with people meters. *Journal of Advertising Research*. **27**, No. 1, pp. 9–13.
4 Miniard, P.W. and Cohen, J.B. 1983. Modelling personal and normative influences on behaviour. *Journal of Consumer Research*. **10**, p. 179.
5 Nicosia, F.M. 1968. Advertising management, consumer behaviour and simulation. *Journal of Advertising Research*. **8**, No. 1, pp. 29–37.
6 Kotler, P. 1967. *Marketing Management*. New York: Prentice Hall.
7 Howard, J.A. and Sheth, J.N. 1969. *The theory of buyer behaviour*. New York: Wiley.
8 Howard, J.A. and Sheth, J.M. 1967. A theory of buyer behaviour. Included in: Enis, B.M. and Cox, K.K. (ed.) Fifth edition, 1985. *Marketing classics*. Allyn and Bacon.
9 Engel, J.F., Blackwell, R.D. and Miniard, P.W. Fifth edition, 1986. *Consumer behaviour*. New York: Holt, Rinehart and Winston.
10 Katona, G. 1963. Rational behaviour and economic behaviour. *Psychological Review*. pp. 307–318. (Reprinted in *Marketing Classics*, see above.)

CHAPTER 9

1 Schein, E.H. 1980. *Organisational Psychology*. New York: Prentice-Hall.
2 Taylor, F. 1947. *Scientific Management*. New York: Harper and Row.
3 Mayo, E. 1949. *Hawthorne and the Western Electric Company: The Social Problems of an Industrial Civilization*. London: Routledge.
4 Trist, E.A. and Bamforth, K.W. 1951. Some social and psychological consequences of the Longwall method of coal-mining. *Human Relations*. **4**, No. 1, pp. 6–24 and 37–38.
5 Schein, E.H. 1980, see above.
6 McGregor, D. 1960. *Theory X and Theory Y. The Human Side of Enterprise*. New York: McGraw-Hill.
7 Burns, T. 1963. Industry in a New Age. *New Society*. No. 18, pp. 17–20.
8 Lawrence, P.R. and Lorsch, J.W. 1969. Organisation and Environment. Homewood, Ill.: Irwin.
9 Likert, R. 1961. *An integrating pattern and an overview. New Patterns of Management*. New York: McGraw Hill.
10 Woodward, J. 1958. *Management and Technology*. HMSO. pp. 4–21.
(*Note*: The 'classic' papers nos. 2–6 and 8–9 are available in: Pugh, D.S. (ed.) 1971. *Organisation Theory*. Penguin books.)
11 Woodward, J. 1958, see above.
12 Schein, E.H. 1980, see above.
13 Robertson, T.S. and Wind, Y. 1983. Organisational cosmopolitanism and innovativeness. *Academy of Management Journal*. **26**, pp. 332–338.
14 Leavitt, H.J. 1951. Some effects of certain communication patterns on group performance. *Journal of Abnormal and Social Psychology*. **46**, pp. 38–50.
15 Sheth, J. 1973. A model of industrial buying behaviour. *Journal of Marketing*. **37**, pp. 50–56.

CHAPTER 10

1 Eysenck, H.J. 1953. *Uses and Abuses of Psychology*. Harmondsworth: Penguin.

2 Herzberg, F. 1966. *Work and the Nature of Man*. World Publishing Co.

3 Hackman, J.R. and Oldham, G.R. 1980. *Work Redesign*. Addison-Wesley.

4 Orpen, C. 1979. The effects of job enrichment on employee satisfaction, motivation, involvement and performance. *Human Relations*. **32**, pp. 189–217.

5 Lawler, E.E. and Porter, L.W. 1967. Antecedent attitudes of effective managerial performance. *Organisational Behaviour and Human Performance*. **2**, pp. 122–142.

6 Greenberg, J. and Ornstein, S. 1983. High status job title as compensation for underpayment: a test of equity theory. *Journal of Applied Psychology*. **68**, pp. 285–297.

7 Schein, E. 1980. *Organisational Psychology*. New York: Prentice-Hall.

Acknowledgements

The material listed below has been reproduced or adapted by kind permission of the copyright holders.

Example 1.1
Pervin, L.A. (c.1980) *Personality*: Third Edition. John Wiley and Sons.
Examples 1.6 and 1.7
Market Analysis Ltd.
Fig. 1.4
Chisnall, P.M. (c.1978) *Marketing: A Behavioural Perspective*. McGraw-Hill Book Company (UK) Ltd.
Fig. 1.6
Baron, R.A. (c.1986) *Behaviour in Organisations*: Second Edition. Allyn and Bacon.
Example 2.1
Narayana, C.L. and Markin, R.J. (c.1975) 'Consumer behaviour and product performance'. *Journal of Marketing*, Vol. 39. American Marketing Association.
Fig. 2.7
Electricity Council, England and Wales.
Fig. 3.1
Atkinson, R.L., Atkinson, R.C., Smith, E.E., and Hilgard, E.R. (c.1987) *Introduction to Psychology*: Ninth Edition. Harcourt Brace Jovanovich, Inc.
Table 3.1
Nord, W.R. and Peter, J.P. (c.1980) 'A behaviour modification perspective on marketing'. *Journal of Marketing*, Vol. 44. American Marketing Association.
Fig. 3.8
Atkinson, R.C. and Shiffrin, R.M. (c.1971) *The Control of Short-term Memory*. Scientific American, Inc. All rights reserved.
Table 4.1
Zuckerman, M. (c.1979) *Sensation Seeking Beyond the Optimal Level of Arousal*. Lawrence Erlbaum Associates, Inc.
Example 4.2
Abbey National Building Society. (Use of logo).
Sun Alliance Insurance Group. (Extracts from promotional material).
Example 4.3
Expression (Magazine) (c.1987): Use of extracts from article 'Going for Gold', September.
Fleet Marketing Plans and Merchandising (c.1987): Use of extracts from letters to clients.
Table 5.1
Joint Industrial Council for National Readership Surveys.
Family Life Cycle (p. 106) adapted from
Engel, J.F., Blackwell, R.D., Miniard, P.W. (c.1986) *Consumer Behaviour*: Fifth Edition. Holt, Rinehart and Winston.
Fig. 6.1

230 ACKNOWLEDGEMENTS

Rosenberg, M.J. and Hovland, C.I. (c.1960) *Attitude Organisation and Change*. Yale University Press.
Fig. 7.1
Cattell, R.B. and Butcher, H.J. (c.1968) *The Prediction of Achievement and Creativity*. Bobbs-Merrill.
Fig. 7.3
Krech, D. *et al.* (c.1962) *Individual in Society*. McGraw-Hill Book Company.
Fig. 7.4
Rogers, E.M. (c.1962) *Diffusion of Innovations*. Free Press (Division of MacMillan, Inc.)
Fig. 8.4
Kotler, P. (c.1965) 'Behavioural models for analysing buyers'. *Journal of Marketing*, Vol. 29. American Marketing Association.
Fig. 8.5
Nicosia, F.M. (c.1968) 'Advertisement management, consumer behaviour and simulation'. *Journal of Advertising Research*, Vol. 8. Advertising Research Foundation.
Fig. 8.7
Howard, J. and Sheth, J.M. (c.1969) *The Theory of Buyer Behaviour*. John Wiley.
Fig. 8.8
Engel, J.F. *et al.* (c.1986) *Consumer Behaviour*: Fifth Edition. Holt, Rinehart and Winston.
Fig. 9.3
Baron, R.A. (c.1986) *Behaviour in Organisations*: Second Edition. Allyn and Bacon.
Fig. 9.4
Ribeaux, P. and Poppleton, S.E. (c.1978) *The Psychology of Work*. MacMillan and Co.
Fig. 9.6
Sheth, J.N. (c.1973) *A Model of Industrial Buying Behaviour*. Vol. 37. American Marketing Association.
Fig. 10.2
Ribeaux, P. and Poppleton, S.E. (c.1978) *Psychology and Work*. MacMillan and Co.

Examination Questions reproduced by kind permission of the Institute of Marketing, and the Assocation of Business Executives.

Index